MW01593507

THE RISE OF THE AMERICAN PEOPLE

A Philosophical Interpretation of American History

BY

ROLAND G. USHER, PH.D.

AUTHOR OF "PAN-GERMANISM," "THE RECONSTRUCTION OF THE ENGLISH
CHURCH," "THE RISE AND FALL OF THE HIGH
COMMISSION," ETC.

NEW YORK
THE CENTURY CO.
1914

KESSINGER PUBLISHING'S
RARE MYSTICAL REPRINTS

THOUSANDS OF SCARCE BOOKS
ON THESE AND OTHER SUBJECTS:

Freemasonry * Akashic * Alchemy * Alternative Health * Ancient Civilizations * Anthroposophy * Astrology * Astronomy * Aura * Bible Study * Cabalah * Cartomancy * Chakras * Clairvoyance * Comparative Religions * Divination * Druids * Eastern Thought * Egyptology * Esoterism * Essenes * Etheric * ESP * Gnosticism * Great White Brotherhood * Hermetics * Kabalah * Karma * Knights Templar * Kundalini * Magic * Meditation * Mediumship * Mesmerism * Metaphysics * Mithraism * Mystery Schools * Mysticism * Mythology * Numerology * Occultism * Palmistry * Pantheism * Parapsychology * Philosophy * Prosperity * Psychokinesis * Psychology * Pyramids * Qabalah * Reincarnation * Rosicrucian * Sacred Geometry * Secret Rituals * Secret Societies * Spiritism * Symbolism * Tarot * Telepathy * Theosophy * Transcendentalism * Upanishads * Vedanta * Wisdom * Yoga * *Plus Much More!*

DOWNLOAD A FREE CATALOG
AND
SEARCH OUR TITLES AT:

www.kessinger.net

TO

THE FAIREST AND LOVELIEST OF HER SEX

MY DAUGHTER FLORENCE,

ON HER THIRD BIRTHDAY

PREFACE

In these days of specialization, the community is divided for nearly all purposes into only two classes—the specialists and the laymen; and all the specialists are laymen in every subject but their own. In those manifold subjects in which he is a layman, the modern reader demands a lucid, vivid account of results and not of processes, a brief statement of the meaning of the development, which can be deduced from the array of facts and dates marching down upon him out of the past. Assuming these facts to be true and important, what do they mean, he asks? Assuming these to be the essential parts of the puzzle, what is the picture like? A specialist himself, the reader knows the value of processes, but he has neither the time, inclination, nor skill to perform the historical process for himself with even adequate materials. He asks for results first, for broad outlines and fundamental factors, and is willing to waive for the moment the question of authorities and the verification of data. He wishes to learn at once what competent authorities consider to be true and cares comparatively little by what precise road they reached their conclusions.

In writing this book it has therefore been my aim to give the reader a lucid account of results and not of processes; to explain briefly the meaning of the facts of national development, rather than to chronicle the mere sequence of events—for, from my point of view, the founding of colonies, the granting of charters, the battles, debates and constitutions are not in themselves history, but simply the material

out of which history must be made. I conceive it to be my
business, not to describe the pieces of the puzzle-picture, nor
to tell the reader their number nor even their relationship,
but to give him some point of view where the pieces cease
to be pieces and blend together into a picture. I believe that
the essential and elementary "facts" in history are not the
actual events but the more complex conclusions which are to
be deduced from a series of such events.

My indebtedness to the instruction and writings of my
teacher, Edward Channing, to the works of Rhodes, Van
Tyne, Beard, Turner, Hart and many others will be only too
manifest. Here and there I have added foot-notes to expand and elucidate the text but without any idea of furnishing adequate information of the extent or whereabouts of the
available or valuable material upon the subject. *The Guide
to American History* by Channing, Hart, and Turner, the
bibliographies in Hart's *American Nation,* will give the
reader, anxious to verify or expand my narrative, access to
the literature of the subject. I have used only material that
is accessible to all, except on a few minor points, and I do
not claim any novelty or originality for this volume or for
the ideas expressed in it, beyond the general point of view
and a much fuller treatment and different emphasis than is
usual in brief histories upon such topics as States' sovereignty, the growth of nationality, commercial relations with
the West Indies, the influence of economic and geographical
factors, and the growth of democracy.

Washington University, St. Louis, January, 1914.

CONTENTS

CONTENTS

CONTENTS

CONTENTS

CONTENTS

CONTENTS

CONTENTS

CONTENTS

CONTENTS

THE RISE OF THE AMERICAN PEOPLE

THE RISE
OF THE AMERICAN PEOPLE

I

THE MEANING OF AMERICAN HISTORY

WHEN, in the year 1890, within our own memories, the frontier in the United States officially ceased to exist, the great westward march of the Aryan race, begun thousands of years ago, came to an end and definitely closed the only period of the world's history which man himself has recorded. The tide of westward movement, which had streamed out of the East into the West for so many centuries, breasted the peaks of that lofty mountain-range which Benton used to call the "shining mountains," and West met East. The history of the United States is the story of the last and geographically longest stage in this westward progress of the Aryan race. Considering the vastness of the area reclaimed from the wilderness and the development there of an advanced civilization within the brief space of three centuries, the achievement is without parallel in the records of the race. Such is the place of the United States in universal history.

A nation becomes, however, a great factor in human development as much by the splendor of its ideals as by reason of its actual achievement. Homer placed the Elysian Fields, the abode of supreme happiness, in the West, the land of the setting sun. Out to those unknown regions, where Phœbus Apollo stabled his steeds at evening, went Odysseus to talk with his father's spirit; out into the West Virgil led Æneas to see the dead heroes, riding and leaping in the green

3

meadows under perpetual sunshine. The grim sagas of the Norsemen tell us how the dead chieftain was laid upon a couch on board his long ship; how the great sail was hoisted and how the raven standard flapped sinister wings against the mast; how the flaring torches flung a beam of light to guide the ship on its last long journey out into the West across the great water to that shore where Odin waited to welcome his chosen warrior to the halls of Valhalla. Some prophetic impulse led the bards to make the West symbolic of the hopes and ideals of the Aryan race. There, the dreamer of dreams has built his castle; there, the seer of visions has beheld great empires, boundless wealth, inconceivable happiness. The dull eyes of struggling European peasants have for three centuries seen in the United States the Elysian Fields. The search for them in the West had been unremitting; only from America came back word that Elysium had been found, a land truly flowing with milk and honey. America has been the hope of the despairing, the refuge of the pursued; here the homeless have found shelter; the hungry, food; the sick at heart, courage; and the oppressed, liberty. No one who has asked in faith has been turned empty away. The United States holds the unique and superb position of embodying for millions of men and women the racial vision of an abode of the Blessed in the West. Such is her place in the history of Western Europe.

But for this deep and abiding racial belief in the location of the Elysian Fields, the present United States would not exist. The first explorers would never have agreed that their hopes could find realization in the cotton fields and rice swamps of the South, in the wheat fields of Dakota and in the cod fisheries of New England. The incentive for the toil and suffering indispensable to the discovery and exploration of this continent came rather from the expectation, firm in the minds of Spaniard and Englishman, that he would next day see gleaming upon the distant horizon the silver walls of the Seven Cities of Cibola, or the deep red glow of the enormous carbuncle that lighted the broad halls of the wondrous palace of Prester John. The expectations of standing upon the shores of the sea that washed the island of Cipango, where the streets were paved with sheets of solid gold, lured Champlain up the St. Lawrence and brought La Salle into the Mississippi Valley. The search for the fabulous wealth and mythological personages did not cease until the eighteenth century. The dreams and visions of men, the persistent search for a will-o'-the-wisp can alone explain much of the exploration and development of the United States. Only the dissatisfaction of men with what they found, their abiding faith in something better further west could have colonized a great continent in three centuries.

This splendid westward progress which gives us our place in the history of the Aryan race, the ideal of liberty and freedom which has created for us a unique place in the history of Western Europe, are not the chief facts in American history. The history of the United States is in the truest sense the story of the assemblage of the crude materials for a great people and of the development in them of a national consciousness. We shall entirely miss the most vital fact about this story if we allow ourselves to assume even for an instant that anything deserving the name of nation existed in North America in 1660, in 1760, in 1789, or even in 1861. American history does not describe the life story of a nation, nor even the development or growth of a nation, but the very birth of the nation, which, as such, is still in its infancy. The fortuitous collection of many individuals upon the same sea-coast does not of itself create a nation, nor do these people become a nation when they first grudgingly permit a common government to perform certain limited functions which none of them could individually perform at all. A nation is not made by the adoption of constitutions nor by obedience to law; its existence is not manifested by conventions nor legislatures; for it is a spiritual bond between the people of a community and does not exist simply in the physical, geographical, economic, or constitutional factors necessary to its existence and expression.

A nation exists only in the spiritual consciousness of a great people and consists literally of the ideals, aspirations, hopes, and fears which they have in common. Nor is this nation made with hands. Its constituent parts think the same, not because they vote to agree, but because they do agree in very fact. They possess the same aspirations and ideals, are loyal and patriotic to their common government, not from policy or from desire, but because such psychological factors are realities. Until this spiritual bond exists, until the people become conscious of its actuality, no sentient, conscious national existence can be predicated. No amount of fervent wishing by individuals that it might be, no eager attempts to make it so, can be accepted as proof of its existence. A nation either is or is not. It cannot be "created"; it must grow into being. Certainly, the very least we can demand as proof of its existence, is the expressed conviction of all classes of the people in all parts of the country that a national tie is desirable and possible. So long as men could fiercely debate, as Washington phrased it, "whether we are one nation or thirteen," so long as one great section of the community could maintain with threats and at last with arms its complete independence of and difference from the rest of the people, no true national bond could exist.

But no one who reflects can be surprised that nationality is as yet young in this country. We have scarcely possessed for decades the outward physical and political expressions of nationality which most European countries have had for centuries:—territorial unity; continuous settlement throughout the whole area; something approaching stability of population;—which can alone make possible the actual experience in living together from which community of sentiment must come. For two centuries and more, the American people has been struggling into physical existence and has needed all the energy of its members to cope with the essentials of individual and community life. Nationally, we have been undeveloped rather than wrongly developed; we have lacked national consciousness from the same inevitable reasons that prevent the man from preceding the child. In Burke's expressive phrase, we were "a people still, as it were, in the gristle, and not yet hardened into the bone." We had to become a nation by feeling, thinking, living, and by developing through the experience of decade after decade that unity of ideals and aims whose expression is patriotism. As a nation, we have yet to share each other's crusts, drink to the dregs the cup of national humiliation, be welded one to another by the devastation of sword and fire, by those horrible catastrophes that make nations old in experience before their time. As yet we have suffered as parts, never as an entity; we have not yet rejoiced as a people with such a delirious, spontaneous outburst as thrilled England after the defeat of the Armada or Germany after the victory at Sedan.

Ours has been a growth, unspoiled and lovely, the natural, normal growth of the child, protected from luxury in its adolescence, furnished with every necessity as manhood approached; lacking experience, not knowing how or when to utilize his resources, but sane, strong, courageous, indomitable. There is something of an epic splendor about this growth to rugged physical manhood of a great people. Like Antæus, we drew our strength from the ground. We built our house with our bare hands and fashioned our national physical body in an incredibly short time out in a cleansing wilderness far from the sins and lusts of the race and out of materials unstained by the drums and tramplings of European conquest. Thus were we purged of the dross and freed from the subtle temptations of the old world. Our sins were the animal cravings of the boy for too much food, too many clothes,—the revel of the child in the riotous pleasures of the race, from curiosity rather than from wickedness.

The events of American history are more obviously concerned with the relationship of entities than with their attempts to unite into a whole. Perforce we study Massachusetts and Virginia, the ideas of the North and the views of the South, not as parts in relation to the whole, but as separate entities whose relation to each other has yet to be defined. The debates in Congress were occupied with the interests of sections of the country, not as parts of a whole but as antagonistic entities whose common interest and bond must be discovered and could never be assumed to exist. Indeed, it is impossible, as Webster and Lincoln pointed out, to reconcile the ideas of States' sovereignty and of Nullification with any other conception of a central government than that of a fortuitous, anomalous, and technical bond of dubious value.[1] The theory of States' rights meant nothing if it did not assert the superiority of the interests of a single State over those of the aggregation of States; Nullification was an empty form unless it meant that each State possessed vital interests so widely divergent from those of other States that its very existence would be at stake if it was to admit the right of the central government to adopt and enforce any policy which a majority of the other States might deem expedient. Both States' rights and Nullification premised the absence of that normal community of interests, of that essential uniformity of thought and ideals, upon which alone one nation in the proper sense of the word could be based. They denied the existence of a whole of which they were severally parts; they solemnly affirmed the existence of a formal relationship between entities absolutely complete within themselves. Secession stated in actual words the contention of a great section of the country that two nations really existed within the bond of the Federal Government and that the formal recog-

[1] "The tendency of all these ideas and sentiments is obviously to bring the Union into discussion, as a mere question of present and temporary expediency; nothing more than a mere matter of profit and loss. The Union is to be preserved, while it suits local and temporary purposes to preserve it; and to be sundered whenever it shall be found to thwart such purposes. Union, of itself, is considered by the disciples of this school as hardly a good. . . . They cherish no deep and fixed regard for it, flowing from a thorough conviction of its absolute and vital necessity to our welfare." Webster, first reply to Hayne, Jan. 20, 1830. *Works*, III, 258-9. "Again, if the United States be not a government proper, but an association of States in the nature of contract merely . . ." Lincoln, First Inaugural Address, Nicolay and Hay, *Abraham Lincoln, Complete Works*, VI, 174.

nition of this obvious political and constitutional fact was so vital to the well-being of the South that those States were prepared to demand its acceptance at the point of the bayonet. The doctrine of the constitutionality of secession affirmed that the separation would be legal according to the Constitution because there had always been entities in America, not an organic whole. The Civil War was not a fight for the preservation of the Constitution or of a technical political bond called the Union, but a war to remove the last and greatest obstacle in the way of the formation of an American nation—the belief of nearly one-half the country that a single nation not only did not exist but was neither possible nor desirable. The great number of Southern men who accepted the action of their State as superior in obligation even to their own personal conclusions that the war was wrong, proves absolutely the lack of a distinctly national consciousness in 1861.

The result of the Civil War was, therefore, something infinitely grander than the preservation of a constitutional form known as the Union. The North was inspired by the vision of "a noble and puissant nation, rousing herself like a strong man after sleep and shaking her invincible locks, as an eagle mewing her mighty youth and kindling her undazzled eyes at the full mid-day beam"; the vision of a nation one and inseparable, in which the rights of the whole should never be sacrificed to an individual or to any body of individuals. Just as the greatness of Webster consisted in the fact that he made the North see this vision, so the greatness of Lincoln's achievement lay in the fact that he made North and South alike realize that the aim of the war was not so much the abolition of slavery or the denial of States' rights [2]

[2] "I have, therefore, in every case thought it proper to keep the integrity of the Union prominent as the primary object of the contest on our part. . . . The Union must be preserved." Lincoln, Message to Congress, Dec. 3, 1861. See also the First Inaugural Address, the first paragraphs. "My paramount object in this struggle is to save the Union, and is not either to save or to destroy slavery." Lincoln's letter to Horace Greeley, August 22, 1862. Nicolay and Hay, *Complete Works*, VIII, 16. See also Grant's correspondence for 1861 in *Letters of U. S. Grant*, edited by J. G. Cramer. (1913.)

as the creation of a mighty nation, powerful in her grasp of a continent and two oceans, rich in the fruits of united endeavor, invincible by reason of her consciousness of a noble and splendid ideal. The superiority of the whole over the parts, the splendor of the aspirations born of designs based upon the unity of the people, were the decisive factors in favor of the North. The War made Southerners and Northerners Americans. The essence of American history then is this achieving of nationality by a great people. Than this no subject could be greater or more fascinating to the student. It is the only instance in all human history where we can watch the consciousness of nationality actually dawning in the individual mind.

II

SPANISH AND FRENCH FAILURES

WE owe the first knowledge of this continent to Norse rovers, to Breton or Portuguese fishermen, who told of its fish and grapes, but never deemed its existence of greater moment. We owe its real discovery to the mistaken geographical notions of the earth's size and form, prevalent in Western Europe at the end of the fifteenth century, which filled a tall, ruddy-haired Genoese sailor with visions of incalculable wealth and of the salvation of souls unborn, and led him to embark a crew of adventurers and criminals in three small, leaky vessels for a voyage to find a sea route to India and China by sailing west. We owe the name America to an adventurer, contractor, and sailor, who wrote the first account of the Mundus Novus which attained much circulation or notoriety. Nevertheless, neither the date of the discovery, the person of the discoverer, nor the nation he represented exercised then or since any appreciable influence on the history of the United States. When the English settlers landed at Jamestown in 1607, the Spanish had long relinquished the exploration and settlement of the northern Continent and had left within the limits of the present United States only a handful of soldiers and settlers in Florida and New Mexico whose continued existence was made precarious by pestilence, famine, and hostile Indians. A century of Spanish effort hardly provided the English who followed them with the knowledge that land of continental dimensions existed here.

Yet if Spanish discoverers and explorers contributed nothing of value to the history of the United States, it was not for lack of diligence nor of prodigious effort. They sought Cipango with the greatest tenacity among the islands in the

Caribbean, hunted the South and Central American coasts with assiduity, and even attempted wild guesses at the relation the scattered islands and bits of continent bore to the maps of Asia already published by travelers and geographers. It was plain to most that the great land south of Cuba was a part of Asia. Then came Balboa. He pushed across the Isthmus of Panama and found the sea on the western side (1513). Was the Mundus Novus then in the South and was it Asia itself that lay to the North? Magellan in his long voyage around the Horn and across the Pacific (1519–21) demonstrated that South America was not connected with Asia and for the first time gave Europeans some notion of the magnitude of the Pacific Ocean, and of the true size of the globe.

Then came to the shores of the northern continent strong expeditions, with infantry and cavalry, generals and priests, seeking everywhere the great countries of Asia which Marco Polo had seen and described. One skirted the northern coast of the Gulf of Mexico and saw the mouth of a great river; others sailed along the Atlantic coast and made at least one attempt to settle on the James River; two traversed the continent from Florida west to the Pacific. Coronado pushed north from Mexico through the Zuni pueblos to the plains of western Kansas and probably returned through Texas. De Soto, in the east, marched northward from the Gulf into Tennessee, and his men, burying him, a victim to the climate, returned along the Mississippi. The Spaniards had explored the continent from the Atlantic to the Pacific and from the Gulf as far north as the latitude of Virginia and Missouri and yet do not seem to have measured distances or plotted maps to scale or to have realized that a river as large as the Mississippi must drain a land of continental dimensions. Whatever they knew, they kept carefully to themselves and in 1600 the cartographers' knowledge of the interior was still of the vaguest.

The reasons for this failure of the Spanish to colonize are not far to seek. The Spaniards came not to found homes as the English did, but to hunt for gold, for the mysterious fountain of eternal youth, for the land where the Grand Khan, Prester John, Gog and Magog, and the mythical personages described by Sir John Mandeville and other imaginative medieval travelers dwelt in surpassing luxury and magnificence. They had read that there were rivers of diamonds, trees on which grew pearls and rubies, and a huge palace lighted by a single glorious carbuncle. The simple tale of Fray Marcos about his trip to the pueblos in Arizona was elaborated by breathless auditors into statements, greedily accepted, that he had seen a city as large as two Sevilles, where all the women wore great strings of golden beads, where all the men were silversmiths, and where the very lintels of the doors were studded with emeralds and rubies. Such cities the Spaniards had expected to find; for such expeditions money and men were forthcoming. Their disappointment was great, for they found some adobe pueblos, into whose door-jambs had been pressed with a no more skilful instrument than the Indian's thumb, rough uncut topazes and garnets. The inhabitants were darkskinned men and women clad in dirty woolen blankets and wearing a few bracelets and anklets of rough-beaten gold and red copper. To the north, Coronado found only huge herds of "humpbacked cows"; to the east, other explorers found the arid plains of Texas, and the swamps of Louisiana and Florida. They stood in the treasure house of the new world, in the Elysian Fields the race had so long sought, in the abode of wealth, liberty, and hope; and they knew it not. They sought the wealth of Inde and of the Grand Khan of China; they were ready with Benedict to "fetch you a toothpicker from the farthest inch of Asia; bring you the length of Prester John's foot; fetch you a hair off the Great Chan's beard; do you any embassy to the Pigmies"; but they were not ready to work. They turned to Mexico and Peru where the gold, silver, and precious stones they had come for were to be found.

At the same time, the failure to colonize was not due merely to the aims of the men who came. The cutthroats and down-at-the-heel gentlemen of Europe, looking for sudden riches, were indeed far from good material for settlers, but they came to spots unsuitable for permanent colonies and they came utterly without preparation for settlement and indeed without even the faintest notion of what the mainland was like. The swamps and lowlands of the Gulf States, the hot fields of Texas are not favorable spots for white men to live in, and the population there is still sparse. Unfitted for permanent residence, the voyagers were not able to maintain themselves for any considerable time. A Spaniard clothed in leather jerkin, heavy cuirass, helmet, leather boots to his knees, and an arquebus weighing twenty pounds was not ready for a march through a Florida swamp on a torrid summer's day. The horses sank to their knees in the ooze and were burdens rather than aids to progress; the insectivora swarmed; yellow fever, malaria, and dysentery carried off the unfortunate explorers at a rapid rate. Narvæz and his men, driven mad by disease, hunger, and the swamp pests, finally killed their horses, made boats out of the skins, embarked on the Gulf and perished miserably trying to reach Mexico.

In addition, the Spanish landed one and all among fierce and well-organized Indian tribes. The Zuni and Moqui pueblo confederacies in Arizona and New Mexico and the Creeks and Cherokees on the Gulf coast, though less advanced than the Aztecs and Peruvians, were yet the strongest bands on the Northern continent and extended their influence to the north until it met that of the Iroquois in Pennsylvania and Illinois. None of them were civilized in any degree as we use the word. They were, in fact, in middle barbarism, two ethnical periods, of some thousands of years apiece, behind the European explorers in development. Not having attained the knowledge of smelting iron or the use of the alphabet, their warfare, agriculture, architecture, and domestic life were those of people who, for lack of hard implements, must be content with axes whose edges turned, with plows and hoes of use only for scratching the surface, and with houses built of mud and wattle or of soft limestone. Their social organization too was most primitive: they traced property and descent through the mother instead of through the father, had no private ownership of property, no domestic animals save the dog. They were utterly unfit to cope permanently with the white men, with whom they could not amalgamate and whom they could not in the long run successfully oppose; but they were stalwart, entirely void of physical fear and sufficiently well-organized to give the Spaniards infinite trouble in this first encounter.

Nevertheless, with ordinary prudence and moderation the Spaniards might have fared well. They considered the Indians, however, to be heretics fit only for slaves. Coronado's men snatched the blankets from the very backs of squaws and even of chiefs; De Soto outraged Indian notions of dignity by compelling chiefs to carry burdens. One and all the Spaniards scoffed at the Indians' worship and to all this they added treachery and cruelty. From greed, violence, and slave-catching could come only one result. The Spaniards were attacked and ambushed, their water and food destroyed, their horses killed, their guns stolen. The Indians, who had been ready to find among the first Spaniards the white Messiah their legends told about, came to detest them with a deep and strenuous hatred. Moreover, coupled to the selfishness, greed, and insubordination of the rank and file were the rivalry, jealousy, and treachery of the leaders. Indeed, the existence of such factors makes the failure of the Spaniards to influence the history of the United States seem not surprising, but inevitable.

Nor was Spain the strong united nation needed to mother a sturdy race of colonists and protect their infancy. Her unity was seeming rather than real; her loyalty to the king questionable; the prevailing idea of her prosperity based upon the economic fallacy that the silver she began to get from Peru in such enormous sums was real wealth. From the dynastic visions of Charles V and Philip II came weakness, not strength. Throughout the century she was occupied either with war with France, or with subduing revolts in Germany, in the Netherlands, or in Spain itself. Her rulers had, in fact, neither energy, money, nor men to devote to the creation and development of a new Spain in the temperate regions of North America.

The exploits of the French Huguenots in Florida and South Carolina and the work of French fur-traders and fishermen in the St. Lawrence region had also led by 1607 to no results of permanence. The same causes which made the Spanish settlement difficult, plus the enmity of the Spaniards themselves, effectually crushed all the enterprises in the South, while the inclement winters of the North, and the difficulty of raising food in the brief summers caused the fur-traders and fishermen to erect only factories which they visited yearly. Along the Great Lakes, too, the French met the fierce and well-organized Iroquois, who effectually prevented them from playing a significant part in the history of the United States. The existence of the French colonies in the eighteenth century rather than the dramatic exploits of explorers in the seventeenth is of importance in our national development.

Thus it fell out that when the English queen issued a patent of colonization in 1578 to Raleigh and Gilbert, her notions of what she was granting were of the vaguest. Fairly accurate maps had been made and published showing the continent and its main features of coast-line; but side by side with these there flourished many maps representing all sorts of conceptions of the new land, and the men of the time had not yet *proved* to their own satisfaction which of these ideas was right. Without actual experience, no one could tell beyond a doubt which was valuable and which was worthless. The English appear to have believed that the Atlantic coast was in places only a couple of hundred miles wide, and that on the other side of this narrow strip was the China Sea and the cities Marco Polo had described. So naïve too were their conceptions of natural forces that the first Virginia settlers were ordered by the English capitalists, who financed the expedition, to sail up the rivers till they came to the spot where in a storm the waters of the China Sea washed over into the head waters of the James and the Potomac. Even after it became known that land and not water lay to the west, the expectations lingered of finding marvelous cities and, at the very least, a water-way to China. Champlain thought the La Chine rapids were all that blocked his path; La Salle fully expected to sail down the Ohio into the Pacific, and, after being disappointed in this, long believed that the Mississippi led thither; in fact, as late as the Revolution, the Rev. James Maury, made famous by the Parson's Cause, predicted a glorious commercial future for Virginia because of the water-way through the Potomac, Ohio, and Missouri Rivers to the Pacific and the Chinese trade. Magellan had demonstrated the fact that a new world existed, but it remained for the French and English gradually to ''discover'' the confines of the present United States by living in it for nearly three centuries.

No proper conception of the area and configuration of the continent was definitely attained and spread generally through the community until the days of Jefferson when Lewis and Clark returned from their long journey to the Pacific coast. The effective discovery of the present United States was, then, a long and difficult process, which was so far from begun when the first English colonists came here that the name Virginia, applied by the English at that time to the whole Atlantic coast, was still one to conjure up to the excited imaginations of adventurous men all sorts of wondrous possibilities. This ignorance of actual conditions and the resultant color it lent to glorious legends and fables was probably no less important a factor in producing English emigration than had been Columbus's misconceptions of geography in causing the discovery of the Western Hemisphere. Had either known precisely what they would find here, had either dreamt of what they would suffer here, neither would have come at all.

III

THE ENGLISH GENESIS OF THE UNITED STATES

OF the many events that happened on this continent only those are a part of the history of the United States which vitally influenced the fortunes of the people who ratified the Constitution at the end of the eighteenth century, and who have since, by the friction and strife of a century's earnest endeavor, at last welded themselves into a nation, possessed of unity of language, laws, and ideals, and whose advanced corporate consciousness entitles it to the respect and admiration of the world. During the colonial period the elements of this nation were brought into a wilderness; the Revolution separated those elements from England and left them to forge themselves into a nation without European interference; the history of the country since 1789 is the story of fusing and welding discordant political and economic interests into unity. The Civil War completed the nation whose first elements came hither in the *Susan Constant* and the *Mayflower*. The genesis of the United States consists, then, of those things which made it possible for Englishmen to come to America; of those things which made them willing or anxious to come; and of those things which made it possible for them to stay.

The present United States was made possible by the victory of the English fleet over the Spanish Armada at Gravelines in July 1588. The victory was itself the product of the genius of the English race for naval architecture and the legitimate result of the development of a new type of fighting ship that could sail as well as fight. The Channel pirates and the daring voyages of Hawkins and Drake to the Spanish Main gave the men of the English South Coast a knowledge of seamanship, a reckless courage, and a contempt for Spaniards. But after all the fact that the English won by sheer efficiency and bravery was of less consequence in the history of the United States than the fact of the victory itself. The Spanish fleet was vanquished—England became mistress of the seas—and the new land to the west lay open to English enterprise. That one day's valiant work, far more than the voyages of Cabot, the reiterated claims of Mary and Elizabeth, and the patents of James, gave the English a right to the soil of the New World. The control of the ocean highway to America was the indispensable prerequisite of possession.

A great outburst of energy in the last years of the sixteenth century and the first of the seventeenth betokened the loosing of the pent-up strength stored away in England by the domestic peace and economic growth of the preceding century. Population and wealth had increased enormously. The fetters which decadent feudalism and the gild and open-field systems had placed upon agriculture and industry were stricken off. With the enclosing of fields and the turning of arable land into pasture for sheep came an improvement in the old wasteful methods of agriculture and stock-raising which doubled and trebled the output of the realm. The dissolution of the monasteries placed a vast property which had been hitherto administered merely for subsistence into the hands of men who utilized it for profit. Means of exchange increased; the middleman appeared and the broker in grain; trading-companies, most significant for the development of the new world, and ready money seeking investment. The old economic fabric had given way before a new. The victory of the Armada seemed to be the occasion for suddenly displaying the great progress made since the Wars of the Roses. A taste for literature and the drama, fine clothes and houses, music and art began to invade the middle class. Not only the control of the sea but the energy and wealth stored away by the English nation during the sixteenth century made the colonization of America a possibility. Nor was it less important that the settlement of domestic and foreign quarrels allowed the subjects of James to spend money upon enterprises which would have been hazardous in the extreme in any previous ten decades.   In 1606 the moment was indeed propitious for colonization.

Out of the economic tangle of the sixteenth century came two varieties of men interesting to us: the capitalists with money to invest, or, as the phrase went, "to adventure," and the "planters," the men anxious to try their fortunes in a new land. The rise of towns, the distribution of the monastic lands and of the huge estates which escheated to the Crown during or after the Wars of the Roses and which were mostly granted to gentlemen without titles, the new agriculture, the new manufacturing—all produced a new class of men with ready money. The prodigious success of the Muscovy, Levant, and East India Companies made this class willing to risk a great deal for the hope of large profits. The very same events had turned tenants from their fathers' fields; had left monks homeless; had deprived apprentices and journeymen of their own tasks, and had thus created a class of unemployed men whose vigor and ambitions were great. Then the vast amounts of silver poured from the mines of Peru had, by a sort of poetic justice, provided men with good reasons for emigration to the new continent whence the silver came. The value of money had declined, prices had risen in consequence and were in 1600, as a result of this and many contributory causes, two or three times what they had been in 1500. Every one whose income was derived from money payments lost, of course, a large proportion of their means of support, and many families turned out to make their own fortunes the younger sons they could no longer afford to maintain. Not only had the economic crisis made the English nation rich enough to undertake the colonization of America, not only did the political situation allow it thus to divert its energies, but the two had together produced the individuals needed to occupy the new country.

The great movements of the time had also worked to pre-

pare individuals for migration to a new land where the possibilities of economic and personal development were not
cramped by relics of feudal law, the limitations of scholastic
philosophy, or the creeds of Rome. The Renaissance had
brought to the individual a sense of power utterly foreign to
the medieval man and, as well, a new restlessness, a reckless
curiosity, and a love of adventure for its own sake. The sixteenth century man was sure that knowledge was power; that
omniscience was possible; and that any man might attain it.
His delight in physical existence, his confidence in his own
ability, led him to look upon the unknown, and indeed the
unknowable, as the only field "whereby a notable mind," in
the words of George Beste, "might be made famous and
fortunate." The greater the danger, the larger the risk; the
larger the compensation, the greater the glory. To those
eager to obtain fame and wealth in the conquest of the physical world, the Reformation added a number of admirable,
pious men and women desirous of finding a place where there
were no fetters upon freedom of speech and of worship, and
where, in consequence, they might work out their own salvation in the way they believed God had directed, without
interference from either those who thought them heretics or
those who called them fools. And they sought not a place
where every one should be free to think as he liked and do as
he pleased, but a place where all men should agree upon
fundamentals and whence all others could be expelled. The
saving of their own souls, their own obedience to God's commands as to temporal and spiritual observance, were the
reasons for their coming. The self-same arguments that
drove William Bradford and John Winthrop from the English Church led them to exile Roger Williams and the Quakers
from Plymouth and Boston.

Curiosity, the spirit of adventure, an eager search for the
Northwest Passage to China led the first English explorers
to American waters, but their reports of the possibilities of the
land rather than their own experiences fired the minds of
"adventurer" and "planter" alike. The returned navigators

described the surpassing climate whose warmth raised expectations of growing lemons and olives in Maine! Wine could certainly be made in large quantities, they declared; the silk worm would flourish; spices of all sorts either abounded or could be cultivated; gold was plentiful but would have to be mined. These samples of the saner predictions made were all proven true to the average mind by the enormous profits made from a cargo of sassafras bark brought back by Gosnold. That they knew much more about the country than we can prove they knew, is certain. Laudonniére and other Huguenots who escaped from Fort Caroline were in London as early as 1566 and lived with Raleigh and the Gilberts; three of Hawkins's men who made their way across the continent from Mexico to Maine and were brought home by French fishermen were closeted with merchants and promoters. Walsingham, the Secretary of State, Peckham, and others listened to what they had to say and studied carefully the records of Verrazano's voyage along the Atlantic coast in 1524, of Cartier's voyage to the St. Lawrence ten years later, and no doubt many maps and narratives which are since lost. Gilbert even consulted the famous astrologer and alchemist, Dr. Dee, as to the possibilities of the new land, and, as Dee records in his diary, "I, Mr. Awdrian Gilbert, and John Davis went by appointment to Mr. Secretary Beale his house where only we four were secret, and we made Mr. Secretary privy of the northwest passage." Nevertheless, despite the explorers and the writing in the stars, the limitations of their knowledge were astonishing. Gilbert, for instance, seems to have believed the new country peopled by fauns!

Impelled by some such considerations as these, heartened by the tales of explorers, a body of merchants and gentlemen contributed a considerable sum of money, secured in 1606 the charter of a joint-stock company from the Crown, permitting them to exploit and settle the new Virginia, as the whole Atlantic coast was then called. After some delay, one hundred and twenty men sailed from the Thames in December 1606, in three ships furnished by the London part of the Virginia

Company. Landing in May 1607, they began the first permanent settlement in the present United States, at Jamestown, in the very sort of locality which the sensible instructions they carried explicitly warned them against. They put up the first rough shacks on a little peninsula in the James River, near a strip of woods affording Indians an excellent cover for attack, and besides a pestilential bit of marsh and stagnant back-water. The "planters" too, for the most part adventurers and down-at-the-heel gentlemen anxious to make a fortune, all of them a thoroughly unpractical lot, had not come to work for a living but to become rich without working. When, therefore, they found that pearls and nuggets of gold were not to be picked up on the banks of the James; that the inhabitants had little worth stealing; and that the Virginia rivers did not lead to China, they sulked and shirked and became mutinous. The food began to get low; once rats broke into the granary; once fire consumed both houses and food. One year after the founding of Jamestown, only fifty-three out of one hundred and ninety-seven persons who had landed there were still alive, and the quarrels of the leaders, the hostility and thievery of the Indians, and the lack of food seemed certain to destroy the colony. The situation seems to have been saved by the one man of sense on the ground, a professional soldier fresh from a romantic life as a free lance in Hungary and a galley slave in Constantinople, whom the capitalists in England had hired to accompany the expedition, Captain John Smith. He hanged the mutinous; pacified the Indians and bought corn from them; and forced the laggards to work by explaining that the Company's rules provided that all should share in common both the food and the work, and that he who would not work should not eat. The Company in England, taught by experience, sent over artisans and laborers to replace the lazy, adventurous spirits who had succumbed to malaria and fever; and finally put in charge of the Colony in 1611 another professional soldier, Sir Thomas Dale, who governed the settlers by the military rules then in use in European armies and produced not only order and industry, but church-going and perhaps piety!

Meanwhile, in the North, the Plymouth branch of the Virginia Company had explored the New England coast and had planted one colony in Maine, which stayed out the winter of 1607–8 and promptly returned in the spring with harrowing tales of the severity of the climate and the definite information that lemons, olives, and the silk-worm did not flourish there. Scarcely a year followed, however, without bringing some voyager to the northern coasts, among them Captain John Smith, Samuel Argall from Virginia, Champlain from the St. Lawrence, and many Dutch traders from the tiny factories they began to establish about 1614 in the neighborhood of Long Island Sound. Permanent settlements there were none between the James and the St. Croix, but the whole coast was alive with fur-traders and fishermen during the long summers, a few of whom at times stayed out the winter, and all of whom were doing a valuable work in charting the coast and in making known to Englishmen its peculiarities and resources. The shores of Massachusetts Bay were by no means an unknown region when the *Mayflower* with about one hundred souls on board came to anchor off Provincetown in December 1620.

Thirty-five members of a congregation of Englishmen at Leyden had left Holland, not because they could not worship there as they wished, but because they found it hard to make a living, saw their children losing their English speech and habits, and feared that the renewal of the war with Spain might actually put their lives in danger. In the new country, they could not fare much worse, they argued, nor run much greater risks and would probably be, in the end, far freer and more comfortable. They had arranged with some London merchants to finance their expedition, in return for which they agreed to put the proceeds of their labors into a "common store" for seven years, at the expiration of which land should be assigned to each family and a proportional division made of the joint property of the merchants and the settlers. Some of their friends in England had been induced to join them and a good many laborers and craftsmen had been hired by the merchants to accompany them to work on the latter's behalf. The little colony at Plymouth was by no means homogeneous, in character or in aims, and the strict religious life of the Pilgrims irked the laborers sent by the merchants. The common stock was a failure, as it had been at Jamestown, and, after some years of suffering and privation, as severe as that at Jamestown, though not by any means as fatal, Plymouth was sheltering a fairly prosperous band of about three hundred men and women.

Soon after their arrival, the adjacent shores of Massachusetts Bay were dotted with little villages of log huts, housing such fur-traders and adventurers as Thomas Morton of Merrymount and Robert Gorges of Wessagusset; a small band of men settled at Dorchester and another at Salem, all under grants from the Council for New England, to whom James I had delegated in 1620 the right to grant to colonists the land between the fortieth and forty-eighth parallels. Most of these settlements were soon absorbed into the Colony of Massachusetts Bay, founded by the arrival of the Great Emigration at Boston in 1630 under John Winthrop and Thomas Dudley. In contrast to the fur-traders, who had money and servants but were not colonists, and to the Pilgrims, who possessed numbers but few worldly goods, the Puritans were well provided with both and came for the express purpose of founding a new state in the wilderness on the model laid down in the Bible. Several of them had held positions of prominence in England, most of them had some property, and, with their retainers, furniture, and domestic animals, they soon established around Boston a number of small but thriving towns, whose population was constantly augmented by new arrivals from England.

Indeed, so marked was the strength and wealth of the Bay Colony that its malcontents seceded and founded Providence, Rhode Island, the River Towns, New Haven, and New Hampshire, without hindering its own rapid growth. The settlement of New England was in a sense merely the expansion of Massachusetts. Meanwhile, Lord Baltimore had founded in Maryland a colony meant to be a refuge for Roman Catholics persecuted in England; the Swedes had set up factories along the Delaware; the Dutch had extended their trading-posts along the Hudson and Long Island Sound. By 1640, the whole Atlantic coast was fringed with colonists all of whom had arrived in a single generation, the great bulk of whom had come within the single decade, 1630–1640, to a land on which it had hardly seemed possible in 1588 that an English colony would ever exist.

The explanation of this rapid growth and of the permanence of the English colonies is to be found partly in the extremely advantageous character of the land for the purposes of settlement. The soil was fertile, the climate temperate, the rainfall varied and dependable, making possible a great variety of crops and in particular allowing the production of all the staples to which the colonists had been accustomed in Europe. The change in their mode of life was not, therefore, too violent, as had been the case with the Spanish and the French. The numerous rivers were so many highways opening the country for miles inland to exploitation at a time when the making of roads would have opposed insuperable obstacles to its exploration and settlement. The influence of the land upon the people who came was good. It attracted serious, hard-working men and women, looking for homes, whose energy and resourcefulness were developed by life in a climate too cold to make existence easy. From the elements that had fatally distracted the attention of the Spaniards—precious metals and luxuriant vegetation—it was entirely free, and forced the colonists to develop profitable industries by their own labor. The treasure-seekers, the merely adventurous, the lazy, the stupid were soon eliminated and the population was recruited only from the more desirable European emigrants.

Nor was it without a deep thankfulness and sense of its

significance that Winthrop wrote, "God hath cleared our title." Perhaps the character of the land, perhaps chance, had made the coast Indians weak, and they had been further decimated by pestilence just before the English settlers appeared at Jamestown and at Plymouth. In addition, numbers were swept off by strong drink which acted upon their unaccustomed frames like virulent poison, and by the measles and smallpox which they caught from the whites and which raged as epidemic fevers, deadly as the plague. While it is not probable that the English were influenced solely by a desire to insure the Indians' welfare, the fact remains that one and all they treated them with courtesy and did not rouse their antagonism. Henry Hudson, in particular, so entertained the chiefs along the Hudson in 1609 when he explored that river, that the Iroquois were ever after firm friends of the English. No doubt the attack upon them by Champlain on the Richelieu River that same year and the prodigious fright they received from the firing of his blunderbuss contributed to the general result. In time, however, as the coast Indians learned that settlement by the English meant not only fire-water, guns, iron hatchets, and kettles so superior in operation to their own crude tools that life became a pleasure, but the loss of their land and the destruction of the game, hostility developed apace and gave rise to sporadic outbreaks which were with one or two exceptions crushed by the colonists without great difficulty. On the whole, it is true, that only in the first years of the century were the Indians a menace to the existence of the English settlements.

Nevertheless, had it not been for the founding of Massachusetts Bay and the presence around Boston of thousands, where at Plymouth and Jamestown were only hundreds, the fate of the United States might have been different. Massachusetts was a tower of strength to the people of New Haven and the River Towns in their resistance to the encroachments of the Dutch. The little collection of huts inside the rough palisade at New Amsterdam was rather a trading-post than a permanent settlement, for its population were Indian traders, sailors, and the cosmopolitan crew which had haunted the New England coast until dislodged by the settlers who had not scrupled to eject them bag and baggage as undesirable tenants. From Holland were sent out by the Dutch West India Company "governors" whose duty it was to control the fur-trade and make money for the Company. Yet weak as New Amsterdam was, had it not been for the existence of Massachusetts, the attempts of Kieft and Stuyvesant to get control of the Connecticut River valley might have been successful, more settlers might have come, and the English conquest of 1665 might have added to the other elements already in America a really considerable amount of Dutch blood and tradition. To the south, the Swedes succumbed to the Dutch. Thus, little more than half a century after the first English settlers arrived, about eighty thousand people were scattered along the coast from Maine to North Carolina, all of whom recognized the English King and the English law and the vast majority of whom had come from England itself.

The most vital fact, however, explaining the permanence of English possession is found in the existence of maize, an indigenous and nutritious food-plant, which could be cultivated successfully where the European foodstuffs could not be grown. Wheat, barley, rye, or oats needed a cleared field, deep ploughing, and constant labor. A hole made with a sharp stick in the open fields or in any forest clearing, a bit of fish dropped in and covered with a little dirt knocked in with the foot, a few kernels of maize covered in a similarly primitive manner and the whole process of agriculture was finished. Neither the Jamestown nor Plymouth colonists nor many and many a trader would have lived to tell the tale but for this maize which they could raise or buy from the Indians. At first serious discussions, which amuse us, took place over the edibility of shell fish, turkeys, and blueberries, and grave doubts were felt about the safety of drinking the water, instead of the "small-beer" to which they had been accustomed in England. These doubts were vanquished by a little experience induced by necessity, and it is hardly an exaggeration to say that the great majority of the colonists supported life even during the first half century largely from indigenous food-products.

But America would never have counted many inhabitants had it not provided them with a profitable return for their labor in the shape of commodities which could be sent to England in exchange for the clothes, shoes, books, and luxuries to which they had been accustomed. The market was soon overstocked with sassafras, but tobacco furnished the Southern colonies a marketable staple whose importance in the upbuilding of the United States cannot be exaggerated. The simplicity of its cultivation, the possibility of employing unskilled labor, the simple method of curing it discovered about 1616 by Rolfe, made it the decisive influence in ensuring the growth of the young colony on the James. By this time, it was well known in England that olives, wine, and silk were as legendary as gold and pearls, and expectant colonists for New England needed to be assured of the presence of some tangible asset. The cod, whose dense schools stopping the progress of ships had attracted Breton and Portuguese fishermen as early perhaps as 1450, now became a staple of the thriving trade of Boston and Plymouth, where the pious Bradford and his lieutenant, John Alden, developed an amazing commercial sagacity for men who had renounced worldly aims. Along the New England coast the supply of fur-bearing animals was soon too much reduced to make the trade profitable, but New Amsterdam and Fort Orange (Albany) rivaled Tadousac, Quebec, and Montreal as fur centers. The Hudson and Mohawk tapped the home land of the great Iroquois tribes and were the natural outlet for their spoils of the chase. By all these varied factors, the advantages of the site, the absence of powerful Indian occupants, the value of maize, tobacco, fish, and furs, the permanence of the English colonies in America was assured as early as 1640. The preponderance of the English

over all other elements of the population made it clear
that they would mold the destinies of the growing nation
and absorb foreign elements rather than be themselves
absorbed.

THE ECONOMIC GROWTH OF THE COLONIES

In 1665, the whole Atlantic coast passed finally into English control; in 1776, the coast colonies declared themselves independent of England. The chief task for the historian of colonial history is the explanation of this latter fact—the most important single fact in our annals—the depicting of the forces which enabled us to deserve and to win our independence. The fundamental cause of the Revolution lies in the rapid economic growth of the colonies which made them in 1775 strong enough and wealthy enough to stand alone. Independence was necessarily an accomplished fact which no fiat could create and which was in 1776 a condition resulting from the operation of forces in the decades just past. The Revolution by no means created thirteen States; it declared the already accomplished fact that those thirteen States were independent entities, distinct from England in ideals and interests, strong enough to maintain themselves against the rest of the world, experienced in self-government, and imbued with the spirit of liberty. The premise of the Revolution is the preceding century of colonial history, and, unless we study that century of growth from the point of view of its most significant result, we shall be closing our eyes to some of the most vital facts in our history. These are the extent and character of the economic growth which made us strong enough to resist; the system of self-government which had enabled us to manage our own affairs so long without assistance that the severing of the political and constitutional ties with England was accomplished literally by writing a few words on paper declarative of the existing facts; and the relations of the colonies to the mother-country out of which grew those tangible constitutional and political issues which roused so great an antagonism on either side of the ocean as to result in actual warfare. The growth of the colonies, the rise of American democracy, States' sovereignty, these are the chief topics of colonial history between 1665 when the Atlantic coast became English and 1776 when the colonies declared themselves independent.

The most important fact about the growth of the thirteen colonies is its extent. Within three generations, a few scattered groups of people had grown by natural accretion and by immigration into the elements of a nation. When the *Susan Constant* anchored in the James River in 1607, a few hundred fur-traders and fishermen were in the habit of spending the summers on the Atlantic coast; by 1640, the English settlers already numbered thousands, nearly 16,000 of whom were in the Bay Colony alone; and by 1660, about 80,000 souls were building homes in the new continent. Within a century, the number of colonies had doubled, and the population, as nearly as it can now be estimated, was twenty times as large as in 1660, having reached the astounding figure of 1,600,000. Clearly, if this development be any criterion, the period preceding the Revolution was not one of acute suffering and distress. And the Revolution itself only stimulated the resort of people thither, for thirty years later the first census of the United States claimed a total population of 4,000,000. Here, in fact, lies the fundamental cause of the Revolution: a century of growth had made the colonies strong enough and wealthy enough to stand alone. Of this the leaders were thoroughly aware. As the Declaration of Causes of July 4, 1775, finely and truly said: "We gratefully acknowledge as signal instances of the divine favor towards us that His Providence would not permit us to be called into this severe controversy, until we were grown up to our present strength, had been previously exercised in warlike operations, and possessed of the means of defending ourselves."

The story of this most significant growth, however, does not describe the settling of thirteen colonies which normally developed by the increase of population and interchange of ideas into the thirteen States of the Revolutionary epoch. It tells of a scarcely broken stream of new emigrants from Europe, with varied customs, ideals, and traditions; of a constant and vital *transformation* decade after decade of every aspect of colonial life. The colonies in 1760 were not only collectively and individually bigger and richer; they were individually totally dissimilar in population, in government, in ideals from the tiny communities extant in 1660. The first settlers, indeed, far from giving final form or even definitive direction to the various States, in most cases merely began the formal existence of that particular political entity, which, after a century and more of transformation and astonishing growth, ultimately became one of the States which declared themselves sovereign in 1776. To suppose that the Massachusetts of 1640, the New York of 1689, the Pennsylvania of 1700 was in anything more than a technical political and constitutional sense the father of the State of 1776 is to lose sight of the most significant fact in colonial history, to forget the growth which made the Revolution possible. In addition, it indicates our failure to remember that the difference in development during that century of those who came to America and those who remained in England was perhaps the main cause of that disagreement out of which the Revolution ostensibly grew. The very extent of the transformation is a cardinal point to stress. In 1760, the thirteen colonies were not English; they were already American.

While there is always danger of exaggerating the extent of the change and of thus seeming to forget that fundamental qualities of the people and basic notions of government can be directly traced to the influence of the first settlers, it is nevertheless only necessary to remind the reader that dancing, card-playing, and theater-going were common amusements in Revolutionary Boston to show him how great a change had taken place since the strict days of John Cotton.

Indeed, Harvard College, founded as a bulwark of the theology dominant in 1640, had by 1700 already become the home of liberal thought to the utter dismay of the orthodox, and the leaven had so spread in the community that even the Great Awakening of 1745 was wholly insufficient to stifle the theological dissent from the older Calvinism. In Pennsylvania, a militia, courts, a hierarchy of judicial officials, and a police force in Philadelphia bore eloquent testimony to the extent of the departure from the ideals of Penn.

The very elements of the future nation, much less the nation itself, were not on this continent in 1660. Six of the thirteen colonies, New York, New Jersey, Pennsylvania, the Carolinas, and Georgia, came into existence after the Restoration.[1] To the Pilgrims, Puritans, and Cavaliers were added other elements of which several outnumbered the original English settlers. There were probably more Quakers around Philadelphia in 1690, and more Germans in New York and Pennsylvania in 1715, than there were English on the whole continent in 1634. The Salzburgers, the Palatines, the Huguenots, the Scotch-Irish from Ulster, the Portuguese Jews were racially and religiously dissimilar from the Pilgrims and Puritans and brought (except the Scotch-Irish) totally different languages, political traditions, and social customs whose marks are still as distinct in the districts where they settled as the impress of the Puritans upon Massachusetts. Most of these dissimilar elements settled along the coast after 1700 and no small proportion came after 1740. The growth which the colonies had attained by 1760 was due less to the normal increase of those already here in 1660 than to direct immigration from Europe.

The character of the individuals who came was also vastly different. With the Pilgrims had come many laborers sent over by the merchants who financed their expedition; Winthrop and his partners had also paid the passage of many

[1] New York, of course, belonged to Holland before 1660, and the abortive settlements of the Swedes along the Delaware seem scarcely worth reckoning.

artisans and farm-hands, and the settlers alive in Virginia were largely descendants of men and women induced to come by the Virginia Company's promises or payments. Still, the proportion of the well-to-do who paid their own transportation and came to the new country with seeds, cattle, tools, and ready money was much greater before 1660 than it was after that date. By 1700, the first extravagant expectations of great wealth and wine-growing had long been definitely abandoned; the Seven Cities of Cibola had been transplanted to inaccessible spots in the interior, and navigators had found the Northwest Passage unpleasantly elusive; the Atlantic coast was rapidly being stripped of fur-bearing animals and the new Hudson Bay Company had monopolized the trade with northern Canada. The possibilities of abnormal profits in trade with the new continent had disappeared, and the capitalists who had financed colonies were disappointed with the small returns and declined to "adventure" more money.

The emigrants were with every decade more and more recruited from those driven from Europe by their individual poverty. Many came as "indented" servants, who in return for passage allowed the ship-captain to auction them off to the highest bidder, binding themselves to serve him for five or seven years. Most of the labor in the tobacco fields of the Chesapeake colonies and in the grain fields of Pennsylvania and New Jersey was of this type. At the end of the term of service, the colony gave him land and his late master furnished him with clothes, seeds and tools. He began life anew; the social stigma hitherto attached to him soon disappeared and he became a full-fledged citizen. Many political prisoners of excellent and desirable stock were shipped over by Cromwell and by James II, and the English government also attempted to mitigate the severity of the criminal code by giving those condemned to death or to long terms of imprisonment the option of transportation to the colonies. More of these were sent to the Barbadoes and the West Indian sugar colonies than to the continent; those guilty of the petty offences then punishable by hanging were hardly what we should call criminals; but these unfortunates as well as the indented servants and political prisoners were very different material for a new nation from the stern, capable, educated men and women who followed Winthrop and Bradford, Hooker and Davenport, Calvert and Penn. In addition, many and many a cosmopolitan adventurer of the type of Morton of Merrymount, many a smuggler and illicit fur-trader, who fretted at the restrictions of society, came to the new land and formed with kindred spirits, at first along the coast and later in the interior, numerous settlements whose business, good and bad, was in volume out of all proportion to their size. These were "the stumbling blocks" in New England's Canaan, the tares sprung up among the wheat. But these dare-devil, careless frontiersmen formed an important element among the new people and in actual numbers cannot have been negligible; we must not forget that they too left descendants. In fact, it was their spirit rather than that of Puritan and Cavalier that became the dominant note of American life in the days of Jackson.

These emigrants to the new world, however their object in coming changed from time to time, were, in 1760 as in the beginning, a sturdy race of enthusiastic, resourceful radicals. Otherwise they had not come. Whatever the motive which led them to America—the difference of creed, the desire to invest capital, the lack of opportunity to make a living at home, ambition, adventure, restlessness—it was invariably their discontent with what existed, and their faith in their own ability to better their fortunes which led the emigrants thither. The result was striking. Gradually the population of Europe was sifted, as Stoughton said, that "We might plant choice grain in the wilderness." Gradually as the more venturesome were drawn into the colonies, the more conservative were left at home. Those whose hatred of the pressure of creed, of social convention, or poverty, had been sufficient to drive across three thousand miles of ocean into an unknown wilderness were not likely to rear there descendants who would brook much interference. The children of such men, in the Governor of Pennsylvania's vivid phrase, "rode restive." They preferred the possible dangers of change to the continuance of slight grievances. Their cousins in England were normally of the opposite mind. They were the descendants of the men who had preferred to endure what they knew rather than face perils yet unknown,—those too contented at home or too lacking in initiative to leave. A century and a half of emigration had cast the characters of the two sections of the Anglo-Saxon race in different molds. It had created in Americans a spirit, a temper of different metal from that which the stirring events of the same period had produced in the mother-country. The very growth itself furnished the possibility and almost the certainty of a fundamental disagreement between the colonies and England.

Despite its rapidity this growth in population had not resulted by 1760 in a fringe of continuous settlement from Maine to Georgia, but had produced rather a collection of little communities dotted along the coast, reaching in places a hundred miles inland, all effectually separated from each other by days of traveling by water or land.[1] A week spent between Boston and Newport, between Providence and New York, or between New York and Philadelphia was by no means an uncommon experience of travelers on horseback unincumbered by heavy baggage; and the various little communities were in point of fact in far more constant communication with London and the West Indies than with each other. Indeed, even in New England the settlement was very sparse; the acreage of primeval forest still great; the roads poor or non-existent. Connecticut was composed in 1760 of three or four little groups of towns widely separated; New York of a little cluster around the city, another around Albany and a third up the Mohawk, with a few scattered farms along the rivers. Pennsylvania strung out along the banks of the Delaware and its tributaries, or pushed down the fer-

[1] See the notably careful and accurate map in Channing's *History of the United States*, I, 510.

tile valleys of the Blue Ridge. There was in 1760, and indeed in 1790, no geographical or economic basis for a single nation or a single government. Nor did these scattered groups, already acutely conscious of their political identity, possess any economic interest in common or any economic bond of a positive character. They had grown strong as thirteen units, not as a whole; and, though they soon came to realize that some sort of coöperation would be necessary to secure that freedom from English interference they coveted, they desired freedom individually, not collectively.

The only economic conditions common to them all were negative in character: the lack of a medium of direct exchange with Europe and their common dependence upon the West India trade.

The three thousand miles of ocean separating America from Europe and the proximity of the continent to the West Indies are two of the most obvious and cardinal facts in American history. With them are vitally connected in some fashion nearly every economic and governmental issue in our history—not only colonial trade and development, but the Revolution, the Jay Treaty, Louisiana, the War of 1812, the Tariff, the Monroe Doctrine, and much more.

Except for Virginia's tobacco and South Carolina's indigo (cotton was not grown for export till after the Revolution), the colonial products were too bulky for export and were in addition not sufficiently salable in Europe to make it worth while to pay the freight thither. At the same time the very general lack of manufactures in the colonies [2] left them dependent upon Europe for nearly everything which the members of the household could not produce with their own hands. A little iron, some glass and cutlery were made in America, but not enough in quantity to supply even local demand. Pins, nails, thread, stationery, tape, knives, and the like, as

[2] "The genius of the people in these colonies is as little turned to manufacturing goods for their own use as is possible to suppose in any people whatsoever." Stephen Hopkins, *Rights of the Colonies Examined*, 13. (1765.)

well as French millinery and English broadcloth, were regularly imported by American merchants. For all this, they must pay, and, with little currency in the colonies and that so debased that the English would not accept it at face value, with no commodities in most colonies which the English wished in exchange, the merchants were forced to undertake a round of regular trading ventures in order to pay their European bills.[3]

The West India colonies, owned by England, France, Holland, and Spain, were producing great amounts of sugar, then scarce and correspondingly expensive in Europe, and were therefore making huge returns to the owners of plantations. The planters preferred to buy food and necessities from the continental colonists rather than divert the labor needed to produce them from the infinitely more lucrative work of cane cultivation. The colonists were equally glad to find so near at hand a market in which to exchange what they raised for the sugar, molasses, and rum so highly valued in Europe. The ordinary method of exchange between Boston and England was therefore via the West Indies. The New England ship loaded at Boston with salt fish for the slaves' food on the sugar plantations, with staves for the barrels and hogsheads in which the sugar and molasses were to be shipped, with boards, window frames, and all the various pieces needed for constructing the planter's house. At St. Christopher, she would load with sugar and molasses, proceed to London, load with manufactured goods, and so return to Boston, clearing ordinary between fifty and one hundred per cent profit. We know of a captain who made

[3] The difficulty of making remittances to England at all, even by means of a round of trading voyages, is admirably illustrated by the correspondence between William Penn and his American agent, James Logan. "If thou canst not get silver . . . by the Madeiras directly thither, as well as by Barbadoes with Madeira wine, send as fast as thou canst turn our cheap corn, flour, and bread into wine, and some wine into sugar, home for supply." Penn to Logan, 1704. *Penn and Logan Correspondence*, I, 340. (Pennsylvania Historical Society, Memoirs, IX.)

eight hundred per cent profit off a cargo of salt taken into Baltimore, and we find merchants considering themselves defrauded if the net profits of the carrying trade fell below one hundred per cent. Even if such cases were not as common as the evidence seems to indicate, there can be no doubt that the legitimate profits from this triangular trade were very large.

Another triangular trade, of which the West Indies were a significant factor, was far more lucrative and hence even more popular in New England. A ship-load of inferior molasses converted into Medford rum in the numerous distilleries in Massachusetts and Rhode Island would purchase from the sodden chiefs of the West African Coast a crowded ship-load of "black ivory," whose value in the West Indian sugar plantations or the Virginian tobacco fields transcended many times the costs of the enterprise. Rum, molasses, and slaves became the solid basis of many a colonial fortune and there can be no doubt that men and women, who believed themselves even more attentive to the calls of conscience than their descendants who are prompt to censure this nefarious traffic, saw in it absolutely nothing objectionable. This attitude toward slavery and the slave-trade in the eighteenth century needs to be most carefully borne in mind by those who undertake to assign the moral responsibility for negro slavery in the South in 1860. It is also incontestable that the Massachusetts men who engaged in this traffic were not one whit different from those sterner men who wrote in the Body of Liberties in 1641, "There shall never be any bond slaverie villinage or Captivitie amongst us, unless it be lawfull Captives taken in just warres, and such strangers as willingly sell themselves or are sold to us."

The significance and importance of the existence of the West India Islands in the colonial and revolutionary periods can scarcely be exaggerated. So great were the profits, so completely did any commerce whatever rest upon one or the other triangular trade, that by 1760 the colonists had come to Defoe's conclusion, that without that trade they would perish.[4] To their minds, the results from it in the cases of individuals and of communities alike were so tangible and convincing that they had almost ceased to believe that any other forces had been behind the exhilarating growth of the past decades.

The number of ships clearing from New York had increased from 64 in 1717 to 477 in 1762; the exports to England which had been according to a seemingly trustworthy source £18,000 in 1701 were in 1767, £61,000; and the imports into New York from England, which were of course the direct fruits of the West India trade, had risen from £31,910 in 1701 to the enormous figure of £417,957 in 1767. A glance at such a balance-sheet as this made clear to colonial merchants how great a demand for English goods existed in the colonies, and how utterly incapable they were of carrying on any direct trade with the mother-country. Indeed, they knew well enough that the English cared little for their exports; but would be panic-stricken at the idea of losing a market for English goods of which the total imports were annually well into the millions of pounds. Above all, they were afraid of losing so convenient a method of receiving the West India products at their own doors and of there selling their own manufactures, a trade from which they derived great profit and in which the colonial shippers shouldered the risks of loss or capture at sea.

That the Navigation Acts were intended to confine this lucrative trade to English and colonial ships, and were meant,

---

[4] "The very Being and Subsistence of New England in matters of Trade consists in and depends wholly upon their Union with and Subjection to Great Britain, as the Growth [i. e., products] of their Country, which is the only Article that supports their Commerce, is taken off by the British Colonies only. . . . Without this Export those Colonies would perish. It is true, the Islands [in the West Indies] would starve for want of provisions too, at least at first; but on the Continent, if the Islands did not take off their Product, their Lands which they have been at a vast Expense to cure and clear and plant would lie useless and uncultivated. . . . Their Plantations would produce more of everything than their mouths could devour or than they could find markets to vend them at." Daniel Defoe, *A Plan of English Commerce.*

as well, to handicap the foreign sugar islands by compelling them to provide themselves with the food, lumber, and live-stock which the English tropical colonies obtained from the continent, this, too, they well understood. Nor, while the continental colonies were weak and the surplus available for export was small, were the Navigation Acts needed to prevent the colonists from seeking a market elsewhere. The logic of the situation and the obvious advantages which colonial ships possessed for carrying the sugar and tobacco to England were sufficient to prevent any very considerable breach of the spirit of the acts, however zealously the colonial captains labored to evade paying the customs dues.

But as the eighteenth century progressed, the productive capacity of the colonies grew proportionately faster than did the needs of the English West India colonies. Probably not later than 1700, the English West India markets were over-stocked with colonial goods at times when the French, Dutch, and Spanish islands were ready to pay high prices for the same commodities. Inevitably, the colonial captains threw the statutes to the winds and sought the better market. The easy sale and the large profits, the willingness of officials and ship-masters to overlook statutes and regulations, and the lack of any coercive force to compel obedience resulted promptly in the development of a brisk and regular smug-gling trade between the foreign sugar islands and the colonial merchants. Fraudulent clearance papers, and the posses-sion of several sets of false certificates by most ship-captains lent a specious legality to these practices, and colonial ships were soon doing business with Hamburg and Middleburg as well as London. The illicit business grew indeed at such a rate that by the time of the Revolution apparently trust-worthy authorities stated the volume of trade between Ham-burg, Holland, and New York at a quarter of a million pounds.[5] While such statistics are probably inaccurate, there can be no doubt that the direct trade with Europe was

[5] H. B. Dawson, *New York City During the Revolution*, 38, and the statistics and authorities there quoted.

very large and that these figures represent the belief of both English and colonial merchants as to its extent and value. To the colonist, it was the sum of which the English government meant to rob him in order to put it into the pockets of Englishmen; to the London merchants, it represented the sum of which they had already been robbed.

This economic interest, however, was not in any sense of the word national, nor did it constitute any positive bond of union between the colonies. In fact, individuals and not entities were affected; and not by any means all individuals. The growth of wealth, like that of population, had not been evenly spread throughout the colonies or even throughout any single colony. Those towns which lay even a short distance from the sea or from some river remained, like Braintree, Massachusetts, nearly static in population and wealth, dependent largely for what they possessed on the work of their own people. Vast and noticeable as was the increase in general wealth, individual merchants and planters, individual towns, and even colonies possessed more than a proportionate share. The handsome mansions around Boston and along the Chesapeake, the imported clothes and conveniences of certain individuals soon marked them as a class apart from the rest in the city or town. With ready money to lend, with goods to sell, with positions to fill, they soon became the creditors of many in the same community who were not so well off. The rich were, in sooth, not as wealthy, nor the poor as destitute as those classes in Europe; the actual distance between them was slight, but it was unmistakably there, and must never be forgotten by one who hopes to understand the history of the Revolution. The merchant was the only purchaser of colonial produce, and the only importer of the coveted English goods. His profits as middleman, then as now, were grudgingly paid, and the fact forgotten that the great profits on a successful voyage were balanced by equally heavy losses when a cargo of grain spoiled, the ship was wrecked, or was captured by pirates or privateers. Unquestionably, there had grown up in the colonies a hatred of the creditor class by the debtor class.

Similarly, the inland towns and hamlets, the "frontier," were usually heavily in debt to the coast towns for salt, seeds, tools, and numerous commodities they had grown accustomed to but could not make. So we find a distinct feeling of hostility nourished by the farmers in the Berkshires against the Boston merchants; by the farmers in the Blue Ridge against the coast towns in Pennsylvania and Virginia; and the beginning of the present antipathy between the counties and the city of New York. In these "debtor" districts, really primitive conditions existed, and the people, shivering in homespun around the great fire in the log cabins, supposed that the merchants and planters must be extremely comfortable, clad in broadcloth and ensconced in a plastered house, decorated with the expensive "china paper." That the latter were also exceedingly uncomfortable, the farmers did not know and would not have believed had they been told. The creation of these great creditor and debtor classes was one of the chief results of the character of colonial growth. Their existence is one of the cardinal facts needed for a comprehension of the Revolution; for that war was fought quite as much between two parties in America as between England and the colonies, and the Loyalist and Patriot parties coincided far more closely with the lines of creditor and debtor than has generally been supposed. The Civil War was not over in 1781; it continued during the Critical Period; the adoption of the Constitution marked the victory of the creditor party, which was promptly crushed in 1800 by the debtors enrolled as Anti-Federalists. Indeed, the fact that the East has been normally the creditor of the West has been one of the fundamental facts in our history and is the explanation of most of our economic phenomena. Colonial growth not only provided economic interests sufficiently powerful to cause the breach with England, but it resulted in the creation of the two economic interests which have been dominant in this country ever since, those of the settled country and of the frontier.

V

THE ORIGIN OF AMERICAN DEMOCRACY

PROVIDENTIALLY, the English settlers began their new life so far from home that active assistance or interference from England in local government was out of the question. American democracy originated in necessity: the settlers did their own work because there was no one else who could by any possibility do it. By 1775, they had governed themselves so long in every particular and with such complete success that the breach with England caused and involved absolutely no administrative difficulties or changes. The fact that the colonists had governed themselves was conclusive proof that they were not dependent upon the mother-country, that merely formal and superficial obstacles stood in the way of complete independence. In this we find a second fundamental cause of the Revolution, scarcely less significant than the economic strength of America.

The width of the Atlantic Ocean, the fact that a very few thousand people were scattered in tiny groups over a thousand miles of sea-coast, the absolute lack of kings, feudal barons, or administrative organs of any sort created by past generations to perform the community's work for it,—these were the primary causes of the origin of American democracy. Nor need we look further than the exigencies and circumstances of the moment for an explanation of its early character. There seems to have been no conscious choice between alternative forms or models, no consideration of theories. Naturally, emigrants did not forget such habits and traditions of local government as they brought with them, but the needs of the moment rather than theory and precedent shaped the Virginia parish and the New England town. It

is only too evident from the records that the first governments grew into being rather than were consciously created.
The circumstances of settlement, permitting no great extremes of wealth or poverty, of education or ignorance, naturally provided the very conditions best adapted for democracy. Indeed, any other form of government would have
been an anomaly, and the various schemes, worthy and un-
worthy, concocted by capitalists and theorists, from the complicated system of councils proposed by Sir Thomas Smith
to the elaborate dreams of John Locke and the constitutional
experiments of William Penn, one and all promptly and in-
gloriously failed. The conditions were right for democracy and were therefore wrong for feudal palatinates and
aristocratic lordships. No one tried to plant democratic
governments; nothing else could be made to grow.

The beginnings of self-government in the town of Dedham,
Massachusetts, furnish a most interesting example of this
natural evolution. The settlers brought with them the traditions of the medieval parish and of the close town-corpora-
tion of Elizabeth's time, with a full panoply of ideas about
nobles and kings, and little or no actual experience in government. The strongest influence was that of the "Church
covenant," then in vogue amongst the Puritans and Separa-
tists, an agreement to abide by the common decision which
did hold the seed of democratic self-government, but which
certainly was not intended to sanction anything we should
recognize as democracy or administration. This was the only
precedent they seem to have found useful. In 1636, twenty-
two "proprietors" signed a simple "covenant" or agreement
to abide individually by the decision of the majority, and
the community then continued for some weeks to exercise its
sovereignty by performing the work of the miniature State
with its own hands.[1] It gave neither itself nor its members
titles nor powers; it discussed neither laws nor theories, and
formally recognized no necessary governmental relationship

[1] The Records of the Town of Dedham have been published and this
information is drawn from them.

with any other body of men in the world. The "executive" business consisted of allotting lands; and the first ordinance was thus recorded: "Ordered that the next Fair day every man of our society shall meet at the footway and assist to mend the same, and soe many as can bring whelbarrowes." The sovereign was at one and the same time executive, legislature, and judiciary, but found spades and wheelbarrows more useful than the pen and the gavel. The only office created during the first four years was that of collecting the fines due from those who came late to the town-meeting, after the beating of the town drum.

On May 17, 1639, the town adopted its first "constitution," and there is no good reason to suppose that Winthrop at Boston was consulted. They acted of their own grace and motion and recognized no authority as higher than their own. "Whereas it hath been found by long experience that the general meeting of soe many men in one meeting of the common affayres thereof, have waisted much tyme to noe small damage, and business is thereby nothing furthered: it is therefore nowe agreed by generall consent, that these 7 men heerunder named we doe make choice of and give them full power to contrive, execute, & performe all the business and affayres of this our wholl towne." The sovereign delegated the whole of its authority for the space of one year. Surely no such "constitution" was ever thought of in England nor ever would have been by these same men had they stayed in England. Nor would they have thus tacitly assumed their complete legal independence of all other authority, had not the miles of wilderness between them and the Governor at Boston compelled them to act on their own initiative. The conditions of the new world fairly thrust the scepter into their hands. It is perfectly clear that the annual town-meeting resumed all authority at the close of each year, and instead of electing new incumbents to these offices, literally created the offices over again. In 1640, a town-clerk and surveyors of highways were elected; and the selectmen appointed the first administrative officials,—fence-viewers, wood-reeves and hog-reeves. The title, "selectmen," does not appear in the records until 1648.

No doubt the close organization of the New England town was largely influenced by the severity of the climate. The long winters forced the people to cling together, not only for sociability, but for the juster and easier distribution of the scanty store of food and fuel. Then too the proximity of the Indians made scattered settlement dangerous. Nor was there much temptation to stray far from the town. No agriculture was profitable in the North until much labor had been expended in clearing the land and most men were unwilling to put so much time into a few acres which were not favorably situated for trade and intercourse. The land around the town seemed in most cases as likely to be fertile as that further away, and the difficulties of clearing and cultivation made comparatively few acres all one family could really use.

In the South, the conditions exacted by the tobacco-culture created, aided by the traditions of English county and parish government, a very different type of local organization. The culture of tobacco consisted in sowing the seed in small beds, in transplanting the young plants into the earth loosened with a hoe between the stumps in a clearing, in hoeing them regularly, and in pinching off the shoots and tops which developed the stalk at the expense of the leaves. The heat of the sun, the arduous and continuous toil, the simplicity of the work made profitable the employment of forced or slave labor. The mild winters, which left the ground open to cultivation nearly if not all the year round, and the necessity of constantly clearing new fields to take the place of those which could not be artificially fertilized, all tended to make the work of the plantation continuous and to tempt the settlers to draw further and further apart in their eagerness to increase the size of their individual holdings. Here were conditions as different as could well be conceived from those in New England but which no less powerfully worked for the growth of self-government. Obviously, the owner of a plantation, living with a couple of overseers and from a dozen to a couple of hundred forced laborers or slaves, on a tract some thousands of acres in size, miles from his nearest neighbor, needed desperately authority of a peculiarly broad type. But in the nature of things there was no one to whom this authority could be delegated or who could effectively use it save the planter himself. Where all citizens were in such a position, local government was necessarily less concerned with the regulation of the behavior of citizens than it was with that of their servants or slaves. Misbehavior and crime committed by the slave or indented servant had to be punished by the master as the only possible delegate of the community's authority, and his right to decide what was or was not to be punished and what penalty ought to be inflicted had to be made as absolute as the imperative necessity of preventing insubordination and revolt among the laborers. Elaborate local government was not needed for there was practically no community life; nor, while the plantation system lasted, was there likely to be a community life whose needs could not be met by the simplest possible arrangements. Legislation dealt chiefly with the relation of employer and employee, of master and slave; the difficulties between masters were few. The whole business of the county was little more than the collection of the quitrents due the Crown, the recording of land titles, and the trying of the few law cases arising between planter and planter, and could be transacted to general satisfaction by at most three officials, whose combined powers were not infrequently vested in the same individual.

Such conditions naturally induced the belief that government ought to interfere with the individual as little as possible; that its sphere of usefulness was so limited that the less it did, the better,—a view based upon the undeniable fact that in Virginia, in Maryland, and in most places where an agricultural population was widely scattered over a great area of land, there were very few things which the individual imperatively needed, which he could not do for himself more promptly and efficiently than the community could possibly do them for him. In fact, the need for coöperation was slight, and the advantages were obvious of complete control over the laborers without too much investigation by others as to the justice of the planter's administration of the laws. Amid such surroundings, grew up the men whose descendants believed so firmly in loose construction, in Jeffersonian democracy, and in States' rights. Under utterly different conditions, which made coöperation as valuable to the New Englander as individual discretion was to his Virginian cousin, grew up the men whose descendants believed as firmly in the benefits of a strong centralized administration, in Federalism, and in National government.

While apparently a less natural evolution than the local governments, the State governments were as little the result of design and as much the creatures of conditions. Many of the first settlers came to the new land as employees of an individual or of a trading-company and the royal charter delegated to the grantee certain powers over them. That anything more elaborate would be needed than some method for deciding simple civil and criminal cases was not anticipated. A handful of men in a wilderness would hardly need special legislation or complicated organs of administration. Even the most intricate schemes of the idealists provided no separation of functions and usually delegated authority and complete discretion from one body of men to another. The responsibility was to be shared rather than the actual work of administration. Self-government by men whose very presence in the new land betokened their economic dependence on some one else was not even thought of as a possibility. An adventurer, like Morton of Merrymount, "governed" the laborers he had hired, and left to his partners the "government" of their laborers. The Virginia Company delegated part of their governmental authority to a council in the colony; the merchants who financed the Pilgrims gave them authority over the laborers sent with them; while Winthrop and the few members of the joint-stock company which began the colony at Boston, expected to exercise and certainly did for some years exert all the authority there was. In most colonies, something like autocratic or military rule was the actual government of the state for a lengthy period. Smith at Jamestown and Dale after him practically put the colony under martial law; the Dutch governors in New Netherlands were forced to do the same; and in all the colonies, even in Massachusetts, the real control remained in the hands of a few men until well toward the close of the seventeenth century.

At the same time, practically without an exception, the autocrat was compelled to share his power with the settlers on a basis which was far removed from the sort of government intended by the King who granted the charter. Indeed, most colonial charters were little more than the record of English ignorance of American conditions, and scarcely one of them had after half a century more than a nominal relation to the form of government actually in operation under it. It is, indeed, hardly accurate to speak of state or colonial government as distinguished from local government before 1660. Outside of New England, the settlers were either so few or so scattered that the whole colony was in practice simply the one large town, which governed the whole geographical entity, so far as it was governed at all, with some spasmodic assistance or interference from the nearest settlers. Indeed, the trouble and expense of sharing in the government of the colony, the obvious preference of each individual for spending his whole time in the promotion of his own economic welfare, the pressure of necessity which forced him to solve for himself the more formidable difficulties, left the majority of the settlers long indifferent to the form or policy of the nominal unit to which they belonged. The growth of the community and that alone forced upon a reluctant people State government.

In every colony, however, there grew into being during the seventeenth century some sort of a representative assembly into whose hands fell eventually the direction of the government. The most rapid growth was attained in Massachusetts, where alone existed before 1640 enough towns near enough to each other to make possible some intercourse and to render advantageous some share in the direction of the common affairs. The Charter was not meant to provide for a government in the colony but it did not forbid it. It did not provide for representative government at all: it directed the election by the freemen in person (and it was assumed they would remain in England), of the usual officers of a joint-stock company, called then the Governor and Assistants (the modern President and Directors), who were to exercise the entire authority vested in the company, subject only to the approval of the stockholders at the meeting of the General Court. By-laws could of course be passed; the officials in America would of course enforce the English civil and criminal law, and make such arrangements as the exigencies of the occasion might dictate. Winthrop, Dudley, and the few stockholders who came to America accordingly voted themselves, before landing, the extensive judicial and administrative powers of an English justice-of-the-peace. Some opposition promptly became apparent; their interpretations of the English civil and criminal code and their levy of taxes were questioned, but Winthrop's coolness and the ability and essential fairness of his administration silenced the objectors. He and his associates were forced, however, to admit to membership in the trading-company some hundred men who applied for admission in 1631. Their rights to a definite share in the economic advantages possessed by the company could not be denied and the certainty that they could easily obtain title to lands and goods in some other part of New England counseled acquiescence. But Winthrop and his friends forbore to mention to the new freemen that the Charter invested them with broad powers of administration, and continued therefore for three years longer to admit new freemen from time to time and to exercise such legislative, executive, and judicial functions as they deemed advisable.

Meanwhile, local governments in the various towns around Boston sprang into vigorous life and their propinquity to each other resulted in an organized movement among the resident freemen for a share in the government of the stock company. Executive orders and demands for taxes had come from Boston to these new sovereign communities, and excited in their members some wonder as to the authority Winthrop possessed. Finally, a committee of investigation appeared in Boston in 1634 and demanded sight of the Charter, which had up to this time been sedulously kept secret. One reading opened their eyes. The freemen, thus apprised that they possessed a voice in the common affairs equal to that of the Governor and Assistants and the right to elect those officials yearly (who had hitherto elected themselves to office), proceeded immediately to avail themselves of all their privileges, and from that moment began the transformation of the trading-company into democratic representative state government. The continued use of names and forms, the claim that the Charter authorized these proceedings need not blind us to the fact that the General Court from the first transacted business never before performed by commercial companies (whose governing heads were normally resident in England) and by methods which Charles I certainly never contemplated when he approved the docquet of the Charter. At the same time, the language of the Charter was so broad that few things were done which could not be read into its inclusive phrases.

The direct exercise in person of authority at quarterly meetings in the performance of a routine business yearly growing in volume soon became a burden on men whose individual affairs necessarily claimed constant attention and unremitting toil. Various expedients were tried for securing the exercise of the freeman's authority without his presence in Boston and yet without forcing him to forego the careful consideration of the matter in hand for which his vote stood. The use of proxies merely allowed the men who did go to vote all the proxies on new business as they saw fit and thus really deprived their friends of their votes. The freemen then tried balloting for officers in their home towns and sent the "papers" to Boston; but as this compelled them to vote in the dark and caused many votes to be wasted, the expedient was adopted of holding what we should call a caucus at the end of the session of the General Court, at which the freemen present prepared what we should call a "slate" to be submitted to all the freemen in all the towns. The freemen soon fell into the habit of designating the man to go up to Boston to perform these important functions in behalf of the rest. Soon, they saw the obvious advantage of investing him with full authority to act for them as his judgment dictated in all matters of common interest. They could not go in person, and, unless they were to sacrifice their power altogether, they must delegate it. Thus, the pressure of circumstances created in Massachusetts out of the nominal machinery of a trading-company a representative assembly, an upper house, and an executive of limited powers. Moreover, the fact that there were freemen in every town soon changed the emphasis of representation; the first deputies were the representatives of the freemen only, but their constituents soon came to act as a town rather than as freemen, and the assembly soon actually represented the proportional strength of the various local entities in that geographical district originally granted to the trading-company. Thus was an articulated state created utterly unlike anything in existence in Europe.

The emigrants from Massachusetts, who founded the other New England colonies, erected everywhere the sort of government already developed in Massachusetts. In fact, the famous "written constitution" adopted in Connecticut in 1639 was nothing but the description of the forms in use in the Bay Colony. In Virginia some twenty years earlier, in 1619, the Governor had summoned an assembly which was the first truly representative body in America; but the loss of the Charter in 1624, the broad powers vested in the new royal governor, the difficulty of coöperation on the part of people so widely scattered and the efficiency of the county government made representative institutions weak till into the eighteenth century. Bacon's Rebellion in 1676 was an unsuccessful protest against the autocratic rule of Berkeley. In Maryland and the Carolinas, where quasi-feudal power was vested in the proprietors, similar pressure of circumstances prevented them from exercising it and forced them to share it with the colonists. In Pennsylvania, Penn was most anxious to establish representative institutions, and, after some dispute and difficulty, came to an agreement with the people. After 1689 ensued three-quarters of a century of rapid development in self-government, which is in some respects the most important fact in colonial history, for the colonists learned how to govern themselves in state as well as in local affairs. So thoroughly did the Atlantic Ocean and the wilderness do their work, that the Declaration of Independence was in very truth merely the statement of an existing political and constitutional fact.

Nor was this all. The uniformly primitive conditions had everywhere developed institutions in an essentially similar manner. Differences there were, by no means unimportant, but on the whole the similarity was so great that all the Americans thoroughly understood one another's methods of procedure and action. There was no fundamental constitutional or political obstacle in the way of the formation of a single nation out of the English colonies. "I find," wrote John Adams to his wife, "although the colonies have differed in religion, laws, customs, and manners, yet in the great essentials of society and government, they are all alike." Simple, axiomatic, obvious as this vital fact seems to the modern American, its transcendent importance can hardly be over-emphasized. The possibility of political union was a direct result of the constitutional development of the colonial period. From this political experience came the precedent for the Constitution and as well for those two notions of the proper function of a central government which, under the names, broad and narrow construction, have been such permanent bonds of political association ever since.

In the working of colonial governments, too, we meet from the very first with a good many of those traits which have lately received so much notice and vilification. Not only have most people assumed that our colonial ancestors discovered the true frame and form of democracy which later generations in their wickedness perverted to strange uses, but they have steadfastly believed that the conduct of our ancestors was impeccable. The evidence is overwhelming in amount and conclusive in character to show that the evils as well as the virtues of American democracy are a legacy from the colonial period. One of the earliest Massachusetts elections was held in Cambridge instead of in Boston as usual, in order to increase the attendance of Winthrop's supporters who lived in the adjacent smaller towns and to put the formidable obstacle of several hours' journey in the way of the attendance of Mrs. Hutchinson's Boston friends. The latter, when they realized the success of Winthrop's manœuver, tried obstruction and filibustering in hope of using up the time and preventing the Court from reaching the election at all. For many decades, black and white beans were used in many colonies at the polls, and it was a common practice for a man to carry a few up his sleeve, which he slid into the box when he inserted his hand to vote. Repeating was common. John Adams calmly recorded in his diary the defeat of a friend at the polls because, after voting for "the first time," the candidate's friends went over to the tavern and when they returned to vote again found the polls closed! The Governor of Rhode Island publicly complained more than once that the assembly of that colony was unblushingly for sale. In Boston and most surrounding towns, the real government was in the hands of a "ring" of politicians of the ultra-modern type. John Adams wrote in his diary for February 1773, of "the Caucus Club" which met in a certain garret, where they put "questions to the vote regularly, and selectmen, assessors, collectors, wardens, forewards, and representatives are regularly chosen before they are chosen in the town."

If the political development of the colonies had made them decade by decade more alike, it had steadfastly carried them in another direction from that which English constitutional development had taken. In 1760, the Americans understood each other; they did not understand the political phrases used in England nor did the English understand those common in America. The pressure put upon the Americans by the wilderness vitally to alter the habits of action they brought from Europe is not more difficult to appreciate than the changes in England resulting from the Revolutions of 1640 and 1689. In America, democracy both in town, county, and State, had been actually created; in England, had risen the House of Commons and Cabinet government. Between such divergent ideas a breach was inevitable. Yet American and Englishman saw in his own ideas fundamental notions invested with peculiar sanctity by a century and more of tradition; and both were right. The fathers and grandfathers of both had lived and died espousing the notions he proclaimed in 1760; both were honest, both were sincere; each misunderstood the other; each believed the other was trying to deceive him and was wittingly making propositions which he knew to be false. Nothing short of a century of divergent constitutional development could have produced a breach of such magnitude between honest men and a difference of opinion too fundamental for compromise, explanation, or apology. Had it been less serious, the strong peace party on both sides of the water in 1775 might have successfully averted war. The constitutional development, which gave the colonists the political experience indispensable for independence, also resulted in the divergent constitutional ideas which caused the breach with the mother-country. In a double sense, American democracy made the Revolution possible. In a very real sense, it is the rock upon which this nation is built.

These same decades of quiet colonial growth and development had produced and trained the generation of men who were to fight and win independence from England. Historians have long unanimously agreed that for ability, probity, learning, and unselfish devotion to a great ideal, the men of the American Revolution and of the constitutional period will bear comparison with the men alive during any crisis of any country's history. The achievements of the colonial period were really stupendous. The successful work in coping with the many exigencies and needs of colonial life was the only thing which could possibly have fitted the leaders to meet the astonishing difficulties of the Revolution, the Critical Period, and the organization of a central government. The prosperity of the colonists alone could have allowed them to accumulate those fortunes which permitted them to devote their lives to the new cause. Washington was the richest man in America; Franklin, John Adams, Jefferson, Madison, the Randolphs, Hancock, and many more were men of independent means. It is hardly possible for us to conceive what their adhesion to the cause in 1775 meant; it completely disproved though it did not dispel the notion, then widespread in England, that resistance was the work of a rabble who had nothing to lose.[2]

George Washington was born, as he thought, to poverty, and trained himself therefore to make his own way in the world. When he unexpectedly inherited a great fortune, he was therefore singularly fitted to make the best use of it. To years of hard labor and outdoor life, he owed his vigorous constitution and physical endurance; his Indian campaigns and service under Braddock made him the only man in the colonies with any considerable actual experience in military matters and the only man acquainted with the effect upon British troops of the conditions under which a war would have to be fought here. He knew from experience the hopelessness of conducting a wilderness campaign upon the

[2] A Committee of Congress, appointed to report on the conduct of the English troops in America, declared in April 1777, that the British conducted themselves as was to be expected towards "a people, whom they have been taught to look upon, not as freemen defending their rights on principle, but as desperadoes and profligates, who have risen up against law and order in general and wish the subversion of society itself. . . . The same deluding principle seems to govern persons and bodies of the highest rank in Britain." *Journals of the Continental Congress*, Ford's ed., VII, 279.

European model, and he never forgot it. The final victory in the war we owe to his keen use of the topography of the country to create an impregnable defense. To him we owe the victory. He was one of those rare men who loom gigantic before the eyes of their contemporaries. He was not as impeccable in little things as he has been represented to be by the garrulous Weems and a century of school text-books. He was fond of cards, was not a total abstainer, and, though a deeply religious man, was by no means devout. Possessed of an extraordinary temper, like Henry VIII and Oliver Cromwell, he had it under that same extraordinary control. Somehow he possessed that thing rarer than genius, more intangible than magnetism, a superlative sanity and probity. He gave the Revolution a watchword unique among rallying cries: "Let us raise a standard to which the wise and honest can repair." Scarcely a dozen men have ever possessed in all history the confidence of a great body of men to the degree he did. Their willingness to follow him without asking explanations or expecting comprehension of the reasons is one of the decisive factors in the movements of the time. His personal influence kept an army in the field during the war, held the jarring statesmen together till the Constitution was formed, and then set the new government on its feet. One cannot conceive of the Revolution without him. He is in the truest sense the father of the present nation. Had colonial America never developed into the United States, it would still be famous in history because it had produced such a man.

No sooner had the first tentative movements in the quarrel with England begun than the need of a foreign ambassador was felt who possessed sufficient ability, foresight, and information to meet the statesmen of the old world upon their own ground. Colonial America had made such a man out of a boy born in Boston in 1706, the fifteenth child of a poor Boston soap-maker. Benjamin Franklin had been a printer in Boston, Philadelphia, and London by the time he was twenty. His "Poor Richard's Almanac," the "Pennsylvania

Gazette,'' the printing of the Pennsylvania paper currency started him on a business career so successful that he retired upon a competence at the age of forty-three. He entered local politics and was soon sent to England to negotiate with the Penns for a settlement of the old dispute about the quit-rents. His tact and finesse attracted such attention that he became the Massachusetts agent, and then the general colonial agent at London, where he remained till the outbreak of the Revolution. He was acquiring that diplomatic experience of which his country stood in need in 1776 when an alliance was to be proposed to France. He also brought to the service of America a European reputation for scientific achievement of the first order, gained by his epoch-making experiments with electricity. It is certainly an extraordinary fact that ''the wilderness,'' as the Europeans called America, should have produced a man who was not only a philosopher and scientist of the first order, but who was clearly the equal of the European diplomatists matched against him, and who, as it was remarked with astonishment, was not abashed in the presence of kings. The reputation of Franklin in Europe for wisdom, sanity, and probity enabled him to borrow vast sums of money on no better security than his personal assurance that some day they would be paid. That such a man should be the American ambassador went a long way towards convincing the French that we deserved independence. If the character of Washington was our army, that of Franklin was our treasury.

VI

STATES' SOVEREIGNTY

THE impartial student who reads without prejudgment the evidence of the colonial period will hardly be able to avoid the conclusion that, whatever nominal bond the individual colonies recognized as binding them to the Crown or to a lord proprietor in England, they considered themselves sovereign States in all but name.[1] The tiny Confederation of Portsmouth and Newport formally declared in 1641 that "the Government which this Bodie Politick doth attend unto in this island and the Jurisdiction thereof, in favor of our prince, is a Democratic or Popular government; that is to say, it is in the power of the Body of freemen orderly assembled, or the major part of them, to make or constitute just laws by which they will be regulated." The Crown is mentioned merely by courtesy; no other authority than that of the freemen themselves is recognized; and not only do they speak of "this Bodie Politick," and denominate it a "confederation," both of which terms proclaim sovereignty, but they declare "this Bodie Politick" to be a "democratic or Popular government." There could scarcely be a more implicit renunciation of English sovereignty. When the Long Parliament had firmly grasped the scepter of empire, its leaders

[1] The use of the word "colony" seems to me objectionable for many reasons, the chief of which is that it continually reminds the reader of a legal superiority of England over them which the Americans never recognized in actual practice except when convenient. Until independence was actually declared, however, the word "State" is hardly correct, because it denies a relationship to England which in theory the Americans gladly recognized. The usage of students sanctions "colony" and forbids "State," and I have felt it better to employ the familiar word except in cases where I have deemed it essential to emphasize the fact of States' sovereignty.

61

intimated to the Puritans in New England that they would be glad to pass any desired legislation. It is an extremely significant fact that Massachusetts declined the offer for fear of creating a precedent for legislation by Parliament at some subsequent epoch when the men in control at Westminster might not be so favorably disposed towards the colony. This same idea of the proper relationship between England and the colonies was writ large in the preamble of the Articles of the New England Confederation of 1643. By the outbreak of the Civil War, they say: "We are hindered both from that humble way of seeking advice, and reaping those comfortable fruits of protection which at other times we might expect." And from whom could they more reasonably have expected "advice" and "protection" than from their co-religionists? Already the New England colonies saw themselves as States independent of the mother-country in all but name, the only connection with England being their right to seek advice and protection. Of English rule, of English right to interfere in colonial administration, we find no recognition. The very word "colony" is rare except in the most formal documents and is almost invariably coupled with the term commonly employed, "jurisdiction." After Edmund Randolph had been in Massachusetts some months in 1676 this fact became very clear to him. "In this as well as in other things," he wrote, "that government [of Massachusetts] would make the world believe they are a free State and [they] act in all matters accordingly." In very truth, the position which the States assumed in 1776 was the same they had held throughout their earlier history. They never had recognized more than a nominal right of England to interfere in America and they did not propose to accept at the dictation of George III a theory in regard to their status which their fathers had uniformly rejected as untrue and inexpedient. The Americans in 1776 took their stand upon the solid basis of history as they knew it to have happened.

In sooth, though the English government was early informed of this tendency by the enemies of the colonists, and though it several times felt the matter important enough to deserve investigation, the exigencies of the situation in England itself gave Charles I and his sons little real opportunity to press the matter to a conclusion. The attitude of Massachusetts at these times is extremely significant from the point of view of the Revolution. When the news arrived in 1634 that the King meant to appoint a new governor for the colony, the General Court ordered the harbor fortified, appointed a commission of war and called out the militia, in expectation, they announced, of "danger from the French." There is no fact in colonial history more remarkable than this: that four years after the founding of Boston, the men of Massachusetts were prepared to fight England in maintenance of their liberties. The spirit of 1776 is merely the recrudescence of the spirit of 1634. When the royal commissioners were expected in 1664, the General Court ordered out the militia, and appointed a committee to hide the Charter. The Commissioners learned to their amazement that they were expected to land with only a few men, unarmed, and that, instead of receiving the royal representatives with joy, the community was holding a day of fasting and humiliation. A good deal of verbal willingness to meet the King's demands was expressed, but the numerous delays and the excessive amount of discussion which followed every request soon roused the suspicions of the Commissioners, who at length formally asked whether the General Court recognized the validity of their commission. The Court replied that it wished respectfully to know wherein the colonists were at fault, and, after much pressing, finally said: "We humbly conceive it is beyond our line to declare our sense of the power, intent, or purpose of your commission. It is enough for us to acquaint you what we conceive is granted to us by his Majesty's royal charter. If you rest not satisfied with our former answer, it is our trouble, but we hope it is not our fault." The Commissioners rebuked them and notified them that they proposed next day to avail themselves of their commission and try a case. The next morning they found a

messenger of the General Court on their doorstep, warning
the people by the "allegiance that they owed to his Majesty,"
not to aid or abet them, for they were usurping powers which
were not rightfully theirs. The General Court a few hours
later tried that case itself.

Some very plain language reached the Commissioners' ears:
" They say that so long as they pay the fifth of all gold and
silver according to the terms of the Charter, they are not
obliged to the King, but by civility;" "they say they can
easily spin out seven years by writing, and before that time
a change may come." They had solicited Cromwell "by one
Mr. Winsloe to be declared a Free State, and now style and
believe themselves to be so." Charles replied with a royal
order to send the officers of the colony to England. The
General Court, when shown it, expressed doubts as to its
authenticity and asked proof that the signature was really
the King's! Charles, however, was unwilling to press the
matter and allowed it to drop. Had he shown George III's
determination to force from them an acknowledgment of
England's sovereignty, is it difficult to imagine the result?
In the other colonies, the same leaven was at work. Penn's
agent wrote him in 1704: "This people think privileges their
due and all that can be grasped to be their native right. . . .
They think it their business to secure themselves against a
Queen's government."

In fact, the colonies saw in 1776 that the declaration of
their independence would involve no real administrative difficulties, because they had in very truth never been actually
governed by England at all. As Franklin ironically told the
House of Commons, the colonies before 1763 had been easily
governed at the expense of only "a little pen, ink, and paper;
they were led by a thread." Nor did his hearers perceive
that he spoke the literal truth. There was, indeed, in the
colonies in 1760, as there had been throughout the preceding
century, a prodigious admiration for England, a feeling that
it was "home," and, as Franklin said, "to be an Old England man was of itself a character of some respect and gave

a kind of rank among us." Even the early Puritans had considered the English Church their mother-church, had attended its services when in England, and had spoken of it with evident affection. At the same time, paradoxically, the colonists felt no gratitude was due the Crown or Parliament for their existence or prosperity. The Address presented by Massachusetts to Parliament in 1661 declared significantly that they had transplanted themselves at their own expense and owed their present condition to their own efforts in the preceding thirty years during which they had been undisturbed. The attempts of the Crown to collect quitrents in Virginia, the energy with which the Baltimores and the Penns had attempted to collect their rents, were conspicuous features of life in those colonies, and had roused even by 1700 a resentment, often openly expressed, against these attempts to derive a revenue from the colony. The Penns were told more than once that the colony was not a private estate which owed them rent, but a body politic, whose members possessed the right of self-government, and of which the proprietors were members, like other citizens. The citizens objected to the payment of rent not because its amount was excessive, but because they did not feel themselves bound by law or gratitude to pay it at all. And these facts were prominent in the minds of the leaders who fought the Revolution. "The settlement," wrote Jefferson in 1786, "was not made by public authority and at the public expense of England, but by the exertions and at the expense of individuals." Colonial experience had taught the colonists that they owed England no gratitude for what they had not received.

The fault was not altogether that of intention at Whitehall. As soon as Charles II was firmly seated on the throne, he created a committee of the Privy Council to supervise the colonial governments, which was continued under various names and did all that was done to govern them until 1763. This was in truth little, but it is difficult to see how it could have been more. The average voyage to England consumed six weeks and the colonists knew, therefore, that they could not receive a reply to an appeal for advice or protection, even if acted upon at once, in less than three full months at the soonest. A little experience showed them that they must wait for a reply nearly a year. After their petition reached London, it must be read, the facts investigated, their request considered and passed upon by a number of busy men, who ordinarily had before them awaiting action a score of matters equally urgent. As was usual, the work of the committee devolved upon one man, its secretary, William Blathwayt, whose diligence and energy were remarkable, but were completely overwhelmed by the physical labor of merely reading the mountain of papers concerning administrative routine voluntarily submitted by the colonies. Anything like effective supervision was practically impossible. If an order was sent to a colony, the committee well knew that the colonists would have a full six months to disobey it before proceedings could be instituted against them or even information of their delinquency brought to London. A law, "repugnant to the laws of England," and forbidden therefore by the charters, would usually have been in full operation for months if not years before the London office discovered its repugnancy. With twelve legislatures producing laws on the Atlantic coast, the work of reading them became a formidable task, and the difficulty of detecting and dealing promptly with objectionable laws exceedingly great. Well aware of these facts, the colonists easily prevented any supervision at all over important matters by passing laws for one year only, which would no longer be in force when read in England, and which could easily be repassed year after year by the legislature without fear of the effectual exercise of the royal veto. The second Massachusetts charter required the submission to the English authorities of all "acts," so the General Court submitted a long list of unimportant "acts," and transacted all important business by means of "resolves" which were not required to be sent to England. In Pennsylvania, all acts were required to be submitted every five years to the English authorities, a provision easily evaded by passing acts likely to be vetoed for periods not longer than four years and six months. Dummer, the Massachusetts agent in London, wrote home in 1716 that the Secretary of State had told him that "by several votes and resolutions of the lower House, printed in their journals, we showed an inclination to be independent of the administration here [in England] and that we treated the King's commands as waste paper."

No sooner had the authorities in England become aware of this propensity than they undertook to overcome it; at first by the supervision of the Committee of Trade and Plantations, and then by the appointment of governors who would accomplish on the ground what could not be done by officials in England. The colonists were equal to the emergency. Without coming to an open breach with the Crown, they managed to nullify the work of the royal governors and other appointive officials, or, in those colonies which chose their own officers, succeeded in evading supervision. Massachusetts held governor after governor helpless by refusing to vote him a salary or make any regular allowance either for the expenses of administration or for his household. They paid him from time to time by allowing him to sign a bill voting him a present after he had affixed his signature to the bills the General Court wished passed. Strict orders were sent from England prohibiting the acceptance of anything but a salary, for the authorities rightly saw that much might be expected from a governor financially independent, and nothing at all from a man dependent upon the assembly's votes for the very bread on his table. Yet governor after governor found it impossible to resist this pressure from the legislature.

There seems to have been a general recognition of the right of judicial appeal to the Privy Council from the colonial courts; but, though frequently used by individuals, it was chiefly confined to cases where the colonial judges patently were not sure what decision to render.

The only series of general regulations made by the mother-country were systematically disregarded from the moment they

were made. The Navigation Acts, passed during the reigns
of Charles II and William III, restricted the trade of the
mother-country with the colonies and that of the outside
world with her colonies entirely to English and colonial ships.
The more important colonial staples—sugar, molasses, tobacco, dye-woods—were to be carried only to other English
colonies or to England. Trade with foreign countries or with
their West India colonies was forbidden. Not only were the
detailed regulations of these acts disobeyed, but even their
general intent was nullified. The coast was crowded with
smugglers; sugar and molasses were openly sold at more than
one place for less money than the duty; most ships carried
several sets of false papers, and traded at will with the
foreign sugar islands in the West Indies and with Europe.
The English calculated in 1767 that a trade worth more than
a quarter of a million pounds sterling was being carried
on by America with Germany and Holland. Attempt after
attempt to stop the smuggling was of no avail; new acts,
new regulations, were simply waste paper, and few or no
men could be found in America who were willing to accept
an appointment as customs officer, so excessively unpopular
was the service and so determined were the colonists to evade
the regulations. Randolph was astonished at the lengths to
which they went in Boston in 1676 to thwart him. They
landed their goods at night and when he appeared to investigate arrested him for breaking the curfew rule; they landed
the goods on Sunday, and arrested him for working on the
Sabbath. The courts would issue only special search warrants permitting him to search only for specified articles in
a specified place. He found that the merchants had built
a series of connecting warehouses, and, after they had seen
his warrant, kept him standing at the door while they rolled
the sugar and molasses into the next warehouse. When there
was nothing he could seize left in the place he was allowed
to search, they admitted him. Their intention to disobey was
an open secret. Violence was not unfrequent in later years
where the customs officers showed any real determination:

heads were broken, ships burned, officers tarred and feathered, ridden on rails, or even murdered. It is easy to understand the fierce objection to the Writs of Assistance in 1761, which permitted the search and seizure of dutiable goods wherever the officer could find them; they made all the familiar expedients for evasion useless. Another difficulty was experienced in the jury trials of such men as were arraigned. It was almost impossible to secure a conviction from any local jury and the English admiralty officials were anxious to obtain the right to try such cases in some other colony than that where the offense was committed. As few men were innocent and few cases were tried where the party was not caught *flagrante delicto*, such a removal of the trial was tantamount to certain conviction, and the penalties for breach of the acts were extremely severe. The colonists therefore resisted these proposals stoutly. It is extremely interesting to note the similarity of the measures which roused such indignation after 1760 to those which had excited active opposition during the colonial period. The outbreak after 1760 was due not only to the fact that the English government was making a systematic and persistent attempt at enforcement for practically the first time, but also to the new consciousness of the colonists of their growing strength and of the actuality of their independence.

The favorite idea in England for the solution of all these difficulties was that of a colonial union of some sort, and many schemes were evolved and proposed. Some provided for a common administrative and judicial machinery; others contemplated some sort of a general legislative body with more or less limited powers; but one and all established a central machinery intended to be directed by the Crown, even when its officers were not actually to be appointed in England, and patently meant to supersede the authority of the individual colonies in many matters of importance, and perhaps to outvote the unruly by means of the more peaceable. One such scheme was actually put into operation with disastrous results. Sir Edmund Andros was appointed Governor of New

England, New York, and New Jersey, with broad powers and
unusual privileges to take the place of the charters just revoked in 1684. Some opposition was expected, and probably
nothing but the knowledge of impending changes in England
prevented an actual rebellion before 1689 when, on pretense
of casting out the Stuarts, Andros was put in jail and the
old charter governments restored. William III was not altogether blind to the fact that enthusiasm for him had not
been the chief motive at work, and only after great suspense
and some difficulty were much less favorable charters obtained. This was, however, until the Revolution the only
attempt to institute any uniform administration.

The reply of the colonies to the other schemes for centralization and for a central government was an unqualified negative. No scheme won colonial approval which was not based
upon the conception of the several colonies as sovereign States.
The New England Confederation, formed in 1643, was a
league of States for offense and defense, and contained in
one of its first clauses an explicit reservation of the liberties
and privileges of each "jurisdiction." In their dealings with
each other, the colonies always preserved scrupulously this
attitude and signed "treaties," made commercial regulations,
granted letters of marque, coined money, declared war and
peace, and performed most of the varied acts customarily
reserved to the sovereign. In some cases, the language of the
charter lent directly or indirectly some color to these proceedings, but it is safe to say that they were not undertaken
because of the existence of any such permission, nor limited
to powers authorized by even a liberal interpretation of any
document. Whatever they were in law or in name, the
colonies were and always had been individually sovereign and
they had in 1760 and 1776 absolutely no intention of sur-
rendering that independence to each other, to a central administration, or to England. Several schemes were suggested
by colonists for three or four sectional governments and these
met with some favor. At Albany, in 1754, representatives of
the colonies finally agreed upon a scheme for a general govern-

ment, which was much disliked in England because the powers
allotted the general government were too few and those reserved to the individual colonies too many, because the central
administration was not strong and the thirteen colonies in-
comparably too independent. It found equally little favor
in America because it gave the general government the power
of taxation and the control of commerce. The one the individual colonies had always had, the other they had always
coveted. In truth, one cardinal fact of the colonial period
is the legal and actual independence of the several colonies of
each other and their actual independence of England.
States' sovereignty was the only idea which possessed much
precedent in 1775, and the only idea of coöperation ever tried
and widely approved had been that of a loose confederation
of sovereign States, which had control neither of taxation
nor of commerce, and whose central authority was little more
than a general agent whose masters from time to time indicated their wishes. Surely it is significant to find the
Parliamentary Commission of 1652 conceding to Virginia in
exchange for her submission, that "the Grand Assembly as
formerly shall convene and transact the affairs of Virginia,"
and that the Virginians should have freedom of trade "as
the people of England do," and should "be free from all
taxes, customs, and impositions whatsoever, and none to be
imposed upon them without consent of the Grand Assembly."
"The bottom of all the disorder," wrote Hutchinson from
Massachusetts in 1772, is "the opinion that every colony has
a legislature within itself, the acts and doings of which are
not to be controlled by Parliament, and that no legislative
power ought to be exercised over the colonies except by their
legislatures." The Revolution was fought by precisely that
sort of an organization which colonial experience had shown
was the only one for which the general consent could be
gained.

There was naturally no accepted idea whatever of a nation
as we now conceive it; there was indeed no sentiment in
favor of nationality; each colony wished to be independent

not only of England but of its neighbors, and would not have entered the struggle on any other terms. The strong bond of economic interest which was later to furnish such cogent reasons for nationality was as yet non-existent because the colonies were as yet contiguous only "on paper." The colonial period, from the point of view which we apply to later history, is the study of the foreign relations of the separate States with each other and with England. In no colony was there a majority in favor of a national government superior in obligation in its relations to the individual to the latter's duty to his colony. When Patrick Henry declared himself not a Virginian but an American, he proclaimed not a fact but a vision.

VII

THE IMMEDIATE CAUSES OF THE REVOLUTION

THE fundamental causes of the Revolution are writ large in the history of the colonial period. The rapidly increasing population of the colonies, their growing wealth, the dependence of the West India Islands upon their produce, their long experience in self-government, their determination not to submit to dictation or control from England or from each other, had made them more and more conscious with each succeeding decade of the weakness of England's control over them, of the almost insuperable difficulties which the width of the Atlantic interposed in the way of schemes for strengthening it or for making it more effective. They saw, indeed, that they had always stood alone and they naturally concluded that they might now as well declare the fact. The longer they studied the story of the settlement of the country, the less they felt themselves bound to the mother-country by ties of gratitude for an aid in money or in men which she had either been unwilling or unable to send. The Navigation Acts on their very face were intended to benefit only the citizens of England itself, for Ireland and Scotland were expressly excluded from their privileges; the royal governors had imposed expense upon the colonies and, instead of rendering valuable service in administration, had done their best to prevent the transaction of the public business in the ways which experience had taught the colonists to be the most expedient. Not the suffering, but the prosperity of the colonies, not their weakness but their strength, not the tyranny of an autocratic government but the obvious lack of any effective supervision at all, caused the Revolution. They had grown to a realization of the truth of Berkeley's warning to the Virginia Assembly in 1652. "What is it can be hoped for [from the Parliament] which we have not already? Is it liberty? The sun looks not upon a people more free than we are from all oppression. Is it wealth? . . . Industry and thrift in a short time may bring us to . . . it. . . . Is it . . . peace? The Indians, God be blessed, round about us are subdued; we can only feare the Londoners."

The immediate causes of the outbreak are to be found in the changed conditions after the close of the Seven Years' War and in the events of the years from 1760 to 1775. The result of the Seven Years' War was of transcendent impor- tance: the departure of the French from Canada removed the only external reason the colonists had for valuing the con- nection with England. The existence of the French colony rather than its history, its loss rather than the method of its loss indicate the salient influence of the French upon the history of the United States. Before the fur-traders had been long settled in the St. Lawrence Valley, they discovered that it lay just north of the corn-belt and that the existence of a colony there would always be precarious because of the diffi- culty of ripening a full crop of the only indigenous grain. The attempts to escape from the Valley are the most vital part of the history of French Canada. Through New York lay a splendid road down the Richelieu River and the lakes to within a few miles of the Hudson and the Atlantic Ocean. Through the Connecticut River valley lay another desirable road. Along both lay fertile fields in a climate which made the cultivation of maize as successful as it was precarious around the St. Lawrence. The knowledge of this eagerness to secure possession of New York or New England rather than their actual strength in Canada caused the abiding fears of invasion in the English colonies, which bound them firmly to the English allegiance for a century and more. To the Congregationalists of New England, the greatest danger was to be feared from Catholicism, and a stock part of every war scare in the eighteenth century were the lurid tales of the ship-loads of inquisitors and instruments of torture which were following in the wake of the great French fleet, coming from France to coöperate with an army from Canada in an attack upon New York or Boston.

Had Champlain not offended the Iroquois in 1609 the history of the United States might have been different. That powerful confederacy of the ablest and best organized Indians on the continent held sway over a vast territory ranging from the Alleghanies to the Mississippi and from southern Tennessee to the Great Lakes. Their home land was in New York and their determined opposition to the French and persistent friendliness to the English, despite promises, bribes, and missionaries, interposed an impenetrable wall between the French and the fertile fields of the Atlantic coast, and thus condemned Canada to insignificance. The only hope lay to the west in the Mississippi Valley beyond and behind the influence of the Iroquois. There were fertile fields and a vast supply of furs. Yet, while striving to build up this empire in the west, the French never quite abandoned hope of reaching the Atlantic Ocean. But the alliance between the Iroquois and the English was so firmly cemented in 1684 by Governor Dongan of New York that only the New England colonies remained exposed to the attacks of the *coureurs de bois* and the Indians of the St. Lawrence region. So strong was New England that nothing more than marauding expeditions was to be feared unless assistance should come in force from France. More than once such a great expedition was planned; at least once French regiments from Canada reached the neighborhood of Albany undetected and could have captured it; and, if small scouting parties could unchecked ravage the very heart of New England, the decisive success of an attack in force was more than probable.[1]   Under such circumstances,

[1] How strong these fears were is shown by the statement prepared by Commissioners of the colonies assembled at Albany in 1754. "That it is the evident design of the French to surround the British Colonies, to fortify themselves on the back thereof, to take and keep possession of the Heads of all the important Rivers, to draw over the Indians to their Interest and with the help of such Indians, added to such Forces as are already arrived and may be hereafter sent from Europe, to be

nothing could save the colonies but an English army and an English fleet. Nor should we ever forget that between 1660 and 1763, France was accounted easily the most powerful nation in Europe. This potentiality the victories of Wolfe definitively removed, and, as travelers and English political writers had busily prophesied for more than a decade, England lost what Kahn considered "the best means of keeping her colonies in due submission."

A series of events had also practically ended the dangers of attack from the coast Indians. As decade by decade the colonies grew larger in population, and extended further and further into the interior, the Indians were of necessity pushed nearer and nearer the mountains; the whites began actually to outnumber them in most districts, and the possibility of anything more than sporadic outbreaks disappeared. Peace and quiet were assured even more certainly by the growing scarcity of fur-bearing animals along the Atlantic coast, by the consequent decay of the fur-trade, and by the concomitant disappearance of the illicit traders who had so threatened the existence of the infant communities by distributing fire-arms and fire-water. Such trade as remained the colonists were able strictly to regulate. In addition, the founding of the Hudson Bay Company in the middle of the seventeenth century and the exploration by the French of the Mississippi Valley opened a vast and virgin field of operations for the fur-traders, and thither hastened the adventurous spirits, thus ridding the Atlantic coast of the very men whose dealings and behavior had so frequently given the Indians just cause for offense.

A century, too, had greatly altered the Indians' ideas of the white men. At first, the notion of private property in land was new to the savages, and the superiority of iron hatchets and kettles, to say nothing of guns and liquor, over anything

in a Capacity of making a general attack upon the several Governments. And if at the same Time a strong Naval Force be sent from France, there is the utmost Danger that the whole Continent will be subjected to that Crown." *Colonial Records of Pennsylvania*, VI, 103.

the Indian possessed was so marked that few chiefs hesitated before assenting to deeds of sale whose purport they did not understand. The white man wanted land for corn, grass for his cattle, wood for his wigwam; and they supposed that, like the Indian, he would soon move his habitation when the land became exhausted. The very idea of permanent possession was not grasped at first, and when such Indians as Philip comprehended it, a fierce hatred for the intruders led them to begin a crusade of extermination. The ease with which the outbreaks of 1675 and 1676 were suppressed dampened the ardor of the savages and reassured the whites. By 1760, the colonists knew themselves capable of coping with any Indian uprising. No aid from English troops was needed. Indeed, the colonial scorn for Braddock's methods and troops was ill concealed, and his defeat rendered extremely unlikely any subsequent requests to the mother-country for assistance.

This precise moment, when the colonists for the first time felt free from the dangers with which the French and the Indians had so long menaced them, was selected by the English ministry as opportune for the introduction of uniform administrative regulations, which could not fail to raise questions of the character and value of the colonial relations with England. Of economic, political, and social conditions in America, George III and his advisers knew little; of the colonial hostility towards England, they were aware but thought it merely insubordination. That the colonies possessed any vitally different economic interests from those of England and Englishmen, that English political ideas and phraseology would connote very different things to the colonists than they did to Englishmen, they do not seem to have suspected. They knew indeed that no real control of the colonies had hitherto existed, but they deemed it a result of the stupidity and inertia of their own predecessors and of the stubborn spirit of the Americans rather than a consequence of fundamental geographical factors, which still stood in the way of the establishment of any efficient administration. Indeed, the fact that no effective control had existed was to them an admirable reason for creating a system which should make English sovereignty more than a name.

Indubitably, the conquest of Canada caused England seriously to consider the status of her possessions in America, and forced upon her attention the fact that the growth of the continental colonies during the past half-century had vastly changed the problem of dealing with them. The few scattered settlements had become States whose size, prosperity, and spirit forbade the longer continuance of the old policy of *laissez-faire*. The new English policy aimed at centralization, at "the weaving of this land into our system . . . so that Great Britain may be . . . a grand maritime dominion consisting of our possessions in the Atlantic and in America united into one Empire, into one center where the seat of government is." To this end Charles Townshend proposed to replace the varied forms of colonial government by a uniform system of local administration which would furnish a firm basis for an efficient central administration over them all. Experience showed the necessity of taking from the colonial legislatures the power of the purse and of providing by customs duties and stamp taxes, collected by royal officers appointed from England, a sufficiently large revenue to support an army, pay the salaries of executive and judicial officers, and in general defray the expenses of colonial administration. Only in this way could any independence be secured for the royal officials and obedience be ensured to the administrative regulations which should weave England and her colonies into one great articulate Empire. If the Navigation Acts and the Sugar Acts could be actually enforced, the revenue would be considerable and the remainder of the necessary sum could be obtained by indirect taxes whose incidence would be extremely light. Disobedience and evasion of explicit royal orders, smuggling and piracy, trade with foreign colonies and European countries, none of which could continue without disrupting the new Empire before it was born, would all cease; order, harmony, and efficiency would take the place of the old haphazard rule.

If we assume with Townshend that the colonies were merely dependencies of England, to be governed by the Crown in accordance with the legislation passed by Parliament, if we find glorious as he the vision of a greater entity built out of the mother-country and colonies for the ultimate benefit of both, then we shall agree with his conclusion of the justice, equity, and expediency of such a scheme. If, on the other hand, we take as our premise the actual condition of colonies which had been for more than a century sovereign States in all but name, we shall begin to understand the instantaneous opposition which those proposals roused in America. To a people, most of whom had never been even asked for any taxes beyond their local levies, few of whom had paid even the quitrents to which the holding of their land obligated them with any regularity and without constant protest, the proposal to establish a series of taxes, however mild and judicious, could not fail to be regarded as an innovation deserving of the keenest scrutiny. And the purposes for which this revenue was to be spent were undoubtedly of questionable expediency. The institution of a uniform centralized administration for all the colonies, directed by the English ministry, composed of officers whom they appointed and paid, certainly involved the complete overthrow of the system of government which had been in existence ever since the colonies were founded. The colonial legislatures had been practically supreme and had directed and controlled the English governors with little regard for the technicalities of constitutional law, for instructions from kings, or for protests from the Board of Trade and Plantations. Each legislature had tightly drawn the strings of the colonial purse and had never paid a penny to an English appointee without first being assured of his performance of their wishes. The colonies had virtually controlled their own policies and their own legislation, and, realizing, as the Massachusetts men told the Commissioners of Charles II, that they could "easily spin out seven years by writing," had recked little of English policies and royal displeasure. Undoubtedly, the colonies had passed a vast number of conflicting regulations; the franchise, taxation, local government, the criminal and civil codes were alike only in their fundamental notions, and interposed a very real barrier in the way of administrative efficiency as the English understood it. Yet these same local peculiarities were regarded by the colonists in 1765 as the most characteristic and admirable feature of American development. Each little community was eager to preserve intact the right to adapt itself to such exigencies of its economic and political needs as the practical demands of the moment might dictate. Uniform regulations were suited to uniform conditions; a single policy to a people whose interests and aims were identical; but were highly inexpedient for thirteen communities whose dissimilarities were more striking than the similarities. The majority of Americans, in fact, did not believe a uniform administration desirable or possible. Had their fathers struggled hard to avoid paying the governor a fixed salary and to prevent the regular collection of the proprietor's rents, that they might yield the control of the purse without a protest? Had their fathers overthrown Andros, negatived every English plan of organic union to cling fast to the idea of a league of sovereign States, only that the sons might in their folly permit the establishment of the very type of government which their fathers had deemed inexpedient? Had the work of the legislatures ever been so inefficient, had the royal governors ever demonstrated such conspicuous ability as to justify the transfer of the real direction of colonial administration from the one to the other? Nor could the colonists believe that a standing army in America, instituted at the very moment when the real dangers of the past century were clearly at an end, could be intended to cope with anything but the resistance of the colonists themselves to the new arrangements. Whatever pleas for a new and more glorious British Empire might be used to lend a specious splendor to such proposals, their acceptance certainly meant the renunciation of the virtual sovereignty and independence which each colony had undoubtedly enjoyed ever since it had been founded.

If the administrative result of the English reforms would be the overthrow of local administration, the economic results certainly threatened to bankrupt the colonies. An efficient central government meant the actual enforcement of the Navigation and Sugar Acts, and meant the cessation of the lucrative smuggling trade with the foreign sugar colonies on which the very prosperity of the continental colonies was believed to rest.[2] The Sugar Act of 1733 had been intended to prevent the direct importation by the continental colonies of molasses, rum, or sugar from the foreign West India Islands and had imposed customs duties meant to be prohibitive and penalties for evasion believed to be severe enough to intimidate offenders. Yet, from the first, the Act was null and void in America. Sugar had been openly sold in Boston for less than the duty and the English government had with difficulty collected £2000 of revenue annually at an expenditure of £7000 for perception. The Sugar Act of 1764, by far the most offensive of all pre-revolutionary acts, made the Act of 1733 perpetual, increased the amount of the duties and the severity of the penalties, and provided for the exercise by English naval and customs authorities of such plenary powers for the detection and punishment of

[2] The Sugar Act of 1764 "will put a total stop to our exportation of lumber, horses, flour, and fish, to the French and Dutch sugar colonies; and if any one supposes we may find a sufficient vent for these articles in the English Islands in the West Indies, he only verifies what was just now observed, that he wants truer information. Putting an end to the importation of foreign molasses, at the same time puts an end to all the costly distilleries in these colonies, and to the rum trade to the coast of Africa, and throws it into the hands of the French. With the loss of the foreign molasses trade the codfishery of the English in America must also be lost and thrown also into the hands of the French. . . . This, nor any part of it, is not exaggeration but a sober and most melancholy truth. . . . Ministers have great influence and parliaments great power: can either of them change the nature of things, stop all our means of getting money and yet expect us to purchase and pay for British manufactures?" Stephen Hopkins, *The Rights of Colonies Examined*, 12, 13. (1765.)

offenses as are now exercised by the United States Revenue officers. To this, the colonists paid and intended to pay no more attention than they had always paid to English acts which seemed detrimental to their welfare.

To their wrath and astonishment, however, the English ministry promptly evinced a hitherto unheard of amount of energy and decision, and introduced first a Stamp Act and then various revenue bills to raise money to maintain in America an administrative and military corps capable of enforcing the Navigation Acts, new and old. The Stamp Tax was not indeed a bad form of taxation and was then in operation in England without objection, and has since been frequently used in the United States; the duties were extremely moderate, and all the varieties of commercial paper which the ordinary man was likely to handle were exempted altogether. The opposition in America came from the clear evidence afforded by the Act itself of the purpose of its passage. The Commissioners were to be appointed by the Crown; their powers were broad, their discretion unlimited; the culprits could at discretion be tried outside their own colony by an Admiralty judge, sitting of course without a jury, and proceeding by the rules of the Admiralty law, instead of by common law. In addition, the duties were payable only in sterling money at London rates; the colonists, long hampered by the scarcity of coin in America, declared it a conspiracy to strip the country of specie.

The purpose and not the tenor of the Stamp Act was as much responsible for the opposition in America as it was for the satisfaction in England. There can be little doubt that the mercantile community on either side of the Atlantic was responsible as much for the policy of centralization as for that of resistance. Both were actuated by the fear of bankruptcy. So long as the carrying trade between England and her own sugar colonies could be restricted to her own colonial shipping, so long as the continental colonies supplied the English colonies with food and necessities and compelled the foreign sugar colonies to divert valuable time and labor

from raising sugar-cane to raising food for their own maintenance, the English sugar colonies possessed a very considerable economic advantage over their rivals. For the continental colonies to supply the latter with food on the same
terms at which they supplied the English sugar colonies
meant the loss of this very important advantage. When,
in addition, the New England merchants traded freely with
Amsterdam and Hamburg and took back to America Dutch
or German goods, the English merchants in England had
lost just so much of their normal market. The pressure upon
the ministry to put an end to this "robbery" was persistent,
and, from an English point of view, entirely justifiable.
That the repression of this illicit trade and open smuggling
was oppression, never occurred to George III and his advisers.
But the Boston and New York merchants, who remembered
that the English West India Islands consumed each decade a
smaller and smaller proportion of their produce, and furnished
fewer and fewer of their numerous ships with full cargoes
to London, who realized that their profits depended on their
ability to market the whole of the colonial output somewhere and that the only possible additional market for bulky
and perishable goods was in the foreign West India colonies,[3]
saw in these regulations nothing but a fixed design to strangle
colonial trade and to ruin colonial merchants simply in order

[3] The Remonstrance of the Colony of Rhode Island to the Lords Commissioners of Trade and Plantations against the Sugar Act of 1764
stated that Rhode Island imported annually £120,000 of British goods
and raised in the colony £5000 worth of goods capable of being sent to
England, "and, as the other goods raised for exportation, will answer
in no market but in the West Indies, it necessarily follows that the
trade thither must be the foundation of all our commerce." Thirty
distilleries turning molasses into rum are "the main hinge upon which
the trade of the colony depends," and use 14,000 hogsheads of molasses
annually, of which 11,500 come from foreign sugar plantations (of
course in inviolation of the Navigation Acts). "The British West India
Islands are not, nor in the nature of things ever can be, able to consume
the produce of the said colonies." To Africa, the colony annually exported 1800 hogsheads of rum and with the proceeds made remittances
to England valued at £40,000. *Records of the Colony of Rhode Island
and Providence Plantations, in New England*, VI, 378-383.

to increase the profits of British merchants. The fact that this trade was necessary to colonial prosperity proved to the Americans that the English statutes and regulations were exceedingly unjust, and were, therefore, illegal and unconstitutional. Parliament never could have intended to commit such hideous injustice; any such reading of the acts must be wrong. The continued insistence of the English ministers upon this very interpretation, the passage of further acts and regulations to enforce it seemed to prove only too clearly that England actually intended to compass the ruin of her own colonies. "Single acts of tyranny," wrote Jefferson in the *Summary View of the Rights of British America,* "may be ascribed to the accidental opinion of a day; but a series of oppressions, begun at a distinguished period, and pursued unalterably through every change of ministers, too plainly prove a deliberate and systematical plan of reducing us to slavery." The growth of the colonies had developed by 1760 an economic interest diametrically contrary to the interests of England, and over its continuance, not over its rightfulness, the Revolution was fought. The Americans conceived the economic bondage to Europe, which pressed so hardly on them, to be the result of the political tie which bound them to the mother-country; if that tie were once loosened or could be changed, all would be remedied. When they found it impossible to alter the conditions which so hampered their development, they determined to get rid of the political connection entirely and thus become free.

The prompt nullification of the Stamp Act by the Americans only convinced George III and his advisers the more firmly of the necessity of such measures. They knew little of the commercial necessities of the continental colonists; still less of the actual facts about colonial self-government. They correctly saw that the conditions in America were entirely at odds with the legal and constitutional relationship between the mother-country and her colonies; they correctly saw that if the authority of the Crown and of Parliament was not to become a mere figment of the imagination recognition of it must be extorted from the colonies as soon as possible. With the coöperation of the colonies, a magnificent future lay before the British Empire; but until so anomalous a condition of affairs was changed, coöperation would be impossible. As Wilson later phrased it in the Constitutional Convention of 1787, "The fatal maxims espoused by her were that the Colonies were growing too fast and that their growth must be stinted [checked] in time."

Accordingly, in June 1766, Townshend announced the policy of the ministry. "It has long been my opinion that America should be regulated and deprived of its militating and contradictory charters, and its royal governors, judges, and attorneys be rendered independent of the people. I therefore expect that the present administration will, in the recess of Parliament, take all necessary previous steps for compassing so desirable an event." There would be "a different police (policy) founded on and supported by force and vigor." With these words ringing in their ears, the Americans learned of the proposed organization of a really efficient American customs service, of the imposition of duties on glass, painters' colors, and tea, all to make "more certain and adequate provision for the charge of the administration of justice and the support of civil government" in America, and to be spent by the English ministry. The low duties, the studiously careful taxation of nothing but luxuries, the excellence of the provisions for administrative efficiency, the fact that the Tea Acts permitted the sale of tea in America from 30% to 40% cheaper than in England was nothing to the Americans, who were, as always, furiously opposed to the payment of any taxes at all intended to make the English officials independent of the colony, and firm in their opposition to the establishment of an efficient English administration. Was this to be the result of the long battle between Massachusetts and the Crown over the Governor's salary? Was Massachusetts thus tamely to surrender and make him independent of her legislature? Were the colonies themselves to pay the money necessary for the creation of an administration intended to destroy their prosperity by enforcing the Navigation Acts? The reorganization of the Admiralty courts, the legalization of general search-warrants for smuggled goods, the new efficiency of the English army in the colonies only increased the dangers apprehended from such measures by the extent to which they rendered the proposed administration more efficient.

The resistance was prompt and for the most part was a resort to the old habits of evasion and violence so common in the relations of the populace and the customs officers. The breaking of heads, burning in effigy, riding on rails, the sacking of houses, the forcible landing of goods in defiance of the revenue officers were as old as the colonies themselves. Conscious of their strength, the crowds indulged in more striking manifestations of their determination, dancing round liberty-poles, burying the Stamp Act with mock gravity, and boycotting or threatening the English officers till they left the colony. There was here no organized resistance; the participants belonged to the poorer and rougher elements of the populace; and their deeds were openly deprecated by the colonial leaders and legislatures. In fact, few were anxious to do more than nullify the English acts or supposed that such proceedings could lead to a separation from the mother-country. "The ideas of people," wrote John Adams, "are as various as their faces."

There was, however, for the first time talk among the leaders of legal or constitutional resistance to the English measures and a great turning of books and consideration of precedents to discover what the legal relations of the colonies to England really were. Firm in their English traditions, the Americans refused to believe that the law obligated them to the performance of anything actually detrimental to their welfare. Out of the voluminous correspondence, speech-making, and tract-writing, there finally appeared about 1774, a coherent American notion of what the British Constitution was and what were the privileges of the colonies under it. In the writings of James Otis and of Stephen Hopkins, we find it clearly expressed, but, above all, we see it in the *Summary View of the Rights of British America,* written by Thomas Jefferson in 1774.

The Americans assumed the existence of an English Constitution superior in obligation to acts of Parliament, based upon an original compact between the King and people and containing "those rights which God and the laws have given equally and independently to all." The British Empire consisted of England, Scotland, Ireland, Massachusetts, Virginia, and the rest of the colonies, all of them equal in rank, each provided with a legislature and an administration supreme within its own sphere. The King was, as Jefferson said, "chief magistrate of the British Empire," "the chief officer of the people, appointed by the laws and circumscribed with definite powers, to assist in working the great machine of government, created for their use and consequently subject to their superintendence." The King was of course subject to the Constitution; Parliament was the legislature of England as the General Court was the legislature of Massachusetts or the General Assembly that of Virginia. Parliament possessed by the Constitution no more right to legislate for Massachusetts than the General Court possessed to pass laws for England. The right of free trade was the inalienable possession of each "part of the Empire"; the Constitution sanctioned no laws whatever on that subject, and all those passed by Parliament, being therefore in contravention of the Constitution, were void.

Such notions obviously bore no relation whatever to any conceptions of the English constitution ever entertained in England. That Americans should advance what George and his counselors deemed ludicrous travesties as constitutional defenses for their extraordinary behavior, only confirmed the latter in their opinion of the "factious" intentions of the Americans. The American notions were, however, the logical result of the application of States' sovereignty to the British Empire; and were simply a plain statement of actual conditions in 1774. The separate States were sovereign and recognized the King's headship of the Empire for what it had been,—an ornamental constitutional feature. They assigned both King and Parliament purely nominal parts because neither had ever regularly exercised any actual authority in America. But neither King nor colonist realized that the difficulty lay in the fact that the legal status and the actual condition of the colonies no longer agreed. The English concluded that, because the law said so, they were still dependencies to be dealt with at the discretion of King and Parliament; the Americans assumed that the Constitution must have been always in force and obtained their definition of the Constitution from what they knew to be true about government in America and about the actual relations of the colonies to England. Both the English idea of American government, and the American idea of English government were therefore astonishing misconceptions. And each firmly believed in his own particular variety of misconception because the facts of everyday life with which each was familiar proved its validity; each scouted the other's notions because neither could credit the existence of such conditions as were claimed to be found on the other side of the Atlantic. How were Charles James Fox, rake and gamester, wit and littérateur, the stolid Farmer George, the routine-ridden Graftons and Townshends to comprehend life on the American frontier or to appreciate the virtues of a Washington or the ability of a Franklin? The personal experiences of the leaders had been too utterly diverse for them to comprehend the motives which swayed their opponents.

Starting from such opposite premises, argument and discussion only intensified the differences of opinion and convinced each of the other's wilful intention to falsify and misrepresent. The little phrase, "taxation without representation," which soon became the decisive point of most practical discussions, was clearly understood by each in a sense which made nonsense out of the other's contentions. The English Parliament was elected by the counties and such boroughs as had always had the right to send. In them, the franchise was based upon a variety of accidental and inconsistent notions, completely lacking in regularity. Many great cities were not represented; many rich men had no vote; while tiny hamlets and barren hillsides returned two members to Parliament, and more than one nobleman and wealthy landowner returned a score. A majority of the House of Commons were put in their seats by about two hundred and fifty individuals. Thus Parliament did not contain a single member who represented any uniformity of qualification of any sort. Nor, as Edmund Burke told the Electors of Bristol, was that important. He was not their member and what they thought or wanted was naught to him; he and every other member sat for all England, for the men who did not vote and for the boroughs which sent no members, as much as for the few men who voted. Parliament legally represented every man, woman, and child in England, and whatever it did was law beyond appeal. Any one taxed by Parliament, was legally taxed. Such was and still is the theory of the English Constitution.

In America, on the other hand, the franchise was uniform, though not everywhere the same; while nearly every colony demanded property and moral or religious qualifications, every man might hope to fulfil them. The apportionment in America was strictly according to population and was regularly changed to keep pace with its ebb and flow. There was, therefore, in America no idea whatever that an individual or a town could be vicariously represented; if the man or town deserved representation, it would be freely accorded. To say, therefore, that the colonies had a perfect right to representation and were in fact already represented in Parliament, sounded to the Americans like nonsense, while the American claim to be taxed only by a body of men for one of whom he or his town had voted seemed to Englishmen worse than presumption.

One bit of American logic particularly irritated the Englishmen and seemed to them most cogent proof that the Americans were wrong and knew it. The latter, entirely ignorant of English conditions, save of course for the better informed who were promptly stigmatized as Tories, kept insisting loudly that they were "justly entitled to like privileges and freedom as their fellow-subjects in Great Britain." Magna Carta declared against taxation without representation, and, despite it, Parliament, in which they were not represented, persisted in levying taxes. But, as William Knox keenly said, if they had been living in England, would they not have been bound by Acts of Parliament, would they not have been deemed fully represented? Should they claim all the rights of Englishmen in England and shirk their duties? Should they be awarded the privileges without assuming the obligations?

If we start from the obviously correct notions of the legal relationship prevalent in England, we shall agree with George and his ministers that the measures they proposed were eminently just, equitable, and moderate. We shall perforce acquit them and the English people of any intention of tyrannizing over the colonies, of imposing any formal or legal obligations not binding on Englishmen in England, of demanding any type of taxes not long collected in England, of levying sums in excess of those laid upon the English themselves. Constitutional arguments have, however, rarely succeeded in adjusting the legal and political fabric to conditions manifestly antagonistic. The real issues were not constitutional but economic and administrative, and concerned not law but expediency. Did the continental colonies need a larger market than the English sugar colonies offered? Was it not most inexpedient for them to consent to taxes and regulations which proposed to enforce a policy which they believed certain to result in the destruction of their prosperity? Both issues were old and the colonies, individually and collectively, had invariably answered both in the affirmative. The Revolution did not grow out of new issues and new claims. The colonies merely reaffirmed with emphasis the position they had already many times assumed. The justification of the American Revolution lies in the fact that the colonies were strong enough to stand alone, had governed themselves successfully for a century and more, and could see no economic, ethical, or constitutional advantages in such a connection as the English proposed. Whatever the law was, they were in fact free agents, sovereign powers, able to accept or reject measures and policies as they thought best. The logic of facts was with them; the law as they honestly understood it supported them; they asked for nothing which their fathers had not in substance possessed. They were free and they claimed the right to make the fact clear.

VIII

THE ORGANIZATION OF RESISTANCE

ARMED resistance was by no means the result of a spontaneous outburst of indignation from a united nation. Indeed, the candid student, who will read the documentary evidence with the colonial passion for States' sovereignty in his mind instead of the national ideals of the Federal Convention, will be compelled to admit, unpalatable as the fact may be, that the Revolution was not a national movement at all. Loyalty and devotion to the States was strong, fervid, and freely expressed; the determination to maintain with force, if necessary, each State's independence of England was unquestioned. But both were as old as the colonies: in 1634 and 1664 Massachusetts had manifested precisely that same determination. Of national feeling in the present sense, there seems to have been among the people in general very little, and that little was manifested only by individuals. At the Stamp Act Congress and all other gatherings of men from more than one colony, the sentiment in favor of complaint was strong, but that in favor of united action was weak. The advocates of a central colonial government of some sort were listened to with tolerance but hardly with approval. Was not a central administration, robbing the individual colonies of part of their power and initiative, the very thing against which they were protesting?

Among the colonial leaders a strong party counseled delay. Franklin pointed at the rapid growth of the colonies in wealth and population since 1760 and predicted that if war could be averted for another decade or two the very growth of the colonies would totally change English policy. "Our security lies in our growing strength, England will soon value our friendship for it.'' ''Bear England's infirmities a little and gradually they will come to treat us well.'' The commercial relations with England were too valuable and too necessary to the prosperity of the colonies to risk their rupture by a war. ''England is worth preserving and her safety may in a large degree depend upon ourselves. Hence she must soon grant us all.'' Nor was actual fighting necessary. The English were prevented by circumstances too fundamental ever to be changed from exercising a control over the colonies sufficiently effective to rob them of the actual independence which had so long been theirs. George III and his ministers must soon realize how insuperable a barrier the width of the Atlantic actually was. In fact, the belief was very general before 1775 that organized resistance would not be necessary. It is hard for us to remember that in 1768 most colonists felt for ''The King'' fervent loyalty, which was not infrequently coupled to an active dislike for George III and which has been often confused with a lack of patriotism to their own country. They still thought as their fathers had, and saw not the slightest incompatibility between a desire to cling to the mother-country as long as possible and a firm determination to disobey all rules and regulations which they did not approve. They saw the familiar aspects of the old colonial quarrels with England, realized that their fathers had found petitions, vigorous protests, and a nullification of the objectionable acts by passive resistance invariably effective, and they were naturally unwilling to go further without more serious provocation. England had hitherto never done anything more than insist, and, if they vigorously wrote and talked, they might in the meantime have their own way. The landing of troops at New York in 1765 and at Boston three years later somewhat shook their complaisance, but as the months passed by and found the trade with the foreign West India Islands still brisk and profitable, as the obnoxious new acts were promptly repealed, and the older ones not enforced, the average man saw no need for action.

In John Dickinson's *Farmer's Letters* published in 1768

we find those ideas which seem to have most nearly expressed the views of the vast majority of the people. Of the unjustifiability of English policy, he has no doubt; but he cannot think it represents the mature opinion of King and people. "I cannot yet believe they will be cruel or unjust. . . . Let us complain . . . but let our complaint speak . . . the language of affliction and veneration." He dilated upon the value and importance of England to the colonies: "The prosperity of these provinces is founded in their dependence on Great Britain;" the obvious economic dependence of America upon England does not seem to him to prove necessarily the desirability of the English interpretation of the political bond, but merely the advisability of caution, patience, forbearance. In fact, he denied that a new issue was being thrust upon the colonists, or that other measures than passive resistance and nullification would be necessary to meet the crisis. The importance of correctly estimating the attitude of Dickinson and his numerous supporters can hardly be exaggerated, and we must above all beware of assuming that they approved of English policy or were any less patriotic in their attachment to their States than were the adherents of the War party, or were any less determined to resist in the eventuality of the failure of compromise. Such motives held the vast majority of the population inactive throughout the war, and led to the prompt formation after Bunker Hill of a strong peace party, opposed to the war not because it was wrong, but because it was unnecessary.

Actual resistance previous to 1775 was, on the whole, individualistic and sporadic, and had no close connection that can now be traced with the later movements for armed organized resistance or for independence. The cases which furnished Otis and Henry with the texts for their famous speeches on the Writs of Assistance in 1761 and on the Parsons' Cause in 1763 were essentially local and the effect of the speeches less general than has usually been supposed. Neither led to open resistance. The violent demonstrations around Boston in opposition to the Stamp Act and to the Townshend Acts were for the most part the work of mobs, whose actions were decried and discountenanced by the leaders. A press gang went ashore in Boston and had a fight with the crowd. The revenue officers who attempted to inspect Hancock's sloop, the *Liberty,* were locked up by the crew, who landed the cargo and made false entries in the books at the customs house. The subsequent seizure of the vessel brought out the old Boston gang, which had long been accustomed to oppose the revenue officers, and which sacked the houses of the inspector and controller of customs in most approved fashion. A cargo of wine was landed at/night in March 1768 and escorted through the streets by forty men armed with bludgeons. At Providence a customs officer was tarred and feathered, and at Newport a revenue cutter was burned at the dock. Some years later a body of men went down Providence harbor in row boats and burned the revenue cutter *Gaspee* which was aground on the mud flats. Such "opposition" was pretty common but was not essentially different either in purpose or degree from the violence offered to the revenue officers in America ever since the days of John Randolph, or from that which the English revenue officers had to contend with at the same epoch in England and Ireland. Certainly, these brawls were not generally considered at the time to be steps towards independence or even as the first events in armed resistance.

There was also a great deal of violence growing out of the continually strained relations between the debtor and creditor classes of the community. Of these cases, that of the North Carolina Regulators in 1770 is thoroughly characteristic. A considerable body of men, armed with clubs, attended the session of the Superior Court and demanded from judge and attorneys, "justice" in the decision of their cases, meaning apparently a decision in their favor. A good many lawyers were badly beaten; several gentlemen of property (the creditors who were trying to collect their debts) were chased out of town, and the Judge "took an opportunity," as he wrote the Governor, of making his escape "by a back way." This same determination to prevent the collection of debts and the foreclosure of mortgages by interfering with the sittings of the courts was common before the Revolution, continued throughout the war, and finally reached its climax in the very general movement against the creditor class which was one of the most prominent features of the Critical Period. Such demonstrations had vital results in hastening the formation of strong State governments, and, in particular, in producing sentiment in favor of the strong national government advocated by the Constitutional Convention of 1787, but they were not primarily directed against England nor against her officials or acts.

Inflammatory speeches and articles became common after 1765 and people talked energetically about "liberty" and "independence." The lofty appeals of the leaders constitute a distinct feature of these years, but it is sufficiently clear that their words in most cases fell on deaf ears. The non-importation agreements of 1767 and 1768 roused more general fervor than anything else, and the demand from England for the rescinding of the *Massachusetts Circular Letter* of 1768 caused a most exciting debate in the Massachusetts Assembly in which Otis compared the colonists to Pym and Cromwell and predicted that England would lose America unless the Acts were repealed. The Assembly was carried away by enthusiasm and voted, 92 to 17, not to rescind the letter. They resolved that the letter was modest and innocent, respectful to Parliament and dutiful to the King! The Governor next day dissolved the legislature. Throughout the colonies, the sensation was profound. Massachusetts had openly defied the Crown. It was just the time when the famous "No. 45" of Wilkes's *North Briton* was so conspicuous in the agitation for liberty of press in England; "92" and "45" became talismanic numbers: 92 patriots drank 45 toasts; 45 candles were lighted and 92 cheers given; 92 Sons of Liberty set up a pole 45 feet high. The colonies generally resolved to support Boston, where the enthusiasm ran so high at a mass meeting that Cooper and Samuel Adams declared it the most glorious day they had ever seen. At this juncture, the troops were ordered to Boston, and, as in 1634 and 1664, the Town-meeting voted "at the utmost peril of their lives and fortunes, (to) maintain and defend their rights, liberties, privileges, and immunities." They ordered a day of fasting and prayer, and resolved to provide themselves with arms for fear of war with France!

Everything except a truly revolutionary spirit had manifested itself: the traditional hatred of the water front for the press-gang, the revenue officers, and the soldiery; the traditional opposition to an efficient executive; the war of debtor against creditor. But this was not revolution. Resistance was organized and the Revolution really foisted upon a reluctant people by the work of Samuel Adams and his Committees of Correspondence. Such committees were in themselves old and premised merely the coöperation in a common cause of some few towns around Boston, whose leaders kept up an indefatigable correspondence with individuals elsewhere. In 1763, self-constituted, unauthorized committees sprang into being in many places and began corresponding with each other to secure an interchange of sentiments and, if possible, an agreement. None of them had any particular organization, or assumed executive or directive powers. Most of them lasted but a short while, and even in Massachusetts there was a constant succession of committees rather than one committee with a permanent personnel. Indeed, by 1772, no definite results of any sort were visible. "The dispute between the kingdom and the colonies," declared the *Massachusetts Gazette,* "ceases everywhere except in this province." "I shall not fail to exert myself," wrote a warm patriot in Plymouth to Adams, "to have as many towns as possible meet, but fear the bigger part of them will not. They are dead; and the dead can't be raised without a miracle." This Adams did not believe, yet even he could not but admit that "the people are at present hushed into silence." His cousin, John Adams, wrote: "They are still and quiet at the South and at New York they laugh at us." Hardly a year before Bunker Hill, he wrote: "I am of the same opinion that I have been for years, that there is not spirit enough on either side to bring the question to a complete decision. . . . Our children may see revolutions and be concerned and active in effecting them, of which we can form no conception.'' There was, indeed, no general feeling in favor of resistance in 1772, and, until Bunker Hill was fought, not even the leaders dared to believe the colonies would resist.

Samuel Adams and those about him, however, did not lose heart. They had long been prominent in Boston affairs, had usually controlled the town-meeting, and were well acquainted with the leading spirits of the surrounding towns. Their plan was bold: ''I wish we could rouse the continent,'' wrote Adams. Still, he dared not hope for the reality: ''If our design (for committees) succeeds, there will be an apparent union of sentiments among the people of this province, which may spread through the continent.'' Clearly, no general spirit of armed resistance was apparent to him in 1772. In November of that year, Adams and his supporters succeeded finally in carrying a vote by a very narrow majority through a thinly-attended Boston town-meeting for the appointment of a committee to correspond with other towns and ''state the rights of the colonies.'' Thus did the men who really began the Revolution obtain a small grant of authority from their timorous and grudging supporters. Most of the members of this Boston Committee, which set the torch to the bonfire, are little known, and outside of Adams, Otis, Warren, and Quincy, were not men of the first ability nor of social standing or wealth. John Adams, Faneuil, Hancock, Gerry, Paine, as yet declined to countenance so radical a step. The Tories scoffed at the Sons of Belial who came together and asked each other, ''What can we lose? Peradventure by our craft we may gain something.'' ''And so Samuel, the Publican (Adams) and William, the Scribe (Cooper) . . . with other the sons of Belial set themselves to oppose Francis, (Bernard) the Governor, . . . and drew much people after them and the land was disquieted.'' Within a few months, the Committee had clearly proved the existence in a good many towns of a considerable

number of men ready to resist, and, on the strength of that, secured a much more definite grant of authority from the Boston
Town-meeting.

But the movement lacked numbers and needed an opportunity to rouse the people by some dramatic act of defiance.
In 1770, an attempt of the roughs of the water-front to "bait"
the redcoats had resulted in a scattered involuntary fire from
the comrades of the men assaulted.   There is no reason to believe that the affair was anything more than one of the ordinary rows then common in garrison towns; but Adams and his
ilk put great pressure on the governor to remove the troops
and utilized the funeral of those killed for a tremendous
demonstration.   Sober second thought told the Bostonians that
the soldiers were innocent, but Adams and his friends seized
upon the "Massacre" as the first blood spilt in the war they
were predicting and held services of commemoration which
naturally became the occasion for inflammatory denunciations
of English rule.

When, however, came from England news of the Tea Act
of 1773 and the determination of the ministry to make the fate
of the cargoes consigned to the four principal ports a test
of the spirit of the colonies, Adams realized that the golden
opportunity was at hand.   A general grievance had been provided which by a miracle enabled Adams to put behind his
new plea for resistance to England the old established habit
of eluding the Navigation Acts.   The campaign against the tea
was worked up by the various committees with the greatest assiduity in newspapers, meetings, and alehouses, and the country strewn with placards.   The consignees in Charleston, S.
C., resigned at the request of a public meeting.   But the consignees in Boston refused to resign.   The Town-meeting voted
executive power into the hands of the Committee of Correspondence, which called in the committees of the neighboring
towns, and sat "like a little senate," wrote the disgusted
Hutchinson.   The tea-ships arrived on November 28, 1773, and,
after every expedient to have them sent back or to prevent
the landing of the tea had failed, the Committee called a great

meeting to take action. Opposition to violent measures was expected and in case the meeting refused to authorize the destruction of the tea, a large band of men, whose identity is still unknown, were ready, disguised as Indians, to take matters into their own hands. After a long and stormy session had proved the opposition too strong, the signal was given; the "Indians" rushed out of the warehouse in which they were concealed, whooping as they hurried toward the harbor. The audience at the meeting and a large part of the population who were not at the meeting rushed after them, and from wharves and warehouses, passively watched the "Indians," silently but rapidly, dump the tea into the harbor and disappear.

As a demonstration, the Tea Party was an overwhelming success and produced precisely that impression of organized, concerted, popular action which Adams had long been most anxious to give. The identity of the opposition of the years 1760 to 1772 with the older phase to which the English had long since become accustomed had effectually concealed from them what had been slowly coming to a head in America. The passivity of the great majority of the people, the lack of united action and of concerted effort, of numbers and of education and wealth among the members of the Committees of Correspondence had very naturally led the King, the ministry, the mercantile and educated classes in England to conclude that the movement was the work of a small faction of radicals, whose stand was disapproved by the vast majority of the people. That the vast majority of the American people could heartily disagree with Samuel Adams and yet even more vehemently disagree with himself, seems never to have occurred to George III. The English, in fact, greatly exaggerated the numbers of their own supporters in America and belittled the extent of the opposition to them. They supposed, as it is rapidly becoming the fashion to assume now, that every man not in favor of armed resistance was a Tory. From the clear evidence of colonial jealousies, they concluded that active and efficient coöperation between the colonies was out of the question. The reception accorded the tea rudely shook this complacency. George III declared that act a subversion of the Constitution; Lord North deemed it the culmination of rioting and confusion, and Parliament solemnly voted it actual rebellion. Indeed, the English at last saw that the Americans objected to their acts and taxes, not because they were unjust, but because the Americans intended never to recognize any such relationship to England as those acts and taxes assumed to exist.

To take no action was to lose the colonies without an effort for their retention, to sanction a revolution. Tyranny was not to the taste of George III; but a supine surrender of what he fully believed were the rights of Empire was as little to his liking. The intentions of some Americans were clear, but he could not yet learn that more than a handful had taken any decided stand or that the colonies were ready to act together. General Gage returned from America and privately assured him that "they will be lions whilst we are lambs; but if we take the resolute part, they will undoubtedly prove very meek." The repeal of the Stamp Act, concluded the King, "was a fatal compliance." So, in the Coercive Acts of 1774, England took "the resolute part," closed the Port of Boston to injure its trade; annulled the Massachusetts Charter and instituted government by men appointed from England; provided for the trial in England of men accused of treason, and erected a new province of Quebec that robbed all the colonies of the lands west of the Alleghenies whose value they had just come to realize. "The die is now cast," wrote George to Lord North, "the Colonies must either submit or triumph."

Had Samuel Adams himself dictated the English measures, he could not have devised any better calculated to rouse the indifferent and lukewarm to the necessity for action or which would have given him and his colleagues greater prestige and authority. He made excellent use of the varied motives now working in his favor: strong State patriotism, love of self-government, and belief in States' sovereignty, even if it involved a breach with England; the hatred of the Boston mob for the troops quartered there; the traditional opposition to the revenue officers; the traditional determination not to pay enough money to the English officers to render them independent of the colony. The Boston Committee had promptly arrogated to itself in 1773 executive powers and now began in 1774 a persistent attempt to create and mold public opinion, and to concert and execute measures of resistance. It collected powder, lead, and muskets; instituted companies of minutemen, who drilled more or less regularly; and appointed watchers and messengers to carry word of the movement of troops to the districts threatened. With the annulling of the old Charter, the Boston Committee became the only body capable of acting with consent of the people without directly exposing all its members to the penalty of high treason. It openly took upon itself the government of the State, the supplying of Boston with provisions, local administration, and the organization of revolt.

Nothing remained but to convince the men around Boston that the only course left them was open resistance. Parliament furnished it in the Act for the exclusion of the colonies from the Newfoundland Fisheries. Salt cod was the chief staple of New England's trade with the rest of the world, and, if they were excluded from the principal source of supply, the New England colonies would be ruined whether the foreign sugar islands were open or closed to colonial trade. The news of this Act arrived on April 2, 1775, and Adams and his followers at once saw that the decisive factor had appeared and was in their favor. From that moment, they determined to force the issue, confident that Massachusetts would support them. In full consciousness of the strength and excellence of the new organization, rather than in any spirit of prophesy, Joseph Warren wrote on April 3, 1775, "America must and will be free. The contest may be severe; the end will be glorious. We would not boast, but we think, united and prepared as we are, we have no reason to doubt of success."

General Gage soon provided an admirable opportunity for a demonstration. Despite the activity of Adams and his Com-

mittees, there were few places in New England and few in
the other colonies where their adherents were really in the
majority and determined to fight. There were still fewer
places where any preparations for armed resistance had been
actually made. But along the highroad from Boston to Concord, the shire town of Middlesex County, and the market
town for the whole district around Boston, were a series of
towns where Adams's propaganda had met the most enthusiastic response of any place in America. An overwhelming majority of the men were determined to fight, had been
organized into companies and provided with arms, a considerable store of which, with powder and lead, had been collected
at Concord. In the previous February the British had seized
cannon at Salem; in March had captured cartridges and cannon-balls that were being smuggled into Boston in candle-boxes
and hay-wagons; and though fights with the populace were
averted by the narrowest of margins, the fact was beyond dispute that no outbreak had taken place. But when General
Gage determined to send his troops to Concord on the night
of April 18, to seize the stores collected there, he thrust his
men into the one place in all America where adequate preparations for their reception had been made.

The alarm was spread by the people themselves and reached
Lexington and Concord far ahead of the messengers, of whom
only John Dawes reached Concord. At two in the morning,
more than a hundred minute-men were waiting on Lexington
Common, but no one came, the night was cold, and they dispersed. At three the alarm was in Concord. Five o'clock
found about a hundred minute-men, armed with muskets,
assembled again on Lexington Common and they soon saw
the red-coated column approaching. Both they and the English seem to have been somewhat non-plussed, and some moments passed in indecision; but a company of the red-coats
was detached from the column, which, without waiting, started
for Concord. The company deployed on the green and fired a
volley at the minute-men, who returned a few scattered shots
and then dispersed, carrying their wounded. The company

fell back into the column and the British marched on to Concord, where they met an unexpectedly stout resistance. The minute-men actually drove back into town a small detachment who were guarding a bridge, and followed them with a persistence that astonished the British. After some powder and shot had been destroyed, the British officers, who had been strictly ordered not to rouse the country, determined to return to Boston. A large body of Americans returned with them, annoying them with a deadly flanking fire from the little hillsides fringing the Boston road, but not offering enough resistance to draw upon them an attack in force. The British column, we now know, voluntarily returned in obedience to orders; the minute-men could not have driven them from the field had they chosen to stand their ground; but the minute-men and the countryside deemed it a retreat before superior force. The effect was incalculable; recruits poured into the camp in the Cambridge marshes; the other New England States promptly started their militia for Boston. Most of the accounts which spread through the colonies were false, but glorious;—the British army had been driven into Boston and was there besieged! The news "will plead with all America," wrote Mrs. John Adams in May, "with more irresistible persuasion than angels trumpet-tongued."

The more completely to invest Boston, the project was adopted by the patriots of erecting a redoubt upon the highest part of Charlestown Hill, the whole of which was then known as Bunker's Hill. On the sixteenth of June, a body of several hundred men under Colonel Prescott marched across Charlestown Neck and began a redoubt on the lower of the two hills, and that nearer the water, since called Breed's Hill. From a military point of view, the error was great: the English fleet, anchored off the Neck, could have cut off their retreat and compelled their surrender to the regiments, who could easily have been landed in the rear of the entrenchment, which was wholly commanded by the hill on which the monument now stands. All this was seen by Gage and Howe, but was cast aside in favor of a demonstration. They would land in front of the redoubt and rail fence stuffed with hay, and show the farmers and the colonies in general that resistance was hopeless even when the British voluntarily gave the farmers every possible advantage. Up the slope, with flags flying, went the British line; down again in haste it came. Twice the assault failed, and then was successful largely because the farmers, finding their ammunition low, began to retreat. They were allowed to escape unmolested by the astonished regulars. The country was electrified. The most diverse reports went broadcast about the numbers engaged, the casualties, and the narrative of the action. Many blamed the patriots for fighting at all. John Adams accurately summed up contemporary opinion: "Considering all the disadvantages under which they fought they really exhibited prodigies of valour." But Bunker Hill, from a military point of view a crushing defeat for the Americans, was a moral victory of the first importance. A miracle had happened:—the farmers had stood their ground, unabashed by the line of redcoats. Bunker Hill "instantly convinced us," wrote Ezra Stiles, President of Yale College, "and for the first time convinced Britons themselves that Americans both would and could fight with great effect."

IX

FIRST ATTEMPTS AT PERMANENT ORGANIZATION

THE hostilities at Lexington and at Bunker Hill had been the work of the Committees of Correspondence and their adherents, and not that of a regularly constituted State or local government, and, even if the people of Massachusetts did finally accept responsibility for what had been done, nothing was clearer to the leaders in the other colonies than that they themselves had not been and would not be in any way obligated even by such action. Their relations to Massachusetts, to each other, and to England were still to be decided by such notions of law and expediency as careful consideration should show to be important. At the same time, the strong sentiment in favor of supporting the gallant stand of the Massachusetts men caused the leaders throughout America promptly to begin the thorough discussion of ways, means, and methods.

They soon found themselves seriously at odds over the most expedient method of securing English recognition of American claims. One party declared war inexpedient and a settlement agreeable to America easily obtainable by negotiation and passive resistance, while their opponents insisted upon armed resistance as the only means of convincing England of the generality and seriousness of American opposition. The former and larger party stood upon familiar colonial ground and espoused methods which had long been successful, and to it naturally flocked the conservatives and the timid, afraid of compromising themselves and of thus endangering their lives or property. Their opponents insisted that some sort of legalization of what had been done by the institution of a definite revolutionary organization was imperative, not only to make resistance effective, but to give the movement a legal status which would enable its supporters to claim the rights of belligerents and permit them to recruit their ranks from those whom the fears of confiscation and execution would otherwise hold passive. The anxiety of the very men who had fought at Lexington to free themselves of liability by denying that they had "resisted" at all warned Adams and his friends of what was otherwise to be expected even from the boldest. Indeed, without assuming a definite object of some kind for which to fight, without in some way defining their future legal relations to England and to each other, it was clear that no general coöperation of colonies or individuals was to be expected. It was highly probable that, unless some public pledges sufficiently definite to make difficult the desertion of the common cause were soon obtained, some States, if not the majority, would make their peace with England individually and leave the few to bear the brunt of the mother-country's displeasure.[1] The greatest obstacle in the way of resistance soon proved to be the exceedingly divergent notions about the future relations of the various States in America to each other, the sort of coöperation needed, the kind of central administration required.

The obvious inadequacy of the existing arrangements, administrative and military, caused at once the greatest perplexity and concern. The committees of correspondence, which were now pretty generally spread throughout the country, were at most empowered only to investigate, correspond, and suggest, and could not claim to have been authorized by local or State governments to commence a revolution. In several colonies, they had been unable to secure any open recognition at all and were voluntary associations of men, entirely extra-legal, whose organization would certainly not confer upon them or their abettors the belligerent status so obviously desirable. In Massachusetts, to be sure, the rescinding of the colonial charter had furnished the Boston Com-

[1] The Journals of the Continental Congress and Force's American Archives are full of material on this point.

mittee of Correspondence an opportunity to oppose the British officials with the open approval of the populace, and this Adams had interpreted as a legalization of the Committee's work. The English government would certainly not agree with him on that point, and it was by no means sure that the people of Boston would if their movement failed of instant success and prompt support elsewhere. Outside Massachusetts, the authorities of the several States had clung to their charters and had held carefully aloof from the committees and their propaganda.[2] Nor did the people of the colonies in general manifest clearly any desire for independence of England. "Until after the rejection of the second petition of Congress in 1775," wrote John Jay, "I never heard an American of any class or any description express a wish for the independence of the colonies." Not only was there in June 1775, no definite State or national organization pledged to opposition to England, which could not easily have been disowned, but there was apparent no sentiment in favor of the creation of such a body or bodies.

The Continental Congress could not claim any such position. It represented the radical elements in the various States rather than the organized governments. Indeed, many of the delegates, both in 1774 and 1775, had been appointed by the committees of correspondence without even a pretense of election by the people. Some States were not represented at all, and others were only partially represented. The Congress was in truth a body of ambassadors from confessedly extralegal associations and possessed no status which the States in America or the Crown in England would in any way be compelled to recognize. Further, it was by no means certain that the majority of Americans favored a central organization of any kind.[3]

[2] This whole subject has been treated by Agnes Hunt, *Provincial Committees of Safety*. Much evidence is in Force's *American Archives*.

[3] The student should in particular read the anxious debates in Congress in the fall of 1775 and spring of 1776 upon the formation of a new government and note the direct testimony of the reluctance of the people to act. Most of the authorizations to members of Congress in

What Lexington and Bunker Hill had not been able to accomplish was consummated by the rejection of the Olive Branch Petition by George III in the summer of 1775, and after the arrival of the news there was in the fall of 1775 a very general acquiescence in or tacit acceptance of the revolutionary organization already in existence, though the leaders were keenly alive to the fact that this sort of recognition pledged neither States nor individuals to the continuance of the war. New executive officers were chosen in Massachusetts in defiance of the English statute of 1774; but in most States the actual business of the country was still transacted through the colonial governmental structure. If the voice had become the voice of Jacob, the hands were still those of Esau. The nearly universal acceptance of the members of Congress in Philadelphia by the people or the popular choice of new members soon gave that body a quasi-legal status as a congress of ambassadors and enabled it to act with something approaching legality or regularity as a central organ of some indescribably vague variety. The appointment of Washington as Commander-in-Chief of the army at Boston in July 1775, and the presence of various officers and regiments from several States in that army was more definite evidence of coöperation between the States for resistance, and enabled Congress to claim in the fall of 1775 support in nearly all sections of the country. But no definite general action had been taken; no formal sanction of resistance had been given by States or people. Their approval referred rather to past than to future action. The people in the States expected to take further action when they thought it necessary; the States intended to reserve their approval of further resistance and the legalization of coöperation until they should make up their several minds; they reserved complete right to recall their citizens from the army or from Congress whenever they should deem it necessary.

This uncertainty crippled no branch of the revolutionary

favor of independence carefully omitted instructions on the question of further organization.

fabric as much as it did the Congress. In the nature of things, the latter possessed no definite grant of authority. Above all, it must not alienate any section of its supporters, for nothing would so quickly ruin the movement as the open defection of some strong State. Congress must, therefore, find the definition of its powers in the instructions of its members rather than in the needs of the moment. It must somehow steer the middle course between the radicals, who threatened to leave the movement if more was not promptly done, and the conservatives who threatened to desert if one step more was taken. The Congress must follow rather than lead; it must do what seemed likely to be approved rather than what was expedient or necessary.[4] The administrative difficulties of the Revolution must be more thoroughly understood if we are to realize how splendid an achievement our independence is.

The difficulties in the way of permanent coöperation seemed to contemporaries almost insurmountable, and attracted more attention abroad than any single aspect of the situation. The distances sundering the States had effectually prevented rapid or frequent communication and had produced almost as great

[4] Every page of the Journals of Congress proves only too clearly the truth of this statement. See, for instance, the attempt to deal with the pressing problem of deserters in Feb. 1777, and the obvious inadequacy of the resolve passed to solve the difficulty as they saw it. "An obstinate partiality to the habits and customs of one part of this continent has predominated in the public councils and too little attention has been paid to others. . . . It has been my fate to make an ineffectual opposition [in Congress] to all short enlistments, to colonial [i. e., State] appointment of officers and to many other measures, which I thought pregnant with mischief; but these things either suited with the genius and habits or squared with the interests of Some States, that had sufficient influence to prevail [in Congress] and nothing is now left but to extricate ourselves as well as we can." Robert Morris to Washington, Dec. 23, 1776. MS. letter, quoted in Sparks's *Washington's Writings*, IV, 237, note.

"It is a fact too notorious to be concealed that C[ongress] is rent by party—that much business of a trifling nature and personal concernment withdraw their attention from matters of great national moment at this critical period." Washington to Mason, March 27, 1779. *Washington's Writings*, Ford's ed., VII, 383.

a lack of acquaintance between parts of America as between America and England. Indeed, many more Americans had been in London than had traveled in the colonies, and the constant receipt of letters, papers, and books from the mother-country had kept each colony more keenly aware of what went on in England than it was of what happened in its own vicinity. In fact, the States were contiguous only on paper and were really separated by great stretches of wilderness, sowed with rivers and bogs and almost devoid of roads. Actually, they were independent of each other as well as of England, and there was not as yet sufficient pressure of circumstances to make coöperation seem imperative rather than merely desirable. The possibilities of agreement, moreover, seemed slight. To most Americans, the superficial differences of customs and religion were more striking than were the great fundamental similarities which attracted the attention of the leaders and gave them confidence in the ultimate outcome. New England was Congregationalist, Virginia Episcopalian, Pennsylvania Quaker; and the religious disputes, in particular those growing out of the threatened severance of relations with the Church of England in case the States should attempt actual independence of the mother-country, were serious obstacles for a time in the way of a permanent organization. The old traditional disputes had been revived: Pennsylvania and Maryland, Maryland and Virginia, New Jersey and New York, Rhode Island and Massachusetts, South Carolina and Georgia had long cherished grievances against each other and now lost no opportunity to pursue the quarrel. Then, a century of development had allowed certain colonies to outstrip the others in size and wealth; had created the jealousies between the large and small States which were in 1787 so significant. All these differences had long prevented the adoption of any scheme of central government in colonial America and they seemed still to present almost insuperable obstacles to permanent coöperation.

They were, however, less serious than the social differences. The fact that the Atlantic coast was everywhere accessible from the sea and was well-furnished with deep parallel rivers had early produced a pretty general settlement of the coast regions and the lower reaches of the rivers all along the seaboard. Subsequent development had pushed this long thin line of settlement westward, until there existed in 1776 a fringe of thoroughly established towns and counties along the coast and a wider belt inland where conditions were still those of the frontier. Between the two districts there had always been a certain antagonism, based on the inevitable dependence of the interior upon the coast for the sale of its own produce and for its supplies of salt and manufactured goods. The frontier, being therefore nearly always in debt to the coast, resented keenly the latter's economic position and assumption of social superiority. Thus developed the distinction between the settled communities and the frontier, between the East and the West, between the creditor and debtor communities, which is one of the most fundamental lines in American life and one of the oldest.

At this time, however, it was less a dividing line between States than a cleft in every State, tending to create social distinctions and foment internal discord. It tended to coincide in each State with the line of rich and poor, creditor and debtor, and made it difficult to institute strong government in the States themselves; and particularly stood in the way of the adhesion of the States as a whole to any scheme of strong central government, because of the determination of the debtors to oppose the development of governmental machinery likely to facilitate the collection of debts. The Revolution was not only a war between England and America, not only a struggle of political parties in both countries, but a civil war in America, some of whose aspects were those of a social war of classes. To this many of the most characteristic manifestations of the Revolution were partially due —the early mob violence, the opposition to English administration, the treatment of the Loyalists. To it are due most of the aspects of the critical years just previous to the adoption of the Constitution. Like every great event in history, the Revolution was a struggle of many motives and many interests, and was concerned not only with the authority of England over America, but with the relations of Americans to each other in the several States and in the central government.

At just this juncture, when in the winter of 1775–76 everything hung in the balance, when energetic united action seemed improbable, and defeat for Massachusetts unless promptly supported seemed certain, the union between the revolutionary movement and the war between debtor and creditor gave a mighty impulse to open resistance by securing the adhesion of large numbers of men who had hitherto held aloof. Naturally enough, among the more adventurous and radical spirits, who had at first flocked to the committees, had been men who had not so much to lose that fears of confiscation weighed heavily upon them. A farmer could easily enough retrieve the loss of his acres by moving on and taking up a new claim. The men who had held back had been not only the conservatives, but the merchants and the creditor class, in general men who were likely to lose heavily by the interference of the outbreak of hostilities with the regularity of trade. Such an alignment of debtor and creditor was natural enough and has always appeared at the beginning of great wars. It was probably as little in evidence during the Revolution as in any period of change in history, but it certainly played a significant part. Indeed, so largely did the debtor class preponderate in the early movements that, until the adhesion of Hancock, Washington, Franklin, John Adams, and other men of wealth and station became known, it was widely claimed in England and America that resistance was merely the work of a crowd of disorderly men who refused to pay their debts or who had nothing to lose.[5]

[5] The evidence is too voluminous to be cited in so brief a book and will be found literally in all directions. An example or two must suffice. Johnston, one of the North Carolina radicals, wrote to a friend

Then, when the tacit recognition of the Revolution by the people permitted the extension of organization, the ablest and most prominent men were at once drawn into the service of the States, of the central administration, or of the army, and local government fell into the hands of the most radical and least experienced men connected with the movement. Nor were their acts likely to be questioned or their discretion hampered from above, as they well knew. The men at the helm in the State had staked their all upon success and were not receiving such universal support as to make them willing to quarrel with the local leaders for being too outspoken or too energetic in maintaining the cause. Graver business, too, prevented really adequate supervision of the local committees, whom the exigencies of the situation thus invested with literally absolute, unrestricted authority.

The men into whose hands this vast power fell were for the most part debtors and they promptly began to use it against all who had for a variety of reasons not yet openly joined the Cause. John Adams and others have recorded opinions that not more than a third of the people openly espoused the movement, but the great majority of those who held aloof were by no means British sympathizers. "Some are [hostile] from real attachment to Britain," said a letter written by a secret committee of Congress; "some from interested views, many, very many, from fear of the British forces, some because they are dissatisfied with the general measures

in December 1776, that the members of the Constitutional Convention of North Carolina who had the least pretensions to be gentlemen were regarded with suspicion by the others (who were in the majority) and who were "a set of men without reading, experience, or principle to govern them." The members of the first legislature he characterized as "fools and knaves, who by their low Arts have worked themselves into the good graces of the populace." *North Carolina Records*, X, 1041; XI, 504, 627; and elsewhere. The crew of an American war vessel were thus described: "His people really appear to me to be a set of the most unprincipled abandoned fellows I ever saw." *American Archives*, Fourth Series, III, 1378, 1658. (1775.)

If such was the testimony of patriots, one can readily imagine the opinions of loyalists and Englishmen.

of Congress, more because they disapprove of the men in
power and the measures in their respective States.'' The
''Patriots,'' however, dubbed all these men ''Loyalists'' and
began to deal with them all as professed enemies of the Cause.
Avowed supporters of England and English officials were
promptly driven out of the district, their property confiscated, and such as were captured were subjected to indigni-
ties and such physical abuse as tar and feathering. The
timid soon discovered, therefore, that the consequences of not
abetting the Revolution were more tangible and quite as
terrifying as those of opposing England, and the committees
of correspondence thus convinced very large numbers of people that George III was a tyrant.

But the exercise of authority grew by what it fed on and
demanded new victims. The ease of employing this new
weapon to pay off old scores and to further selfish interests
was too great for many to resist the temptation. Thus self-
interest and the spice of hatred and traditional antipathy
between the debtors and creditors gave the Revolution a
mighty impulse and the deeds done in the name of Liberty
committed many thousands to its cause by methods which
only eventual success could condone.[6] A good many men

[6] The minister of Longmeadow, Massachusetts, a patriot, gives the
following account in his Diary of 1776: "April 9.—I hear of tumults
and disorderly practices; stupidity, hardness of heart, atheism, and
unbelief prevail. The British ministry breathe out cruelty against the
colonies still. . . . July 24.—A number of people gathered together,
some dressed like Indians with blankets, and manifested uneasiness
with those that trade in rum, molasses, sugar, etc. I understand that
a number went to Merchant Colton's and have again [note this significant word] taken away his goods. I don't see the justice or equity
of it. Many don't approve of it, but have not resolution enough to
interpose and endeavor redress. . . . Nov. 30—Military Co. called together at a minute's warning to go wherever called. People don't
appear forward. . . . Our soldiers begin to return that enlisted for a
stated time, and people seem engaged to get money, and I fear by oppression and unjust measures." Hart, *American History Told by Contemporaries*, II, 456, 457.
    A bibliography of the loyalists and their sufferings is in C. H. Van
Tyne, *American Revolution*, 338-340. Particularly interesting is Samuel
Curwen's *Journal and Letters*.

of wealth were promptly declared loyalists and their property seized and distributed, although they protested that they were not English supporters at all. Imitations of the Tea Party gave excuse for the robbing of stores and warehouses; local regulations and even state laws required the payment of coin by loyalists to patriots and the acceptance of depreciated paper currency at its face value from patriots in exchange for goods. The property of all the exiles, voluntary and involuntary, was at once distributed. In time, this war of the debtor upon the creditor class culminated in that union of the propertied class throughout the country in favor of strong government which was largely responsible for the adoption of the Constitution. In the meantime, this onslaught upon the creditors pretty generally brought about their adhesion to the Revolution or their organization against it. After 1776, the loyalists were in the minority in New England; in the South, they were in the minority along the coast and in the majority in the interior; while in the Middle States they equaled if they did not outnumber the patriots. Thus, throughout the country, the existence of a stanch opposition to the Revolution, in many districts thoroughly successful, became evident.

It has been difficult for posterity to realize that a considerable portion of the people did not support the Revolution; it has been even more difficult for us to realize that their opposition to the movement was based upon differences of opinion for the most part American in their origin and effect, which did not in the least indicate a desire for English rule or a dislike of American independence. The opposition was the normal result of the civil war in America.

The issue raised by the war, as contemporaries saw it, was not as much the desirability or possibility of independence of England—upon this the agreement was so general as hardly to admit of debate or require argument—but of the desirability and expediency of obtaining that independence by means of a central administration whose very existence would necessarily deprive the States of some of their

cherished sovereignty. Not loyalty to England, but States'
sovereignty was the formidable obstacle in the way of the
Revolution preventing permanent coöperation. Many and
many a man seriously feared the results of a victory over the
British won by Washington at the head of an army, which
might then be strong enough to erect a central government
more powerful, and therefore more obnoxious, than the British
government had ever been. States' sovereignty and State
independence were the supremely desirable things and the
great majority had no more intention of sacrificing them to
erect a revolutionary organization in America than they had
of submitting to the rule of George III.

Independence meant, as Paine phrased it, ''a continental
form of government (which) can keep the peace of the
continent and preserve it inviolate from civil war.'' Significant words, these; significant, too, his omission of all
mention of England. John Adams, writing to his wife in
April 1776, defined independence as ''government in every
colony, a confederation among them all, and treaties with
foreign nations to acknowledge us as a sovereign State, and
all that.'' Of a nation in our sense of the word, composed
of individuals and governed by a central administration,
superior in obligation to the State governments so far as
the individual was concerned, there seems to have been little
talk. The idea, if it occurred to many, seems not to have
been seriously discussed. The ''continental form of government'' meant one which provided explicitly for the sovereignty
of thirteen separate States. Some of the States declared
themselves independent of England in the spring of 1776; the
rest afterwards followed suit, while there seems to be good
reason to believe that the County of Mecklenburg, N. C.,
declared itself independent as early as May 1775.[7]

The expediency of any central government, the exact form
of the new government, its probable powers, its relation to
the States, the necessity or desirability of forming new State

[7] Hoyt, *Mecklenburg Declaration*. The Resolves of May 31 are undoubtedly genuine; the document of May 20 is now generally rejected.

governments, all these were really the issues behind the question of independence, which was so widely and actively discussed throughout America from the summer of 1775 to the summer of 1776. Public meetings thrashed it over; delegates traveled the length and breadth of the States to learn the trend of opinion; and a pretty general conclusion was reached in the States by the people themselves in June 1776, in favor of a general declaration of independence of England by the States as sovereign entities.[8]

Congress really registered the opinion of the country in Lee's famous Resolutions and the even more notable document drafted by Jefferson to embody them. On July 2nd, Congress adopted the principle of independence; on July 4th, it discussed, amended, and accepted the document prepared by the Committee, and referred it back to those gentlemen for final verbal revision. The document, with which we are familiar, was completed by the committee some time during the night of July 4th and 5th and was printed and published next day by order of Congress. The signing of the document was an afterthought; the full delegation of some States had not been present on July 4th and there was some fear that subsequent misfortunes might set the various States seeking loopholes through which to escape equal responsibility. Most of the signatures were appended on August 2nd, though a few were affixed as late as November.[9]

The Declaration of Independence was a statement of the

[8] The evidence has been printed by J. H. Hazelton, *The Declaration of Independence, Its History*.

[9] The Journals of Congress are quite explicit on all these points. John Adams believed that July 2 would be the day celebrated. Mellen Chamberlain was the first to explain how July 4 came to be the day. The secretary of Congress when he came to write up the Journal saved himself the labor of copying the text of the Declaration by pasting into the Journal under July 4 one of the printed copies of the document with all the signatures appended which had been issued in the autumn of 1776 to give it publicity. When the Journal was printed afterwards, this printed copy with the names was included in the official account of the proceedings of July 4 as historians and the general public received it. *Proceedings* of the Massachusetts Historical Society for November 1884.

evident fact that the American colonies were in reality and long had been independent of England; that they had governed themselves in the past without assistance and could do so in the future; that their interests were too different from those of the mother-country for them to accept her decisions in regard to policy. The Declaration of Independence was also unquestionably a verdict in favor of a central organization of some sort, and might even be argued to have declared some such government essential. But it was an even more explicit affirmation of the point most important to Americans in 1776—the absolute sovereignty of the individual States over their own citizens and their complete independence of each other. The capitalization of the title was itself freighted with meaning: "A Declaration by the representatives of the united States of America, in Congress assembled." The phrases of the document, which followed the long preamble, were even more explicit: "The Representatives of the united States of America," "by authority of the good people of these colonies, solemnly publish and declare, That *these* United Colonies are, and of Right ought to be Free and Independent States." [10]

The plunge once taken, the solemn pledge of the independence of the individual States of each other and of the central government once passed, the business of permanent organization began. Naturally enough, the lines of policy already laid down by the opposition to England were followed, and such permanent action as was taken at once was local and not national. Some of the States had already formed new governments; the others began to make constitutions in the summer and fall of 1776. That there might be no excuse for misinterpretation, most of them explicitly declared their independence of all other authority in the world in the preambles of the new constitutions. The Pennsylvania Convention expressed its approval of the Declaration of Inde-

[10] This quotation is from the parchment engrossed copy in the Department of State at Washington. The word "United" in the last clause is omitted in several of the manuscript copies.

pendence and went on to declare "this, as well as the other United States of America, free and Independent." The Connecticut Assembly voted "that this Colony is and of right ought to be a free and independent State." The power of the people, the necessity of their confirming the work of the conventions, a strong bi-cameral legislature, a weak executive, the separation of powers, these other legacies from the colonial period definitely shaped the form of the new State governments. Experiments were tried, and, in these successive State constitutions, each of which attempted to include the good points of those already in operation and to avoid the unsuccessful expedients, we see gradually taking form the Constitution of the United States.

Congress set to work in 1776 upon a plan of central government, and, in the meantime, appointed various new committees to struggle with the obvious administrative questions whose solution was imperative. These were chiefly military or connected with supplying the army and navy with necessities. Ambassadors to the chief European nations were promptly appointed: Franklin to France; Adams to Holland; Lee to England; Jay to Spain. The framework of a temporary central administration was thus erected. Gradually the Marine Committee, under the able guidance of Robert Morris, assumed chief place, and began to develop a system of administration through agents in the principal ports which soon became adequate for most purposes. These Continental Agents, as they came to be known, were primarily appointed to receive and forward to the army the supplies brought from Europe or captured by privateers, but they soon were busy with various types of work and formed a network of officials throughout America upon whom Congress more and more was forced to depend and who became a connecting link not only between the administration at Philadelphia and the States in America, but between Congress and the Ambassadors and agents abroad.

From the first, the importance of recognition by the European nations was appreciated. The knowledge that it could

not come until America had definitely declared the purpose
of the war and pledged itself to independence had been a
prime factor in securing the consent of the timid to the
Declaration of Independence. Somewhat to their dismay,
the leaders were informed that the Declaration was not regarded in Europe as sufficient to entitle the United Colonies
to recognition. Franklin had been despatched to France to
obtain recognition and an alliance, but wrote that fears of
the inability of Washington's army to cope with the English
and doubts as to the stability, permanence, and efficiency of
the alliance between the States were nearly insuperable obstacles to the conclusion of a treaty. Congress was still only
a body of delegates, whose decisions were at any moment
likely to be reversed or disavowed by the sovereign States,
a body therefore limited to those decisions which it had
reason to believe would not be repudiated. This lack of a
definite grant of authority, the entire lack of certainty that
their commands would be obeyed, vitally weakened the central
government at a moment when the exigencies of the war
required prompt and decisive action. It was naturally not
a body upon whose solemn pledge the European governments would rely.

The defeat at Long Island, the disaster at White Plains,
the continued loss of position after position during the summer of 1776 and Washington's retreat across the Jerseys
upon Philadelphia in the fall only too clearly weakened
support at home and rendered aid from abroad unlikely.
Indeed the continued existence of the army was problematical, and the battle of Trenton was fought on December
25th, 1776, in order to use the army before it should melt
away.[11] That overwhelming success put new life into the

[11] "The present exigency of our affairs will not admit of delay. . . .
Ten days more will put an end to the existence of our army." Washington to the President of Congress, Dec. 20, 1776. See also the letter
of December 24. *Writings of Washington*, Ford's ed., V, 113; 124-5;
127; 129. "The militia must be taken before their spirits and patience
are exhausted." Reed to Washington. Reed, *Life of Joseph Reed*,
I, 273.

army and into Congress and convinced the English and the French that their first conclusions had been mistakes. ''Mr. Washington'' had arrived to stay.   The failure of the Americans to do more than hold their own in the spring of 1777, the failure to adopt some form of central government to take the place of the anomalous multiple executive at Philadelphia, and the invasion of Burgoyne from Canada, all had a most unfavorable effect upon opinion at home and particularly abroad.   No nation was anxious to recognize a movement likely at any instant to be crushed; to make terms with a central government which was as yet confessedly a make- shift and which seemed each month liable to dissolve from internal dissensions; or to sign a treaty with a number of States which were obviously unable to agree upon as funda- mental a point as the expediency of having a central govern- ment powerful enough to enforce upon them all a common agreement or decision.

The surrender of Burgoyne in October 1777, decided nearly all the outstanding questions.   The Congress at Phila- delphia adopted the Articles of Confederation in November; in December, the French expressed their willingness to recog- nize the new government and to sign a treaty of alliance; in January, the English began to draw up measures of com- promise and treaties of peace.   Parliament and King were willing to yield anything short of independence.   The matter had, however, now gone too far for compromise; the Amer- icans had agreed upon a new central government from which much was expected; they were offered an alliance with the most powerful nation in Europe, England's oldest and bitter- est foe.   They considered the successful conclusion of the war to be mainly a question of time.   Congress, therefore, rejected the English offers without much hesitation, and ac- cepted the alliance with France.   Many and many a dark day was still to dawn, when even the stoutest heart was destined to quake from fear that all was lost; but from the spring of 1778, the ultimate outcome of the war seems really never to have been in doubt.

X

WHY WE WON THE REVOLUTION

The winning of the Revolution long concealed the essential truth about its military aspects. When historians and patriotic speakers considered its trend at its twenty-fifth and fiftieth anniversaries, the fact that we had won proved to them conclusively that our victory was due to superior military ability. It was to them inconceivable that the successful conclusion of a great war, fought for so high a stake as the independence of a continent, should have been accomplished by any less decisive factors than the best general and the most numerous army. The "survivors" of Lexington, Concord, and Bunker Hill, who appeared in 1825 on the occasion of Webster's memorable oration, which itself "made" history, were also sufficiently numerous to cause men to believe irresistibly that we must have had a large army upon the field. Moreover, the victory, besides demonstrating our military efficiency, was naturally supposed to prove that the history of the war was the tale of a triumphant march toward the goal of independence, of which their fathers had been proud, whose glories the sons must venerate with enthusiastic and sincere devotion, and whose reverses could only add to the martyristic halo already shrouding the patriots who fought in it.

So strong indeed is the predisposition of every loyal American to accept these conclusions as true, that historians have long been afraid to emphasize the real aspects of the war for fear of being charged with disloyalty and a disposition to destroy patriotic ideals. No serious student now denies that we won the war with an army much less numerous and efficient than the British force and with generals certainly

123

not comparable to great European leaders like Cæsar and Cromwell. Indeed, we lost, with some striking exceptions, every battle of note. Lexington, Concord,[1] Bunker Hill, Long Island, Brandywine, Germantown, Camden, Guilford's Court House, were all defeats, and in the battles we did win, Trenton, Bennington, Saratoga, Yorktown, the Americans outnumbered the English. The glories of victory over Burgoyne are somewhat diminished by the knowledge that some six or seven thousand British, without adequate provisions or ammunition, were surrounded in the woods by some twenty thousand Americans well supplied with food and powder and constantly reinforced from the surrounding countryside. During the campaigns, the English invariably marched where they pleased, and, except at Saratoga, the Americans retreated before them or followed.[2] From the military point of view, as C. F. Adams and others have shown,[3] the Revolution is disappointing to the student and patriot alike. Nor were the English ever driven out of the country;[4] they ended the

[1] In the technical military sense, the side which remains in possession of the field is the victor and there can be no question of the ability of the British to have remained as long as they liked on either field. The country was overjoyed because the Americans had not been expected even to attempt resistance.

[2] Note for instance the war from Long Island to Trenton; the campaigns of Howe against Philadelphia; the campaign of Cornwallis in the South. Washington stated in a circular letter to the States, dated Oct. 18, 1780, when the American army was stronger and better disciplined than at any previous period of the war, that "the enemy [are] at full liberty to ravage the country wherever they please."

[3] C. F. Adams, *Studies Military and Diplomatic*, 1775–1865. (1912.) The evidence is well summarized and the foot-notes contain an adequate list of authorities.

[4] The fact itself is patent: the British army occupied New York and other sections until after the Treaty of Peace. Washington had made up his mind as early as 1780 that the Americans alone could not drive them out. "I should not advise to calculate matters on the principle of expelling [the British] without the coöperation of the French navy. . . . I imagine we must of necessity adopt the principle of a defensive campaign." Washington to Baron Steuben, Feb. 8, 1780. *Writings of Washington*, Ford's ed., VIII, 194. "You know our inability to expel them unassisted, or perhaps even to stop their career." Sparks's *Washington's Writings*, VII, 200. Again at 206.

war, not because they were defeated, but because they were convinced of the impossibility of ever holding the country without subduing it, and of the impracticability of trying to conquer and hold in subjection a land of continental dimensions, three thousand miles distant from their own source of supplies.

If we add to this a picture of the American army at Cambridge when Washington took command, armed with pitchforks and clubs, and without powder for such guns as they did have; of the army, naked, hungry, and shivering at Valley Forge, while the Pennsylvania farmers carried their produce into Philadelphia to exchange for British gold; [5] of the wholesale desertion of companies and regiments at critical moments; [6] of the intrigues to injure Washington's reputation by allowing him to be defeated and so to secure his removal and to appoint Lee or Gates in his stead; we shall understand better the gloomy forebodings which filled the leaders' letters all through the war. [7] The real atmosphere of the time is not triumph but despair. "I have seen without despondency even for a moment," wrote Washington to George Mason, as late as March 27, 1779, "the hours which America have [sic] stiled her gloomy ones, but I have beheld no day since the commencement of hostilities that I have thought her liberties in such eminent danger as at present. . . . Where

[5] On this whole topic see L. C. Hatch, *The Administration of the American Revolutionary Army.* (1904.) The trade with the British soon became extensive and open. "While our army is experiencing almost daily want, that of the enemy in New York is deriving ample supplies from a trade with the adjacent States . . . which has by degrees become so common that it is hardly thought a crime." Washington to the President of Congress, Nov. 7, 1780. Sparks's *Writings of Washington*, VII, 286-7; and a longer and more explicit statement on p. 401.

[6] "The militia, who come in, you cannot tell how, go, you cannot tell when, and act, you cannot tell where, consume your provisions, exhaust your stores, and leave you at last at a critical moment." Washington to the President of Congress. *Writings of Washington*, Ford's ed., V, 115 (Dec. 20, 1776); also VIII, 290, 292, 503, 506. An instructive document is the report of a committee of Congress on deserters in Feb., 1777. *Journals*, Ford's ed., VII, 115-118.

[7] For instance, *Writings of Washington*, Ford's ed., VIII, 503-4.

are our men of abilities? Why do they not come forth to
save their country? Let this voice, my dear friend, call upon
you—Jefferson and others—do not . . . let our hitherto noble
struggle end in ignom'y."[8] Is it likely that George Washington would have written as strongly as this to as prominent
a man as Mason and named a man like Jefferson if the response from the country had been as spontaneously enthusiastic as the older accounts assume? "I have seen in this
world," wrote John Adams, "but a little of that pure flame
of patriotism which certainly burns in some breasts. There
is much of the ostentation and affectation of it."[9] These
words from the men in America who certainly should have
known the facts are of great significance. The Revolution
was not a time when the exaltation of continuous victory and
the sense of superiority buoyed up the American leaders in
campaigns of constant success, but a time when the keen
knowledge of the army's weakness,[10] of the lukewarmness of
the people,[11] and the bitter realization of the ability of the
British general to march whither he would made even Washington despair of a favorable outcome of the war, long after
Trenton and Saratoga had been won. He remembered, as we
have too often forgotten, that the men who fought at Bunker
Hill were anxious to conceal their presence; that Parker vigorously denied having fired at Lexington upon the British at
all; that the victory at Trenton had been since deprecated in
Congress and his own generalship seriously questioned. The

[8] *Writings of Washington*, Ford's ed., VII, 382.

[9] *Familiar Letters*, 214. August 18, 1776. This was written a little
more than a month after the passage of the Declaration of Independence.

[10] Washington periodically doubted until 1781 whether the army
would be in existence three months hence.

[11] A French traveler thought that "there is a hundred times more
enthusiasm for the Revolution in the first café you choose to name at
Paris than there is in all the United States together." Stedman,
American War, I, 387. "The enemy are daily gathering strength from
the disaffected," Washington wrote on Dec. 20, 1776. *Writings of
Washington*, Ford's ed., V, 114. Also pp. 124-5. "The contest among
the different States now is not which shall do most for the common
cause but which shall do least." Washington to Fielding Lewis, July
6, 1780. Ford's ed., VIII, 335.

Revolution was a time of defeat and despair, and Washington
least of all believed that the final victory was due to the winning of campaigns by a ragged and ill-disciplined army over
a well-equipped and thoroughly disciplined force. He well
knew that many factors contributed to the final result.

Yet the difficulties of the situation, far from robbing Washington and his aides of the glory that has been so long accorded them, only increases and intensifies it. The laurels,
given a leader whom all conditions favor, whose army is
strong, whose countrymen throng round him with joy, are
in no way comparable to the crown to be awarded the general
who wins his war without a strong army and in the face of
the hostility and suspicion of his countrymen. Washington
and his generals won the war by the use of the weapons
they did possess, which were amazingly effective, despite the
fact that some of them appeared in military annals for the
first time and others were hardly military at all. So far
as it can be true that any one man ever did win a war,
George Washington won the Revolution single-handed. He
did not so much lead the American people, as drag them
after him to a victory and an independence which they had
not entirely made up their minds to seek. Scientific research
has heightened, not diminished, the reputations of the leaders.

Unquestionably we won the Revolution because the English did not push the war in 1775 and 1776. Possessed of
an immensely superior force, well-equipped and highly disciplined, Lord Howe dallied around Boston and New York
when he might have been laying waste New England and
the Middle Colonies without any danger to himself. The
reasons for his inaction were at the time as little understood
in England as in America. A tract called *A Succinct Review of the American Contest*, printed in London in 1778,
blamed generals and ministers severely. General Howe had
not prosecuted a war at all, declared the author, but had
merely attempted "to determine a military wager between
him and Mr. Washington, whom he, at the head of a limited
and small body of English, had undertaken to fight, with all

the Americans together in any part of America that Mr. Washington should choose; and that, to give the Americans fair play, he had obliged himself to do nothing that should obstruct their assembling.'' The British, he complained, had respected the property of the Americans who took the field, and had not interfered in the least with the occupations of those who stayed at home. His brother on board Howe's fleet had written that two thousand men landed in Virginia ''would easily lay waste the whole province, but it seems to hurt the Americans without loss or danger to ourselves is not the present system of politics.'' Had Howe taken the field in this spirit our ragged and ill-disciplined army, which Washington kept in existence only by the greatest of exertions, must soon have been destroyed. Indeed, as General C. F. Adams has shown, only Howe's slowness prevented its complete annihilation at Long Island. The control of the sea would have enabled him to land troops on every side of the American position and would have made impossible the escape by sea of any who slipped through his cordon on land. The total lack of both a continental military and administrative machine when the war began; the jealousies of the States;[12] the refusal of the militia to serve outside their State; their enlistment for six weeks or six months only; the lack of powder and shot; the quarrels in Congress, must all have proved fatal to us[13] but for this forbearance of the British.

[12] "Unless the bodies politic will exert themselves to bring things back to first principles—correct abuses and punish our Internal Foes—inevitable ruin must follow. . . . Our Enemy behold with exultation and joy how we labor for their benefit," Washington to Mason, March 27, 1779. *Writings of Washington*, Ford's ed., VII, 382. "One State will comply with a requisition from Congress; another neglects to do it; a third executes it by halves; all differ either in the manner, the matter, or so much in point of time, that we are always working up hill and ever shall be. . . . We shall ever be unable to apply our strength or resources to any advantage. . . . I see one head gradually changing into thirteen." Washington to Joseph Jones. *Ibid.*, VIII, 304, May 31, 1780.

[13] "Nothing but the supineness or folly of the enemy could have saved us from [ruin]." Washington, circular letter to the States, Oct. 18, 1780. *Ibid.*, VIII, 503.

It has often been called folly but was really based upon a most careful study of conditions.

The English view of the American situation is not contained in the speeches of Burke or Chatham nor in the tyrannical notions of George III and Lord North about representation, but in the ideas of the latter about the factors in America which had produced the revolt. The King, the ministry, and the educated classes were firmly convinced that the movement was the work of a small faction, which was not supported by the majority of the people. That the colonies should forget their own jealousies and differences long enough to unite was to George improbable, and that the few leaders should be able to weld together permanently such inconsistent elements was unthinkable. The weakness of the malcontents, the stanch loyalty of a large majority to England, and the jealousies of the States would soon end the struggle, if only the English army did not by plundering and marauding force the waverers into opposition and compel them in very truth to defend their own firesides. Given time and a little assistance at precisely the right moments, the loyalists in America would themselves crush out this selfish uprising. Furthermore, a military conquest of America by an English army was highly inexpedient if harmonious relations with the colonies were to be eventually restored. George and his advisers were anxious to retain the allegiance of the colonists, and were well aware that men who had been excited to the point of armed resistance by the mild acts Parliament had just passed were certain to be antagonized for long years by the burning of their homes and the death of their loved ones. The King was aware that a strong minority in the American Congress favored peace at any price, that a strong party in his own Parliament and ministry also favored conciliation, and that the American army was barely kept alive by the most desperate expedients.[14] The

14 "They [the British] believed that when one army expired, we should not be able to raise another; undeceived however in this expectation by experience, they still remain unconvinced, and to me

pressing of the war, then, until it should become perfectly
clear that peaceable overtures were futile and the loyalists
too weak to overpower the patriots, was the most certain
method of promoting the very thing the war was being
fought to prevent, the loss of the colonies' allegiance. The
English must win the war without alienating the Americans.
A victory obtained in any other fashion would be as deadly
as a defeat. Throughout the first two years of the war,
therefore, the English ministry expected to end the war as
much by "compromise" or negotiation as by a successful
campaign. Lord Howe was to win a decisive victory if he
could and the sooner the better; but he was not to allow
"Mr. Washington" to disturb the forces working in America for a peaceful settlement, nor was he to take any risk
of disturbing them himself, without a practical certainty
of ending the war by a crushing defeat of the Americans.

Thanks to this politic forbearance, we were given the time
necessary to evolve an army and a central administration out
of nothing. The natural difficulties of the situation were
enormous. Powder, shot, arms, clothing had to be imported
and were not only difficult to obtain but exceedingly difficult
to distribute when secured. As the British controlled the
sea, everything had to be carted overland, and this difficulty
of communication proved at times literally insuperable. The
lack of good currency, the lack of credit due to the absence
of faith in the successful outcome of the war, prevented any
general acceptance of the colonial paper money for food and
such few supplies as could be had in America. Despite all
difficulties, however, by 1778, when the English took up the
war in earnest, Von Steuben had drilled the army into something like efficiency; Nathanael Greene had put the quarter-

evidently on good grounds, that we must ultimately sink under a system which increases our expense beyond calculation, enfeebles all our
measures, affords the most inviting opportunities to the enemy, and
wearies and disgusts the people. This has undoubtedly had great influence in preventing their coming to terms and will continue to operate
in the same way." Washington, circular letter to the States, Oct. 18,
1780. *Writings of Washington*, Ford's ed., VIII, 505.

master's department on its feet; Robert Morris had organized, through the Marine Committee of Congress, a series of Continental Agents in the important ports who had developed a method of exchanging products, by which the army was supplied with what they received from Europe and from the English supplies seized by American privateers. Washington had learned from experience to avoid his first blunders and to take advantage of the natural forces fighting for us, as well as of the French army and navy who soon appeared on the scene. Indeed, without their aid and the money and arms Franklin secured in Europe, it is probable the Revolution would still have failed; even the tact and influence of Washington could not have kept an army in the field longer without arms and money from abroad.[15]

The strategical geography of the eastern Atlantic coast plus the three thousand miles of ocean were almost as decisive factors in our favor. The North Atlantic is always difficult for sailing-ships, and at that time a month or six weeks was considered a quick passage. The English general, therefore, knew when he began the campaign in the spring that three months at least must elapse under favorable conditions before he could receive instructions or assistance. He also knew that the preparation of an army. for the voyage was a long task, needing two months or more; for the beef had to be killed and salted; the grain bought, carried to the sea-coast, ground, and baked into bread; the soldiers enlisted, their clothes made, their guns provided, powder and shot prepared. To allow himself to be defeated or outmanœuvered in the early summer meant the possibility of annihilation before help could arrive. Howe and Clinton campaigned therefore in the fall when the coming of winter would naturally limit Washington's ability to take advantage of possible successes. After all, they were to win battles if they could, but at all costs to keep an army in the field.[16]

[15] See Washington's letters during 1780.
[16] "Yet it is a fact, they [the British] are as much afraid and cautious of us as we can be any of us of them." Col. Smallwood's report

Both protested and Howe complained energetically that the army he had was not in the least adequate for the military occupation of the continent. In truth, he and his generals soon discovered that the Atlantic seaboard lacks a strategic spot like that of the Netherlands, which, when taken, opens the gates into several countries and menaces half Europe. They found instead a seat of war a thousand miles long, intersected by many large rivers whose courses lay parallel to each other, thus cutting the country into large sections and making long overland marches most difficult. The English, at first, thought Boston the strategic point, but were soon disabused: it did not help them to hold a foot of land outside the lines of their own fortifications. Prolonged residence in New York and Philadelphia at last convinced them that there was no charmed spot in America whose possession ensured the conquest of the whole. Instead they found their armies constantly out of touch with each other, often on their own resources, and were, so far as they could see, no further advanced toward the conquest of the continent by all their marching and countermarching than when they began. As early as the fall of 1776, Howe realized the truth and wrote home that 10,000 men in New England, 20,000 in New York, 10,000 in the South, and an additional army of 10,000 men to operate against Washington would be necessary to finish the war.[17] He was laughed to scorn by the English ministry who knew that the total American forces in the field did not number 10,000, who were divided among several armies and were all likely to go home at any moment. When the course of events reluctantly brought them to the same conclusion in 1781, they gave up the struggle,[18] for the maintenance

to the Maryland Council of Safety, Oct. 1776. Quoted in H. B. Carrington's *Battles of the American Revolution*, 233.

[17] H. B. Carrington, *Battles of the American Revolution*, 254, 279.

[18] "That one great point [of Howe's plan] is to keep us as much harassed as possible with a view to injure the recruiting service and hinder a collection of stores and other necessaries for the next campaign, I am as clear in, as I am of my existence." Washington to the President of Congress, Dec. 20, 1776. *Writings of Washington*, Ford's ed., V, 113. This would end "the British hope of subjugating this

of a permanent army of 50,000 men to keep America in subjection was too expensive a proposition to be thought of. After all, they reflected, if Adam Smith was right, the American trade, which was really the only benefit they could secure from the possession of the colonies, would come to them anyway.

While the length of the seat of war and its intersection by large rivers furnished the Americans with problems in transportation and in the manœuvering of armies fully as difficult as those the English experienced, these factors immensely reduced the discrepancy between the size and discipline of the armies. The discipline of troops who cannot reach you is unimportant; and the fact that England possessed greater resources in men and money was neutralized by the difficulty the Atlantic interposed in the way of their utilization. The two parties were by no means as ill-matched for a long struggle as at first seems. There were, moreover, numerous natural factors which left the balance enormously in the Americans' favor and which in the long run as much as any single factor contributed to bring about the result.

The very fact of the British army's discipline and organization became a hindrance the moment they left the open fields about the Hudson and Delaware and advanced into the wilds of Lake George and the hill-country of North Carolina. A couple of thousand farmers in their shirt-sleeves and without any artillery and baggage would straggle across fields, scaling fences, penetrating woods and losing little if anything of their efficiency in the process: they had little in fact to lose, for the only method of fighting they understood called for men behind trees and stone walls and not arrayed in line of battle. A British column, on the other hand, could not advance without roads, for the trampling of many feet and the wheels of the artillery and baggage-wagons soon

continent either by their arms or their arts. The first, as I have before observed, they acknowledge is unequal to the task; the latter I am sure will be so if we are not lost to everything that is good and virtuous." *Ibid.*, VII, 389.

rendered even a dry field a quagmire. Fences, rivers, woods were insurmountable obstacles. Burgoyne spent days on the march south from Canada in 1777 building roads and bridges in order that he might advance at all, and consumed in reaching the Hudson as many weeks as Schuyler's men had used days. Inasmuch as few roads in America were sufficiently well made to stand the travel of an army, the Americans possessed a positive advantage over the English in manœuvering, which would have given them victory after victory, had not the very lack of organization that helped them on the march been a fatal deficiency on the field of battle. The British, therefore, could rarely be dislodged, but could always be eluded. After the first two years, the American generals thoroughly appreciated this fact and kept the campaigns in territory which offered the English the maximum difficulty. European strategy, which assumed the existence of roads to march upon and level, unobstructed fields to manœuver upon was useless to a general conducting a campaign which was really a series of contests with the country itself. "Almost every movement of the war in North America," wrote General Howe, "was an act of enterprise clogged with innumerable difficulties."

Then appeared the necessity of supplying the armies with food. Here too the very factors about which Washington at first chiefly complained were the Americans' salvation. Their armies were, except for the few regiments of regulars under Washington himself, nothing but collections of minute-men, who assembled at the news of the British approach, bringing powder and shot and food enough for ten days or a fortnight. When any distance had to be traversed, they marched, like the North Carolina detachment en route northward, driving a herd of cattle before them with sacks of meal across their backs, milking the cows and killing the steers as need dictated, with the belief that the herd would last as long as the march. Naturally the speed of the march was limited to the slow pace of the cows. Once on the field they worried the English column as long as their supplies lasted and then went home, leaving the task of defense to the minute-men of the next county; and, inasmuch as they were all equally innocent of tactics and discipline, Burgoyne or Cornwallis found himself constantly face to face with a fresh body of men, quite as efficient as those who had just gone home. Desertions and short enlistments in fact worked little permanent injury to the American cause. On the other hand, the fact that the English forces consisted of regular troops whose identity could not change, whose food must be supplied them, brought all the British generals into contact with formidable problems. The difficulties were great enough in the settled parts of the country, because enough food was not always for sale; but when the campaign was carried into the wilds of the Hudson and the hills of the Blue Ridge, Burgoyne or Cornwallis found that the sagacious Schuyler or the wily Greene had either carefully collected all the food or led him where there was none to collect. Nor could the British generals cheerfully sit down to roasted sweet potatoes as Marion did, or cabbage and bacon with Washington. They traveled with their wines and scorned the homely but nutritious dishes of cornmeal mush, and the peas, beans, and turnips to which the Americans were accustomed; such food, declared one irate officer, was fit only for swine. The soldiers, too, refused such fare and grumbled and became mutinous if the grog ran short. Before the Saratoga and Southern campaigns were over, however, they were all glad to eat anything they could get.

In addition, the rough ground on which the Americans offered battle puzzled the English, and the American generals, quickly noting this trouble, began soon the systematic use of hills, fences, woods, and field entrenchments for the first time in organized warfare. Nor were they ashamed to do what the English thought cowardly—"hide" in ditches and behind walls; nor to do what the English declared contrary to civilized warfare,—pick off sentries and troops on the march. Gates at Boston was extremely indignant to find sharpshooters in the Cambridge marshes shooting at his officers walking on the ramparts for a little fresh air, and Burgoyne at Saratoga was vastly annoyed at the constant popping of guns through the night which disturbed his slumbers and at the cannon-balls that swept his dinner from the table. But the Americans were not playing a game, where among the forces on the other side were also mercenaries, like the Hessians, and where neither army was, therefore, desirous of exposing the other to any risks not unavoidable. They were fighting to win and considered any means legitimate that would gain the end in view. Instead of being taught in the European style, that the musket was too inaccurate a weapon to be of use except for volley-firing, and that therefore anything more than an approximate aim was valueless, Morgan's sharpshooters were accustomed to a style of fighting where they had to kill their man or be killed themselves.

The tactics of the Americans, however, were not nearly so deadly in effect as the result of the rough ground on the British tactics. There were no orders in the manual for climbing fences or for sending parts of the column around opposite sides of the same boulder, and the formations of the regulars were usually so disorganized by the obstacles nature had left in their path that the weight of the charge had been expended before the moment of impact. The equipment of the British, complete and admirable for a European campaign, was also a positive hindrance in America. The red woolen shirts, the heavy fur or felt hats, the heavy knapsacks and boots were not intended for a hot July day with the thermometer at ninety degrees. Burgoyne ordered a body of heavy dragoons, men so heavily equipped that they were meant always to ride, to march on foot through the hills and fields of southern Vermont in midsummer. By the time they reached Bennington they were exhausted from the heat of their clothing plus the heat of the sun and were in no condition to fight a battle with Colonel Stark and his men clad only in jeans and shirt-sleeves.

The most puzzling thing to the English, however, became, as the war progressed, the willingness of the Americans to lose the battles. They had expected the "farmers" to run at the first fire, and the Americans had entertained similar anticipations. The patriotic joy over Concord and Bunker Hill brushed aside what seemed minor features, such as the fact that the English voluntarily withdrew to Boston and that Bunker Hill was a great defeat, in its elation over the fact that the minute-men had dared to follow the English into Boston, and had compelled the regulars to dislodge them from behind the rail fence. No one at the time thought either battle accomplished anything, but nearly every one entertained the wildest expectations of future prowess. Long Island and White Plains, however, convinced Washington and Greene that pitched battles were undesirable except as demonstrations of the American determination to resist. They perfectly well understood that the most essential thing was to keep an army in the field until aid could come and until the natural factors working in our favor should become effective; [19] they well knew that in every pitched battle they risked losing the cause without a proportionate chance of winning it. They realized, too, that the English did not dare injure them too much and that conquest attained by laying waste the country was not to be feared. Whatever might be done as an example of possibilities, there would be no general campaign on such principles. They came in fact to see that so long as the army remained intact, the loss of the battle involved merely a shift of position. Greene reduced the losing of battles to a science in his operations in the South in 1780. Realizing that a third of his raw army would run at the first fire,[20] he

[19] "On our side, the war should be defensive (it has even been called a war of posts) that we should on all occasions avoid a general action, nor put anything to risk, unless compelled by a necessity into which we ought never to be drawn. . . . Experience has given her sanction. . . . Being persuaded it would be presumption to draw out our young troops into open ground against their superiors both in number and discipline, I have never spared the spade and pickaxe. I confess I have not found that readiness to defend even strong posts at all hazards, which is necessary to derive the greatest benefits from them. . . . The wisdom of cooler moments and experienced men have decided that we should protract the war if possible." Washington to the President of Congress, Sept. 8, 1776. *Writings of Washington*, Ford's ed., IV, 392.

[20] The militia seems always to have been unsteady. "Every measure

placed them in the first rank with orders to fire one volley before they ran or the second rank would shoot them.   The second and third ranks, placed at wide intervals, were to let the
fugitives through, and when the English appeared, offer some
resistance themselves, and then retreat before they themselves
were harmed.   The third rank, composed of experienced
troops, would cover the flight of their less enthusiastic comrades.   The battle would always be lost, but ten miles up the
road, Greene would find his army quite as before, save for the
breath lost in running.   Thus a blow was struck at the British
without danger to himself, Cornwallis was led further and
further from his source of supplies in the fleet cruising along
shore, was decoyed into the hills where there was little if anything to eat, and further and further north toward the general field of action where Greene could expect some support.
The whole campaign is a marvelous example of how wars
can be won without good armies and without winning
battles.

  After six years of fruitless operations, each of which found
the Americans better equipped and drilled, more strongly
placed, and with a better administration and a larger body of
supporters, the English came to the conclusion that, to succeed, a conquest of the country must be executed with the utmost severity by an army double in number their total force
then in the field and that a huge army of occupation must then
be left behind.   Such a price was out of the question, and
there were serious doubts in London whether the payment even
of that price would attain the object of the war.   To conquer
America at the point of the bayonet would effectually put an
end to all harmonious relations.   The Treaty of Paris signed
in 1783 recognized the independence of the thirteen States, and

on our part, however painful the reflection is from experience, is to be
formed with some apprehension that all our troops will not do their
duty." Washington to the President of Congress, Sept. 8, 1776. *Ibid.*,
p. 391. "The militia fled at the first fire"; they are "incapable of making or sustaining a serious attack." Washington, circular letter to the
States, Oct. 18, 1780. *Ibid.*, VIII. 506. See also the emphatic statements in letters of 12 and 15 September 1780.

handed over to them the continent south of the Great Lakes, east of the Mississippi, and north of a rather indeterminate line very nearly that of the present southern boundary of Tennessee.

XI

THE RESULTS OF THE REVOLUTION

IN 1781, John Adams, then Minister to Holland, prepared a pamphlet called *Twenty-six Letters* to explain to European bankers that the astonishing but entirely desirable result of the war had been to enrich and strengthen the thirteen States. The number of men was, he declared, scarcely impaired; the resources of the country barely touched; the economic development of the older communities had not been retarded; the westward march had continued at an even more rapid pace. "America, notwithstanding the war, daily increases in strength and force." "America could indubitably maintain a regular army of twenty thousand men forever." Subsequent investigation has amply confirmed these observations. The highest estimate of population in 1760 put the figure well under two millions; the first census of 1790 estimated it at four millions. There was not even a forswearing of luxuries, if the observation of contemporaries is trustworthy.[1] "The extravagant luxury of our Country," wrote Franklin in 1779, "in the midst of all its distresses, is to me amazing. When the difficulties are so great to find Remittances to pay for the Arms and Ammunition necessary for our Defence, I am astonish'd and vex'd to find upon Enquiry, that much the

[1] "I could demonstrate, to every mind open to conviction, that in less time, and with much less expense than has been incurred, the war might have been brought to the same happy conclusion, if the resources of the continent could have been properly drawn forth; that the distresses and disappointments, which have very often occurred, have in too many instances resulted more from a want of energy in the continental government than a deficiency of means in the several particular States." Washington, circular letter to the Governors of the States, June 8, 1783.

greatest Part of the Congress Interest Bills come to pay for Tea, and a great Part of the Remainder is ordered to be laid out in Gewgaws and Superfluities.'' At least as much tea was being bought as before the war, an amount, he thought, not short of £500,000 a year. ''Five Hundred Thousand Pounds Sterling annually laid out in defending ourselves, or annoying our Enemies, would have great Effects. With what Face can we ask Aids and Subsidies from our Friends, while we are wasting our own Wealth in such Prodigality?'' [2] Washington complained bitterly and repeatedly of the farmers who declined to sell grain to the American army and carted it to Philadelphia and New York to sell it for British gold.[3] He wrote of ''officers, seduced by views of private interest . . . to abandon the cause of their country.'' [4] ''If I were to be called upon to draw a picture of the times and of men, from what I have seen, heard, and in part know, I would in one word say, that idleness, dissipation, and extravagance seem to have laid fast hold of most of them; that speculation, peculation, and an insatiable thirst for riches seem to have got the better of every other consideration and almost every order of men.'' [5] ''The spirit of venality,'' wrote John Adams, ''is the most dreadful and alarming enemy America has to oppose. . . . I am ashamed of the age I live in.'' [6]

Nor is the seeming inconsistency of this most striking result of the war hard to reconcile with our earlier notions of the result. The picture of war which naturally rises before our eyes depicts murder, pillage, and general desolation. An army would, of course, devour everything. During the Revolution, however, the armies were at no time large and, therefore, were not unduly burdensome to the community in the

[2] *The Life and Writings of Benjamin Franklin*, A. H. Smyth, VII, 391, 291. See also pp. 83, 258, 408.

[3] See *supra*, p. 125, note. See also *Connecticut Public Records*, I, 528; *Rhode Island Records*, VII, 388; *Delaware Session Laws*, May 20, 1778.

[4] *Writings of Washington*, Sparks's ed., V, 305, 312, 313, 322, 351; VI, 168.

[5] *Writings of Washington* Ford's ed., VII, 388.

[6] *Familiar Letters*, 232.

strictest sense of the words. Both realized that pillage or foraging would throw many waverers into the ranks of their enemies, and, from motives of policy, both conducted the war with a view to avoiding all possible cause of complaint from non-combatants. Indeed, far from being a hardship to the Americans, the presence of the British army was a positive blessing. For the first time in colonial history, a large and steady market for the produce easily raised in America was located at the farmer's very door; and the British paid him not in bills on London which turned out to be bad, or in depreciated silver or in paper currency, but in gold at sterling rates. Probably there was more actual coin in America in 1783 than ever before.[7] The farmers charged war prices, sold more than ever before, and waxed rich as the war continued, especially in the Middle States where the British occupation lasted several years. The American armies also paid, and their paper promises were not long afterwards funded at par. Business was good during the Revolution; the community undeniably grew wealthy.

At the same time, many and many an individual suffered severely. English privateers captured the merchants' vessels; committees of correspondence confiscated the estates of exiles and loyalists, and compelled merchants to accept the nearly worthless paper money from the patriots at a tariff which in many cases amounted to the confiscation of the goods. "Persons who refused to sell their lands, houses, or merchandize for nearly worthless paper were stigmatized as misers, traitors, forestallers, and enemies of liberty. . . . Stores were closed or pillaged; and merchants were mobbed, fined, or imprisoned,"[8] tarred and feathered, or ridden on rails. The war automatically suspended the collection of debts owed by Ameri-

[7] "Tho' the public treasury was so very poor and distressed, yet the States were really overrun with an abundance of cash: the French and English armies, our foreign loans, Havanna trade, etc., had filled the country with money, and bills [of exchange] on Europe were currently sold at 20 to 40 per cent below par." Peletiah Webster, *Political Essays*, 267. Philadelphia, 1791.

[8] Bullock, *Monetary History of the United States*, 66.

cans abroad,[9] and, as these liabilities far exceeded in amount the money which foreigners owed Americans, the country as a whole was again made richer by the war, for no arrangement was ever subsequently made to liquidate any considerable part of the pre-revolutionary debts. Of course, the debts owed the loyalists and exiles were promptly repudiated or confiscated. In all these ways, very considerable amounts of property changed hands, and made many individuals much richer than before at the expense of a comparatively small number of other individuals. The transfer from loyalist to patriot, of course, in no way lessened the total assets of the community, while the repudiation of foreign debts actually added great sums to the community's wealth.

The general fall of values and the equally general rise in prices coupled to the existence of large amounts of depreciated currency suggested to many of the unscrupulous,—whose existence in past epochs is a constant source of amazement to many who are familiar with the existence of that type of man to-day—the payment of debts incurred at the old scale of prices in the new paper money. Guardians and trustees accounted in paper for the funds entrusted to them in specie, and thus were able to embezzle the greater part. "For two or three years," wrote Witherspoon, "we constantly saw and were informed of creditors running away from their debtors, and debtors pursuing them in triumph and paying them without mercy!" The lack of a suitable medium of exchange thus deprived all people dependent on a salary or on a fixed income from investment of the great bulk of their fortunes. Every one, too, in whose hands paper money depreciated in value lost considerable sums. These indirect consequences of the

[9] There was no reason why it should have done so, save that most Americans believed themselves no longer liable because political independence would effectually prevent collection through the English courts or by English law, and naturally, until the war was over, no new system for collection would be erected. The general sentiment in favor of repudiation of public and private debts was overwhelmingly strong in 1783. With these difficulties the Confederation struggled feebly and in vain.

Revolution certainly brought distress to many, who usually least deserved it, but who were on the whole best able to bear it.

During the Revolution, then, the general resources of the community were enormously increased by agriculture and commerce; the war destroyed little and added appreciably to the wealth of the country and to its store of gold; the wealth was redistributed and in general equalized among individuals, very much to the advantage of those who had been poor, very much to the detriment of those who had been rich. The latter seem to have been the ones really to suffer from the war, and were chiefly loyalists and in many cases exiles. They and the foreign and domestic creditors of Congress and of the States paid for the Revolution, for the confiscated property was never restored, and most of the original holders of the Revolutionary debt sold their bonds or certificates at heavy loss, when the very general repudiation of the Revolutionary indebtedness at the end of the war convinced them that the debt would never be paid and that they would do well to sell before the evidences of their loans lost all market value.

The Revolution had been a war between England and America, between parties in England and between parties in America, and the issue had been the institution of a central administration in America sufficiently powerful to enforce the new policy which Parliament had adopted for the creation of a greater Britain. Something more had divided parties than the bare question whether or not England should play a part, decisive or otherwise, in the settlement of questions in America. The immediate result of the American victory was, therefore, something more than the decision that the two countries should hereafter be separate and that Americans should formulate policy for themselves without British assistance or interference. In England, the American victory was a victory for the peace party who had throughout declared the policy on which the war had been conducted a mistake. The winning of the war gave control in America to the radicals, to the anti-national party, opposed on principle to the adoption of the English notion of strong central government. It also immensely strengthened the anti-national party and weakened in numbers, in wealth, and in the proportion of capable and educated men amongst them, the creditor and conservative parties which believed in strong government.

The number of loyalists expatriated was probably about one hundred thousand, most of whom had been people of culture and property, who had normally counted on the side of law, order, and justice. Very considerable amounts of property had also been changed during the war by both political and economic forces from the hands of the conservatives to those of the radicals. The proportion of educated men in the country was not as large as it had been; the total wealth of the conservative class was far less than before. The radical party had not only gotten into the saddle in State, town, and county, but had possessed itself in all probability of the bulk of the movable property, and was anxious to continue conditions which worked so greatly to its advantage.[10] The party of strong government and especially of national government, as we understand it, had been completely vanquished by the party of loose government and of States' rights. The victory of the radicals in the "civil war," in fact, was too complete, as was soon to appear.

Had the Revolution, however, decided the various issues over which it had nominally been fought? Had it proved England wrong in all her contentions, shown George III to have been a bloodthirsty tyrant and Lord North an oppressor? Were the loyalists all traitors and was their property forfeit? The radicals insisted with vehemence that victory had demonstrated the truth of all their contentions, legal, historical,

[10] "It is more consistent with the views of the speculators—various tribes of money-makers and stock-jobbers of all denominations—to continue the war for their own private emolument without considering that their avarice and thirst for gain must plunge everything, including themselves, in one common ruin." Washington to George Mason, March 27, 1779. *Writings of Washington*, Ford's ed., VII, 382.

political, and ethical. The legacy of the Revolution was a hatred of England and of English ways which for many decades colored all policies and politics.

The war had been fought with England over an issue of administration and organization. It had been a war to maintain the superiority of State governments over any central government, a war to prevent the erection of a central government, a war to support a distinctly anti-national policy. To the radicals, therefore, the winning of the Revolution decided that the States were supreme and a central government inexpedient. Were the patriots who had fought and bled for the independence of their own particular States to admit that the war had succeeded and had vested in King Congress the powers of King George? If so, they had exchanged a tyrant three thousand miles away, who was, after all, slow and stupid, for a many-headed hydra at their very doors, insatiable in its demands for money and authority. For what, then, had they fought? Again, the war had been waged to prevent the exercise by any central authority of the right of taxation and the right to control commerce. Had not the winning of the war definitely vested the exclusive exercise of these powers in the several States, and as definitely decided once and for all that no central government ought ever to possess them? If the Revolution had not settled the issues in these ways, what had it decided? Nothing?

Nevertheless, the Revolution actually decided none of the great questions out of which it had arisen. It decided merely that England and the conservatives in America should have no share in their decision. The anti-national party assumed the direction of policy and was not slow to announce and apply its characteristic remedies to the solution of all difficulties. Were the men who had won the Revolution unable to cope with the problems of freedom? The key they applied to all perplexities was the old colonial conception—States' sovereignty. Neither the Revolution itself nor any specific act done during it or because of it seemed to the radicals to have created a nation or to have even established the desirability of creating one.[11] "It seems certain that at no time during the Revolution was there a stronger desire for national unity than for the continued sovereignty of the several States."[12] The central government was to be rather a common mouthpiece, a sort of formal head, a convenient method of expressing the decisions of the States, than a government empowered to act for them.

During the war, the States had one and all exercised the familiar attributes of sovereignty.[13] Virginia made and ratified a treaty with France; established a clerkship of foreign correspondence; sent over an agent to various countries to borrow money and buy arms; negotiated formally with Spain for a war loan; sent George Rogers Clark into the West to take possession of the land in the name of the Commonwealth of Virginia. Nine of the States built navies of their own and all enlisted armies; all of them struck coins and issued paper money; most of them regulated commerce by the imposition of tariffs and of embargoes. These powers they continued to exercise after the Articles of Confederation had been formally ratified in 1781 and after the Treaty of Peace had been signed in 1783. Neither one event nor the other, to the thinking of the men in control of the State governments, produced any change in the relation of the States to each other or to a cen-

[11] "A selfish habitude of thinking and reasoning leads us into a fatal error the moment we begin to talk of the interests of America. The fact is, by the interests of America we mean only the interests of that State to which property or accident has attached us. Thus a citizen of Philadelphia, when he harangues on the rights and liberties of America, is not aware the while that he is merely advocating the rights and liberties of Pennsylvania. And our fellow-citizen here, . . . lead him to the westernmost banks of the Hudson . . . and his heart is as cold and unconcerned as to the interests of Kouli Khan or the Nabob of Arcot." *New York Packet*, August 30, 1784. Quoted by McMaster, *History of the People of the United States*, I, 136.

[12] Van Tyne, *The American Revolution*, 177-8.

[13] C. H. Van Tyne has given an admirable resumé of the evidence in the *American Historical Review*, XII, 529-545. See also the selections quoted in Hart's *American History Told by Contemporaries*, III, 124-137. Even a casual reference to any source of the period will hardly fail to be rewarded with significant examples.

tral government.   Congress was to assume the position which
the radicals had desired George III to occupy:—that of as-
sisting and advising the several States.   Indeed, there was
little disposition to admit in America that the Declaration of
Independence had done more than enounce the actual condition of affairs or that the war had accomplished more than
the prevention of the unwarranted extension of authority proposed and attempted by England.   The States were still
sovereign as they always had been; in their several hands
rested the solution of the difficulties, and they believed themselves as capable of deciding upon and executing such measures as their own welfare and safety demanded as they had
already been for a century and more.   That the growth of
the country during the preceding century and even during
the war had made some common action and agreement indispensable, only a few individuals seem to have grasped.

The solution proposed by the radical anti-national party
was, therefore, simplicity incarnate,—the States should individually deal as they thought best with such matters as
seemed to them to require action, and should signify to Congress what action they deemed necessary in questions requiring coöperation.   There seems to have been a rather general expectation that the remedies for the various difficulties
would evolve themselves from circumstances, for no action
was taken on most questions.

The fear that the Americans would be excluded from the
West India trade and the Newfoundland fisheries had been
one of the motive forces of the Revolution.   The war over,
most men seem to have expected that the old status would be
reëstablished and that the Americans would continue as before to smuggle at will, unhampered now by English revenue
officers and administrative restrictions.   They had fought to
obtain that privilege, and, having won the war, was the suggestion to be credited that the prize was not theirs?

The pay of the army which had won the war was some
years in arrears, and the officers and men, who had been
held together by promises of prompt payment upon the suc-

cessful conclusion of the war, were already manifesting something more than impatience at the non-fulfilment of the
promises. The interest payments on the debts incurred during the war by Congress and by the several States were already overdue, and in many cases payment of the capital had
been promised on the successful completion of the war. A
uniform and stable currency was desperately needed to replace the worthless paper which no longer circulated at all.
In addition, the Treaty of Peace contained promises made by
Franklin and other ambassadors, concerning the payment of
the debt, public and private, the restoration of the property of
loyalists, the repeal of the acts passed during the war which
deprived the latter of all rights, legal or social, in the community, and the prompt adjustment of the boundary difficulties in the West.

Incredible as it may seem, the anti-national, States'-sover-
eignty party was in favor of disbanding the army without pay
and without the fulfilment of one of the many promises made
to both officers and men. The army very naturally refused
with considerable heat to disband and remained in the neighborhood of Philadelphia for some years, grumbling and threatening Congress, while the States blithely continued to disregard their obligations to the men who had actually fought the
war. Inasmuch as none of the various creditors, foreign or
domestic, possessed any method of exacting payment of the
principal or the interest of the Revolutionary debt, the
radicals calmly repudiated all their obligations and declined to
vote a penny to Congress for any such purpose, or indeed for
any purpose at all.[14] To cap the climax of this policy of

---

[14] On Nov. 5, 1786, Washington wrote Madison a description of conditions in New England as reported to him by General Knox, who had
been sent by Congress to investigate the situation. "Among other
things he says: 'Their creed is, that the property of the United States
has been protected from the confiscation of Britain by the joint exertions of all; and therefore ought to be the common property of all;
and he that attempts opposition to this creed, is an enemy to equity
and justice, and ought to be swept from off the face of the earth.'
Again: 'They are determined to annihilate all debts, public and private,
and have agrarian laws, which are easily effected by the means of

laissez-faire, none of the States executed the solemn promises of the Treaty of Peace and enough were always opposed to any action on the part of Congress to prevent fulfilment by the Confederation. From whatever motive, whether from policy or from preoccupation with other problems, nothing whatever was done. The consequences of this universal application of the anti-national remedy of States' sovereignty to the difficulties confronting America were all too soon apparent. "How melancholy is the reflection," wrote Washington to Madison on November 5, 1786, "that in so short a space we should have made such large strides towards fulfilling the predictions of our transatlantic foes! 'Leave them to themselves and their government will soon dissolve.' Will not the wise and good strive hard to avert this evil? Or will their supineness suffer ignorance and the arts of self-interested, designing, disaffected and desperate characters to involve this great country in wretchedness and contempt?"[15]

unfunded paper money, which shall be a tender in all cases whatever.'"
Writings of Washington, Ford's ed., XI, 81-2.

[15] *Ibid.,* p. 82.

XII

THE CRITICAL PERIOD

From the war, the radicals had expected great things. Once the shackles of the tyrant had been struck off, Liberty would ensure her admirers happiness and prosperity. Yet, with the Treaty of Peace scarcely signed, with the policy of the thirteen new sovereigns barely promulgated, and the perpetuity of the new Confederation between them little more than declared, it became only too apparent that the country was worse off than it had been before. Whatever might be the theoretical merits of the new type of government, certainly its practical results were disastrous. The policy of *laissez-faire*, of disregarding problems, simply did not work. The army refused to disband and continued to live in the vicinity of Philadelphia to the great discontent of the farmers of the district. The difficulties resulting from the lack of a stable currency grew steadily worse and not better. The failure to pay the interest or principal of the old debt made impossible the borrowing of money. The English were by no means willing to dispense with the fulfilment of the promises in the Treaty of Peace about the western lands, while the all-important trade privileges in the West Indies and off Newfoundland could not be obtained by a weak and discredited government, which had thus far defaulted every payment and broken every promise.

The pressure of national, State, and local issues for settlement was great in 1783 and was growing obviously greater; the economic and social problems demanding honest and sincere effort were numerous. The chief difficulties were, however, two:—the lack of honest, able, consistent administration in the States and in the central government, and the existence of the first commercial crisis, due partly to the economic tangle caused by the war, but largely to the lack of a reliable medium of exchange either with Europe or between the various States. In fact, the difficulties were economic rather than administrative, were indeed superficial rather than fundamental, and resulted from administrative carelessness and inefficiency, from the policy of repudiation and of ignoring vital problems. The truly fundamental difficulties lay in the economic position of the States in relation to each other, to the West Indies, and to Europe. Nor would the administrative deficiencies alone have been so serious had they not coincided with the commercial crisis. All the difficulties, temporary and fundamental, economic and administrative, were accentuated, magnified, and multiplied by the attempts of the radicals to solve them. Before peace was a year old, it was clear to the leaders and was constantly becoming apparent to a larger and larger section of the community, that the radical solution, based on the theoretical and administrative contentions over which the war had been fought, was a hopeless and irredeemable failure.

The economic crisis was the result of production far in excess of local needs coupled with a very general lack of adequate means of exchange and distribution. As has already been explained, the Atlantic coast produced chiefly staple goods—cod-fish, lumber, flour, horses,—for which no adequate market existed in other colonies, which were (except for tobacco) too bulky to ship to Europe, and which would usually be sold only in the West Indies. At the same time, the manufactured articles, upon which the Americans depended and which they bought so largely, must come from Europe. We were then in the extremely unfortunate economic position of producing what we could not consume and what the makers of the only articles we really wished to buy would not accept in exchange. The prosperity of the new sovereign States was absolutely dependent upon the ability to sell in the West Indies and to purchase the sugar and molasses which Europe so greedily bought. A principal incitement to resistance in 1775 had been the knowledge that all the West India sugar islands together barely furnished the Atlantic seaboard with an adequate market for its growing volume of produce, and that the exclusion of the Americans from the foreign sugar islands and the restriction of their trade to the English sugar colonies would prevent the further expansion of American trade, if it did not immediately glut the market and send prices tumbling. To retain the freedom of trade with all the West India Islands, English, French, Spanish, Dutch, and Danish, had been the best reason for the refusal to obey the Navigation Acts, the Sugar Act of 1764, and the English administrative regulations, and was one of the really cogent reasons for fighting the war at all.

Apparently, the Americans had expected their victory to result in a more complete freedom of intercourse with the rest of the world, and they learned with scarcely feignable astonishment that they had lost their rights in the English sugar islands and in the cod-fisheries off the Grand Banks without gaining any rights in the sugar colonies of other nations.[1] They found that they had no rights anywhere; that every American vessel in the West Indies was seizable by virtue of some European regulation; the English proposed to allow no ships to trade with their colonies except English vessels, and the American ships were now "foreign." The loss of their rights on the Grand Banks in particular was a heavy blow to the New England states, the more severe because it had apparently not been foreseen; it robbed them at a stroke of their staple for export and hence stopped their trade at its source. The Americans had fought the war to avoid commercial ruin; had won it, and found themselves doubly and trebly ruined, worse off for exchange than they had ever been before.

During the war, the armies had eaten and utilized an appreciable part of the produce of the country; the smuggling trade had been briskly plied to the West Indies and the war prices had helped to lessen the distress. But the astonishing

[1] Channing, *History of the United States*, III, 408-413.

prosperity of the country during the war and the good market at home had stimulated production, and the output in the last years of the war and immediately after was far too great to find vent through the smuggling trade. America was producing more than could be sold at a profit, and prosperity itself caused a fall of values and of prices and resulted in a widespread distress which the Americans could not at all comprehend. The old system of exchange with Europe and between the various States had been completely dislocated by the war. The English privateers and cruisers had captured many merchantmen and had thus preceptibly weakened the American merchant marine. Many prominent merchants, whose ability and experience had made the complex round of voyages a profitable and adequate outlet for American produce, had been exiled, robbed of their property and position, and their places were either not yet filled or were occupied by *nouveaux riches* quite incapable of rendering the same service.

To reëstablish the old routes proved to be unexpectedly difficult. The very general failure of American merchants, whether from inability or design, to meet their obligations in England contracted before the war, caused a not unnatural reluctance on the part of the English houses, who had lost heavily, to reopen old accounts or accept new, and deterred others from engaging in American exchange. From the numerous loyalists and exiles in London came tales of robbery and confiscation which made even speculators pause before trusting Americans. Nor was the English ministry willing to concede the Americans as successful revolutionists the very terms which the latter had rejected in 1778. They listened coldly to the proud colonists who had disdainfully tossed one side, as if of no value, their unlimited privileges under the Navigation Acts, and who were now suing for some very limited rights in the West Indies and off the Grand Banks. The English deeply resented the American attitude towards the mother-country, and were especially indignant over the really unjust and tyrannical treatment meted out to the loyalists. They were hardly in a mood to grant favors. Moreover, as long as the States obstinately refused to accede to the continued requests of Congress to fulfil the terms of the Treaty of Peace, and as long as the Congress was only too obviously helpless to execute what it had solemnly agreed to perform, what reason was there to sign new treaties or even to discuss further arrangements which would still depend for validity upon the honorable intentions of the Americans? Administrative reform in America was an indispensable prerequisite to the securing of such terms from England as would relieve the economic pressure on the new States.

Administrative reform and a change in policy were also indispensable if trade between the States was to be reëstablished. Nothing more prejudicial to it could well be conceived than the legislation passed during and just after the war. The States seemed indeed to be animated by the determination to injure each other as much as possible and to prevent interstate commerce by every means in their power. Port regulations, embargoes, tariffs were passed by State after State, discriminating against their neighbors and frequently admitting English ships and English goods on more favorable terms than American.[2] Inasmuch as few of the States were in any position to deal directly with Europe and were ordinarily compelled to export their produce by a series of exchanges in various American ports, the difficulties sown in the way of commerce by these contradictory and hostile acts can be easily imagined. Most merchants soon came to realize that the enforcement to the letter of the proposed English acts, whose stringency had been alleged as adequate cause for re-

[2] "Massachusetts, in her zeal to counteract the effect of the English navigation laws, laid enormous duties upon British goods imported into that State; but the other States did not adopt a similar measure; and the loss of business soon obliged that State to repeal or suspend the law. Thus when Pennsylvania laid heavy duties on British goods, Delaware and New Jersey made a number of free ports to encourage the landing of goods within the limits of those States; and the duties in Pennsylvania served no purpose, but to create smuggling." Jedidiah Morse, *The American Geography*, 1789. Quoted in Hart's *Contemporaries*, III, 136-7.

volt, would in all probability have injured trade far less. Why then, merchants began to ask, had the war been fought? Who had benefited from it?

Nor was there a common medium of exchange in America by means of which trade was facilitated between the States. There had never been any considerable amount of coin in the country, and the British and French gold paid by the armies had been quickly hoarded or had flown away to Europe. Paper money in vast amounts had been issued by Congress, and each State had its own peculiar variety. The bulk of it, in Ramsay's phrase, "gently fell asleep in the hands of its last possessors." Men exchanged the actual cloth and shoes and grain and meat as in the Middle Ages before a money economy existed. However adequate this might be for local trade, it meant the complete disappearance of the budding commercial structure which seemed so important to Americans. Yet, without agreement among the States, without authority in the central government, how was a uniform currency to be had? Administrative reform in America was from this point of view also indispensable.

Another pregnant cause of the commercial crisis lay in the general dislocation of business by the attitude of the radicals and the debtors towards property, the courts, and the collection of debts. When the first loyalists had left New England with Howe in 1776, and when the confiscation and distribution of their estates had whetted the appetite for more, a pretty general indictment of "loyalists" had taken place all over the country, and large amounts of property had changed hands. The outbreak of hostilities had naturally reacted unfavorably on business; the sale of confiscated property, paper money, and the like had produced a vast amount of speculation and gambling in land, certificates, and loans which had also discouraged legitimate business.[3] Not only was it suspected that much robbery and con-

[3] "Paper currency . . . operated in the most powerful and malignant manner. . . . Every sordid passion of man was stimulated to the most vigorous exertion. Wealth, for such it seemed to the fancy, was ac-

fiscation had been thinly covered with the allegation of loyalism, that men had been exiled and brutally treated because they were rich or creditors of many of the mob that dealt with them, but the passage of acts by the legislatures condoning such offenses, the practical repudiation of the pre-revolutionary debts owed to English merchants, the evident unwillingness of the radicals to agree that the Revolutionary debt was a valid obligation, the evident liking for paper money and the imposition of heavy penalties for its refusal, all caused the more serious to fear lest this occasional misdoing should be organized and legalized by the new State governments. As the months elapsed and became years, these fears became greater instead of less, and were amply confirmed by the determination in Rhode Island to provide ''cheap'' money and plenty of it, by the use of force throughout the States to prevent the courts from collecting debts. ''We are fast verging,'' wrote Washington, ''to anarchy and confusion.'' ''I am uneasy and apprehensive, more so than during the war,'' declared Jay. ''If faction should long bear down law and government, tyranny may raise its head and the more sober part of the people may even think of a king!''

While throughout America a crisis was apparent and the

quired with an ease and rapidity which astonished the possessor. The price of labor and of every vendible commodity rose in a moment to a height unexampled. Avarice, ambition . and luxury saw their wishes anticipated. . . . It soon became impossible for upright men to determine whether their bargains were honest or oppressive. . . . The general sense of right and obligation, in buying and selling, was gradually lowered; and the pride of making good bargains, a soft name for cheating, gradually extended. Whatever was not punishable by law multitudes considered as rectitude. . . . The existing government was peculiarly unhappy. All regular public functionaries lost during this period either the whole or a great part of their proper efficacy. In their stead, committees of inspection and correspondence assumed an extensive control over both the public and private affairs of their country. The powers of these bodies were undefined, and therefore soon became merely discretionary. Yet they were the tribunals by which almost every cause was decided. In most instances they were composed of men, unlearned in law and unskilled in public business. . . . Very many and very great evils were actually produced by this government.'' Dwight, *Travels in New England and New York*, IV, 369-371.

friends of decency and order feared for the worst, nowhere did the radicals succeed as well as in Massachusetts, and in no State would their success have excited more alarm either among its own people or in other States. Massachusetts had so long been the largest Northern State; its wealth and conservatism, its virtue and honesty, had already become so commonly accepted as unalterable, that the outbreak of Shays's Rebellion in the western part of the State in the fall of 1786 caused the people of less orderly and stable States to believe that the deluge was near. The lawyers had for some time been assailed in Massachusetts as "pickpockets" and "bloodsuckers" because they were aiding creditors to recover the debts due them; but these ebullitions of temper became serious when conventions met in various towns, voted lawyers a grievance, and demanded their abolition. At Hatfield, a convention voted to abolish the court of common pleas, which meant the abolition of the machinery for the collection of debts and for the recovery of land. It also declared in favor of an immediate issue of paper money and against the granting of any money to Congress. Mobs prevented the sitting of the lower courts in several counties, and Shays with nearly six hundred armed men prevented the session of the Supreme Court at Springfield. For some weeks, he and his disorderly crew terrorized Massachusetts but were finally scattered by militia from Boston. "Our distress was so great," said Smith, speaking of this time in the Massachusetts Convention of 1788, "that we should have been glad to snatch at anything that looked like a government."[4] Such acts had occurred before and during the Revolution, the North Carolina Regulators in 1770 being an especially noteworthy case, but in 1786 the crisis seemed to have come. Most men concluded that the alternative lay between a strong central government and anarchy.

It was only too patent that the States had been unable to cope with the difficulties and would never be able satisfactorily to solve them, because the problems were not local

[4] Elliott, *Debates*, II, 103.

but general, and required for their solution unified action based upon a unanimity of opinion. Thirteen States could not negotiate for fishing rights off Newfoundland or privileges in the West Indies, though both were directly or indirectly necessary for the welfare of all. From bitter experience it was clear that the States could not be induced individually to vote money to pay the army and to meet the obligations of the Confederation. The thirteen might conceivably agree upon uniform tariff regulations and upon a uniform currency, but surely a negotiation conducted through "ambassadors" in Congress was the most roundabout and cumbrous method of reaching such an agreement. Had the States not been so violently at odds with each other, something might have been done. Had there been any alignment of States by which the large and the small could have combined or the States with western lands have united against those without, something might have been achieved through sectional governments. But the accident of geography and of settlement had made us, as Gerry happily said, "neither the same nation nor different nations."[5] The large States were not contiguous and were also at odds over the western lands; the small States were hopelessly separated from each other by the territory of the large States, were neither all with or without western lands and other obvious local interests. In all, the line of debtor and creditor, of patriot and loyalist, was sharp, and men were even beginning to complain of an opposition of interests between the Northern and the Southern States. The vital difficulty was that no two of these lines coincided; that the country was not divided geographically into sections, vertically into creeds, parties, or interests, horizontally into classes. Each tiny group in every State hoped to secure timely assistance from its sympathizers in other States. There was no basis on which the jarring interests could divide: they must perforce unite and somehow work out together a livable compromise.

Nor should we forget the powerful incentive to strong cen-

5 Hunt's *Madison's Notes*, I, 302.

tral government furnished by the growing belief among the conservative, orderly, propertied classes that they were in the numerical minority in every State, and could escape destruction only by a union of their forces and by the assistance which a strong central government could lend any individual State-government which should be too hard pressed. Private interests seemed likely to be more injured by the continued complete sovereignty of the States than they could possibly be by even sweeping and dictatorial authority in the hands of a central government. If only a government could be established whose policy would be the payment of the debt and of the army, the fulfilment of the promises in the Treaty of Peace, and adequate provision for foreign trade, it could rally to it the creditors and moneyed men throughout America.

It was, however, clear beyond a shadow of doubt that the existing Congress did not and could not, under any such document as the Articles of Confederation, occupy any such position or furnish any such protection. The Congress in fact merely multiplied the difficulties and accentuated the differences between the States, because it could only reflect the divisions of the States themselves. To most of the leaders, it was clear that States' sovereignty and its corollary, a weak central government, was the root of the trouble and made it insoluble. "The great and radical vice in the construction of the existing Confederation," declared Hamilton, "is the principle of Legislation for States or Governments in their Corporate or Collective capacities and as contradistinguished from the individuals of which they consist."[6] The very attempt to discuss the general issues in thirteen different places and to record the conclusion in a fourteenth was in itself a problem of the first magnitude. "The world must see and feel," wrote Washington in 1785, "that the Union or the States individually are sovereign as best suits their purposes; in a word, they are one to-day and thirteen to-morrow."[7]

[6] *The Federalist*, XV.
[7] Marshall, *Life of Washington*, II, 97.

"The confederation appears to me to be little more than a shadow without the substance." [8] "If you tell the legislatures they have violated the treaty of peace and invaded the prerogatives of the confederacy, they will laugh in your face." It was facetiously said that the Americans had outdone the Trinity by making the thirteen one while leaving the one thirteen.

The Confederation, in fact, was a league of friendship and amity rather than a government. The central body was really a multiple executive unable to act of itself, and compelled to wait instructions from its numerous masters before it could act at all. So long as the vote was taken by States, and State delegations disagreed or were absent, there were always States who were able to claim that they had not consented to this or that resolution and were therefore not bound by it. Although the lack of authority over commerce and of the power of direct taxation were almost insuperable obstacles in the way of efficient administration, the chief trouble —if any one thing among so many could be claimed to be the stumbling block of offense—was the inability of the Confederation to compel the States to observe any "law" upon any subject, however indifferent or minute. "They (the Congress) may make war," wrote Jay, "but are not empowered to raise men or money to carry it on. They may make peace, but without power to see the terms of it observed. They may form alliances, but without ability to comply with the stipulations on their part. They may enter into treaties of commerce, but without power to enforce them at home or abroad. They may borrow money but without having the means of repayment. They may partly regulate commerce, but without authority to enforce their ordinances. They may appoint ministers and other officers of trust, but without power to try or punish them for misdemeanors. They may resolve, but cannot execute, either with despatch or with secrecy. In short, they may consult, and deliberate, and rec-

[8] *Writings of Washington*, Ford's ed., XI, 1.

ommend, and make requisitions, and they who please may regard them." [9]

Two things, each in itself insignificant, indicate how helpless and powerless was this Confederation. During the last two or three years of its life, there was not money enough in the treasury to provide the secretary with the pens, ink, and paper needed to keep a record of its deliberations! Since the close of the war, the army, still unpaid, had lingered in the neighborhood of Philadelphia, and one day a small band of about eighty men escaped from their officers and marched on Philadelphia to demand their pay from Congress. Into the city they marched and to Liberty Hall, where, after some shouting and disorder, they threw stones through the windows. Not a hand was raised to protect the central government, and the members of Congress ignominiously crawled out of the windows or escaped through the back door and fled across the river to Trenton. That was indeed a spectacle which confirmed the worst fears of Americans and the predictions of Europeans. "To be more exposed in the eyes of the world," wrote Washington, "and more contemptible than we already are, is hardly possible." [10]

The remedy, as the leaders saw, lay in the institution of a central government possessed of powers for direct taxation and the regulation of commerce and with a sanction of force behind it of sufficient weight to insure obedience to its orders. Men like Peletiah Webster propounded in pamphlets which attracted wide attention various forms which such a solution might take. From the growth of the last century and, indeed, of the last generation, had emerged compelling facts arguing the expediency and profitableness of union. Rapid emigration, westward movement, the general prosperity, had certainly quadrupled the number of people in America in 1700, and had easily doubled the population since 1760. From this growth inevitably resulted a degree of propinquity which had never before existed. When the colonies were

[9] Ford, *Pamphlets on the Constitution*, 67.
[10] *Writings of Washington*, Ford's ed., XI, 77.

merely little groups of people scattered along a thousand miles of sea-coast, separated by long miles of wilderness devoid of roads, and dependent on tedious sea voyages for inter-communication, it was easy for them to maintain their sovereign independence of each other; there were few interests or antagonisms in which they affected each other's welfare vitally. Nature had separated them and made them thirteen and not one. But in 1783 the States impinged upon each other, at least along the coast, and forced upon each other the consideration of this matter and the decision of that. The lack of natural barriers between them, of geographical divisions of the Atlantic coast, the fact that they all occupied contiguous sections of the same watershed, drained by parallel rivers, gave them, whether they would or no, certain common problems which had to be settled either by discussion or by force. Partly because of the accident of settlement, partly because of the ignorance of geography and of the sort of entity desirable for a single State, the colonial charters had accentuated these facts by making the important rivers the boundaries between the States. New Hampshire and Massachusetts were separated by the Merrimac; New York and New Jersey by the Hudson; Pennsylvania, Delaware, and New Jersey by the Delaware; Virginia and Maryland by the Potomac; South Carolina and Georgia by the Savannah. By law and custom, they owned together the only common roads into the interior before the days of railroads, and normally therefore came into contact with each other the moment the area of settlement attained any dimensions at all. Even where there were no disputes as to what the boundary was, the common use of the rivers made necessary some sort of a general consensus of opinion as to the rights of each State in the natural highways.

On the whole, too, by reason of the common economic dependence of the whole Atlantic coast upon Europe for manufactured articles and of the total lack of a medium of exchange with Europe, the interests of all the States were sure to be furthered or injured together by the sort of relationship now to be established with foreign nations. The fact that economic conditions forced all the States to trade with each other and with Europe *via* the West Indies gave them the most powerful of possible common ties, a strong self-interest which could best be preserved or extended by a general agreement and common action. If the New Englanders could not fish off the Grand Banks, how could they buy Pennsylvania flour or Virginia tobacco? Common action, a general agreement as to rights and policies were clearly the best methods of furthering and protecting the economic interests of individuals and of the several States.

Moreover, the jealousies of the various States of each other, the fact that nearly all of them were at loggerheads with more than one of their neighbors, made them equally unwilling to leave the settlement of the more obvious problems to the States most nearly concerned. For all, the free navigation of the rivers without militating and conflicting regulations and preferential duties was most advantageous, and seemed wholly impossible unless the common highways could be handed over to a central government which might arbitrate and represent equally the claims and interests of all.

But the western territory between the Alleghanies and the Mississippi, ceded by England in the Treaty of Peace, presented the greatest difficulty. It was quite clear before the ink on the treaty was dry that the separate States would not be able to settle this question by agreements with each other. Before the war, settlers from Virginia and North Carolina had begun pushing over the mountains, and, after the war had begun, Patrick Henry, as Governor of Virginia, had directed the "conquest" of the land north of the Ohio by a Virginia "army" under Clark. One of the old charters was then exhumed whose plausible interpretation vested in Virginia the title to the whole interior of the Continent north of 36° 30′. Whereupon, New York produced a claim to the same extensive district on the ground that it was the property of the Iroquois tribes, and was therefore included in the grants to the Duke of York by Charles II. From Connecticut and Massachusetts came loud cries of protest and claims to the whole northern part of the Missisippi Valley based upon their own charters. That the acceptance of any one claim excluded the other three was undoubted. If their respective claims were valid at all, they were mutually exclusive.

The other nine States, however, resisted vehemently any attempt at compromise which should divide the property between the four. The solid cause of their opposition came from the fact that some of them had already smaller territories than these four States and that the existence of all the remainder would be vitally endangered by such an extension of the territory of a few. Rhode Island and Maryland feared conquest or absorption. Had not Plymouth and New Haven already been swallowed by Massachusetts and Connecticut? New Jersey declared herself a cask tapped at both ends by New York and Pennsylvania and therefore certain to be dry. Nor were such fears slow to produce arguments from history, law, and expediency. All the charters on which these claims were founded had long since been specifically revoked; the Proclamation Line of 1763 had definitely restricted the thirteen coast colonies to the eastern slope of the mountains; if the acts of the English Crown were to decide the question, the four claims were undoubtedly all bad. Furthermore, had not the Treaty of Peace ceded the land in question to the thirteen States in common? Had anything been said about the revival of charters or the extension of existing boundaries?

So evident was it that no division of the territory could be devised satisfactory to the four principals, and that no retention of it by any of them on any terms would be countenanced by the rest of the States, that the claims of the four were finally ceded to the shadowy central government. Thus the territory between the mountains and the Mississippi became common property and its existence aided immensely the cause of union and of strong government. From one source and another had come tales of the wonderful fertility of the land, of the incalculable value of its trading privileges, while a good many of the legends so influential in encouraging the early explorers showed a surprising vitality and persistence. The new land was valuable, and every State began to take thought about the proper method of ensuring the safety of its interests in the common property.

Finally, union was as eminently possible as it was desirable. Throughout America the population was substantially homogeneous. The Teutonic stock and the Protestant religion easily predominated; the English common law was universally accepted; State and local government were essentially alike in form and in operation. There were no fundamental geographical, economic, racial, religious, or institutional obstacles to be overcome. The difficulties were superficial, not fundamental, matters of form and detail, not matters of substance. Indeed, adequate administrative regulations and corporate honesty alone were needed to remedy a situation which seemed to superficial observers desperate. From the pens of keener men we have words which indicate that the situation was as thoroughly understood in Europe as in America. "The reflections which I have just had the honor of submitting to you," wrote a European envoy, "scarcely conform to the vague and exaggerated reports with which almost all the European and American publications are flooded in regard to the situation of the United States. They confound the uncertainty of a people which has not yet chosen its form of stable and permanent government with disorder and internal anarchy, but this uncertainty is only felt abroad or in their political discussions without affecting in any way the tranquillity and industry of the citizens. If one studies ever so little the general prosperity, individual comfort, the well-nigh inconceivable growth of all parts of the republic, one is tempted to believe that this one has taken the longest strides towards opulence and formidable power."

The convention which drew up the Constitution grew out of the attempts of Maryland and Virginia to settle their private disputes by conference and compromise. After a thorough discussion of the situation, the delegates of both States agreed that the adequate solution of their peculiar quarrels involved

the decision of too many other interstate quarrels to admit
of the attainment of a satisfactory conclusion by themselves
alone.   Accordingly, the several States were invited to send
representatives to Annapolis to discuss the various issues with
a view to permanent settlement.   Five States responded, whose
delegates abandoned any attempt at agreement and counseled the summoning of a general convention at Philadelphia to amend the Articles of Confederation.   The suggestion was at once adopted by a majority of the States and
the others soon named delegates.   The Federal Convention
which met in 1787, therefore, like most other important
actions taken during the period, was the result of separate
State action and not of an act of the central government.
The claim of the Southern leaders in later days that the
States, and not the nation, made the Constitution was thus
far historically true.

XIII

THE CONSTITUTION

THE wisdom of the members of the Constitutional Convention, which sat at Philadelphia from May to September of 1787, was in no respect more conspicuous than in their determination to debate thoroughly and agree upon the basic principles of constitutional law upon which the government they suggested must be founded. They recognized, furthermore, the truth of Montesquieu's contention that successful governments were founded upon and must be consonant with the economic and social conditions of the time and could not be based merely upon theory or precedent. American political democracy was consciously based upon the economic and social equality which the members of the Constitutional Convention saw existed in this country. While they examined with great care every form of government the world had known and gave particular attention to the Greek, Roman, and Dutch Republics, they concluded that the circumstances in America in 1787 were without precedent and that the results of previous attempts at democracy were therefore without value. The English government many of them admired, and the subtlety of its working they all understood; but Hamilton stood practically alone in claiming that any of its elements could be profitably copied in America.[1] The members of the Convention, in fact, fell back upon colonial experience and the experiments of the States in forming their constitutions during the Revolution for most of the detailed provisions of the Constitution. Presi-

[1] For Hamilton's views, see Hunt's *Madison's Notes*, I, 158; for the contrary opinions of Wilson, Madison, Pinckney, and others see *Ibid.*, I, 50, 51, 98, 225, etc.

dent, Senate, and House, the separation of powers, the pre-
dominance of the legislature, the weakness of the executive,
they tried to copy from American experience. But these
details, the purely formal elements of the new government,
were not its vital forces.

First and foremost in importance stands the fact that
the Constitution founded a democracy in which all men should
be equal before the law and in which the people should be
sovereign. This was indeed merely the legal recognition
of an existing fact. In wealth, in birth, in education, in
privilege, men were already on the same footing in every
colony: the affirmations of the Declaration of Independence,
the vital words of the Preamble of the Consitution were,
as their form indicated, simply statements of existing facts.
"Equality is as I contend the leading feature of the U.
States." "A system must be suited to the habits and genius
of the People it is to govern, and must grow out of them,"
declared Pinckney. "After all there is one, but one great
and equal body of Citizens composing the inhabitants of this
Country among whom there are no distinctions of rank, and
very few or none of fortune. For a people thus circum-
stanced are we then to form a Government. . . . These are
I believe as active, intelligent, and susceptible of good Government as any people in the world." [2]

With this equality of condition, the travelers, already
numerous, had been charmed. A French traveler, De
Ségur, expressed his surprise at the absence of the extremes
of luxury and poverty to which he was accustomed in Europe.
"All the Americans whom we met wore clothes of good
material. Their free, frank, and familiar address, equally
removed from uncouth discourtesy and from artificial polite-
ness, betokened men who were proud of their own rights
and respected those of others." To Lafayette's astonishment,
the inn-keeper and his wife usually sat down with him at
table, and conversed with him intelligently on a great variety
of subjects. He saw no magnificent mansions, with powdered

[2] Hunt's *Madison's Notes*, I, 225; 229-231.

lackeys at the door, rode in no splendid coaches, drawn by prancing steeds (though there were fine equipages in the colonies), but found everywhere houses of wood or brick, simply made, gleaming with clean white paint, and furnished inside with a frugal elegance and an excellent taste which even the fastidious Frenchman was compelled to confess were admirable. The Comte de Ségur was enthusiastic over the scenery and equally loud in his praise of the settled portions of the country. "Sometimes I was admiring a lovely valley, carefully tilled, with the meadows full of cattle; the houses clean, elegant, painted in bright colors, and standing in little gardens behind pretty fences. Abundance, comfort, and urbanity everywhere." Everywhere he found cleanliness, everywhere he found a plenty of the hearty wholesome fare which in Europe was then unknown to the lower classes. In France, many of the peasants of 1787 were eating bread made out of chestnuts and acorns ground fine and mixed with bran. Even the middle class was glad to get rye bread, while fresh meat was a luxury known only to the rich. But in America, the farmer, the laborer, and the carpenter, as well as the merchant and the great planter, sat down daily to a dinner of fresh meat and wheat bread, and not infrequently, as Rowe tells us in his diary,[3] such luxuries as green peas or strawberries and cream, which had already become characteristic American dishes.

Next to the equality of conditions, the simplicity, honesty, and genuineness of life seem to have caused most remark. "Simplicity of manners," declared Lafayette, "the desire to oblige, and a mild and quiet equality are the rule everywhere." "The inhabitants, each and all," wrote the Comte de Ségur, "exhibited the unassuming and quiet pride of men who had no master, who see nothing above them except the law, and who are free from the vanity, the servility, and the prejudices of our European societies." Life was free; the necessities of life being easily secured, all were equal and treated

[3] The Diary of John Rowe (*Massachusetts Historical Society Proceedings*, Second Series, X, 147.

each other like brothers. Education was widespread: most of the people could read, and many could write an excellent hand. The old dames' schools had done well in New England and had spread education, albeit neither very deeply nor very accurately, over the whole community. In the Middle States, the ability to read and write was common and in the South universal among the planters. Furthermore, there is nothing more interesting to note in the mental attitude of colonial Americans than the belief, firmly planted in the mind of each boy, that with work and diligence he could become anything he wanted to be. Witness the youthful Franklin. He desired to become an author. No sooner said than done: he took Addison as a model; he set to work rewriting the *Spectator;* and soon began to send contributions to his brother's newspaper, whose excellence attracted attention. Falling out with his brother, he did not set out for some place ten miles distant, but for Philadelphia, half across the country; and, becoming dissatisfied with prospects there, sailed for England. He had no money; he had no guardian but his own sublime self-confidence; but he neither hesitated nor doubted. Thirty years later he retired from active business, a wealthy man for life.

This American, at once so frugal and so honest, was vehemently interested in politics. Even the servants read the newspapers, remarked one observer. Yes, and understood them too, added another. All classes of the community talked politics in season and out of season. Nor were they interested merely in personalities about the governor or gossip about the love affairs of his daughter. A brief perusal of the *Centinel* or the *Gazette* will show the modern reader that our ancestors read with avidity essays, constitutional arguments, histories of trade, summaries of English and colonial legislation. This habit of reading and the subsequent discussion of tangled questions was of great value in training the Americans for the great experiment of democratic government on which they were embarking.

But in this life and in their politics they were self-centered.

A Massachusetts man lived for Massachusetts, not for England nor for Virginia. He was patriotic but not to any united organization called either the British Empire or the United Colonies. His ignorance of affairs in Europe and even in other colonies was colossal. The Comte de Ségur exchanged opinions with the keeper of the inn where he put up for the night, who called himself a Colonel, and discoursed at great length on campaigns and farming. De Ségur, stating in turn that his father was a general and a minister of State, was astounded to perceive that the Colonel did not at all realize what the rank of General and office of Minister of State implied in France. Outside of trade, the American cared only for politics; outside of the local politics of his own community, he understood little, though ready to discuss anything with anybody.

In the hands of such a people, the makers of the Constitution placed the sovereignty, the right to decide in the last resort all issues of importance. After long and heated discussion, no Bill of Rights was included and no direct statement made that the supreme power was vested in the people themselves. The argument which carried the day was that of James Wilson, of Pennsylvania, to whose keen logical mind and deep understanding of the situation we owe much of the shape of the great document. "The preamble to the proposed Constitution," said he, "'We, the people of the United States, do establish,' contains the essence of all the Bills of Rights that have been or can be devised." The people alone made it; the people alone might change it; the people in making it surrendered no jot or tittle of their power; they remained superior to the Constitution. Furthermore, by writing "the People of the United States" and not "the peoples of the United States," the new government was necessarily made a government where a body of individuals and not a union of States was sovereign. "A Union of the States," said King, "is a Union of the men composing them from whence a national character results to the whole."[4]

----

[4] Hunt's *Madison's Notes*, I, 186. The preceding part of King's

The new government would have jurisdiction over every man in America, the lack of which had been, to the thinking of the Convention, the old Confederation's greatest defect. There was, too, in the minds of the leaders no doubt that the sovereignty of the States which had caused during the Revolution and Critical period so much suffering to every one would be a thing of the past. The wholesale repudiation of debts, the coining of money, making of tariffs to exclude trade from the next State, raising of armies, building of navies and more, were explicitly forbidden, and the wording of the preamble took away the sovereign power of the States as clearly as words could. Indeed, the first drafts of the preamble had read, "We, the people of New Hampshire, Massachusetts," and so on, enumerating the States. The words finally adopted were indeed, as Wilson said, a whole treatise on sovereignty.

The States were to be related to the national government through the people. Wilson explained at length "the two-fold relation in which the people would stand, 1, as Citizens of the General Government, 2, as Citizens of their particular State. . . . Both Governments were derived from the people —both were meant for the people—both, therefore, ought to be regulated on the same principles. . . . The General Government is not an assemblage of States, but of individuals for certain political purposes—it is not meant for the States, but for the individuals composing them."[5] The people, therefore, organized in sections formed the States; the same people viewed as a whole, not as parts, were the basis of the national government. The value and importance of the

speech is enlightening. "He conceived that the import of the term 'States,' 'Sovereignty,' 'national,' 'federal' had been often used and applied in the discussions inaccurately and delusively. The States were not 'Sovereigns' in the sense contended for by some. . . . They could not make war, nor peace, nor alliances, nor treaties. . . . If the States therefore retained some portion of their sovereignty, they had certainly divested themselves of essential portions of it. If they formed a Confederacy in some respects—they formed a Nation in others."

[5] Hunt's *Madison's Notes*, I, 233-4.

States was not lost sight of. "Without their coöperation," Ellsworth reminded the Convention, "it would be impossible to support a Republican Government, over so great an extent of Country. . . . The largest States are the worst governed. . . . If the principles and materials of our Government are not adequate to the extent of these single States;[6] how can it be imagined that they can support a single Government throughout the U[nited] States. The only chance of supporting a General Government lies in grafting it on that of the individual States."[7]

But only the ultimate power was placed in the hands of the people. They were given only three legal duties. They were to choose the representatives directly; they were to vote for the electoral college, which would choose the President and for the state legislatures which were to choose the Senators; they were to vote either directly or by special conventions upon all amendments to the Constitution. But in no other way and at no other time should they in any way themselves participate in administration or legislation. They should not govern; they should not even constantly direct the hands which governed for them. They should choose a President, who, once inaugurated, would possess in himself absolute discretion in the performance of the executive work entrusted to him. During his term of office, no one should control him or dictate to him; he should be supreme. The people, his masters, might at the end of his term censure him for what he had done; they might refuse to let him act again for them; but they should not legally prevent him during his term of office from acting at any time as he thought fit. Similarly, in the hands of Congress was placed the whole legislative power; and in the hands of the judges, the whole judicial power. Each branch was delegated its power by the people; each would be responsible to the people at the end of its term, but during that term the framers intended that each should govern for the people. The share of the

6 That is, are not capable of governing a single State.
7 Hunt's *Madison's Notes*, I, 234.

people should be ultimate, not immediate; they should control the broader aspects of policy, not dictate the details of methods and means.

Nor did the framers understand that they placed this sovereignty in the hands of the male citizens over twenty-one years of age. By a general agreement, the federal suffrage was left in the hands of the States, who were to regulate it by regulating their own. There was not then, and never had been, in any State or colony, manhood suffrage. A property qualification had been nearly universal; oaths of fidelity or allegiance had been common; while throughout New England a man's moral and religious character had been closely scrutinized before he had been granted a share of political power. It was indeed true that the amount of property was not usually difficult to amass, nor the degree of spiritual excellence impossible of attainment; neither birth nor previous condition was a permanent bar. Any man might become qualified for the suffrage; but it was nevertheless a fact in 1789, not much questioned or remarked upon, indeed accepted as axiomatic, that the democracy viewed by the framers of the constitution was limited to men of property, education, and good character. Not till about 1840 did the words "People of the United States" place the sovereignty in the hands of the male majority which now has it. The franchise was in 1789 a privilege conferred by the State on deserving citizens; and the lack of it was not supposed to imply the slightest right to disobey the authorities. Bills of Rights and Constitutions conferred no such privileges.

It was fully recognized that if the Federal Government must govern for the people, its executive arm should have sufficient power to act. The President's term of four years they believed too short to enable him to encroach upon the people's liberties. But that the Convention could not possibly enumerate or even foresee the powers which would in the future need to be in the hands of both President and Congress was freely admitted and the form of the Constitution was in large measure due to the decision, early reached, to sketch only the broad outlines of the government and its powers, and permit executive, legislature, and judiciary to read into its broad clauses the authority which the exigencies of State might render imperative. "The vagueness of the terms," said Mr. Gorham, "constitutes the propriety of them. We are now establishing general principles, to be extended hereafter into details which will be precise and explicit."[8] The Convention contented itself, therefore, with enumerating the obviously necessary things which the President and Congress must do, and in broad terms conferred upon them respectively the executive and legislative power. It is this aspect of the Constitution, as its framers foresaw, which has made it possible for us to live under it for a century and a quarter with so little radical change. It is at present the oldest written fundamental law in the world.

The framers were, however, alive to the fact that such great powers, so vaguely stated, must be controlled. They adopted the doctrine of the separation of powers, so highly praised by Montesquieu, as the basis of the relations of the departments with each other. "It has been agreed on all hands," said Mason, "that an efficient Government is necessary: that to render it such, it ought to have the faculty of self-defense; that to render its different branches effectual, each of them ought to have the same power of self-defense."[9] To fetter the three departments more than this would be to sacrifice unduly the efficiency of administration, they thought. A further safeguard they found in the fact that the problems most vital in the daily life of the community were both explicitly and implicitly left in the hands of the States or the local town or county governments: there would not be many things which the Federal government could do which could much interfere with or directly injure the private citizen. The different conditions in various parts of the country which needed to be met in widely divergent ways made the division of the country into States very fortunate, and they

[8] Hunt's *Madison's Notes*, I, 366.
[9] *Ibid.*, I, 235.

were anxious not to interfere with what they considered so happy a circumstance. In addition, the population of about four million souls was still very much scattered over the Atlantic seaboard in little groups separated still by the wilderness at more or less frequent intervals. A few people in Maine, a few in New Hampshire, and a pretty thoroughly settled district in Massachusetts, Rhode Island, and Connecticut, then a considerable fringe of settlements along the Hudson and Mohawk, and along the Delaware, around Chesapeake Bay and along its rivers, then a gap till the North Carolina settlements came into view, then another gap until South Carolina and its rice and cotton fields came above the horizon to the south-bound traveler. The largest town of the infant country was Philadelphia with some 75,000 souls. New York in 1776 possessed some 2500 buildings, and they pastured cows along lower Broadway. The chief problems were local, not national, and must be dealt with by the States, not by the Federal government. "Were not this great country already divided into States," wrote Jefferson, "that division must be made, that each might do for itself what concerns itself directly and what it can so much better do than a distant authority. . . . Were we directed from Washington when to sow and when to reap, we should soon want bread." [10] These same facts, coupled with the rivalries already conspicuous between the States, would prevent the Federal government from encroaching upon them and, what was better, prevent them from encroaching upon the legitimate powers of the Federal government.

How to put power into the hands of so many people without allowing them to abuse it and destroy the national government and themselves too, seemed to the members of the Convention their greatest problem. That the people were honest and capable of deciding the great issues of State wisely after due deliberation, few doubted. In the long run, they would do right, but the problem of securing sufficient time for them to deliberate and make up their minds was the

[10] *Memoir*, I, 70. London, 1829.

difficult issue. The Convention finally concluded that one duty of the Federal government would be to stand between the people and the consummation of their first passionate desire. The Constitution should be a restraining document, which should create an engine capable of preventing the people from having their way for a number of years. Far from its being intended that the government should facilitate the expression of the popular will, it was in fact shaped so as to make difficult the fulfilment of popular desire. ''Why has government been instituted at all?'' asked Hamilton in the famous fifteenth paper of the *Federalist*. ''Because the passions of men will not conform to the dictates of reason and justice without constraint.'' To some extent this determination to restrain the people caused the Convention to omit mention of explicit powers as granted Congress, which it seemed dangerous to put firmly in the people's hands. As Chief Justice Marshall later phrased it, ''That power might be abused was deemed a conclusive reason why it should not be conferred.''

But the framers were by no means satisfied with omission. To give the Senate a check on both House and President, they made the term of senators six years, and made it a permanent body of men, by allowing two-thirds to hold over at each election and therefore making it impossible for the legislatures to choose more than a third of the Senate at any one time to carry out some particular wish of the people. The House of Representatives which the people elected was given a term of only two years, partly to render it more responsive to the people, partly to allow the President, who sat for four years and the Senate, two-thirds of which would still be sitting, to control it more easily. If all three agreed upon some measure, it would be clear that the nation wanted it and ought to have its way. But if any considerable opposition existed in the country, enough of it would be reflected in Congress to prevent agreement. When all three did not agree, there was to be no method legally provided for putting pressure upon the dissenters. Whether Presi-

dent or Senate opposed, the highest duty of that branch
to the people consisted in maintaining its firm front until
a new election could be held and the people could once more
indicate their desires. In four years at the most, the President and Senate could be brought into agreement with the
House of Representatives, and if the people were decided
enough in their opinion to maintain it for four years, nothing
further could or ought to be done to prevent them from
having their way. To the end that this arrangement should
not cripple the efficiency of the Federal government, however, the executive power was placed unreservedly in the
President's hands: the existing law should be enforced
promptly and efficiently in any case; new laws should be
enacted, new policies adopted, only after due deliberation.
The routine administration was made easy; the adoption of
new legislation was consciously made as difficult as possible.

After four months of anxious debate, from May to September 1787, the Convention submitted its work to the country, requesting that the document should be ratified by conventions or by popular vote in each State, and that when
nine States had accepted it, it should go into operation as
binding upon those who ratified it. A long and bitter campaign was fought in State after State. The old "Patriot
party" of 1775 led by Samuel Adams, Patrick Henry, Me-
lancthon Smith of New York, and George Mason of Virginia
felt that the Constitution sacrificed all that the Revolution
had been fought to win.[11] "Who authorized them to speak
the language of We the People, instead of We the States?"
cried Henry.[12] "I stumble at the threshold," declared Samuel Adams, "I meet with a national government instead of
a federal union of sovereign States."[13] The very strong

[11] The Constitution was the "triumph of the legitimate successors of
the Anti-Revolutionary party of 1775." Judge Chamberlain in *Papers
of the American Historical Association*, III, No. 1.

[12] Speech in the Virginia Convention. Elliott, *Debates*, III, 22, 29,
44, 521-522. "Even from that illustrious man who saved us by his
valor, I would have a reason for his conduct."

[13] Samuel Adams to R. H. Lee. Lee's *Life of R. H. Lee*, II, 130.

objection was also raised that the Convention had exceeded its authority. It had been directed to amend the Articles of Confederation and had proposed a wholly new scheme of government. Nor were men slow to remark that 73 members had been elected, of whom nearly a third never attended and of whom scarcely more than half (39) signed the final document. The boasted unanimity was absent. Detailed objections of all kinds appeared. In Massachusetts, New York, and Virginia the fight was particularly fierce. A series of essays called the *Federalist* written by Hamilton, Madison, and Jay, published in New York but widely read throughout the country, were instrumental in convincing the people of the expediency of the new constitution, which was finally adopted by eleven States in the fall of 1788.

The first elections, held in January 1789, caused a succession of disagreements in various States, which for a time threatened to prevent the choice of a Congress or of presidential electors in time to meet on March 4, the date when the old Congress of the Confederation was formally to dissolve. The presidential electors, however, finally did meet; the news quickly spread that George Washington and John Adams had been elected President and Vice-President respectively; but when March 4 dawned, there was no President-elect in New York to be inaugurated, because the votes had not been officially counted and the President not yet officially elected. Furthermore, there were not enough members of either the House or the Senate in the city to form a quorum to count the votes; the Assembly Hall was still in the carpenters' hands; and Washington and Adams both declined to leave home until they should be officially assured of their election. It is most difficult for us to understand to-day the anxiety and suspense of those weeks in March and April 1789, when, with the old government legally dead, it was as yet more than doubtful whether the new could be even formally put in power. After weeks of alarm and speculation, a bare quorum in both houses of Congress finally assembled on April 6, more than a month after the date set for the inauguration of the new President; the votes were counted; and a fortnight later, on April 30, Washington was inaugurated. Few people remember now that in 1789 it was doubtful for nearly two months whether men could be got together to fill enough of the formal posts created by the new Constitution to make it possible to begin the task of creating a new administration. As the Anti-Federalists derisively declared, the "old man" (Franklin) and "the two boys" (Madison and Hamilton) were all wrong: the old roof had leaked but the new one was not even on the building. "If the system can be put in operation without touching much the pockets of the people," wrote Washington to Jefferson, "perhaps it may be done; but, in my judgment, infinite circumspection and prudence are yet necessary in the experiment."[14]

Fisher Ames has left us a touching picture of Washington at this time. Just after the inauguration, "I was present in the pew (at church) with the President and must assure you that, after making all deductions for the delusion of one's fancy in regard to characters, I still think of him with more veneration than for any other person. Time has made havoc upon his face. That and other circumstances not to be reasoned about, conspire to keep up the awe which I brought with me. He addressed the two Houses in the Senate Chamber; it was a very touching scene and quite of a solemn kind. His aspect grave almost to sadness; his modesty, actually shaking; his voice deep, a little tremulous, and so low as to call for close attention; added to the series of objects presented to the mind and overwhelming it, produced emotions of the most affecting kind upon the members." In the inaugural address Washington had said: "The preservation of the sacred fire of liberty, and the destiny of the republican model of government, are justly considered as deeply, perhaps as finally, staked on the experiment intrusted to the hands of the American people." Such were the hopes and aspirations, such the sense of responsibility, with which the fathers began work under the Constitution.

[14] Washington to Jefferson, August 31, 1788. *Writings of Washington.* Sparks, IX, 426-7.

XIV

THE ESTABLISHMENT OF PERMANENT ADMINIS-
TRATION

WERE it not for our after-knowledge and the realization that the difficulties to be remedied were for the most part superficial and curable, the immediate success of the new government would be as astonishing to us as it was gratifying to its contemporaries. But the Constitution was not, as the vast majority assumed, the cause. The secret lay in the changed economic conditions, in the disappearance of the commercial stringency by the operation of economic factors on which governments and constitutions had no influence. Of this Washington was well aware. "It was indeed next to a miracle," he wrote in 1790, "that there should have been so much unanimity in points of such importance among such a number of citizens, so widely scattered, and so different in their habits in many respects, as the Americans were. Nor are the growing unanimity and increasing good-will of the citizens to the government less remarkable than favorable circumstances. . . . Perhaps a number of accidental circumstances have concurred with the real effects of the government to make the people uncommonly well pleased with their situation and prospects." [1]

Chief among these, he placed the natural reaction from a long period of business depression and confusion, and the result of the frugality and economy which hard times inevitably inculcate. "I expect that many blessings will be attributed to our new government which are now taking their rise from the industry and frugality into the practice of which the people have been forced from necessity. I really

[1] *Writings of Washington*, Ford's ed., XI, 459.

believe that there never was so much labor and economy to be found before in the country as at the present moment. . . . All these blessings (for all these blessings will come) will be referred to the fostering influence of the new government. Whereas many causes will have conspired to produce them.''[2]

Among the ''many causes'' clearly belongs the very great development of the country during the previous generation, —the doubling of the population, the vast increase in the number of acres under cultivation, in the number of ships being built, in the volume of produce seeking a market. A French traveler declared that ''on the whole, it is difficult to conceive the state of increase and the prosperity of this country after so long and calamitous a war.'' Then, at the very moment when America had more to sell than ever before, a new market for grain, naval stores, and all sorts of staple crops was opened in Europe by the outbreak of the French Revolution and the resulting wars. For the first time in history, the Atlantic coast was able to export directly to Europe on advantageous terms. Moreover, the generality of the European war after 1793 deprived most of the continental shipping of its neutral status, exposed it to capture and the cargoes to confiscation, and thus left the American merchant marine the only considerable neutral fleet on the ocean. The really extraordinary impulse to trade and navigation from these sources did not manifest itself clearly in 1789, but followed closely enough upon the inauguration of the new government to cause the people, as Washington had predicted, to ascribe the resulting prosperity to its operations. Economic forces thus gave the new government time to formulate its plans and to establish the administration on a permanent basis without being so much hampered by the exaggerated expectations of the people and the demand for immediate results as Washington and Hamilton had anticipated would be the case. Moreover, as Hamilton very clearly saw, the great development during and since the Revolution proved the country unquestionably solvent and un-

2 *Writings of Washington*, Ford's ed., XI, 279.

doubtedly very prosperous. It demonstrated conclusively that the evils were more apparent than real, superficial rather than fundamental, and of a nature which administrative regulations could easily obviate, if only public confidence could be long enough secured to give them the thorough, honest trial which would be indispensable to final success. If his plans for the opening of trade channels, for the provision of a medium of exchange, and for the funding of the debt could be actually accepted, and better foreign relations could be established by diplomacy, the moneyed and propertied class would be firmly bound to the new government by the solid chain of interest and the stability of the new régime therefore assured. While the immediate success of the new administration was clearly due to fortuitous economic factors, which could neither have been foreseen nor controlled, its permanent success was due to the measures of Alexander Hamilton.

The first session of Congress was mainly occupied with the establishment of the skeleton of a central administration, —the creation of four departments, state, treasury, war, and judiciary; and with such questions as salaries, territorial government, Indians, post-offices, federal courts. The second session, in 1790, was devoted to the discussion and adoption of Hamilton's great measures for the permanent solution of those vital problems which had caused the adoption of the Constitution. Of these unquestionably the most important was the refunding of the entire debt of the Revolutionary governments, state and central. Hamilton declared in favor of paying the entire indebtedness of every sort and variety at par: the certificates constituted a valid legal claim on the new government for the sums mentioned in them; if they were not valid for the whole sum, he did not believe them legally valid at all. It was imperative to establish the credit of the new government at once and enable it to borrow money to meet the probable crises of the future. It was no less imperative to tie to the government the moneyed men and the creditor class by giving them a personal interest in its continuance and in the future of the Federalist party. Refunding had a political as well as a financial purpose. Hamilton's study of English politics had convinced him that the men of property exerted more political influence than any other class and that the union of financial and commercial interests in the new Federalist party would go far to produce that consensus of opinion and union of political sentiment which the new government so obviously needed. If the citizens who held the debts of the government were promised payment at par of debts which they had expected would never be paid at all, there would be little doubt of the ability of the new government to maintain itself.

To the objections of the Anti-Federalists and opponents of assumption, Hamilton returned convincing answers. Although the debt looked large, it was not too large to be paid. Nor was its history to be taken into account; it was a legal obligation and should be treated accordingly. Any attempt to compromise by payment on the basis of a scale graduated to the previous market values of the securities would be fatal to the prime object the refunding was meant to accomplish,—the establishment of the government's credit both at home and abroad. To many this attitude seemed foolhardy and unnecessary. Was it not commonly acknowledged that the bonds and certificates had depreciated in value to almost nothing, and had often been originally issued at a rate far below par? The government would thus pay even more than the original holder had loaned. Was it not even truer that all the certificates had changed hands, so that the original holder would not get the profit Hamilton proposed to allow, while a man not at all entitled to the gratitude of America would calmly pocket the difference between the small sum he had paid and the value of the certificates at par? This argument was strengthened by the knowledge that speculators had been busy for some months buying up certificates in the country districts, imposing on the ignorance and credulity of such original holders as still retained their evidences of indebtedness. The trade in securities in the larger cities was brisk and prices went up and down with rapidity according to the news from Congress. Hamilton was rewarding speculation and encouraging gambling, vociferated his opponents.

The really bitter debates took place over the assumption of the States' debts. Would the country be able to bear the ruinous taxation which would be necessary to pay the interest? Was account to be taken of what had already been paid by the States? Some had paid much; others had paid a little; most had paid nothing. Were the honest then to be taxed for the payment of *all* the debts of the dishonest, when the share paid by the latter of the honest States' debts would be proportionately smaller? Again, was it wise to assume a burden whose size no one knew? There were indeed no reliable figures to show what the outstanding indebtedness of the States was and it seemed almost impossible to draw a wholly accurate line between the revolutionary and pre-revolutionary debts. Several States were heavily involved as a result of paper-money crazes and land-bank schemes during the colonial period, and these debts the other States were vehemently opposed to assuming. The debates were acrimonious in the extreme: taunts over the relative suffering during the war; threats of secession if the debt was not assumed, threats to leave the union if it was, were hurled back and forth with vehemence. A bargain was finally struck at a little dinner-party given by Jefferson whereby the capitol was located at Washington as the Anti-Federalist forces and the Southern States wished and the debt was assumed as the Federalists and the Northern States desired.

The debt of the United States totaled, with the arrears of interest, about fifty-four millions of dollars. Of this, about twelve millions, principal and interest, was owed abroad and was paid at once in full by the proceeds of a new loan. The domestic debt of forty-two millions was to be funded by the exchange of the old certificates at face value for the new bonds at par. No one was to be compelled to make the exchange, but Hamilton believed the terms at which the new bonds were offered were sufficiently advantageous to result in the voluntary exchange of the bulk of the debt, and that the government would be able to buy up the rest in the market. Each creditor received a certificate equal to two-thirds of his indebtedness which bore interest at six per cent at once, and a certificate for the remaining third bearing interest at six per cent after 1800. The device reduced the interest paid on the whole debt to four per cent, but concealed the fact from the public. New bonds to the extent of twenty-one and one-half millions were to be exchanged for the States' indebtedness at par, but only about eighteen millions were ever applied for. To these creditors were given three certificates, one calling for interest at six per cent at once, and one for interest at three per cent at once, and a third for interest at six per cent after 1800. By these devices the total debt was refunded, paid off, or bought up, and the annual interest charge reduced from nearly five millions to something over two. The national revenue and the western lands were pledged for payment of principal and interest.

The refunding was a great success. Within three years, the bulk of the domestic debt had been converted; the interest payments which had seemed so huge in 1790 were easily met by the revenue from the customs; and the government was even able to show a small surplus six years out of the first ten, with one year in which expenses and receipts exactly balanced. Unquestionably, the Federal government was solvent and its credit has never since been questioned. By 1835, the whole national debt had been paid off. And all had been accomplished smoothly, quietly, and with practically no objection on the part of the people. The necessity of not burdening the people with taxes at the first was clearly appreciated by Washington and Hamilton. During the colonial period and the Revolution, the people had paid few or no taxes except to their own local town or county government; the State governments had needed little money. Hamilton insisted that the people must never see a United States tax-collector; that they must pay indirectly by customs and excise, and would then never realize what the amount was. This tradition has been on the whole followed ever since with unquestioned success.

The army was paid off in full either in money, in bonds, or in grants of western land. Measures for the complete fulfilment of the terms of the Treaty of Peace were undertaken. A national revenue was at once created by the imposition of a tariff on imports. The adoption of the Constitution and the establishment of the new administration had abolished at once the State tariffs on exports and imports, had made discriminating duties favorable or hostile to any locality impossible, had given all the free use of the rivers and roads, and had assured the citizens of every State the same civil and commercial privileges in every State as in their own. This freedom of intercourse and the abolition of restrictions went far to remove the artificial obstacles in the way of the growth of trade and of the complete rehabilitation of the credit of State and Federal government.

Some paper or token money had yet to be made, which would pass currently in America but not in Europe, possess a standard value, and be kept in circulation. A sufficiently large amount in notes must be issued to furnish the necessary medium for private and government business, without running the risk of depreciation on the one hand because of the size of the issue, or of the undue scarcity on the other hand which would be certain to result, if the merchants or the government held any considerable quantity of it for even a few weeks. As at the present day, money "flowed" from the coast cities to the interior to move the crops and usually came back again in exchange for manufactured goods, leaving the inland districts pretty well denuded of currency for local business or for government taxes until the next year. Nor must the government collect the money in payment of taxes and custom-dues unless it could immediately return it to circulation.

Hamilton's solution was the first Bank of the United States, chartered finally by Congress after a bitter fight over the constitutionality of the measure, with a capital of ten millions, and a monopoly for twenty years. A mint was established at the same time to standardize the coinage and emit such specie as could be obtained, but the real currency was to be the notes of the Bank, which the latter was to be allowed to issue to an amount not exceeding its capital, and which were to be legal tender for most debts due the government and for all private business. Branches were to be established in convenient cities to enable the Bank to become the government agent in different parts of the country. The stock was subscribed in a hurry and was at once regarded as a good investment. According to the provisions of the law, one-fifth of the capital stock, two millions, was subscribed by the government in its own six per cent bonds; one-fifth, two millions, was paid in by the public in specie; and the remaining six millions by the public in United States six per cent bonds. The public and the government, of course, hoped that the dividends on the stock would exceed the six per cent interest which the Bank itself got from the government bonds it received in exchange for stock; the Bank expected by the loan of the two millions in specie plus the six per cent interest on the eight millions of bonds to make a good profit and to be enabled to declare dividends. Such indeed was the result. The public duly paid in the two millions in specie, which became of course an asset of the Bank. The latter promptly loaned the money to the government at a fair interest and the government too had an ample account from which to meet its first bills. The government then deposited the two millions with the Bank as the government's agent and the Bank also had the specie to use. The Bank then loaned it out to the public, who returned it to the Bank with interest or paid it to the government for taxes. Of course, most of the specie never left the Bank's vaults, and the transactions were really performed by means of notes, checks, or entries on the books of the Bank, but the knowledge that the specie was there gave the note issue stability and this careful utilization of the same small stock of specie by the government, the Bank, and the public, kept it in constant circulation, prevented hoarding, and thus enabled it to meet the country's needs. The existence of the branches and the fact that the Bank was the government's agent, permitted the transaction of the business of the distant sections of the country without the actual transfer of specie and notes from one locality to another and thus left most parts of the country constantly supplied with an adequate amount of currency. By means of the Bank, the government had induced the public to finance the central government during the first years when it must otherwise have borrowed directly sufficient money to meet its pressing needs. The success of the expedient made money for the Bank, the government, and the public, and allowed the government to control the currency and prevent stringency or depreciation far better than it could have through the Treasury itself.

One thing more remained to be accomplished before the permanent success of the central government could be assured,—the vast majority of the people must be brought to believe in its expediency and desirability. Washington had fought the Revolution; Franklin had financed it; Madison and Wilson had framed the Constitution; Hamilton had put it into operation. It remained for Thomas Jefferson to convince the great majority of the people of its excellence and to reconcile them to the existence of a central government which was something more than a name.

The Constitution, as John Quincy Adams later truthfully said, had been ''extorted by grinding necessity from a reluctant people.'' Nothing short of the vivid fear of anarchy and a possible resort to kingship reconciled many of the leaders to the new government, and it may be safely claimed that the people as a whole understood the subtle legal and constitutional points involved as little as they usually have comprehended similar facts at other epochs of history. After we strip away from the Revolution the preconception built around it by the struggles of the Civil War, we begin to realize that it was an anti-national movement, in the sense in which we now use those words. It was a solid protest by thirteen States against the encroachment of England upon their individual sovereignty. It was fought to prevent the institution of a central administration; its success caused the institution of the league of amity between the several States known as the Confederation, whose chief point was the inalienable and imperishable sovereignty of each State. With the Constitution, on the other hand, the people had adopted nationalism as we now conceive of it, the principle of a union between individuals, which made the people as a nation superior to all the States and the central government superior to any State in its obligation upon the individual. We have too long discussed sovereignty and States' rights with relation to a definite document and have laid too little stress upon the fact that the full-blown doctrine of States' rights is anti-national, because it denies the existence, the desirability, and the expediency of a truly national government.[3] If there was no nation in existence in 1776 and in 1783, if the people were unswervingly loyal to the old colonial notion of States' sovereignty until the eve of the adoption of the Constitution, it will be apparent that the adoption of that document did not disabuse them at once of the notions they had so long cherished nor by some occult operation deprive them of their preference for local authority. Whatever the legal effect of the preamble of the Constitution was, whatever the leaders of both Federalist and Anti-Federalist parties conceded it to be, the people as a whole little appreciated the full significance of its adoption and assumed that they had done little

[3] "I am sure," said Patrick Henry, opposing the Constitution in the Virginia Convention, "they [the framers] were fully impressed with the necessity of forming a great consolidated government, instead of a confederation. That this [the Constitution] is a consolidated government is demonstrably clear; and the danger of such a government is, to my mind, very striking. . . . States are the characteristics and the soul of a confederation. If the States be not the agents of this compact, it must be one great, consolidated, national government, of the people of all the States." Elliott's *Debates*, III, 21, 22. As a national government, Henry opposed it.

more than remodel the old Congress and permit it to regulate trade, impose taxes, and pay off the debt.

Miracles had been promised and expected; on the whole miracles happened; but the most marvelous of things become dulled after a thorough acquaintance. Soon the vast majority forgot how much the new Federal government had accomplished, began to clamor for what it could not do, and became dissatisfied. From the Revolution the majority had inherited a hatred of England and an admiration for France, which was much heightened by the outbreak in the latter country of the Revolution and by the proclamation of democratic ideas, which the Americans readily assumed were identical with their own. Because the English promptly disavowed the principles of the French Revolution, and because the Federalists wished to wait for the institution of firm government in France before recognizing the new Republic, the Anti-Federalists concluded that the administration was English, "monarchical," and dominated by "a corrupt Treasury Squadron."

The attempt to live under the new Constitution had revealed the need of definition, and the discretion and latitude of interpretation allowed Congress and the President alarmed the Anti-Federalists; the excise and other new taxes they thought obnoxious; the prompt suppression of the Whisky Rebellion in western Pennsylvania augured a strength in the new government dangerous to the sovereignty of the individual States. Jay's proposed treaty with England in 1794 furnished the occasion for the outbreak of as virulent an attack upon the administration and its motives as has been seen in this country. All things considered, the terms he secured from England were favorable; they were, however, so far below the expectations of the people that the outcry was immediate: the Federalists had sacrificed America to the British interest. In fact, the prompt success of the Federalist measures plus the unexpected changes in the economic situation had suddenly removed the "grinding necessity" which had extorted the Constitution from the reluctant majority.[4] The panic was over

4 "The great number of new and elegant buildings which have been

and the more timid as well as the more venturesome began to wonder whether things had not gone far enough.

The Anti-English, Anti-Federalist, anti-centralization movement found its leader in Thomas Jefferson, who really represented the majority whom Hamilton was seeking to rule. His early experience in Virginian politics and long residence on the frontier had brought him into contact with the sort of citizens who formed the majority in America; his long residence in France as ambassador had familiarized him with Rousseau's ideas of theoretical democracy and with their enthusiastic reception abroad. Soon after his return to America and his entrance into the Cabinet, he became acutely conscious of the antagonism between his notions of right and expediency and those of Washington and Hamilton, and, as well, appreciated the all-important fact that the latter were at variance with the majority of the people. He soon resigned from the Cabinet and went into open opposition. He sensed his own agreement with the people and began consciously to organize the Anti-Federalists and to prepare the way for the overthrow of the Federalists at the coming presidential elections. Through newspapers which he subsidized, through public meetings, private letters, and all other available methods, he carried on a systematic campaign to discredit the Federalist leaders and their policies in the eyes of the people. The arrival of the envoy of the new French Republic, Citizen Génêt, gave Jefferson an admirable opportunity, and he contrived to raise a good many other issues which put the Federal-

erected in this Town [Boston], within the last ten years, strike the eye with astonishment, and prove the rapid manner in which these people have been acquiring wealth. The revolutionary situation of Europe, has made them the most exclusive [extensive] Carriers of the Powers at War with Great Britain—their extensive Fisheries and Lumber Trade, with a great surplus of Provisions and other staple commodities for exportation, which they have been permitted, almost without restraint, to carry to Great Britain and her Islands, have filled them with that Wealth the operative effects of which are so visible in every direction, that they cannot fail to strike the eye of even a superficial observer." John Howe to Provost, May 5, 1808. *American Historical Review*, XVII, 78-9. Howe was sent by the Lieutenant Governor of Halifax to view and describe conditions in the United States.

ist administration apparently in the wrong and so rendered it
unpopular.

Even had the Federalists been supported at the first
by a clear majority of the people, and even if their
majority in the first Congresses and their victory in the first
presidential elections had not been partially due to a
disposition to give the men who had secured the adoption of
the Constitution a fair chance to put it into operation, Jefferson would have had little difficulty in defeating them
eventually, because they soon disagreed with each other over
vital policies. Hamilton, with all his brilliance and ability,
had not the tact needed to handle men who disagreed with
him; the difficulties were enhanced by the attitude of Jefferson and his subsidized press; and Hamilton was compelled
to resign from the Cabinet and direct the government's business from outside. While Washington remained President,
this was not difficult, but the inauguration of Adams at once
made trouble, for Adams personally distrusted Hamilton and
was angry at finding his own Cabinet officers seeking counsel
from Hamilton which he felt they should have asked of him.
The rift in the Federalist party grew greater and greater; the
rivalry for the leadership of its parts began to be keen; Jefferson had now perfected his organization and drew first the
people and then the leaders over to his side.

The presidential election of 1800 was even unnecessarily decisive: the Federalist support simply disappeared. John
Adams in a rage appointed as many officers as he could before the third of March 1801, made John Marshall Chief
Justice of the Supreme Court, and left Washington in high
dudgeon. From the victory flowed surprising results, but
none more astonishing than the complacency with which the
Anti-Federalists began to employ the powers which they had
so often denounced. Once in office, they found that the Constitution could be as easily interpreted to perform what they
thought right as it could to do what they thought wrong.
Jefferson, too, furnished a rule of interpretation which gave
general satisfaction, though its illustrious framer did not in-

variably observe it.   The Federal government should be "the American department of foreign affairs"; the strictest possible construction should be placed upon the broad phrases of the Constitution; the Federal government should do only what was absolutely necessary, never what seemed merely desirable; all else should be left to the States.   On the whole, declared Jefferson, the less government the better.   With the Constitution, thus interpreted, the vast majority were thoroughly well suited, and in general the talk about the wickedness and undesirability of central government disappeared. Jefferson had performed the very great service of reconciling the people to their own Constitution, of fostering that general consensus of opinion that the central government was a good thing and that its form and policy were about right, without which in the long run no government can exist.   He did it by interpreting the document in the light of the people's ideas instead of by the notions of its framers.

XV

THE WAR OF 1812

ONE great difficulty we meet in studying the long period be-between the adoption of the Constitution and the outbreak of the Civil War in 1861 lies in the necessity of remembering that the colonial issues were not completely settled in 1789 and did not then give way to entirely new issues around which subsequent events group themselves. The unity of American history is found rather in the identity of issues throughout our growth and development. The Revolution, the Constitution, and the victory of the Anti-Federalists had not definitely settled anything more than the two cardinal but none the less elementary facts, that England was not to interfere with our internal relations, and that a central government of some strength ought to be maintained. Still pressing for solution were the really fundamental difficulties,—our commercial relations with European nations and with their colonies, an economic difficulty of the first magnitude which the Revolution had only intensified; the relations of the States to each other and to the central government, the national issue; the powers of the central government, what sort of a central government did we want, the constitutional issue.

The Revolution had declared us politically independent of Europe, and the men of 1776 had apparently supposed that the winning of the war would free us from all the disagreeable commercial chains which bound us so closely to England and to her West India colonies. The Confederation had been the anti-national solution of the relations of the States to each other and had been put into effect by the radical party which had won the Revolution. Out of the economic crisis and the failure of the radicals to cope with it had grown the union of the conservative and propertied elements which had made possible the formulation and adoption in the Constitution of a distinctly national solution of the struggle between the States. Yet it was apparent, before the Constitution was adopted, that the national solution by no means satisfied every one and was eminently distasteful to a majority which grew in size and vehemence every year. The War of 1812 was the culmination of a period of unrest and dissatisfaction which had its real beginnings in the Anti-Federalist approval of the Whisky Rebellion and their opposition to the Jay Treaty. It was, like the Revolution, a struggle between forces in America as well as a war between England and America. Its causes were the same fundamental difficulties which had led to the Revolution and which were to lead to civil war in 1861: on the one hand, the economic dependence of this country on Europe, and, on the other, the fact that the States in America were neither one nation nor different nations, had neither the same interest nor different interests, were not independent but interdependent.

To the apparent surprise of the Americans, the Treaty of 1783 excluded them promptly from the English West India Islands and from the Newfoundland fisheries and gave them the status of foreigners, with absolutely no rights at all under English legislation and no privileges whatever under any other nation's regulations. Temporary arrangements, highly unsatisfactory to American merchants, had been made before 1789 with several countries, but the Federalist administration had quickly seen that better terms were essential and had sent Jay to England to negotiate a treaty. After weary months of argument, he was able to secure some agreement in regard to the evacuation of the western lands and other matters not regarded in America as imperative, but upon the vital matter of commercial relations and respect for our shipping on the high seas, so little was conceded that the Senate in high indignation rejected that clause of the treaty altogether. At the same time, considering the almost universal American hostility towards England, our failure to fulfil our earlier treaty obligations, the very general laudation of the French Revolution and of what the English deemed anarchistic sentiments, England was hardly to be blamed for displaying some reluctance at making substantial and valuable concessions which we were scarcely in a position to requite, and which really amounted to nothing less than the voluntary restoration on England's part of that complete freedom of intercourse which the States had long enjoyed as colonies and had so lately rejected with contumely as something quite worthless. Were the English then to forget that the Revolution had happened, to swallow our affronts and insults without resentment?

Moreover, the Jay Treaty episode was scarcely begun before circumstances had entirely altered the situation and every year made more inexpedient the resumption by England of the earlier *status quo,* even had pride and a natural resentment against disloyal subjects not continued to influence the English decisions. By 1800 the new facts were appallingly clear. Since the outbreak of the French Revolution and more especially since the beginning of the general European war in 1793, a market for American staple products had appeared in Europe, and a demand for neutral ships to handle the carrying trade. Both had redounded to the benefit of the United States, had caused our export trade to revive, had furnished us with the much needed medium of exchange with Europe, and had given an impetus to the growth of our merchant marine which made it a factor on the sea to be reckoned with. While the statistics are not perhaps very reliable, it seems reasonably clear that within a decade after 1792 the tonnage of American shipping increased five hundred per cent, from two hundred thousand tons to one million tons. England awoke to the existence of a new commercial rival whose operations threatened to interfere more and more every year with her monopoly of the carrying trade. Nor was it unnatural for her to conclude that we were allies of France and therefore pledged to her own destruction. We were making our chief profit out of supplying her enemies with food and out of carrying their trade in our neutral vessels from one point to another under the very noses of her cruisers. Fuel was of course added to the flames by the discovery that the old plan to annex Canada, which had been so prominent among the early movements of the Revolution,[1] was still alive and was received with great favor in the West and North. In 1789 and in 1804 something more than talk was on foot, though it was not and is not clear how far the matter went.[2] Should the English also supinely surrender Canada?

Accordingly, the English proceeded to treat us as they had treated other commercial rivals and fought us with the self-same weapons which had been so efficacious against the French, Dutch, and Spanish. They proclaimed at once the right to search all vessels on the high seas for contraband goods and refused as before to accept the doctrine that neutral ships make neutral goods. Everything going to France was contraband. In the West Indies and off Newfoundland the British cruisers did their best to enforce strictly the now doubly obnoxious provision of the old Navigation Acts and were more successful than ever before. The treatment accorded American vessels in English ports and American

[1] The attempts to obtain Canada during the Revolution are conveniently summarized by J. H. Smith in *Our Struggle for the Fourteenth Colony*, New York, 1907. Franklin's letters and the *Journal of the Continental Congress* contain pregnant and interesting information.

[2] Interesting material on the situation just previous to the War of 1812 is to be found in the secret reports of John Howe, an Englishman sent to the United States in 1808 to report upon conditions, popular and official opinions and intentions, to the Lieutenant Governor of Halifax, Sir George Provost. He made a very careful and thorough investigation and reported very fully upon what he saw and heard. "But, they say, we can take the British Provinces of Canada, Nova Scotia, and New Brunswick; . . . all the Military preparations in this Country can only have references to the British Colonies. . . . It is amusing to hear them talk here of the extreme facility with which they can possess themselves of the British Provinces." Howe to Provost, from Washington, Nov. 27, 1808. "The Conquest of Canada they contemplate as a matter perfectly easy; and whenever they speak of it they build much on the disposition of the Canadians as friendly to them. . . . Men of all parties think if a War should ensue that the Conquest of these Colonies is certain." Howe to Provost, May 19, 1809. *American Historical Review*, XVII, 342-3; 354.

sailors from the confiscated ships was captious and offensive. In the Mississippi Valley, the English still held important posts and incited revolts among the Indians.

But most obnoxious of all from the American point of view was the so-called "right" to arrest English deserters wherever they could be found and the defense of the operations of the press-gang. The English notion had always been that a man born in England would always be an English subject; they had always declined to recognize any oaths or acts of his as a valid release from his responsibility to England. To prove a man of English birth or to have been an English citizen was to prove he was still one. This notion of indefeasible allegiance therefore denied the right of an Englishman to take an oath of allegiance to the United States which would constitute a valid severance of his connections with England; it was tantamount to a refusal to recognize the citizenship of a very large number of Americans in 1800, who had no intention whatever of returning to England and felt nothing but hatred for that country. Here was of course a subject on which compromise was hardly possible: the right of the United States to protect its citizens was clearly infringed by the refusal of England to admit that large numbers of Americans were citizens of the United States at all.

The necessity for action on the part of the United States was particularly clear because of the operations of the English press-gang. The British navy was chiefly manned by conscripts and by men forced into the service by questionable methods. The press-gang from a battleship would go ashore in any town it happened to be near, whether in England or elsewhere, and seize by main force the sturdy-looking men it met, carry them off to the ship, and compel them to serve as sailors. Poor pay, bad food, strict discipline, degrading punishment, as well as the prospect of being killed in battle, made the service highly distasteful to Englishmen and particularly onerous to the unfortunates "pressed" into it. Desertions were therefore common and it was certainly true that many an American merchant-ship was manned by British deserters and that many and many an American citizen was a deserter from the English navy, who sought to save himself from the severe penalties for desertion by forswearing his allegiance. To cope with the difficulty, the English cruisers landed a press-gang in the various ports they called at and seized on sight and without investigation every man they thought looked like an English sailor. They also stopped American merchantmen on the high seas or in American harbors, lined up the crew, and selected those they thought were British deserters. Had they not also availed themselves of the opportunity to collect all likely-looking men without regard to their previous history or origin, the American case would still have been incontestable. There is no doubt that, by 1812, many men born in America, who had never set foot in England, had been thus forced into the British service. Had the English been willing to confine themselves to the merchant marine, the situation would not have become so intolerable. But the victories of Nelson made them even more arrogant than before and caused the detention of United States warships from which American citizens were taken and compelled to serve in the British navy.[3] A clearer insult to this country could hardly be conceived than this refusal to recognize the citizenship of the men enlisted in its official navy under the United States flag.

The growing tensity of English relations only made more apparent the divergence of opinion in the United States and stimulated the local discord which had for a time been ended by the success of the Federalist administrations. Scarcely had the loss of American privileges in the West India Is-

[3] "I am informed, by a gentleman on whose information I think I can rely," wrote Howe to Provost, "that when she [the famous frigate, *Constitution*,] was paid off here [at New York] and her men discharged, there was not twenty American sailors belonging to her, that her whole crew with the exception of a few other foreigners, was entirely composed of British seamen." June 7, 1808. *American Historical Review*, XVII, 86. Such information naturally encouraged the English government to continue the search. Nor were they displeased to learn from Howe that the majority of the people he met in New England admitted the justice of the English claims and acts. *Ibid.*, 89.

lands and in the fisheries been apprehended than talk of disunion and secession began in the Mississippi Valley. The people who had settled west of the mountains had come to realize that the Mississippi was the only possible outlet for their commerce and that the mouth of the river, and hence control of its navigation, was in the hands of Spain. They believed the Spanish anxious to close the river to American trade, and they so well appreciated the mutual advantages, both to the Spanish and to the Atlantic States, of the establishment of intercourse between the Spanish West India colonies and the Atlantic coast, that they were afraid Congress would allow Spain to close the Mississippi in exchange for commercial privileges in the Spanish West Indies. As early as 1786 this notion was current in the West, and, after the new Constitution had vested in the central government power to regulate commerce and to deal with western lands, the malcontents in Kentucky and Tennessee became sure that such was the design.[4] Negotiations were opened with the Spanish at New Orleans and at St. Louis,[5] and the Virginia and Kentucky Resolutions of 1798 were somehow connected with the agitation for secession.[6] With this western sentiment, the Southern States largely sympathized, and the Anti-Federalists all over the country were disposed to complain vigorously of English insolence and encroachment and to declare themselves in favor of no compromise and of an insistence upon demands to which England clearly would not accede.

In New England, on the other hand, and in mercantile circles all along the Atlantic coast, there was a disposition to insist less and negotiate more. Some sort of agreement with England was far more essential to them and their busi-

---

[4] *Writings of Washington,* Ford's ed., XI, 239; 240 note. Tyler's *Life of Henry* and Rowland's *Life of Mason.*

[5] The Missouri Historical Society, St. Louis, has a valuable collection of manuscript material on this subject. Houck's *Missouri* contains material from Spanish archives.

[6] *Writings of Jefferson,* Ford's ed., VII, 263, 281, 290 note. Jefferson's counsel against secession prevented further action.

ness than it was to the interior and western districts, and they realized far more adequately the impossibility of dictating terms to England, and the very great difficulty under the circumstances of obtaining from her a working compromise, that would give them a part of what they hoped ultimately to obtain. The mercantile community was therefore in favor of minimizing the disputes over the right of search and impressment, which militated against individuals rather than against the country as a whole and on which no compromise was possible, in the hope of obtaining some rights of navigation which would certainly redound to the benefit of the vast majority of Americans. The loud talk of reprisal upon English ships, the insistence upon reparation for insult, the general hostile tone assumed toward England, the laudation of France and everything French, these the New Englanders well knew only made more and more difficult the arrival at any agreement.[7] Even after the overt outrage against the *Chesapeake* in 1807, they hotly protested against anything being done likely to rouse the hostility of England.[8]

And now came in 1800, like a bolt from the blue, the news that Spain had ceded Louisiana to France. How large a territory it was, how far west it extended, what the character of the land was, no one knew, and few had more than the vaguest ideas about it; but one thing all apprehended; the

[7] "On general politics," Howe reported, "they appear more disposed to blame their own Government than ours. . . . The irritation against Great Britain is fast wearing off and the most anxious wish appears to be a renewal of the Commercial Intercourse between the Countries. . . . They feel how necessary her [England's] friendship is to their prosperity." *American Historical Review*, XVII, 79-80. Boston, May 5, 1808. From New York he wrote on May 31, of the feeling in Connecticut: "Here they speak upon the subject [the Embargo] with a degree of boldness that astonished me, and many of them even lamenting publicly that ever they were separated from Great Britain." *Ibid.*, 83.

[8] The *Chesapeake* affair is frequently mentioned by Howe, who concluded that the majority in New England took a stand against their own government. At Philadelphia he found a celebration of the anniversary of the affair, made to excite the people against England. "But it is by all discreet, well-disposed persons here (and this body I am happy to say is very numerous) looked upón with disgust." June 22, 1808. *Ibid.*, 94.

cession included New Orleans and the control of the Mississippi, and the diplomatic world promptly exhausted itself in surmises as to its purpose. Jefferson and his Cabinet, in common with most thinking men in the country, felt that the event in any case portended danger for the United States. "It completely reverses," wrote Jefferson to Dupont in Paris, "all the political relations of the United States, and will form a new epoch in our political course. . . . There is on the globe one single spot, the possessor of which is our natural and habitual enemy. It is New Orleans, through which the produce of three-fourths of our territory must pass to market."

To these fears succeeded the apprehension that England might seize Louisiana herself and thus unite the Gulf and the St. Lawrence by means of the Mississippi. Nor was there much doubt in Washington that the attempt of either France or England to establish a new empire would be promptly followed by the revolt or secession of the settlers in the Mississippi Valley from the United States and their adhesion to the new empire. Too many pledges of their readiness to join the Spanish had already been given to cause Jefferson to hesitate long. The crisis was, he wrote, "the most important that the United States have ever met since their independence [9] and which is to decide their future character and career." [10] An embassy was despatched to France to purchase enough land at the mouth of the river to place its navigation definitely in the control of the United States. [11] Napoleon, however, offered to sell the whole tract, moved perhaps by secret information of Jefferson's opinion that the attempt of France to use that land must force the United States to ally with England. For fifteen millions of dollars, Louisiana was sold. "The sale," said Napoleon, "assures forever the power of the United States and I have given England a rival who sooner or later will humble her pride." "To-day," proudly wrote the United States Minister to France, "the

[9] Note this significant use of the plural.
[10] *Writings of Jefferson*, Ford's ed., VIII, 203; 209, 210.
[11] *Ibid.*, VIII, 206.

United States take their place among the powers of the first
rank.'' [12]

The immediate effect was to bring to an abrupt termina-
tion the plots for the creation of revolutions in the Mississippi Valley, and to make possible the settlement of the difficulties with England without risking the secession of the
western States and Territories. The victory of the English
over the French and Spanish at Trafalgar in 1805, the almost immediate decision to enforce strictly the prohibitions
of the Navigation Acts and to stop direct trade between the
West Indies and Europe, followed by the war of decrees in
which the English and French effectually blockaded all trade
throughout the world so far as paper proclamations could
do it, all forced the United States to undertake negotiations
for a settlement. How hard-pressed the government was is
clear from the treaty negotiated with England in December
1806. The Americans were to be allowed to carry goods to
Europe from the West Indies by paying a duty upon them
to England, and, unless the United States at once resisted the
measures of Napoleon, the treaty would be void. Jefferson rejected it at once. Further decrees militating against American trade appeared in 1807; the frigate *Chesapeake* was fired
upon by the English ship *Leopard* and three American citizens and one English subject were seized from her crew.
Congress had already prohibited the importation of English
goods or colonial produce after certain dates, and now in 1807
an act forbade American vessels to sail for foreign ports.
The most vehement opposition to this Embargo at once
became evident in New England and most shipping-centers;
the act was evaded and even the Enforcement Act of the next
year was unavailing to do more than cause open resistance to
Federal authority along Lake Champlain and the probability of armed revolt in New England. The policy was obviously injuring Americans far more than the English or
French, who openly exulted over the folly of the Embargo;

[12] Note again this significant use of the plural in connection with the
United States.

the act was therefore repealed. After a long series of further attempts at legislation and negotiation, and after the receipt of further insults from the English, war was declared in 1812.[13]

The new policy was the result of the passing of the control to a new set of political leaders—Clay, Calhoun, and later, Webster. They demanded the "extortion" from England of favorable terms; the "avenging" of the slights and insults the United States had suffered; the conquest of Canada and the exclusion of the English from the continent.[14] But, without adequate preparation for defense or offense on land, without a numerous and powerful navy, without money or a definite method of obtaining it, success was hardly possible. Indeed, the same factors fought for us and against us as in the Revolution: the simple difference was that Washington and Greene had understood what those factors were and had used them with consummate skill; the men of 1812 seem hardly to have been conscious of their existence. The distance which separated us from England, the size of the theater of war, which had made it impossible for her to conquer us, made even more impossible the successful prosecution of an offensive war by the United States against England. To be sure, she was engaged in a life and death struggle with Napoleon and could hardly spare ships and armies to fight the United States effectively at the same time. If a decisive rapid attack could have been delivered upon Canada by a large and really efficient army, Canada might have been conquered, and the width of the Atlantic and the wild character of the land would probably have prevented reconquest by England. But the prime cause of the war and its only justification was impressment, the right of search, the

[13] Howe wrote to Provost in 1809: "Mad as Parties are in America, I do not think that a Majority of the Population wish a War with Great Britain. The warmest among them will frankly own, they do not see any benefit they could obtain by it." *American Historical Review*, XVII, 350.

[14] See in particular Clay's speeches during the session of 1813. *Annals of Congress*, 12 Congress, 2 session, especially pp. 667-676.

attainment of commercial privileges in Europe and in the West Indies, the recognition of American ships as neutral carriers, and the concession of a privileged status to all neutral shipping. The conquest of Canada and the destruction of British frigates could not conceivably put sufficient pressure on England to compel her to grant these demands of the United States. The war was foredoomed to failure and the winning of a few brilliant naval victories could not conclude the issue in our favor.

It was even more definitely decided against us by the outbreak of "civil war" in America. Ever since it had become apparent after the signing of the Treaty of 1783 that the commercial question had not been settled, the mercantile community and New England as a whole had more and more vehemently opposed the hostile attitude towards England assumed by the majority, and had more and more consistently declared for a policy of conciliation and the securing of such terms as could be had. The election of Jefferson had convinced the Federalists in New England that little was now to be expected from the central government and that their dearest hopes and most important interests would be sacrificed to the clamor of the mob. The purchase of Louisiana, the rejection of the various treaties framed with England between 1803 and 1812, the Embargo and non-intercourse legislation convinced them as the years went on that their expectations were only too certainly being realized. "We have a country governed by blockheads and dunces," the brother of the President of Yale College told the students; "our children are cast into the world from the breast and forgotten; filial piety is extinguished."

"The principles of our Revolution," wrote Pickering to Cabot in 1804,[15] "point to a remedy—a separation. . . . The people of the East cannot reconcile their habits, views, and interests with those of the South and West. . . . I do not

[15] This whole subject of secession and nullification in New England has been well covered by Henry Adams in *Documents Relating to New England Federalism*. 1800 to 1815. Boston, 1877.

believe in the practicability of a long continued union. The
Northern Confederacy would unite congenial characters, and
present a fairer prospect of public happiness; while the
Southern States, having a similarity of habits might be left
to manage their affairs in their own way." Not only did
the Federalists not believe one nation desirable or possible;
they were perfectly sure that none existed. Indeed, upon
the existence of three nations or groups of interests, they
based their plans and by this "fact" they justified their proposed secession. The annexation of Louisiana "was oppressive to the interests and destructive to the influence of the
Northern section of the confederacy," wrote John Quincy
Adams describing this plan years later, "whose right and
duty it therefore was to secede from the new body politic
and to constitute one of their own." The New England
States, which found the Union very much to their interest in
1860, quite forgot at that time that they had themselves espoused and believed constitutional and patriotic the same ideas
which the Southerners were then promulgating.

Hamilton's decision against the scheme, the discovery that
the immediate fears concerning the shift of influence to the
South and West were not realized, checked the secession movement in 1804. In 1807 and 1808, the disastrous effect of the
Embargo on New England revived it; armed rebellion seemed
almost certain, but the danger was averted by the repeal of
the act and by the expectation of relief from the renewal of
trade. When war was declared upon England in 1812, New
England determined to wait no longer. While the new confederacy was being organized and the movements concerted
which should make its secession final and successful, passive
resistance of the old colonial type was offered to the commands
of the Federal government. The New Englanders declined to
put their troops under command of United States officers, refused to allow them to serve outside the United States and
in some cases outside their own borders. In all these States,
loans were authorized and troops equipped for their own defense, an example followed in 1814 by New York, Pennsyl-

vania, and Virginia. New England was then the moneyed community and from its resources the Federal government had expected to finance the war. The New Englanders declined to loan money to the government and instead gave aid and comfort to the enemies of the United States, supplying the English fleets and armies with beef and fuel [16] and even with the specie to pay the troops.[17] At the crucial moment of the war, two weeks after the English had sacked Washington, one week after they had occupied parts of Maine, the State militia of Massachusetts, 70,000 well-equipped and drilled men, was withdrawn from the armies of the United States. Rhode Island and Connecticut followed suit and the three entered into bonds for mutual defense. Meanwhile, behind closed doors, the Hartford Convention was elaborating a new constitution and concerting measures for the independence of the New England States. The "civil war" in America was not yet over; the anti-national feeling was yet strong; the vision of a single nation was as yet seen only by a few individuals; but a great advance had been made towards nationalism. The old talk of the necessity of the independence and sovereignty of each separate State had disappeared; the thirteen sovereigns had been reduced to three—the East, the South, and the West. The development of the country and propinquity were doing their work slowly but surely.

The seriousness of this crisis has not been fully enough recognized. For some weeks, the fate of the union hung in the balance, for not only was New England clearly ready to secede, but there were grave fears in Washington that the Mississippi Valley would either attempt to secede or would offer its allegiance to England, fears which found ample con-

[16] "Supplies of the most essential kinds find their way not only to British ports and British armies at a distance, but the armies in our neighborhood with which our own are contending, derive from our ports and outlets a subsistence attainable with difficulty, if at all, from other sources." Madison, Special Message to Congress, Dec. 9, 1813. Richardson, *Messages and Papers of the Presidents*, I, 540-1.

[17] So the British authorities in Canada reported to England. See the quotations from manuscripts in the Canadian Archives in Henry Adams, *History of the United States*, VII, 146.

firmation in the news that an English army had been despatched to New Orleans.[18] There could scarcely be any
other reason for such an expedition than the expectation of
winning a great domain with the assistance of the inhabitants.
The fate of the United States was at stake in the winter of
1814 and 1815; the anti-nationalist movement seemed this
time certain of success and the creation of two new confederacies more than probable. At the critical moment came the
news of the signing of the Peace of Ghent with England and
of the victory of Jackson over the English at New Orleans.
The rejoicing was extreme, not in the least because the Treaty
of Peace accorded us the favorable terms which the war had
been undertaken to extort, but because the sectional strife in
America had been decided in favor of the Federal government.[19] The rebellions had been crushed without actual warfare; the union had been preserved without the memory of
deadly combat to stand in the way of reconciliation. The
Hartford Convention dissolved; the talk of secession died a
natural death; New England and the West tried to act as if
nothing had been intended, and the various parties and interests returned to Congress to debate the common problems.
Nothing had been settled; the cause of dissidence was still
present; but for the moment the solution by force or by secession was definitely abandoned by every one. When it was
next mooted, the development of the country had transferred
the seat of discontent to the South.

[18] Howe found in 1809 that "Great apprehensions are excited for the
Safety of Louisiana. A part of the new Levee of 6000 men has been
sent to that Quarter." *American Historical Review*, XVII, 349.

[19] So great was the anxiety in 1808 that Howe concluded that the
Federal government would declare war with England as a last desperate
expedient for holding the union together. "And if our Government
[the British] should not be disposed to let them out of their own Trap
[the Embargo], and the Government of America should continue their
present system, not a doubt can be entertained, but that a separation
of the Eastern States will ensue. If the answer of our Government
should not meet the wishes of the ruling Party, they will then endeavor
*to preserve the Union by plunging the Country into a War with Great
Britain,* in hopes that a sense of common danger, will excite a unanimity, they will have no other means of effecting." *Ibid.*

XVI

"THE AMERICAN SYSTEM"

THE War of 1812 scarcely improved the commercial relations of the United States with Europe, but it had a profound
influence on our history because it gave American statesmen
for the first time a clear conception of the fact that our
fundamental difficulties were economic and not political or
administrative, issues to be solved by the plow and the loom
rather than by the sword. The end of the war in 1815
happened practically to coincide with the close of the Napoleonic wars in Europe and the natural resumption of peaceful pursuits on the continent. Thus disappeared, in a moment, as it were, the market for American food-stuffs and
naval stores and the opportunity for American ships in the
carrying trade. Great as had been the dangers and serious
as had been the obstacles in the way of the complete utilization of the opportunity by Americans, many fortunes had
been built upon it and a really flourishing mercantile marine
had been developed. The resumption of manufactures on the
continent was a great blow to the English manufacturers,
whose business had flourished, not only because of the Industrial Revolution and the use of the new machinery, but
also because the state of war had left them the only manufacturers in Europe, and had given them, despite the militating regulations of Napoleon, almost a monopoly of the
European market. With the return of peace, their market
largely disappeared, a large surplusage of production resulted,
prices accordingly fell rapidly, and English goods at low rates
flooded the American market. The disappearance of our market abroad both during the continuance of the Embargo and
after the close of the war left the American merchants with

a large variety of produce which they could not sell and revealed to the eyes of even the blindest the fact that there was
no home market for what we produced. The flood of English
manufactured goods and the practical lack of anything else
on the American market made it equally clear that we did
not produce much of anything which we ourselves needed.
We were utterly dependent upon Europe to buy what we had
to sell and to produce for us what we wished to buy. And
Europe was three thousand miles away and was subject to
wars and commercial crises!

The period, which began with the institution of the Federal government in 1789 and closed with the War of 1812,
had been one of unusually rapid economic development in
America, and had produced an entirely new alignment of interests in the country. A distinct entity had begun to form
in the South concerned with the growing of cotton, another
in the North chiefly busied with the manufacture of cotton
cloth, and a third to the West intent upon the conquest of the
wilderness by the plow as rapidly as possible.

Cotton had been found by Columbus and had been used by
the early colonists sufficiently to cause it to be enumerated
by the Navigation Act in 1660 as a marketable commodity,
but it had never rivaled tobacco, indigo, or rice as a great
staple crop. A great variety of circumstances, juxtaposited
by chance, united to make it the long-sought medium of exchange between America and Europe, the valuable commodity
the demand for which in Europe should increase as fast as
the ability of America to increase its rate of production. The
pre-revolutionary non-importation agreements and the attempt
to find a substitute for woolens first called attention to it.
Then came the invention in England of machinery for spinning
and weaving cotton; and the accident of fashion created a
demand for the new cloth. At or about the same time (1786),
the first crop of the sea-island cotton, grown near Charleston,
S. C., was marketed, and the extraordinary length and the
soft and silky quality of its fiber was first appreciated. It met
at once with favor and within a few years was selling for a

dollar and even two dollars a pound. Cotton came as a god-send to the South. The Southerners were seeking a new staple crop, for the indigo industry had depended on the English bounty for its profit and had therefore been ruined by its discontinuance in 1775. The rice-cultivation was limited to the swamp lands of South Carolina and Georgia; and the European demand for American tobacco was always distinctly limited, since America did not produce the finest grades. Cotton therefore promptly attracted attention and was tried in many districts, and just as the planters had found that the upland cotton was filled with seeds so difficult to remove that the process destroyed both fiber and profit (the sea-island cotton was easy to clean), Eli Whitney invented a simple machine with which even an ignorant slave could rapidly cleanse huge amounts from seeds. The European demand, the new machinery to use the fiber, the gin to clean it, the need for a new Southern staple crop, all combined to make cotton within twenty years the greatest asset the South had and the most important single product of the Atlantic coast. 9,000 bales were produced in 1791; 211,000 were grown in 1801; and at the close of the war of 1812, 458,000.

Cotton made slavery profitable and therefore permanent. In 1789, it had been the rather general sentiment that slavery was likely to die of inanition and that its extension was hardly likely. In 1815, it was beyond question that a great and a permanent interest of the South had appeared which it did not share with other sections of the country.

As definite an interest, and one as obviously local, had appeared in New England and in the middle States. The Embargo, followed by the War of 1812, had compelled America to do without English goods and the high prices manufactured goods commanded had stimulated the production at home of cotton and woolen cloth, some pig-iron, glass, pottery, and a few other articles. Of all these industries "created" by the war, the most successful was cotton-spinning. In 1805, 4,500 spindles were at work; the imposition of the Embargo raised the number to 31,000 in 1809 and to 87,000 in 1810, while the war resulted in an expansion to 130,000 spindles. Where 1,000 bales of raw cotton had been used in 1805, 90,000 bales were being consumed in 1815. Slater at Pawtucket had introduced the new English machinery for spinning, and Lowell had instituted near Boston, in some of the first true factories in the world, power looms for weaving cotton cloth. All through New England, abundant water-power and unremunerative agriculture produced conditions favorable for manufactures. The new industries spread rapidly. Apparently the war had created industries and a new sectional interest as definite in its needs as the "peculiar institution" in the South.

Moreover, a third section had grown over night, as it were, in the Mississippi Valley. By 1815, on the great prairies where the Iroquois had so long hunted, where in 1783 had been only a few scattered hamlets and a few daredevil adventurers, were four fully organized States, Kentucky, Tennessee, Ohio, Louisiana, and five territories nearly populous enough for admission as States. The band of settlement had spread westward from the Hudson and Mohawk Valleys into the old Northwest Territory, from Virginia and North Carolina through the Cumberland Gap into Kentucky, Tennessee, Missouri, southern Illinois and Indiana, and west from Georgia and South Carolina into the rich river-bottoms of the Gulf country where cotton was most profitable. This last section became soon an integral part of the South, bound to it by an identity of interests, but the more northern districts found themselves above the cotton-belt and west of the mountains, shut off in the great river valley with characteristic problems of their own. The provision of adequate facilities of transportation by means of roads, canals, turnpikes, was seen at a very early date to be the most difficult problem, upon whose solution rested the possibility of an immediate development and utilization of the land. Unless the crop could be moved south or east, there was no purpose in raising more than the individual needed for his own sustenance. But the crop could not be moved and exchanged for manufactured goods without money, and of that the West had little and was never able to retain for long what little it did obtain. Compared to these, the more immediate problems of the division and allotment of land, the institution of administration, the taxation of undeveloped land, the provision for schools and universities were simple and were rapidly and on the whole admirably dealt with.

The net result, however, was the creation of three distinct and varying interests. Calhoun in an interview with Hammond in 1831 thus accurately described the situation. "He then spoke of the three great interests of the Nation, the North, the South, and the West. They had been struggling in a fierce war with each other, and he thought the period was approaching that was to determine whether they could be reconciled or not so as to perpetuate the Union. He was of the opinion that they could. The interest of the North was a manufacturing and protecting one, that of the South, Free Trade, and that of the West was involved in the distribution of the lands and Internal Improvements." This "fierce war" of which Calhoun spoke occupied the period from 1815 to 1840 to the practical exclusion of every other subject and to some extent has persisted throughout American history and is still of consequence. In this guise, the civil strife in America went on.

The great influx of English manufactured goods, which poured into the country in 1815 and 1816, drove the American cotton and woolen goods off the market. Under any circumstances, the new factories could scarcely expect to produce as cheaply as the English merchants could export goods, and certainly were helpless in competition with English goods sold actually at a sacrifice because of the overproduction. The cry went up from the new manufacturers: having created us by the Embargo and the war, you must now protect our infant industries. The logic of facts seemed undeniable. Before the war, no manufactures; after the war, flourishing industries; the Embargo and the war had been equivalent to a protection of 100%; therefore protection could create industries, and by protective tariffs American industries could be enabled to compete successfully with underpaid foreign labor. The argument of course was applied to the encouragement of industries, necessary to the country, sure to be profitable if started, but whose rise was prevented by superficial and artificial difficulties of a nature to be readily overcome by the imposition of a duty on the foreign product equivalent to the difference between the cost of manufacture in America and that in Europe plus the cost of freight. The essential point is that no permanent causes hindered the development of the industry, though it is only fair to add that the enthusiastic supporters of the tariff scouted the notion that there was an industry which could not profitably be pursued in the United States.

A low tariff had been imposed in 1789 and had proved its value as a money-getter by providing a sufficient revenue to meet the expenses of the new administration. Indeed, previous to 1860, the tariff provided nearly the whole Federal revenue. In 1816, a tariff was imposed, however, with the intention of protecting the new manufactures; the duties were all raised and new duties on textiles were imposed, amounting to about twenty or twenty-five per cent of the value of the article. An agitation against the high tariff was at once begun in the South and in many of the interior districts, which had depended entirely on Europe for manufactured goods and which still depended on finding a market abroad for the great staples, tobacco, cotton, and rice. To their thinking, the new scheme was intended to force them to pay for the development of manufactures in the East, to compel them to renounce their own particular interest, which lay of course in complete freedom of trade, and particularly in the ability to bring back into the country as large an amount of goods as possible in return for the product they exported. This they complained was unfair; the interest of one section was favored at the expense of the interest of another.

In 1820 and in 1824, Clay and others fought valiantly

for "the American system" of encouraging home manufactures, and in the end their logic won the day. "We
have shaped our industry, our navigation, our commerce,"
Clay told the House in 1824,[1] "in reference to an extraordinary war in Europe, and to foreign markets which no longer
exist. . . . Whilst we have cultivated with assiduous care our
foreign resources, we have suffered those at home to wither
in a state of neglect and abandonment." "We have seen
that our exclusive dependence upon the foreign market must
lead to still severer distress, to impoverishment, to ruin. We
must give a new direction to some portion of our industry.
We must speedily adopt a genuine American policy. Still
cherishing the foreign market, let us create also a home
market, to give further scope to the consumption of the
produce of American industry. Let us counteract the policy
of foreigners, and withdraw the support which we now give
to their industry, and stimulate that of our own country. . . .
The creation of a home market is not only necessary to
procure for our agriculture a just reward for its labors, but
it is indispensable to obtain a supply of our necessary wants.
If we cannot sell, we cannot buy. . . . We must naturalize
the arts in our country . . . by adequate protection against
the otherwise overwhelming influence of foreigners."

That the protective tariff was likely to burden the South
and West, Clay clearly appreciated and a distinctive part of
the "American system" was the open recognition of the
necessity of protecting the special interests of all three sections. "Now our people," he declared, "present the spectacle of a vast assemblage of jealous rivals, all eagerly rushing to the seaboard, jostling each other in their way, to
hurry off to glutted foreign markets the perishable produce
of their labor. The tendency of that policy, in conformity
to which this bill is prepared, is to transform these competi-
tors into friends and mutual customers, and, by the reciprocal
exchange of their respective productions, to place the con-

[1] This and other valuable papers and speeches on the tariff will be
conveniently found in Taussig's *State Papers and Speeches on the Tariff*.

federacy upon the most solid of all foundations, the basis of common interest." "Our confederacy comprehends within its vast limits great diversity of interests, agricultural, planting, farming, commercial, navigating, fishing, manufacturing. No one of these interests is felt in the same degree and cherished with the same solicitude throughout all parts of the Union. Some of them are peculiar to particular sections of our common country. . . . Here, then, is a case for mutual concession, for fair compromise. . . . It sacrifices the interest of neither section to that of the other; neither, it is true, gets all that it wants, nor is subject to all that it fears."

The peculiar interest of the South had already been a subject of great concern and recognition of its seriousness had already been ample. Profit from cotton cultivation was even thus early seen to depend upon the ability of the planter to shift his slaves from the fields partially exhausted by successive crops to new virgin soil where the proportionate return for the labor was enormously greater. So great was it, that the Southerners regarded in the light of a calamity the arrival of the day when the supply of virgin land should be exhausted and the cotton-culture should be forced to become intensive instead of extensive. By 1819, the whole of the land east of the Mississippi available for cotton had already been settled sufficiently to be divided into States and admitted to the Union. The resort thither of planters was seen to be progressing at a rate which would within a decade or two exhaust the supply of the very best land. West of the river in the great domain of Louisiana, the southern corner had early been settled and admitted to the Union, and now in 1819 a second great State, Missouri, was knocking for admission.

The question of the extension of slavery was not at the time, however, of as momentous consequence as the preservation of the balance of power between the particular interests in Congress. The House, whose members were proportioned among the States according to population, was already controlled by the States which found staple crops unprofitable and which could therefore not be expected to defend either free trade or slavery. In the Senate, where the States were each represented by two members, the balance between the slave and free States were exactly even, and had always been so, due to the admission of the new States in pairs, cne free and one slave. Now Maine and Missouri had both applied for admission, and, should both be admitted as free States, the South would at once be in the minority and the sacrifice of its agricultural interests to the manufactures of the East seemed to be an almost certain result of the loss of political equality.[2] The difficulty was frankly recognized; the right of the South to sufficient power to protect itself, conceded. But the principle itself—that the interests of the three sections of the country were mutually antagonistic, and destructive of each other, and that only a balance of power between them in the national government could

[2] This was a notion long familiar and had been stated in 1811 with great force and clarity by Josiah Quincy of Massachusetts in a notable speech in the House of Representatives. The admission of Louisiana would be, he claimed, "nothing less than [the exercise of] a power, changing all the proportions of the weight and influence possessed by the potent sovereignties composing this Union. [Note this acceptance of States' sovereignty by a Massachusetts man.] . . . This is not so much a question concerning the exercise of sovereignty, as it is who shall be sovereign. . . . The Proportion of the political weight of each sovereign State, constituting this union depends upon the number of the States, which have a voice under the compact. [Hayne used this same word to designate the Constitution in 1830.] . . . I hold my life, liberty and property, . . . by a better tenure than any this national government can give. . . . We hold these by the laws, customs, and principles of the commonwealth of Massachusetts. Behind her ample shield, we find refuge and feel safety. . . . With respect to this love of our union, concerning which so much sensibility is expressed, I have no fear about analyzing its nature. There is in it nothing of mystery. . . . I confess it, the first public love of my heart is the Commonwealth of Massachusetts. There is my fireside; there are the tombs of my ancestors. . . . The love of this union grows out of this attachment to my native soil and is rooted in it. I cherish it because it affords the best external hope of *her* peace, *her* prosperity, *her* independence." This will be destroyed when the western States are admitted, for they will outnumber the original States. Hart, *Contemporaries*, III, 410-414.

preserve the Union—was felt to be fraught with the greatest danger for the welfare of all. That the question should be not simply an issue of morals or of rival institutions but of the political power of great sections of the country whose interests seemed to be and certainly were assumed to be irreconcilable, was seen to contain possibilities which caused all to fear for the future. "The words civil war and disunion are uttered almost without emotion," wrote Clay,[3] while Cobb of Georgia predicted that the Northern men had "kindled a fire which all the waters of the ocean cannot put out, which seas of blood only can extinguish."[4] Clay even predicted the establishment of new confederacies, while John Quincy Adams entrusted to his diary thoughts regarding the desirability of dissolving the union and reorganizing it "on the fundamental principle of emancipation." As to civil war, he went on, "so glorious would be its final issue, that as God shall judge me, I do not say that it is not to be desired."[5] Almost calmly, Northern and Southern men considered the dissolution of the "confederacy" and decided that end not undesirable. Not yet was there anything approaching an agreement that the existence of one government, of one nation composed of all the individuals in America, either existed or could exist or ought to exist. The loyalty of men to their States had been transferred to their sections; it was yet to be transformed into allegiance to the country as a whole.

The difficulty was compromised in 1820 by the admission of Maine as a free State, of Missouri as a slave State, and by the division of the Louisiana Purchase into two zones, one, north of 36° 30', which should be free territory, and one south of that line which should be slave territory.

The West had yet to receive its share of the compromise and clamored for Internal Improvements. In 1808, Gal-

---

[3] *Private Correspondence*, 61.

[4] *Annals of Congress*, 15 Cong., 2 Sess., I, 1204.

[5] *Memoirs*, IV, 531. See also *Writings of Jefferson*, Ford's ed., X, 157.

latin, whose financial ability had gone far to make the Anti-Federalist régime successful, recommended a Federal system of roads and canals to open up the great areas in the Mississippi Valley. These would obviously be of great value if proper facilities of transportation could be provided. As yet, however, their inhabitants did not themselves possess sufficient capital to promote so costly an undertaking. The benefit would really redound to the country as a whole and furnished reason for the adoption of a policy of Internal Improvements by the Federal government. To the declaration that sufficient powers were not vested in Congress by the Constitution, answer was made that the right to charter a bank and to purchase Louisiana were not explicitly mentioned either. There was a general feeling that the development of the Southwest and of the Ohio Valley by Federal money would be a discrimination in favor of those States against the East; but to prove that roads and canals were necessary was to establish, to the satisfaction of the western men, the constitutionality of the power to build them. Was the Constitution made only for the eastern States? In 1817 and 1818, projects were introduced in Congress by Calhoun and Clay for a comprehensive system of internal improvements and in 1818 the national road from Cumberland on the Potomac to Wheeling was finished; but nothing further was done till 1825, when Adams approved of a broad project and over two millions of dollars were voted for the building of roads in the West. A plan was also mooted to distribute the lands reserved to the Federal government in the western States to settlers at fifty cents an acre instead of the rate of two dollars and a half already established.

The appropriation of money for internal improvements and the tariff of 1828, which raised the duties so much that it was promptly dubbed the Tariff of Abominations, roused the South to indignation. Calhoun became spokesman and in his "Exposition" tried to demonstrate that the tariff and the internal improvements were responsible for the low price of cotton and the high price of other commodities. The tariff stole the profit of the cotton-crop by compelling the planters to pay a duty on the goods they bought with the proceeds abroad; the indirect taxes of the government further depleted their incomes to furnish the money to build roads in the West. The attempt of the government to foster the interests of the other sections was injurious to the South. In South Carolina plans were made to "nullify" the obnoxious Federal laws by an appeal to the reserved powers of a sovereign State.

In reality, the general commercial crisis of the period following the close of the Napoleonic wars was the cause of most of the difficulties in the South. The demand for cotton in Europe was not as great as before because the overproduction of the earlier years had been succeeded by retrenchment; the production of cotton at the South had however increased by leaps and bounds and the supply was therefore greater, though the demand was smaller; a great drop in price was inevitable. On the other hand, manufactured goods had been abnormally cheap in the South because of the overproduction in England, the resumption of manufacture in Europe, and the growth of industries in New England. The supply in this direction had far exceeded the demand and had consequently reduced prices. The reduction of the output in Europe necessary to restore the normal balance between the demand and the supply had begun, however, by the time the tariff of 1824 was passed; had raised the prices on manufactured goods considerably, and the increase was of course attributed by the South entirely to the tariff, whose avowed purpose had been to increase the price of foreign goods in America. Furthermore, in the States just north of the cotton-belt, in the tobacco-belt, the border States, as they came to be called, Virginia, Maryland, Kentucky, Tennessee, and Missouri, slavery was no longer as profitable as it had once been, and the commercial crisis had accentuated the planters' troubles until plans were actually proposed in Virginia for the purchase and deportation to Africa of the surplusage of slaves.

To the excited Southerners, the union, the existence of the Federal government, seemed solely responsible for their ills. Did it not allow the North and West to pass the tariff? Did not the Constitution recognize and legalize this sacrifice of the interests of a part and that too without possibility of immediate redress by legislative methods? Of what value was such a union? "I consider the Constitution a dead letter," declared John Randolph in the House of Representatives in 1824. "I have no faith in parchment, sir. . . . If you draw the last shilling from our pockets, what are the checks of the Constitution to us? A fig for the Constitution! . . . There is no magic in the word union." The President of South Carolina College was cheered when he said in a public meeting that the time had come to calculate the value of the Union, and Webster later declared himself convinced in 1828 that the plan for a Southern Confederacy had been generally received with favor by the Southern leaders. Was that whither the United States was tending, to separation into two confederacies? When the value of the Constitution was calculated was there nothing but a piece of parchment, and no magic in the word union?

Senator Hayne of South Carolina had delivered a powerful speech in the Senate in favor of the old anti-national view of the central government. He obviously looked upon the union as a question of present and even temporary expediency, "nothing more than a mere matter of profit and loss," complained Webster; not as the embodiment and representative of a great and glorious nation but as a connection between the States whose beneficial operation was sufficiently doubtful to require constant and careful inspection of its working in order to determine the expediency of its longer continuance. When he declared the Constitution "a compact" to which the States were the parties, he denied that the Constitution had created a nation or that one existed. The States were sovereign, he insisted, had always been sovereign and had never in any way explicitly or implicitly parted with their sovereignty; and were therefore, as parties to the compact, obviously capable of judging whether the compact for the creation of a central government had been observed and whether or not it was expedient to continue under it. The nature of the general government as defined by its own Constitution made it incapable of coercing a State which solemnly and advisedly declined longer to obey the Federal statutes. If the Federal government were to be allowed to interpret the Constitution and decide upon the extent of its own powers, the sovereignty, independence, and liberty of the States would disappear, and the United States would be, what its framers had never intended it to be, an entity in and of itself superior to the States, which would then be bound to obey its behests. To say that the Constitution prevented the Southern States from nullifying the recent oppressive acts of the Federal government would mean that those States had no resource against tyranny, save armed rebellion.

He appealed to the founders of the Republic, to the debates of the Constitutional Convention, to the Virginia and Kentucky Resolutions. His was, he claimed, the historical Republican doctrine, "first promulgated by the fathers of the faith," whose triumph in 1800 had "saved the Constitution at its last gasp." "Give us the Constitution of Jefferson," he exclaimed, "give us the federal compact of independent sovereign States, . . . the Constitution of 1787 as its framers meant it and constructed it, and we shall deem ourselves satisfied and safe." That Hayne had accurately described the idea of the Constitution held by the majority of people in most districts since 1789 it was difficult to deny; that upon those assumptions every section of the country had planned secession and nullified Federal measures was equally incontestable; but, if such were the truth, it was equally clear that no nation existed in America nor could be created so long as a powerful section of the community stood ready to contest the expediency and desirability of its existence. Hayne took his stand upon precedent and history, upon present expediency, and made the welfare of individual States his criterion of the excellence of union. To his thinking, unless absolute unanimity of opinion existed, unless every State were convinced that its interests were furthered by the federal bond as it would itself have advanced them had it been wholly independent, the union was inexpedient.

Webster, in his great speech in reply, delivered early in the year 1830, took his stand upon the Constitution as it was, not as it had been thought to be; the document itself, he said, would clear all controversies. He took as his test of expediency the welfare of all the States and insisted that the welfare of each individual State would be better served by union than by disunion. Above the States, he placed the nation: the Constitution was not a compact between States, sovereign entities, but a supreme and fundamental law created by the people of the whole country, making of them one nation. "The truth is . . . the people of the United States are one people. . . . The very end and purpose of the Constitution was to make them one people in these particulars; and it has effectually accomplished its object. . . . It is the People and not the States who have entered into this compact, and it is the people of all the United States." Webster took the highest possible ground and declared that a nation already existed, had long existed, and that the sovereignty of the States had been surrendered by the adoption of the Constitution. He thus decided in the negative all the issues Hayne had raised. The Federal government and the State governments were both limited in power; both were founded by the people, and controlled by them; but of the two, pending further action of the people, the Federal government was supreme. Upon it, through the Constitution, the people as a whole had conferred the right to decide all disputes as to the meaning of the Constitution. Secession and nullification by any State were under the Constitution impossible. "Sir, the very chief end, the main design for which the whole Constitution was framed and adopted was to establish a government that should not be obliged to act through State agency or depend on State opinion or State discretion.'' From the Union had resulted safety at home, ''national, social, and personal happiness.'' In his peroration, he pronounced as a rallying cry for the men of his own day and of a later generation, the flaming words—''dear to every true American heart''—''Liberty and Union, now and forever, one and inseparable.''

For the first time, the great majority of Americans saw what their Constitution actually said; for the first time they realized that it proclaimed the creation of one nation; for the first time under impressive circumstances, a man of prominence boldly proclaimed the actual existence of *a nation,* declared himself proud of it and eloquently argued for its ''continuance.'' The vision of nationality was seen; it had now to be realized.[6]

It was even doubtful whether it would not be at once authoritatively denied. The jubilation in New England found no echo in the South. What attitude President Jackson would take was not known. At a great banquet to celebrate the birthday of Jefferson, a series of toasts was arranged to put the issue squarely before the President and to force him to declare himself for one nation or for a compact of sovereign States. Amid breathless silence, Jackson pulled his lank form erect and gave his toast: ''Our Federal Union. It must be preserved.''

[6] The truth of this statement can scarcely be better demonstrated than by quoting the conclusions of one of the keenest foreign observers who ever visited this country. Alexis de Tocqueville described what he saw and heard here in 1834–5. "We ought not to confound the future prospects of the republic with those of the Union. The Union is an accident, which will only last as long as circumstances are favorable to its existence; but a republican form of Government seems to me to be the natural state of the Americans. . . . The Union exists principally in the law which formed it; one revolution, one change in public opinion might destroy it forever; but the republic has a much deeper foundation to rest upon. . . . It was impossible at the foundation of the States, and it would still be difficult to establish a central administration in America. The inhabitants are dispersed over too great a space, and separated by too many natural obstacles, for one man to undertake to direct the details of their existence. America is therefore preëminently the country of provincial and municipal government." *Democracy in America*, I, 425-6. London, 1875.

The advisability of national government had been argued, its expediency questioned; statements freely made that a second confederacy was far preferable to a national bond; but there was little doubt that the North agreed with Webster and stood for one nation and rejected the notion of two.

Characteristically, the difficulty was compromised. Where, in 1824, the policy of the satisfaction of all interests had been espoused, Jackson pronounced himself in favor of the restriction of Federal powers and refused to assist any interest. States' rights and nullification he declined to recognize. South Carolina must submit to Federal authority.

At the South there was no desire to force the issue at this time; they felt sure of obtaining what they asked by some simpler method than a test of strength. For the South had control of the Federal government and was growing so fast in wealth and strength that an equally rapid development of the North seemed hardly possible. There was little to gain, they thought, by actual secession and the concession of a victory to Webster in the forum did not seem materially to affect the real issue. The talk of secession was therefore dropped.

To remove the most obvious grievances, the high tariff was repealed and a low one adopted; the internal improvements which the West demanded were declared unconstitutional. As the West and South both objected to the existence of the United States Bank and attributed to its manipulations the scarcity of currency in their territory and their condition as debtor communities, the Bank was also declared unconstitutional, an "un-American monopoly," and was brought to a sudden end as a governmental agency by the removal of Federal deposits in 1833 to certain selected State banks. The government declined to renew the charter, and completely changed the fiscal policy of Hamilton. Finally, after various expedients had been tried and rejected, an independent Treasury was established in 1843 into which the government's funds were to be paid, where they were to be conserved, whence the currency was to be issued and controlled, and by which, in general, the fiscal business of the government was to be transacted. If the advocates of nationality had now a theoretical victory in the forum, the anti-nationalist party had shorn the Federal government of such national functions as it had been discharging and had in large measure reversed many of its most important policies. Webster might be right as to what the Constitution said; but States' sovereignty would be safe until the people as a whole should read the document through his spectacles and should elect an administration to enforce his reading of its provisions.

XVII

JACKSONIAN DEMOCRACY

IT is not possible in so brief a sketch as this to do more than advert to the significant constitutional development of the period from 1789 to 1829 during which the warp and woof of American democracy became thoroughly established, but it is essential at least to enumerate the conspicuous elements which practice introduced into the original concept.

The democratic institutions which to-day exist in the United States are too firmly knit into the "bone and gristle" of the nation and are too clearly adapted to our conditions to have been "created" by any one document or by any one man. Because certain definite stages of development became perfectly clear at certain epochs, because certain men were largely responsible for informing the public mind of the conditions actually existing and for directing its choice of a remedy, we have been in the habit of writing about Hamiltonianism, Jeffersonianism, and Jacksonianism. In reality the theories and concepts, the administrative machinery by which we have actually been governed, are too complex and too numerous to have been produced by anything short of the slow growth of the community. "It is a great mistake," said Mr. Mercer in the Constitutional Convention, "to suppose that the paper we are to propose will govern the United States. It is the men whom it will bring into the Government and interest in maintaining it that is to govern them. The paper will only mark out the mode and the form. Men are the substance and must do the business." [1] The form of the Constitution was evolved in the various State constitutions made during the Revolution; the federal idea came from an

[1] Hunt's *Madison's Notes*, II, 165.

attempt to find some solution for the economic difficulties whose pressure was so seriously felt after the war was ended; the first administrative traditions were created by the pressure of necessity and the genius of Hamilton. Jeffersonian democracy, on the other hand, was the product of the various attempts to interpret the actual document called the Constitution; while Jacksonian democracy, in which we recognize the final product of American genius, was caused by the growth of the country, especially of the West, and by the attempt to "live" democracy.

The Constitution of the United States is a very large document indeed and provides for the doing of many things not foreseen by the framers of the "paper" and for the doing of many things they saw would be necessary, in other ways than those they deemed best. With the passage of the twelfth amendment in 1801, the feature most admired by the framers was practically abandoned. It had not been thought desirable that the people should in any direct way influence the selection of the President, and accordingly an electoral college had been provided which the people should elect and which should then calmly and deliberately vote for the fittest man for the highest post, the candidate receiving the next largest number of votes, indicated therefore in the electors' opinion as most desirable second choice, to become Vice-President. The electors were forced by the Constitution to meet in the various States and to vote in absolute ignorance of what was actually being done elsewhere. After the first two elections, it became apparent that some sort of previous agreement among the electors would be essential to prevent a too great scattering of the votes and the accidental choice by a ridiculously small minority of some obviously unsuitable and objectionable candidate. So completely successful was the attempt at previous agreement in 1800 that Jefferson and Burr received the same number of votes, no candidate received a majority, the election was thrown into Congress, and an unseemly scramble for votes ensued, in which Jefferson, whom nearly every one desired for President, was almost defeated.

An amendment was at once passed providing that the electors should vote for both President and Vice-President instead of simply for President. The provision that the electors should meet in their own States was not changed.

Despite the amendment, the desirability of a previous arrangement, generally understood, in regard to the fittest candidate was still obvious. Otherwise, the electors voted in the dark, practically threw the State's vote away, and permitted the few States who would go to the trouble of a previous agreement to elect any candidate they chose, without giving the rest even a chance to vote against him. The right to defeat a certain candidate was soon seen to be as significant, and perhaps of more practical importance, than the right to select the man really preferred. It had been the habit in the various States from the earliest times to nominate candidates for executive positions in a caucus, composed of the members of the legislature, which met for the purpose after the regular session was over. The voters in the towns and counties could not spare the time to come to the capital and found it much more satisfactory to vote for or against certain men, whom their representatives from the legislative caucus told them were being voted on elsewhere, than it was to vote at random. This flourishing institution, the caucus, long familiar to all the members of the first Federal congresses, was at once employed to solve the self-same difficulty, and to its deliberations we owe the choice of Madison and Monroe. The electors were not compelled to vote for the caucus candidate; but it was safer, for he invariably received enough votes to elect. Other candidates were frequently put into the field, men of excellent character but not widely enough known to cause that sort of unanimous decision as to their fitness which had been responsible for the choice of Washington and Jefferson. Indeed, by 1820, it was seen that no candidate, however admirable, would stand any chance in opposition to the caucus candidate without the same definite previous agreement, scrupulously observed, to vote for him in enough States to command a majority in the electoral college. The congressional caucus had been invoked to prevent haphazard voting and had literally taken the choice of President away from the electors and put it into the very hands deemed most unfit by the framers of the Constitution, into the hands of the legislature.

As each successive election more and more clearly demonstrated the power of the caucus and the fact that its nomination was equivalent to election, the advantages which would result from its manipulation were appreciated by the less scrupulous. In 1820, Crawford, a politician of unsavory reputation and little ability, nearly secured the nomination, and the news thoroughly frightened and aroused the country. The fact that the people did not directly elect mattered little, for the electors had for years never used their prerogative of choice and had nearly always voted as directed by their constituents. The people were really robbed of their right to choose.

To break the power of the caucus, to restore the right of selection to the people (a right which it had already been forgotten had been thought most undesirable by the framers of the Constitution), an attempt was begun in 1822 to obtain by previous announcement and hard work a sufficient consensus of opinion in favor of some one man to enable him to defeat the next candidate of the caucus. Clay was nominated by the legislature of Kentucky two years before the election of 1824 and was soon only one of sixteen or more candidates, all nominated in a similar way, among whom Jackson was clearly most popular with the masses. The caucus, by this time thoroughly unpopular, was thinly attended in 1824 and nominated Crawford and Gallatin. Jackson, Adams, and Clay had all been nominated independently by friends in most of the States and something like a real vote by the people on all the candidates for President took place. Jackson, Adams, Crawford, and Clay all received a considerable vote in the order named, but none had sufficient for a choice, and Congress was after all to choose between them. A great deal of excited discussion and the passing of promises between Adams and Clay finally made the former President. Mr. Clay's adherents were strong in the House of Representatives and he was able to control enough votes to decide the matter in Adams's favor, with the understanding, faithfully observed by Adams, that Clay should become Secretary of State. The result was loudly denounced by Jackson's supporters; the people had been again defrauded. Jackson had received easily the largest popular vote and a plurality in the electoral college, and had been "robbed" of his rights by the "corrupt deal" between Adams and Clay. War to the death was declared; the most elaborate arrangements yet made preceded the election of 1828 and Jackson was triumphantly swept into the presidential chair.

While he received nearly double the number of votes in the electoral college that Adams did, the estimated popular vote showed something approaching equality, and the number of States in which the vote had been close was sufficient to give the opposition hope of reversing the result. The caucus was dead indeed, but it was even more apparent than ever that if the minority were to prevail or the majority maintain their position, both must organize even more carefully than before. The amount of labor involved in the method of nomination pursued in Jackson's case was so great that it seemed hardly likely to succeed again, and much more likely to reproduce the situation of 1824 and throw the election into the hands of Congress. The campaign of 1832, therefore, saw in the field a new organization, nothing more nor less than a caucus or convention chosen by the people expressly for the purpose of nominating a candidate and of formulating a policy. The name "National Republicans" was adopted, Henry Clay nominated for President, and the first party "platform" or policy announced. The Democrats promptly followed suit and by a similar convention nominated Jackson again.

Thus originated the two great national parties, whose influence has dominated Federal politics ever since and which are the most important part of the machinery designed by

Jackson and his supporters to make effective the new democratic maxim, the direct rule of the people. As Calhoun put
it, "Let the people have the power directly." Needless to
add, no idea had been further from the minds of the framers
of the State and Federal constitutions. Colonial democracy had been a limited democracy where the fit acted for the
unfit; it had favored indirect influence by the majority, and
had allowed the people in Federal government even less actual
participation than in State government, restricting their
share to the choice of the presidential electors, of representatives, and of the State legislatures which elected the senators. Indeed, the electors had been by no means infrequently
chosen by the legislatures prior to the Jacksonian régime.
Jackson proclaimed the right of the people to direct influence
in local, State, and Federal government and, whether or not
as a direct result of his campaign, certainly universal manhood suffrage became the slogan in the States, and of course
the States, having in their hands the provisions for the Federal suffrage, promptly projected manhood suffrage into Federal politics.

Herein Jacksonian democracy differed from Jeffersonian
democracy. Jeffersonian democracy had laid stress upon the
proper scope of central government, upon the proper interpretation of the Constitution, upon the relation of the individual to the central government rather than upon the
definition of "the people." On the whole, its august founder
had been content with the limitations upon the suffrage common at the time and had felt that local and State governments were in their existing condition almost ideal. He had
been concerned with guarding the individual from the new
colossus, Federal government, had been anxious to limit its
province as much as possible, with the idea that the less direction the individual received from without, the better; the
freer he could be from all interference beyond what other
individuals had a right to exert by an appeal to the judiciary,
the better it would be for him and for the community.
Could the strict interpretation of constitutions and laws be-

come an actuality, all desirable results would follow. That elaborate machinery would be necessary to enable the people even formally to participate in elections and to influence the policy of the State, he declined to believe. After all, it must be remembered that the form of Jeffersonian democracy was largely due to the fact that it was a reaction from the Hamiltonian notion of a strong centralized administration which should effectively correlate and direct the energies of the individuals who composed the community.

Similarly, Jacksonian democracy was a revolt against the machinery which had been developed to express a decision for the people. The people could act directly, must act directly, and needed no mediator. It was not Jackson, however, so much as Webster who gave the idea immediate currency and stability by showing a delighted and astonished public that their own Constitution vested in the people, in the new Jacksonian sense, the ultimate power of decision. "It is, Sir," said Webster in that famous reply to Hayne of 1830, "the people's Constitution, the people's government, made for the people, made by the people, and answerable to the people." Upon Hayne, he cast the stigma of maintaining a notion repugnant to democracy, that the States and not the people were sovereign. The subtleties of Hayne's doctrine he brushed aside; its historical defense he ignored with magnificent assurance, conscious that for the first time the American people would see that States' rights was in essence undemocratic and contrary to the notion of the supremacy of the people as individuals. That it was also an anti-national doctrine, he declared with eloquence, but this the people did not as yet grasp. It is this reading of the new Jacksonian democracy into the Constitution, the realization of what the words of the document actually said, the failure to know that he was not using the words "the people" in the sense common in 1789, that made Webster's 1830 speech a landmark in our constitutional history.

States' sovereignty was undemocratic! The notion so completely harmonized with the interests and desires of the New

Englanders that it was caught up at once and became the basis of their political thinking. Behind the ideal of nationalism, Webster had definitely placed Jacksonian democracy and a reading of the Constitution whose cogency and accuracy it was impossible to deny. Historical evidence, quotations from the fathers, all were and always will be futile against Webster's dramatic, eloquent reading of the words of the document. Moreover, Webster made the word "union" synonymous with nationalism, and made nationalism equivalent to strong central government, all of which he asserted was provided by this same democratic Constitution. Yet the idea of union was less potent in causing the popularity of the speech than the proof that the Constitution itself already contained the idea of democracy and popular rights, the proof that Jackson was right and the caucus wrong. Jefferson had been able to show the anti-nationalists that the Constitution could be read in their sense and that the grant of power did not necessarily presume its abuse or even its use. It had remained for Jackson and Webster to prove that the Constitution explicitly enthroned radical democracy: —that the interpretation of the document and of the powers granted by it rested not with the States or with the Federal officials but with the electorate.

Along with this fundamental change in the notion of who were the people went the development of legislative, administrative, and judicial forms and traditions. The House of Representatives was soon after 1789 forced by the exigencies of the situation to develop the committee system, the rules for restricting debate, and the enormous power of the Speaker, which really to-day have taken from the House itself the power of legislation. As the Constitution was the work of Madison and Wilson, as the executive departments were the creation of Hamilton, so the machinery by which legislation is actually made in the House was distinctly the work of Henry Clay. In the Speakership, the Rules of the House, and the Committee System, Clay has left an enduring mark upon our national institutions. He made the

Speaker of the House more powerful than the President and raised that office to a height it has never lost. By 1830, too, the transfer of the preponderance of legislative power from the House to the Senate, which has made the latter what it is to-day, the balance wheel of our legislative fabric, was well under way.

The real Constitution of the United States by which we live was largely written by Chief Justice Marshall during his long term of office from 1801 to 1835. The interpretation of the broad phrases and inclusive wording intentionally placed in the document by the framers to enable it to be adapted to the exigencies of times and occasions was a difficult task under any conditions. It was essential that something more than a few specific decisions should be made; the general rules for the consistent interpretation of the document under all conditions had to be developed, tested, and applied to a sufficient variety of cases to provide the country with the definite body of constitutional precedents which alone could give the individual that degree of personal and civil liberty the Constitution guaranteed him. In particular the clause concerning the powers of Congress required most careful treatment. It was at once obvious that only a tithe of the powers which Congress must actually exercise had been enumerated and that only a liberal interpretation of these clauses would permit the Federal government to legislate outside a very narrow range indeed. Jefferson and Madison had declared for the strictest possible construction and the unconstitutionality of every power not explicitly granted. Marshall, however, as Chief Justice, possessed an authority to interpret the Constitution which was denied the President, and the Constitution itself made his decisions binding law. To him we owe the doctrine of implied powers which permits Congress to legislate upon all subjects "necessary and proper" for compassing the ends for which the Federal government was instituted. Under this ægis the most important work of the Federal government has been done. The decisions of Marshall are actually as much a part of the law considered binding in the United States as if they had been solemnly adopted by the Constitutional Convention in 1787.

The movement for the extension of the direct control of the people spread with extraordinary rapidity in the decades following the election of Jackson. In the States, manhood suffrage was generally adopted; the appointment of executive officers pretty thoroughly abandoned in favor of election for short terms; the terms of legislators generally reduced in length; and the separation of powers, long since adopted in theory, actually instituted in practice. Scarcely were these changes completed than the first of the great waves of immigration reached the eastern States and created new conditions in State and especially in city government. Soon the registration laws and laws fixing the qualifications for voters were being altered to admit these newly arrived members as citizens after shorter and shorter periods of actual residence, until, by the outbreak of the Civil War, boss rule, with its accompanying graft and corruption, had become thoroughly established in State, municipal, and local government in most parts of the country.

In Federal government, a new rule concerning executive officials had been instituted by Jackson, patterned on Jefferson's half-hearted measures in the same direction. "To the victors belong the spoils" was the slogan of the army of office-seekers who stormed Washington in 1829. There was no doubt a plausible defense: the chief executive must have around him "friends of the people," who would execute his commands according to the spirit as well as the letter in which they had been given. Washington's and Adams's unsuccessful attempts to create a Cabinet from warring elements had early caused the general acceptance of the necessity of harmony in the immediate circle of the President; but Jackson was the first actually to put into operation the principle of the "clean sweep" throughout the Federal offices. Thus the spoils system entered American politics and became speedily one of its best accepted maxims, whose literal fulfilment was invariably demanded by the impatient cohorts and rarely denied.

The period between 1815 and 1840 was a great formative period when protective and compromise principles were adopted; when legislative, judicial, and executive traditions assumed the form they still retain; when manhood suffrage, appointive officers, and city bosses were changing vitally the aspects of democracy as the earlier generations lived it. Lastly and by no means least, it had been a period in which the bud of national consciousness had been bursting into flower among the people themselves. A new nation was slowly evolving; and here and there an individual, seized with the consciousness of the great developments gradually unfolding, began to express in no doubtful tongue his notion of what that national spirit was and ought to be. Among those who influenced popular thinking, Daniel Webster again stands foremost with his great orations on the Pilgrims and on the Battle of Bunker Hill. He created a new conception of the colonial period and of the Revolution, national in its scope and expression, which was caught up into the school-books children were given to read and on which men who later fought in the Northern armies were nourished. Weems had already produced eulogistic biographies of Washington, Franklin, and other notables, whose ready sale showed the growing popular taste for literature glorifying the endeavors of the men who had been conspicuously nationalists, working not for a single State's welfare but obviously for the good of the whole country. By 1850, the literature of American history had been further enriched by Irving's dramatic tale of Columbus, by Bancroft's intensely "patriotic" and nationalistic description of the history of America to the adoption of the Constitution. Sparks's editions of the writings of the Revolutionary fathers were also intentionally prepared to inculcate a love of the country as a whole and an admiration for the men who had worked for our union under one government as well as for our independence from England. The poets of New England, Lowell and Longfellow especially, gave voice to this growing sentiment of admiration for our national welfare. So far as the new country had any literature, it was written by Northern nationalists, a fact significant in explaining the strong sentiment in favor of nationalism in the North in 1860.

Of an identity distinct from other races, the individual American became acutely conscious about 1830. Truth to tell, an idea that we were different from and better than other people was not unknown in colonial days and became common during the Revolution; but it was then almost certain to reflect as much local pride and satisfaction as a sense of difference between Americans and Europeans. Until 1830, the feeling of a difference between Americans was still too keen to allow it to become apparent that the people of the whole coast had really begun to think of themselves as Americans rather than as inhabitants of certain States. With this acute consciousness of racial difference came at first an arrogance and a conceit which we find only too faithfully reflected in the pages of travelers. The American insisted upon the instantaneous recognition of the superiority of his country, and its institutions, literature, and culture, over all other countries and their qualities and graces. Crude, rough, ill-mannered as this spirit seemed to the sensitive Dickens, it is nevertheless to the historian unmistakable evidence of the dawning of a truly national consciousness, of the disappearance of the harsh lines which had kept the people so separated from one another throughout the colonial period. To be sure, nothing like definitive agreement or a consensus of opinion on any subject had been attained, except on the one fact that America was different from and therefore better than Europe; and until a clear consensus of opinion should reach a point at which the community as a whole became conscious that it existed, until it was no longer a matter of idealism but a plain inevitable fact, no nation, in the modern organic sense of the word, could or would exist. Still, all-unconscious, the nation had begun to try to think, act, and believe.

XVIII

THE TWO DIVERGING SECTIONS

THE economic forces in operation in 1830, which were swiftly producing south of Mason and Dixon's line and of the Ohio River conditions more and more widely divergent from those north of it, are all connoted by the single word—cotton. And cotton connotes slavery. In 1789 neither cotton nor slavery were factors of prime consequence; in 1815 both were clearly of growing importance and were seen to be potentially capable of great extension. By 1830, the increasing demand for cotton, the ease with which the South had been able to meet it, the astonishing profits, proved to the dullest minds that in cotton the United States had at last found the medium of exchange with Europe which it had so long lacked, and which with every decade was becoming more and more adequate. Indeed, many and many an excited planter and New England merchant saw in cotton the means of freeing the country from its long economic dependence upon Europe. They were ready to teach their children, in the words of De Bow, "to hold the cotton plant in one hand and the sword in the other, ever ready to defend it as the source of commercial power abroad and through that of independence at home."

The most obvious result of the cotton-culture had been to render slavery extremely profitable and to put an end to the talk at the South of the desirability of its abolition which had been so common in Virginia and in South Carolina between 1815 and 1825. The vast increase in the cotton crop—from about four hundred fifty thousand bales in 1816 to one million bales in 1826, over eighty per cent of which was promptly exported—of course greatly increased the exports of the United States and facilitated exchange with Europe. Indeed, in the palmiest days of the old pre-revolutionary smug-gling-trade, the ease and profitableness of trade with Europe had never been so great. The loss of the West Indian trade be-came each year of less consequence, and, as the country devel-oped, it became clearer and clearer to Americans that the West India market, even if it had continued open to them, would have been inadequate to consume the whole swelling volume of produce. Thankfully, they realized their deliverance when the abolition of slavery by England in 1833 ruined her West India sugar plantations and hence destroyed at one blow the original source of the commercial prosperity of the Atlantic coast. The problem of our relations to the West Indies had solved itself. There was now no recourse save cotton.

The cotton-culture had also trebled the value of land and of slaves at the South. It was a method of cultivation pe-culiarly adopted to the use of slave labor. The stalks of the previous year's crop were first broken down; the field was then laid off into beds by plowing a furrow between the old rows and lapping on it from four to six other furrows, thus leaving the field in ridges about four feet apart. After the earth had been pulverized with a small harrow, and the center of the ridge split with a plow, negro women sowed cotton seed in the trench at the rate of about two bushels per acre and the trench was closed by dragging a sort of scraper over it. The young plants were thinned out with a hoe, a laborious task, so as to leave two plants about a foot apart, and, until the crop was ready to pick, the ground was constantly hoed or stirred every twenty days. Picking, a long and tedious rather than laborious occupation, consumed months, and when it was over the field gang began to break stalks and plow again the old field or to clear new fields of weeds and underbrush. The simplicity of the work, the small number and rudimentary character of the tools needed, the constant but not exhausting labor all the year round, the profitableness of organizing labor on a large scale and of performing simultaneously the same task by great gangs of slaves, all made the cotton-culture ideally fitted for the use of forced labor. The expense of maintaining slaves in comparative comfort was small in a warm climate where housing, fuel, and heavy clothing were not essential, and where the vegetable food abundantly provided by nature formed an important part of the negroes' diet.

Cotton, however, rapidly exhausted the land, and even virgin soil after two or three years' cropping yielded a perceptibly smaller return. Since manure and fertilizers were expensive and little understood and since new land was plentiful, it became customary to abandon a field after a few years and move the gang of slaves to a new scene of operations. From this grew a tendency towards large plantations of thousands of acres where several shifts of operations could be made on the owner's territory, without leaving the general neighborhood, and then permit a return to the first field, which would have lain fallow long enough to recover its fertility. The profits, too, were indubitably greater from farming on a large scale and great gangs of slaves owned by comparatively few men were soon producing the bulk of the cotton crop.

The extraordinary profit in cultivating the richest bottom lands compared to the more moderate returns from cropping the uplands promptly sent the more adventurous and ambitious into new districts and caused the rapid growth after 1830 of the territory along the Gulf of Mexico. A very large superficial area was at once occupied: the land sales in the five Gulf States in 1834 aggregated nearly three million acres; and in both 1835 and 1836, over five million acres. The rush of capital to the district was equally marked; the number of slaves owned there increased 86% in the decade after 1830, while the production of cotton increased 163%.

From this expansion flowed results of consequence. The preponderance of slaves and of wealth shifted from the Atlantic coast to the Gulf States. In 1790, Maryland and Virginia had owned three-fifths of all the slaves in the country; by 1840 about two-thirds of the slaves had migrated to the Gulf States, and one-half of the total number were absolutely dependent on the cotton-culture. By 1850, nearly 80% of the total number of slaves were in the cotton States. The value of a good field-hand had risen from $200 in 1778 to $600 in 1836. Indeed, compared to cotton, tobacco, the staple crop of Virginia and Kentucky, was not profitable enough to retain the slaves in the district, while in Tennessee and Missouri the profit of using slaves for agriculture was in no way comparable to that of selling them to the cotton-planters. Practically, the enormous success of the cotton-culture in the Gulf States and the consequent high price of slaves made it more profitable for the border States to breed slaves for the Southern fields than to cultivate any crop themselves. "Virginia is, in fact," wrote a Southern professor in 1830, "a negro-raising State for other States." Cotton thus not only perpetuated slavery in the cotton-belt where the slaves could be profitably used for the actual production of the staple; but it perpetuated it in the border States where it made the slave himself a marketable and valuable commodity. "It is believed," said Henry Clay in 1829, "that nowhere in the farming portion of the United States, would slave labor be generally employed, if the proprietor were not tempted to raise slaves by the high price of the Southern markets which keeps it up in his own."

Certainly, too, the cotton-culture made the South essentially agricultural and essentially an agricultural community of one crop. As years went on, the amount of food raised proportionately declined, the amount of manufactured goods, even under the most liberal interpretation of that term, was so very small that the cotton States practically depended on the North, the West, or Europe for literally everything necessary for life. Other industry than cotton-culture and all sorts of manufactures were dwarfed, discouraged, or prevented from developing. Where in 1810 the total value of manufactured goods south of Mason and Dixon's line compared to their value north of that line had been about one-half, it was by 1840 only one-third, and had sunk by 1850 to one-fifth. Some growth there was, but relatively to the growth of manufactures at the

North, the South suffered an actual decline. The two sections were developing in different directions and certainly those geographical and geological conditions, which made the cotton-culture so profitable in the South and which forced the North into manufacturing and varied industry, are mainly responsible for the contrast which plainly existed between them in 1860.

A Southern historian has made a careful study of the condition of Alabama in 1850. Out of 750,000 people, there were 330,000 slaves, owned by 30,000 men, that is, by about seven per cent of the white population. About three-fourths of the total number of slaves, with nearly that same proportion of the land, were owned by less than 10,000 white men, from whose plantations came the great bulk of the cotton crop. The profits can be guessed from the fact that the exports of the State were valued at ten million dollars annually while the imports were under a million. To New England and to Europe, the State sent cotton; from the Northwest via the Mississippi and the Gulf she drew bread and meat. Some 75,000 whites and as many negroes derived a livelihood from manufactures, banking, and the professions. Until just before the Civil War there was no attempt at an organized public-school system. Alabama was a State of small towns and villages, of scattered plantations, with no large cities and little if any community life in the broadest sense. The figures given by the census of 1850 for the South as a whole prove these conditions typical. There were 347,525 slaveholders in the South, and something over three millions of slaves. "Of the large planters owning more than fifty slaves, whose elegance, luxury, and hospitality are recited in tales of travelers, over whose estates and lives has shone the luster of romance and poetry, there were less than eight thousand."

So striking and important a change in the aspect of slavery, in its geographical extent and its economic position, naturally provoked both North and South a vigorous and eager discussion of its cause, its methods, its morals, its expediency, and its justifiability. Societies for the abolition of slavery or for its limitation were old in America, had been common both North and South in the decade following 1789 and in that following the commercial depression of 1816; but the vital changes in the position and importance of slavery, together with the general intellectual ferment which produced as dissimilar movements as the Sunday-school, the Mormon church, temperance and women's rights societies, roused a section of the Northern people to agitate against slavery and led to the formation of a new type of Abolition and Anti-slavery societies by a new group of leaders, of whom the most remarkable were Garrison, Parker, and Phillips. Their propaganda, which seems to modern investigators to have contributed little to the outbreak of the War in 1861, did cause a searching of consciences and in particular of history, the Scriptures, and the census. What was the economic status of slavery; was it profitable; was it fair, equitable, just, ethical, moral; was it cruel, was it as good for the slave as for the master? The discussion was carried on by both parties with a furious intensity, with the uncritical use of so-called "facts," and with that sentiment and prejudice which are so certain to accompany the political discussion of any moral issue.

While it is hardly profitable to-day to consider the detailed arguments advanced by either side, it may be briefly pointed out that the chief difference seems to have lain in the fact that the Southerners lived with the negro and treated slavery as an essentially practical economic question, while the Northern men, by reason of their lack of actual contact with slavery, were able to look upon it with a certain detachment and to apply to its difficulties moral and ethical theories drawn chiefly from their own widely different practical experience. The planter believed that cotton could not be grown without negroes and knew that history as well as the Scriptures provided no other solution of the problem raised by the juxtaposition of a superior and an inferior race except slavery. If any individuals then alive were to blame for the existence of slavery at the South, he felt some share of the blame ought to be borne by the New Englanders whose fortunes had originally been based on the rum, molasses, and slave-trade during the colonial times. That cruel treatment of slaves occurred, he was willing to admit, but he claimed that on the whole slavery at the South in 1850 was as humane and considerate as it had ever been anywhere. Northern opinion more and more came to lay stress upon the moral and ethical issue, upon the claim that any slavery anywhere was of itself wrong, inhuman, and cruel. It pointed out that the trend of human development had been clearly toward the emancipation of the individual, and that the enlightened opinion of Western Europe in 1850 regarded the institution with abhorrence and had everywhere abolished it. Both sides employed many other arguments and illustrations whose truth was stoutly challenged by their opponents.

The trouble about the argument was that the truth on one side did not offset or answer the truth on the other. The Southerner, quoting history and the Scriptures, declined to listen to what he was told was the moral sense of the world. Nor was the claim that slavery in the South was in general humane and that no individuals then alive were in any way to blame for its existence, at all satisfactory to the excited Abolitionists who declaimed against it as a wrong in itself, whose very existence proved it wrong. After the dark days of the Reconstruction, it is hard to convince many sincere men that most negroes were not happier and better cared for under slavery than they have been since under freedom. In fact, the South raised the issue of expediency: how could we or can we do otherwise. The real difficulty was the existence of millions whose actual ignorance and incapacity made them economic slaves, literally unable to care for themselves, and not to be made capable and industrious by fiat. To this the Northern men replied that slavery simply meant the perpetuation of this situation by making it legally, economically, and socially impossible for the children to rise above the position their fathers and grandfathers had occupied. It was the clash between present and future expediency, a choice between the probable evils of emancipation with which men then alive must cope, or the postponement of the remedy for the evils of slavery to a future time. If we confine ourselves strictly to the point of view of 1850, we shall be likely to agree that humane, sensible, honest men might find much that seemed cogent and convincing in either argument and be able consistently to espouse that side with ardor.

Meanwhile, north of Mason and Dixon's line and of the Ohio River, in the districts popularly known as the North and the West, an extremely different type of social economic structure was growing apace. Even before the Revolution, a difference in development between the North and South had been remarked by casual travelers, and by the inauguration of Jackson the contrast was striking; but the following decades saw a truly stupendous growth in the North of diversified industry and in the West of more intensive scientific agriculture, whose reaction upon the social and political life of the community was exceedingly significant. It was not so much an increase in the output of Northern factories and Western farms which attracted attention, though the doubling of the wheat and corn crops and of the production of raw iron and the trebling of the value of manufactured woolens and cottons were sufficiently interesting facts. The normally rapid increase of the population, plus steady immigration, necessarily meant the application of more hands to the soil, enormous sales of land, more acres under actual cultivation, and hence ensured a great increase in total production. The remarkable fact was the undoubted gain in efficiency, the proportionally greater return from the investment of capital and labor than ever before; the increasing variety of the output; the rapid rise of new industries, and the steady development of a home market for home products as well as the manufacture of domestic products to supply the home demand. The North was not only gaining on the South from the more rapid natural increase of the white population; it was gaining immensely by immigration year by year, especially after 1850; and it was utilizing more of its natural resources more skilfully and adequately than was the South.

This new efficiency was largely due to improved methods and to the invention of new machinery to perform the manual labor for which it was impossible to procure hands enough on the Western farms. The cast-iron plow, the mowing-machine, the horse-rake, the reaping- and threshing-machines, the horse-cultivators and seed-sowers, all of which were in use by 1840 and all of which had by 1850 become practically universal in the West, were enabling a few men to do the work of a hundred hand laborers. And the North found that the increased output of raw iron, the better pig iron produced by the new process of smelting with anthracite coal provided the material out of which busy hands in Northern factories could form the machines needed by the West. Then, too, as the years passed, improvements upon the old spinning- and weaving-machinery, the sewing-machine, changes in factory organization, cheaper machines due to cheaper iron and cheaper transportation, increased the proportionate output from the factories and reduced the cost of production.

More people to be reached, living on a constantly greater area of land; more produce to be moved, more markets demanding it, required and secured a tremendous improvement in the facilities of transportation. In 1825, the Erie Canal connected the Great Lakes with the Mohawk and the Hudson Rivers, and was soon linked to a network of canals through the low watershed separating the Ohio River system from the Lake system. By 1840 grain traveled a thousand miles to the Eastern States more cheaply and expeditiously than it could have been moved a hundred miles a decade earlier. A vast acreage of land hitherto inacessible became available and to it flocked the ambitious. Soon canal lines were supplanted by the rapid growth after 1840 of railroad trunk lines which made transportation of all bulky goods still cheaper and greatly fostered the rapid development of diversified industry. Cheap iron of constantly better grade made possible better engines, larger cars, stronger rails, and enabled the railroads to haul longer trains of larger cars, each with heavier loads, in less time at constantly diminishing cost. As transportation became cheaper, districts were able to send grain to market which had never before been able to compete and were consequently able to afford manufactured goods for the first time. The increased supply of food enabled men in the East hitherto dependent on local supply to abandon the farm for the factory and produce the articles the West demanded. Yet, as food and clothes grew cheaper because of the improved process and the development of transportation, the profit to the individual seemed to increase on each transaction, and the bushel of corn bought more manufactured articles, and strange to say a yard of cloth or a pig of iron bought more corn. It was as if some magician had waved his wand and bade them all make one another rich.

As the economic fabric grew in size, it developed in strength and complexity. Corporations of all sorts were formed; by 1860 a goodly number of labor unions attempting organization on a national scale had appeared. Particularly evident and gratifying were the increasing number of banks, the swelling volume of deposits, and the extension of credit facilities in the East. The amount of capital seeking investment had never been so great and proved the unquestioned soundness of the country's development. Exchange through London for trade between the States was long obsolete, and the banking centers were really capable of handling all domestic business transactions. The complexity of the economic life of the North, the proportion of skilled workmen, the variety of industries, as well as the stability of the credit structure, were to be of the utmost consequence in the waging of the Civil War. Most significant of all, the new development depended upon coöperation and was profitable in proportion to the efficiency of that collective effort. This the North clearly saw. In the South, on the other hand, the individual was still isolated and was either unconscious of the greater possibilities of a more complex social life or hindered by adverse conditions from developing them.

In the social structure, too, occurred striking changes between 1840 and 1860, utterly transforming the aspect of Northern society. The population not only doubled but was able to remain practically upon the same area which had supported the previous generation. In earlier decades, no more people could live together in a town or city than the district could support, unless the ease of water transportation and the nearness of a great source of supply enabled them to import their food. But as the efficiency of the new farming by machinery enabled a part to feed the whole, and as the efficiency of the new factories made the labor of a part sufficient to clothe the whole, a larger proportion of the community than ever before was free to live where it pleased and could rely upon the railroads to supply its wants. Thus was made possible a new type of social unit, the modern industrial city, devoted perhaps to the production of a few articles and relying upon the outside world for all else. Concomitantly, the cheapness of wood with which to build houses, of coal to heat them, of gas to light them, of sewers to drain them, of water-works to supply fresh water, made the rapid growth of cities possible and freed these hundreds of thousands of people, huddled upon the same spot, from the old menaces of the plague and the scurvy. The community had time to build cities and public works, and to supply the multifold new economic wants which community life in cities promptly created. It was becoming wealthy, beginning to have traces of a leisure class, able to afford systematically to develop its tastes in a variety of directions not essential to existence but imperative for culture and education. Theaters, magazines, books multiplied; the opera and concerts became popular. Education received more careful attention and a considerable part of the swelling profits were wisely invested in school buildings and equipment, and the children could be, and were, left longer in school than ever before. For those adults whose early opportunities had not been great, the lyceum and the lecture courses provided a variety of informing and instructive material.

In the Mississippi and Ohio Valleys, the gain in population and wealth was proportionately more rapid than in the North, and for the first time a truly complex social structure began to develop west of the mountains. Naturally, it centered round the lines of communication with the East; along the great highway from New York through the Hudson and Mohawk Valleys, along the shore of the Lakes to "the Northwest," as the States northwest of Chicago were then called. Naturally, it was most striking at the various gateways and termini, New York, Albany, Buffalo, the Lake cities, Chicago. New York and Chicago, the eastern and western termini of the railroad trunk lines, of course benefited most. The older centers in the West, Cincinnati and St. Louis, had owed their prominence to their control of the river routes to the South and were therefore outside the new field of development. A shift in the balance of population and wealth took place between the North and West, much to the advantage of the West as a whole, and with it came a concomitant shift of the balance of population and wealth in the West from the Mississippi and Ohio River system to the Great Lakes and the upper Mississippi. And Henry Clay had predicted in 1824 that Zanesville, Ohio, would become the emporium of the West!

Why the only sectional line in American history, which ever threatened to become permanent, should have begun with the old boundary line run by Mason and Dixon between Maryland and Pennsylvania and have continued along the Ohio River and then have passed northwest through Missouri is one of the most fascinating questions of American history, and probably does not admit of a wholly determinate answer.

It is, however, a remarkable and suggestive fact that the southern line of the great ice sheet, which at one time occupied the whole northern half of this continent followed very nearly Mason and Dixon's line, then followed the Ohio River for half its course, passed across Indiana and Illinois leaving a sizable section south of it (where "before the

War" many slaves hired from Kentucky were at work and which were pro-slavery districts in most elections), and then turned sharply towards the northwest, leaving most of Missouri to the south of it. The result of the existence of this great ice sheet and of its melting was to create north of this line a soil richer in chemical elements and hence more fertile than that south of it. Much land south of this line is still "dead soil" and only in the river bottoms, filled with silt brought by the Mississippi from the upper valley, is the soil extremely fertile. The southern half of the United States is not capable of the same variety of crops as the northern. Closely following this same line of the ice sheet is the isotherm of an average annual temperature of 60 degrees, the belt just north averaging 50 to 60 degrees, and that just south, 60 to 70 degrees. But the peculiarity of America is that while the lines of winter temperature slope southward and give the country between the Great Lakes and the Gulf the range of temperature found in Europe between the North Cape and the Sahara Desert, the summer lines expand in both directions and produce greater extremes of temperature in the northern half than in the southern half or in European countries of the same latitude. The temperature of the northern belt, like its soil, is far more varied than that of the southern half, where only those crops can be profitably grown that will thrive in a summer temperature of 80 degrees and above. In addition, the average annual rainfall, so important to agriculture, is from 20 to 40 inches in the belt just north of the line of the ice sheet, and from 40 to 60 inches in the whole district south of it. More than 60 degrees annual temperature and more than 40 inches of rainfall is fatal to the profitable cultivation of many agricultural products, and it is in the belt just north of Mason and Dixon's line and of the Ohio River, that soil, temperature, and rainfall create the most favorable conditions for agriculture. Consequently, the bulk of the most highly developed land, and nearly all the wheat and corn land will be found to-day, as in 1860, north of the line.

Soil, temperature, and rainfall prevent the growth of wheat and corn at a profit in the South and do not permit the raising in the North of staple crops like cotton, tobacco, rice, and indigo, which can be profitably grown with slave labor. The North was prevented by Nature, not by the superior moral and ethical fiber of its people, from developing slavery as an institution. These conditions were true in 1606; they are still true in 1914: they are fundamental conditions which have shaped and always will shape economic and institutional life in this country.

One more fact is of consequence. As the great sheet of ice melted, the Ohio and Missouri Rivers were formed by the streams flowing along its edges into the cleft of the valley; there they united with the Mississippi, cutting a deep channel between the low hills to the Gulf of Mexico. They flowed, however, through a vast plain whose angle of inclination was small, and, except at times of flood, their progress was leisurely and wandering. In this country there would be little water-power for manufacturing. On the other hand, the mountains and rocky northern country created swift rivers with many falls and rapids. All through New York and New England the streams hurrying down the steep hillsides and draining great mountain valleys made possible the water-power upon which the early factories depended. The use of steam as the chief motive power in manufacturing is very recent, and is wholly dependent upon coal as a fuel. The water-power in the rivers enabled the north to develop industries. The same rocky soil and mountainous formation that made the rivers numerous and swift made agriculture on a large scale difficult and unprofitable and influenced the inhabitants to follow other occupations. The climatic and geographical conditions, far more than inherited tendencies or natural ambition, explain the rapid development of manufactures in the North in the half-century preceding the Civil War. The lack of water-power and the profitableness of great staple crops made the South predominantly an agricultural country.

Similarly the geographical and economic fabric influenced decisively the political institutions of each section. The cold winters in the North made agriculture impossible for many months, necessitated the storing up of provisions and led the people living inland to huddle together for company, for sharing the food and fuel in time of scarcity, and for defense against the Indians and French. The shipping and fishing industries similarly encouraged the formation and growth of towns. These factors naturally explain the formation of closely knit coöperative centralized institutions in the North; it was convenient and expedient so to live. In the South, it was as clearly convenient and expedient to live otherwise. Tobacco in colonial times, like cotton after the Revolution, required vast areas of new land, for the crops quickly exhausted the soil and the science of fertilization was not then understood. Each planter owned, therefore, a tract equivalent to a whole New England township, in the middle of which he usually lived with a few white overseers and a large gang of slaves. He tilled only a part of his estate each year and was constantly moving from one field to another. Summer and winter were alike to him so far as food, shelter, and communication went; there was nothing to make him dependent on other planters, or to make close political association necessary. The great plantations were therefore organized into counties in the loosest fashion. The necessary functions of government were reduced to a minimum by the small number of whites and their comparative isolation. The common business was largely judicial or financial and could be performed with ease by one or two men. Only on the plantations was extensive authority in daily use; the population which most needed to be controlled, tried, fined, and legislated about was not the planters but the slaves, and it was inevitable that nearly plenary authority should be vested in the master. Centralized control was a physical impossibility: each planter must govern his own plantation and receive from the county aid and assistance in cases of special difficulty. The State

would settle disputes between planters; it could not undertake to govern the community for the planters.

In the seventy years following the adoption of the Constitution the North developed industry; the South, cotton; the
North became wholly free; the South chiefly slave. Where
in the North, something like centralized government was a
necessity and the object of coöperation was to secure a positive result, in the South the best government was, as Jefferson said, the one which did the least, which interfered only
in the last resort. States' rights had therefore for the
Southerner a solid foundation in the experience of the community. The benefits of union, that is of coöperation, had
to the Northern man an equally firm basis in experience. In
the North, free labor, diversified industry, seemed to be the
very price of existence; in the South, great staple crops
grown by slaves or at least by unfree labor seemed equally
inevitable. To the Northern man slavery was an abstraction,
an excrescence on the life of the community; to the Southern
man, it was as necessary as the soil. That in another part
of the country the factors, accepted in each as axiomatic,
not only did not exist but would have been positively detrimental to the successful administration of public and
private business, neither North or South fully realized.

The Civil War was the result of a misunderstanding between honest, sincere men, in which both were right and
both were wrong, and, it is far truer to add, in which
neither could be either right or wrong. Each did what the
conditions of life seemed to make inevitable, what its traditions sanctioned, and its ideals counseled.

XIX

TEXAS AND THE MEXICAN WAR

By 1835, the profits of cotton-culture were clear to the Southern planters. Apparently the market was exhaustless; the amount of profit obtainable from the labor of slaves on virgin soil in the river bottoms was astounding; unless the land most profitable to cultivate should be exhausted, or the supply of slaves become insufficient to work it, there seemed literally to be no dreams of wealth and power which might not be realized. For the time being, the supply of land and of slaves was ample, but the rapidity with which the westward movement was progressing made the continuation of the same rate of growth improbable unless more land could be obtained than was available in 1835. That the same rate of growth must continue seemed to Southerners of the time an axiom whose truth was too apparent to be disputed by any fair-minded individual. To continue it, there must be more land and more slaves.

The territory between the Alleghanies and the Mississippi was in 1835 already organized into States, the lands had been allotted to private individuals, and the status of slavery had been decided in a fashion which could not be altered. To the north of the Ohio lay the vast plains called the Northwest Territory, which had been organized by the famous Ordinance of 1787, with a prohibition of slavery in the territories and States to be organized out of it. By 1819, Ohio, Indiana, and Illinois had been admitted as free States, and the type of soil, the rainfall, and the climate made it certain that the district was wholly unfitted for the growth of cotton. From every point of view, all the land north of the Ohio was unavailable.

The territory south of that river had been also ceded to the Confederation by England in the Treaty of 1783, but without a very definite agreement concerning the southern boundary. Kentucky and Tennessee had been settled from Virginia and North Carolina and had entered the Union as slave States in 1792 and 1796 respectively. The ownership of a district roughly approximating the present States of Alabama and Mississippi was, however, in dispute between England and Spain, and the former agreed with the latter that if she could make good her claim against the United States, the land should be hers. Georgia also laid claim to the district by virtue of her colonial charter. The difficulty was finally settled by treaties in which the United States bought the Spanish claims to the whole southern part of the United States, including Florida. Mississippi and Alabama had already been settled by Americans and were indeed admitted as States before the Treaty of 1819 was finally ratified. Save Florida, there was no land left east of the Mississippi and south of the Ohio which slavery had not already formally occupied by 1820.

There were, however, in the Gulf States great tracts of exceedingly fertile lands in the hands of the powerful Indian confederacies of the Creeks, Cherokees, and Choctaws. After the breaking of solemn treaties and unseemly and undignified quarrels, which very nearly provoked armed defiance of Federal authority by Georgia, the Indians were expelled from their rich fields, and by 1835 had been located in what are now Oklahoma and Indian Territory. Although the new area thus opened to cotton was large, it was so promptly occupied that before 1840, all the best cotton land south of the Ohio and east of the Mississippi had again been allotted.

As early as 1819 when Missouri and Maine simultaneously applied for admission, the status of the Louisiana Territory was seen to be an issue of the first importance. The southernmost part had become a slave State some years before; it was natural that the district around the Missouri River whither the rich fur-trade had drawn settlers should outstrip the rest of Louisiana in growth and should be large

enough for admission as a State when the rest of the purchase was scarcely settled at all. The Compromise of 1820
admitted Missouri as a slave State, and, while prohibiting
slavery in the broad plains north of Missouri's southern
boundary line, 36° 30', obviously left the river-bottoms of
Arkansas for future expansion. In 1820, the allotment to
the Indians of land south of 36° 30' was not foreseen and
the Southerners felt that they had amply provided for all the
cotton land which could conceivably be needed for decades to
come. In fostering this feeling, the prevailing dense ignorance of western geography played a prominent part. The
expedition of Lewis and Clark, sent by Jefferson to inspect
the new purchase, and the accounts of trappers and hunters
had given no accurate idea of how much land there was to
which the United States could rightly lay claim west of the
Mississippi. The general notion that it was practically unlimited was quite satisfactory to most men. But within
fifteen years, Arkansas was demanding admission as a State;
the Indians had been assigned the rest of the Louisiana territory west of Arkansas and south of the Missouri Compromise
line; and the development of the cotton-culture west of the
great river was clearly proceeding at so rapid a pace that the
limitation of production and the diminution of the degree of
profit hitherto obtained was certain unless new lands could
be promptly secured.

The obvious direction for such expansion was in the Gulf
of Mexico, either in Cuba and the islands or in the vast domain of Texas, contiguous with the cotton States, along the
Gulf between the Sabine River and the Rio Grande. About
this great estate, the United States had hitherto cared little;
it was included in the Louisiana Purchase, though the fact
was not understood in 1803; it was therefore left outside the
boundaries of the United States in the Treaty of 1819 with
Spain, and the omission aroused little comment except in Missouri. Indeed, few supposed we had a just claim to it or that
it was of any particular value. The efforts of the South
American and Central American colonies of Spain to obtain

their independence about 1821 excited much sympathy in the United States, evoked the Monroe Doctrine and practically their protection by the United States from European aggression. With equal promptitude appeared arguments in favor of the annexation of one or more of them, especially of Cuba and Mexico, to the latter of which Spain had ceded Texas. Several attempts to annex Cuba and buy Texas were made before 1830, but came to nothing. Meanwhile, several thousand Americans with slaves hurried to Texas and began raising cotton; at least two attempts were made by Americans to set up an independent republic there; and their determination to break the loose tie binding the territory to Mexico was greatly strengthened by the emancipation of the slaves by the Mexican Constitution of 1827. After several failures, the Americans in Texas succeeded in establishing their independence of Mexico in 1836 and secured recognition from the United States and several European nations the following year.

With so anomalous a status they were by no means satisfied and ardently desired annexation. This, the discovery by the Southern planters of the rapid exhaustion of available cotton land led the latter to support with might and main. The scheme was defeated in 1837. Now it became clear to the Southerners that Texas as an independent State had only to begin the direct importation of cheap negroes from Africa to sell cotton at a price with which the high price of slaves in the United States and the abolition of the slave trade would prevent them from competing. In addition, the rapid exhaustion of the virgin soil available in the Gulf States made it also possible that the profit from cotton would be so reduced that its cultivation in Louisiana and Mississippi might no longer be profitable at all. The remedies were either annexation, which would impose permanently upon the Texans the same restraints to which the Southerners themselves were subject, or the repeal of the constitutional prohibition against the slave trade.

The designs of the Southerners upon Cuba and Texas

roused the suspicions of the Northern and Western men. The anti-slavery and abolition movements were becoming strong; anti-slavery petitions poured into Congress, where they found a stanch and able advocate in John Quincy Adams. What agitation and insistence had not been able to effect in Northern minds, the obvious trend of Southern ambition promptly accomplished. Was it after all right to adopt a policy for the wide extension and development of an institution, the logic for whose extension was by no means as unanswerable as the arguments against interfering with it where it already existed? Did not the South intend to create a new slave empire which would in time sweep into its maw the whole Gulf of Mexico and whose size and wealth would endanger the free States in the North? The fact that the South controlled the chief medium of exchange with Europe— and the only medium since the destruction of the prosperity of the English West Indian Islands by the abolition of slavery in 1833—caused the Northern members of Congress to realize that the commercial situation might effectually chain their States to the chariot wheels of the new slave empire and that it behooved them to look well before they sanctioned its development. But the fear, which seemed at the time well-founded, of the annexation of Texas by England or France and the consequent creation there of a rival State capable of contesting with us the control of the Gulf and of the continent, carried the day. In 1845, Texas was annexed by a joint resolution of the two Houses of Congress.

The boundaries of the new State on the west and south had not yet been settled with Mexico and the territory claimed by the Texans,—a broad band stretching up into the country between the Nueces River and the Rio Grande—was of immense size and probably of commensurate value. Its cession by Mexico could certainly be secured by a little show of force. The latter country was in the throes of an internal revolution and could scarcely resist. War was declared in 1846 and the United States armies soon defeated the ill-equipped and badly disciplined levies of Mexicans. Webster and other

Northern men inveighed hotly against the war as unprovoked and unjust aggression, and only in the South was popular approval widespread and outspoken. Charges were made that the President attempted to buy or annex the whole of Mexico and was forced to renounce his plans by the refusal of England and France to countenance the scheme. However this may have been, a treaty was signed in 1848 which ceded to the United States the enormous territory west of the Rockies, south of Oregon and north of the present Mexican boundary (except a tract in southern Arizona purchased in 1853), —fully a quarter of the present area of the United States.

At about this same time were concluded treaties with England which definitely settled the northern boundary, between the United States and Canada, nearly the whole length of which was in dispute. The real cause of the difficulty lay in the lack of accurate information about the topography of the interior at the time when the Treaty of 1783 and the Louisiana Purchase of 1803 had been concluded. In the Northwest, the United States claimed that Maine extended almost to the St. Lawrence River, while the English declared the highlands mentioned by the negotiators were far to the south and east. In the West, it was found that the terms of the Treaty of 1783 were impossible of fulfilment, and, as well, that much land which it had been evidently intended should belong to the United States was outside its boundaries and that other land it had not been intended to have was its property. Still further west, beyond the Rockies, was the great valley of the Columbia River, which both England and the United States claimed by virtue of title by discovery, and parts of whose valley had been already occupied by trappers and settlers of both nations. The western boundary was settled first, the parallel of the Lake of the Woods being accepted as far as the Rockies and a joint occupation of Oregon agreed upon. In 1842, the boundary of Maine was compromised, and in 1846 Oregon was divided by continuing the 49th parallel to the Pacific.

In 1848, therefore, an enormous accession of territory had

just been made and its organization and status became a burning question in Congress.   Nor were the issues such as would permit of postponement.   The demarcation of the western boundary of Texas was necessary in order to establish a government over the disputed area, which was already occupied, and in which the Texans had immediately begun to assert their authority.   In Oregon, the number and activity of trappers and settlers, the immense value of the fur-trade, as well as the need of authority of some sort for the preservation of order, made prompt action in providing permanent organization no less imperative.   In California, gold was discovered, and in 1849 a rush to the new territory ensued of such proportions that the regulations concerning the number of inhabitants required for admission to statehood were practically met at once.   The prospecting stories which came back were amazing.   A gold-seeker died from starvation and exposure; his partner determined to give up as soon as he had buried the body; in digging the grave he turned up a nugget of pure gold worth $40,000.   A tramp, put off a wagon-train because he had not paid his fare, wandered across the fields, and literally stumbled over a nugget worth $2500.   The idle, the adventurous, the desperate all started for Eldorado and formed a population particularly in need of strong government.

These problems, whose solution was so essential, were at once discussed in the light of previous agitation and grouped themselves with other grievances of the North and of the South.   The satisfactory decision of all seemed peculiarly difficult.   California, already clamoring for statehood, proposed to tolerate no negroes, free or slave; "California for white men" was the slogan.   Even the descriptions of casual travelers in the arid plains of the great district then known as New Mexico convinced the Southerners that cotton could never be grown there and that the profitable use of slaves there for any purpose was highly problematical.   Apparently the Mexican War had been worse than fruitless; it had added enormous reaches of free territory without increasing the available cotton land at all. Again, the war had ostensibly been fought to enforce the claims of Texas to the Rio Grande as a southern boundary and its success was assumed by the Texans to have guaranteed them the land in dispute. The United States, however, found itself heir to the claims of Mexico, and, when Congress began to realize how vast an area was affected by the Texan claims and how strong the Mexican case had been, it soon assumed the extraordinary position of denying the rightfulness of the claims of Texas to establish whose rectitude the war itself had been fought. Here too the issue of slavery appeared. If the territory were adjudged part of Texas, it would at once become slave territory forever; if it were left a part of New Mexico, Congress would then be able to consider its status. Strong objections were at once manifest among the New Englanders to any settlement in favor of Texas.

Into this tangle of interests and prejudices were projected three old issues on which the North was becoming evidently more and more reluctant to allow the Southerners their way. The argument of the Abolitionists had done much to rouse feeling in the North, but had produced little effect compared with the sight of a fugitive slave fleeing from his master and pursued by United States marshals. If he was so happy in slavery, taunted the Abolitionists, why did he prefer to risk being torn to pieces by bloodhounds rather than stay with his "dear master"? If the masters had the welfare and happiness of the slave so much at heart, why did they pursue him with hue and cry the moment he manifested unmistakably his distaste for slavery? The fact that the negro was valuable property, that he was to be returned as a strayed or stolen horse, and was to be returned to forced labor under the lash moved many a Northerner to expressions of pity and abhorrence whom the impassioned utterances of Phillips had never stirred. The fugitive was to him a living illustration, deposited at his very door, of the evils of slavery. The co-operation of the Northern communities in the capture and return of fugitives had been promised in all colonial agreements between the States and occupied a prominent place in the Articles of Confederation and in the Constitution. Congress had more than once enacted legislation at the request of the South which was believed at the time to be sufficiently stringent. After 1840, however, it became more and more difficult to apprehend fugitives and it was well known that an "underground railroad" had been formed by the Abolitionists for passing the fugitive secretly from house to house to the Canadian frontier. In Ohio and Indiana, where slave territory was nearest Canada, the work was best organized and escapes most numerous; but many fugitives were passed through Philadelphia into New York and New England and so into Canada.

To stop this obvious defiance of Federal statutes had long been the object of the South, which was now clamoring for a law so severe as to stop the escape of slaves. In addition, some regularization or recognition was demanded of the "right" of masters to travel through free territory with their slaves or even to remain there permanently without losing their "property." Slaves were thus held in most Northern States before the War, and in Indiana and Illinois they were even numerous, but the sentiment was growing rapidly in favor of the English view that a slave brought into free territory became at once free. To raise this point, the Dred Scott case was at this time begun, whose decision on appeal by the Supreme Court was so very momentous an incident in the development of the crisis which led finally to hostilities.

But to many members of Congress no issue so imperatively demanded settlement as the question of the continuance of the slave-trade in the District of Columbia. Must their debates be interrupted by the cries of auctioneers and of bidders and the clanking of chains at the slave auction just behind the Federal capitol? In the District of Columbia, the slave-trade had no reason to exist because there was no active use of slaves for agriculture there; the powers to prohibit the practice seemed to be vested in Congress, for the District could plausibly be argued to be of different status from the rest of the national domain. Its slave-trade was, said the more radical, a standing and unnecessary insult to the North, kept in existence by the South purely as a demonstration of her domination over the Federal government.

The debates for the settlement of all these issues were long and eminently able, and centered round the Wilmot Proviso which proposed to exclude slavery from the Mexican accessions. The issue was boldly and plainly stated by the Southerners: the adoption of the Proviso would justify secession by the Southern States from the Union. The legislature of Virginia voted that rather than accept the Proviso the people of Virginia would make "determined resistance at all hazards and to the last extremity." Public meetings and conventions throughout the South very generally expressed similar sentiment, and at a great public banquet in South Carolina the toast, "A Southern Confederacy" was received with great enthusiasm.[1] A convention of the Southern States at Nashville resolved in favor of the lawfulness and constitutionality of secession and was believed by many in the North to have met to concert measures for forming a new confederacy in case the North should not yield. It seems highly probable that Calhoun counseled war in 1850 on the ground that the provocation was sufficient, compromise merely a postponement of war, and the South more likely to prevail than she would be later. Indeed, confirmation of this belief is lent by the fact that even after the North yielded in 1850, the newspapers in South Carolina and a convention assembled to discuss the question were practically unanimous in favor of secession with or without the coöperation of other States; and that in Mississippi the State campaign of 1851 was fought on the issue of secession with Jefferson Davis as the secessionist candidate for Governor and Foote as the candidate favoring an acceptance of the Compromise of 1850. There can be little doubt that many understood the alternative to be com-

---

[1] *New York Tribune*, April 25, 1849. "We firmly believe that there are sixty members of Congress who this day desire a dissolution of the Union and are plotting to effect it." *Ibid.*, Feb. 23, 1850.

promise or secession, and that the feeling at the North in favor of nationalism and union was stronger than the dislike of slavery or of its extension.

The Compromise of 1850 was proposed by Clay, and, as finally adopted, provided that California should become a free State; that the land claimed by Texas should be divided and that State compensated for the surrender of a considerable part of her claims by the assumption by the United States of her indebtedness incurred while independent; but that the rest of the land acquired from Mexico should be organized into Territories without stipulation concerning slavery. Slavery in the District of Columbia was abolished in exchange for a drastic fugitive-slave law. This provided for a summary trial without jury (on the ground that every Northern jury invariably freed the negro), threw the burden of proof on the negro, and, where the owner had been compelled to prove the man his escaped slave, forced the accused to prove himself a free man. Above all, the testimony of slaves was excluded. It was "a law," said Emerson, "which no man can obey or abet the obeying without loss of self-respect and forfeiture of the name of a gentleman." [2]

The Compromise was carried by Clay and Webster, who pleaded for union and peace, against Calhoun, Seward, and Chase, who predicted war and secession. As Webster showed, California was determined to be free and was too far away to permit effective coercion; the South might well yield that. The rest of the territory obtained from Mexico was prevented by the laws of nature from becoming slave territory; it was simply a gratuitous insult to the South for the North to insist upon excluding slavery from it by law. The North might easily yield that. The Compromise of 1850 was an understanding, an agreement, and never possessed nor was meant to possess legal status. Specific provisions for the execution of the agreement were passed in the form of six separate bills during August and September, 1850. There was much exultation throughout the country, and it was openly claimed

[2] Cabot's *Emerson*, 578.

that the issues had been settled for good and all:—the South was satisfied; the North was content. Indeed, during the campaign of 1852, the perpetual observance of the existing agreement was constantly promised and campaign orators desecrated the name of the man who should again open the issue of slavery.

But the handwriting was already on the wall, and there were some who saw it. Surely, the States' rights conventions, the approval of the right of secession, the Southern elections hotly contested and carried by narrow margins in favor of the Compromise, were sinister omens and boded ill for its perpetuity. At the same time, none of these incidents were invested by contemporaries with a tithe of the significance we now attach to them because talk of secession, nullification, and actual dissolution of the union had been loud at every crisis in our history, and men had become accustomed to hearing every difficulty between the sections alleged as adequate cause for disunion. It was a truly ill omen that the men who had made the Compromise, who had for nearly forty years controlled the destinies of the country, had all passed away before the settlement was two years old. John Quincy Adams had died in 1848, and Calhoun had followed him in 1850, murmuring "The South! the poor South! God knows what will become of her!" Benton was defeated for reëlection in that same year and retired to private life; Clay and Webster both died in 1852 and it was universally felt that the pillars of the State had fallen. The control passed into the hands of younger men,—Seward, Chase, Davis, Douglas,—on the whole, into the hands of the enemies rather than the friends of the Compromise. It is one of the enigmas of history that men should delude themselves into the belief that the waters have been swept back with the broom of argument at just the moment when the tidal wave, as yet a tiny crest of white along the distant horizon, is rushing towards them with the speed of a race-horse.

XX

THE IRREPRESSIBLE CONFLICT

ONE of the most significant facts in the history of the United States is the growth in the North of the moral conviction that slavery was wrong. The North had become pretty thoroughly convinced by 1850 that the South meant to extend slavery, but, until a clear majority of the people were agreed that slavery was morally wrong, the decision of the South to extend it still permitted discussion and made compromise possible. Until it became clear to both sides that compromise was impossible, a war could not result, and, for the historian of the United States the all important fact to make clear is the reason why two sections of the country fought each other for four years. A disagreement, a fundamental cleavage in the country, was clear in 1850; but disagreements, threats, sectional interests, a belief in the legality and possibility of secession were as old as the country itself. No one considered them in themselves dangerous, and the union had been so many times on the brink of dissolution that men had almost begun to believe it capable of withstanding all shocks and attacks. A change took place after 1850 in the attitude of the North which treated the extension of slavery as a wrong, and which led the North to demand from the South a definite statement as to what the latter proposed to do about the extension of that wrong.

In the very year in which the great Compromise was passed, a book was written by a poor woman in southern Ohio which became the most mighty ethical influence of the decade. *Uncle Tom's Cabin* presented slavery to the North in a concrete, dramatic story, every incident of which was intended to convince the reader that slavery was wrong. Whether or not

269

the book was an accurate or fair picture of the institution is of little significance compared to the fact that within a few years a million and a half copies were sold to readers, an overwhelming majority of whom believed the story true. Not those things which are true, but those things which honest and sincere men and women believe to be true, are the bases of motive forces in history. Still, the North as a whole looked and saw nothing; it listened and read but was not convinced.

Now came three incidents which effectually roused the North and which to the thinking of millions confirmed the facts and pointed the moral lesson of *Uncle Tom's Cabin*— Kansas-Nebraska, the Dred Scott Decision, and the Lincoln-Douglas debates. Books and speeches had left the North indifferent and apathetic because only a fraction of the people had been reached. The "Crime of Kansas" was writ high upon the heavens for him to read who ran.

The vast stretches of the Louisiana Purchase to the west of Missouri and of the territories of Iowa and Minnesota had not yet been organized at all, and the stream of people surging across the plains to California and Oregon now made necessary some sort of territorial government, if only to preserve the peace. There was in this nothing disputable, but the organization of the district instantly raised the question of the status of slavery and evoked from the North the statement that the Missouri Compromise had consecrated that land to freedom. It was evident to the South that, if this was true, slavery was already circumscribed, and that the end of its westward march and of its further development was already in sight, for, with California free, Arkansas and Texas already settled, and the Indians in possession of the only other land south of 36° 30′ at all suitable for cotton, there was no more new land for slave States and, short of the conquest of Mexico, there never would be any. The danger so long warded off was already upon them. The Missouri Compromise, the Southerners therefore argued, had been made when circumstances were entirely different and would now have an effect never intended by its framers. Headed by Douglas, they demanded the opening of the unorganized territory to slavery and alleged that the Compromise of 1850 abrogated the Missouri Compromise, and that the latter had been never valid at all, but had been void from the first because Congress had no power to prohibit slavery in the Territories.

Here was an issue concerned with great men, with great events; with queries not merely political, moral, and religious, to be decided by general principles, and an appeal to logic and reason; but with questions of fact upon which a definitive understanding had existed among statesmen of all parties for more than thirty years. The Northern men brushed aside the constitutional subtleties regarding the invalidity of the Missouri Compromise and declared the new bill the breach of a compact considered sacred by a generation of statesmen.[1] Despite a storm of protest and argument, the Kansas-Nebraska Bill passed, dividing the great area into two parts, leaving the decision in regard to slavery to the vote of the inhabitants ("squatter sovereignty") and declaring the Missouri Compromise null and void. "It annuls all past compromises with slavery," insisted Sumner of Massachusetts, "and makes all future compromises impossible. Thus it puts freedom and slavery face to face and bids them grapple." Chase of Ohio even more nearly touched the keynote of Northern feeling. "You may pass it here," he told the senators, "it may become law. But its effect will be to satisfy all thinking men that no compromises with slavery will endure, except

[1] It was not noted at the time and seems to have been hardly realized since that the Compromise of 1820 had already been broken. The western boundary of Missouri had originally been drawn straight north in continuation of the meridian of the point at the end of the southern line. This line crossed the Missouri River and left a triangular delta between it and the river, which of course did not form at that time any part of the western boundary of the State, a large and rich district coveted by the Missourians. According to the terms of the Compromise, this was free territory, but in 1833 the Federal government made a treaty with the Indians for the cession of that district and by act of Congress made it part of Missouri. If this act was or is legal, the Compromise of 1820 never had any *legal* status beyond that accorded by men to any "gentlemen's agreement." Shepard, *Early History of Missouri*, 111.

so long as they serve the interests of slavery." The Bill passed just before dawn, and, as the senators came down the steps at the Capitol, the morning guns at the Navy Yard were sounding the usual sunrise salute. The Democrats at once exclaimed that they celebrated the victory just won. Chase turned to Sumner and said solemnly: "They celebrate a present victory, but the echoes they awake will never rest till slavery itself shall die."

The excitement in the North was prodigious and the unanimity of condemnation revealed a degree of agreement unsuspected. Douglas declared that he could have traveled from Chicago to Boston by the light of his own burning effigies; one hundred and three ladies in an Ohio village denounced him as a second Judas Iscariot and sent him the thirty pieces of silver for which they declared he had sold his Lord.

Kansas had been opened to slavery; the decision of the new settlers who voted at the first territorial election would decide its status so far as slavery was concerned. Men from all parts of the country joined in the rush to Kansas with the avowed intention of voting on one side or the other. The New England Emigrant Aid Society was formed to encourage the resort of men opposed to slavery and an able man was sent to Kansas to direct the cause of the Free-State men, as they were soon called. From Washington came a Pro-Slavery man as governor, sent by the President of the United States with definite orders to make Kansas slave territory. When the time approached for the territorial election, at which the question of the status of Kansas while a Territory was to be decided, a rough, boisterous, unkempt mob of border ruffians came over from Missouri, voted at the election, and carried Kansas for slavery. There were about 2900 legal voters in the territory; 5427 votes were cast for slavery, proving to many Eastern men that slavery advocates intended to make Kansas "slave" even if it were necessary to resort to foul means to do it.

The Governor accepted the fraudulent votes as valid and

organized a Pro-Slavery legislature. The Free-State men prepared a constitution, elected a delegate to Congress by about a hundred more votes than had been cast for the Pro-Slavery delegate, and asked recognition from Congress as the true majority in Kansas, entitled to govern the territory by any proper interpretation of the recent act. Congress declined to accept their claim and for a while considered requesting the President to suppress them. Meanwhile, the Pro-Slavery men, aided by a large mob from Missouri, advanced upon the Free-State town of Lawrence, intending to sack it, but the Free-State men were well armed and a truce was agreed to by the leaders, cold weather arrived, and the "army" withdrew, carrying three dead bodies,—one man killed by the falling of a tree, one shot by his own guard, and a third killed in a brawl. In Lawrence, one man alone protested against the agreement not to fight,—a tall, slender man with a somber face, fired with intense earnestness, John Brown.

The Pro-Slavery men retired, avowedly but to await a better opportunity. The sheriff a little afterward was in Lawrence, and, a shot intended for some one else coming in his direction by accident, he declared that the Free-State men had attempted to murder him. He impaneled a grand jury which indicted them all for murder, and the marshal gathered a posse of some scores of men from Kansas and a thousand or more ruffians, who came over the river from Missouri, armed to the teeth and well provided with whisky. At Lawrence no resistance was offered; some arrests were quietly made; but the Missourians were not to be balked twice. The town was thoroughly sacked on May 20, 1856.

Two days later, in the United States Senate, Charles Sumner of Massachusetts delivered an eloquent and bitter arraignment of the Pro-Slavery attitude towards Kansas. To wipe out the insult to the South, as he deemed it to be, Brooks of South Carolina approached Sumner, writing at his desk in the almost empty Senate Chamber, and struck him repeatedly on the head from behind with a heavy cane till he fell from his chair unconscious. The news of the sack of Lawrence and of the assault on Sumner reached the country almost simultaneously and caused an outburst of indignation and anger at the North such as had never been known before. The newspapers came out with great black headlines, "The Crime against Kansas," "Bleeding Kansas," "Shrieks from Kansas." The effect would have been immeasurably less profound had not the South openly declared the cause of the Pro-Slavery men in Kansas that of the South itself, and if it had not rejoiced at the assault upon Sumner, tendering banquets to his assailant at which gold canes were presented to him and his health toasted.

Whatever actually happened in Kansas, the North believed that a premeditated design was being executed by fraud and force to make Kansas slave. To secure the opportunity the South had broken so sacred a compact as the Missouri Compromise and had provided that the people who went to Kansas should decide for or against slavery. But finding the majority were Free-State men, ballot boxes had been stuffed, innocent men slain, an unresisting town sacked by a drunken crew of ruffians imported for the purpose. And such actions the President and Congress of the United States had approved by the high authority vested in them and behind these ruffians had placed the sanction of Federal authority! The President had removed seriatim the Governors who declined to obey his partisan orders to support the Pro-Slavery party with Federal troops; the Houses of Congress had declined to accept the government formed by the numerical majority in Kansas. To pass the enabling act they had been forced to descend to perjury and fraud; to prevent the honest execution of their own measure, they had been driven to deceit, arson, and murder. They had been willing to allow the inhabitants of Kansas to vote in favor of slavery; they had no intention at all of recognizing as valid the vote against it.[2]

2 "While the Nebraska Bill was pending, Judge Douglas helped to vote down a clause giving the people of the Territories the right to exclude slavery if they chose." Lincoln, speech at Beardstown, 1858. Herndon, *Life of Lincoln*, II, 99-100.

The following month of June, 1856, saw the first national convention of a new political party, the Republican party, composed of men opposed to the extension of slavery. There can be no doubt that its strength and unity were largely due to the events in Kansas. Throughout the North had sprung up during the preceding fifteen years groups of men, for the most part fragments of the old Whig party, who were trying to organize an opposition to the ruling party, and most of whom had made prominent in their platform a plank either connected with liberty or with some form of opposition to slavery. The movement to fuse them into one party had begun in the Northwest and had been on the whole successful, but was made positive and permanent by the spectacle of "bleeding Kansas." In a great speech at Rochester, N. Y., Seward struck the keynote of the campaign: "It is an irrepressible conflict between opposing and enduring forces and it means that the United States must and will, sooner or later, become either entirely a slaveholding nation or entirely a free labor nation. . . . I know and you know that a revolution has begun. I know and all the world knows that revolutions never go backwards." Frémont was nominated by the Republicans and ran on a platform which opposed the further extension of slavery. Apprehension at the South was keen, and preparations for secession, should he be elected, were said to have been made. The Democrats elected Buchanan President, but they carried only four Northern States and the popular vote gave them only half a million votes more than the Republicans. The moral feeling of the North that slavery was wrong had attained effective political expression in a strong new party pledged to prevent its extension.

Now came the pronouncement in 1857 of the decision of the Supreme Court in the famous Dred Scott case. The issue was essentially simple: Scott, a slave, had been carried by his master into free territory, where he had long resided, and whence he had then willingly accompanied his master back into slave territory. The claim was that his residence in free territory had made him free; but the case took such a form that the only issue for the court to decide was his status at the time of the suit's institution. A majority of the judges agreed that he was then a slave and hence unable to sue in the courts, but disagreed entirely upon the reasoning by which they reached that conclusion. The political significance of the case arose from the fact that some of the judges, notably the Chief Justice, a Southerner, considered in his opinion and pronounced in favor of the South upon the multitudinous constitutional controversies regarding slavery. That Taney acted with high-minded purpose in an attempt to fend off possible war, is clear; that the South proclaimed from the house-tops that the Supreme Court had decided for all time in favor of slavery upon the legal issues, is also clear; that the North utterly declined to accept the new decision as of any validity, is beyond doubt at all. The arguments of the judges roused the North far less than the conclusions which the South drew from them and the significance the South was determined to give them. If Congress had no power over slavery in the States, and if the decision meant that it could not prohibit slavery in the Territories, it had then no discretion at all; it could act only to preserve, extend, and protect slavery. Taney's opinion was soon condensed into an aphorism which obtained great currency at the North,—'that negroes had no rights which the white man was bound to respect.'

The Northern lawyers instantly pointed out that the decision of the court, which alone was of legal obligation, concerned Dred Scott, and that the long arguments concerning the status of slavery were merely *obiter dicta*, which the practice of centuries held to be of no legal obligation whatever. But, even if these statements upon the general controversy were valid, there was no agreement among the judges upon these points, and to declare the individual opinion of the Chief Justice the decision of the court was a flat contradiction of obvious facts. As if to give point to the arguments of the angry Northern lawyers, the Southern Democrats printed thousands of copies of Taney's opinion, distributed them as campaign documents, and openly taunted the Republicans, demanding "Well, what are you going to do about it?" Was it true, the Northern leaders asked each other, that slavery could not be constitutionally restricted, that this wrong was to be perpetuated despite them, was protected by the Constitution itself and defended by President, Congress, and Supreme Court? "Alas," lamented the *New York Tribune,* "the character of the Supreme Court of the United States as an impartial judicial body has gone! It has abdicated its just functions and descended into the political mire. . . . It has draggled and polluted the ermine in the filth of pro-slavery politics."

Now came news in the fall of 1858 that out in the West, the "little Giant," the great Douglas himself, had been bested in a series of debates by a lanky, raw-boned Illinois country lawyer, a mighty plain-spoken man, affectionately alluded to by his admirers, as the "Tall Sucker,"—Abraham Lincoln. What he said was startlingly clear and expressed what many in the country had long been trying to say for themselves. He was able to grasp both sides of the issue; to make every allowance a fair-minded man could ask, but his statement of the crux of the difficulty was illuminating and satisfying.

"I think I have no prejudice against the Southern people," he told his audience at Galesburg. "They are just what we would be in their situation. If slavery did not now exist amongst them they would not introduce it. If it did now exist amongst us, we should not instantly give it up. This I believe of the masses of the North and South. . . . When Southern people tell us that they are no more responsible for the origin of slavery than we, I acknowledge the fact. When it is said that the institution exists, and that it is very difficult to get rid of it, in any satisfactory way, I can understand and appreciate the saying. I surely will not blame them for not doing what I should not know how to do myself. If all earthly power were given me, I should not know what to do as to the existing institution. . . . I have no purpose, directly or indirectly, to interfere with the institution of slavery

in the states where it exists. I believe I have no lawful right
to do so, and I have no inclination to do so. I have no
purpose to introduce political and social equality between
the white and black races. . . . But I hold that, notwithstanding all this, there is no reason in the world why
the negro is not entitled to all the natural rights enumerated
in the Declaration of Independence—the right to life, liberty,
and the pursuit of happiness. . . . In the right to eat the
bread without the leave of anybody else, which his own hand
earns, he is my equal and the equal of Judge Douglas, and
the equal of every living man.'' ''To satisfy the Southerners,'' he said to a New York audience in 1859, ''we must
cease to call slavery wrong, and join them in calling it right.
And this must be done thoroughly, done in acts as well as
words. . . . If it is right, we cannot object to its nationality,
its universality; if it is wrong, they cannot justly insist
upon its extension, its enlargement. All they ask we could
readily grant, if we thought slavery right; all we ask they
could as readily grant, if they thought it wrong. Their
thinking it right and our thinking it wrong is the precise
fact upon which depends the whole controversy. Thinking it
right, as they do, they are not to blame for desiring its full
recognition, as being right; but thinking it wrong, as we do,
can we yield to them? . . . If our sense of duty forbids
this, . . . let us be diverted by no sophistical consequences—
such as groping for some middle ground between the right
and the wrong, vain as the search for a man who should be
neither a living man nor a dead man; such as a policy of
'don't care' on a question about which all true men do
care.''

Lincoln's reputation spread; the East wished to hear him
and he spoke in many parts of the country, always to the
same purpose, always leaving behind him a deep impression
of his fairness, honesty, and sincerity. Above all, he was
a ''plain man,'' who used plain language. If slavery was
right, why not extend it? If slavery was wrong, why consider
its extension at all? How could one coolly propose to per-

petuate a wrong? Should the South be allowed to destroy the Missouri Compromise, commit arson and murder in Kansas, drag the judicial ermine in the mire, to extend and perpetuate a wrong? He gave the Northern people an ethical test to apply to the situation which at last enabled them to make up their minds.

At this juncture, a book written by a "poor white" in North Carolina, *The Impending Crisis of the South*, raised squarely the most significant issue of all, as was promptly recognized both North and South. If slavery was so good a thing, *for whose good was it?* Helper emphasized with relentless force the facts in the United States census, that the direct benefits of slavery accrued to only a part of the whites at the South; that the splendor, luxury, and culture of the South, which had been so praised, were the possession of a small minority of the whites, who ruled for their own particular benefit six million whites and nearly four million blacks. The problem, he showed, was not one of two dimensions, concerned only with the master and his slave, but one of the three dimensions, concerned with master, slave, and the poor whites, the overwhelming majority of the white people at the South, who had no vital interest in slavery and no hopes of possessing any. Pitilessly he exposed their poverty, their lack of economic, social, and political rights, and demanded the abolition of slavery in the name of the majority of the whites in the South, as the only means of restoring to them their true freedom and privileges, as the only means of providing a market for their labor and their produce. *Uncle Tom's Cabin* had told of the wrongs done to the slave; Helper dwelt upon the wrongs done to the white man. Great piles of the book became a familiar sight in Northern book stores; the Republicans circulated it as a campaign document; the Southerners further advertised it by their efforts to secure its suppression. The query began to form in Northern minds: is not this fear of discussion, this desire to prevent investigation and comment fathered by the knowledge that the facts are not as favorable to slavery as they allege them to be? Had the poor whites in the South been able to read and understand the book, it would have spelled the fall of the slave-power.

Nor did the clamor at the South for the reopening of the slave-trade fail to furnish Northern minds with corroboration of the arguments of Lincoln and Helper. In 1858, a convention in Alabama gave its entire attention to the subject; a general convention at Vicksburg in 1859 voted two to one in favor of reopening the slave-trade, while in the legislature of Louisiana bills were under consideration for the importation of "black apprentices," and some thousands of negroes were actually smuggled into the country from Africa. *The Charleston Mercury,* one of the most influential papers in the South, championed the cause ardently and declared that the decay of cotton-culture in South Carolina was wholly due to the prohibition upon the importation of slaves.

And now sounded through the land what many felt was the voice crying in the wilderness, shouting the battle-cry of freedom. A man came forward calling for action: "These men are all talk—what we want is action—action!" Men were needed, he said, who would "break the jaws of the wicked and pluck the spoil out of his teeth." John Brown nourished himself upon the avenging clauses of the Old Testament and believed himself called to be the soldier of the Lord, called to wreak God's vengeance upon the Pro-Slavery men. He had been in Kansas and had murdered men in cold blood in the name of Truth and Justice. Now he believed that the knowledge among the slaves that a haven of refuge existed in the mountains of Virginia, where they would be protected by force from capture, would lead to a general attempt to escape and perhaps to a slave insurrection. The remarkable thing about Brown's raid is the philanthropists of national repute whose support he secured, and who provided him with money and arms. After all has been said, there must have been something remarkable about the man. The raid failed; he held the arsenal at

Harper's Ferry for a few hours, and then was captured by Federal troops.

The news of an attempt to rouse and arm the slaves caused in the South a paroxysm of terror and a demand for justice on the perpetrator and protection for the South from the Federal government. The North was stirred as never before by the sight of a man who voluntarily, cheerfully, laid down his life for the principle that slavery was wrong. "The cry of the oppressed," he said in prison, "is my reason and the only thing that prompted me to come here." "I feel just as content to die for God's eternal truth on the scaffold as in any other way." All his sins were forgotten in his atonement. To the Northern Abolitionists, he was a martyr. To them, the moment for the downfall of slavery was near,— a man had died for the cause! "This will be a great day in our history," wrote the poet Longfellow in his journal under the date of John Brown's execution, "the date of a new revolution quite as much needed as the old one." Four years later, when on the battlefield at Gettysburg, the last gallant charge of Pickett's brigade faltered, broke, and fled, the Union soldiers on Round Top swung their caps in the air and chanted in mighty chorus, rolling out over the valley filled with the flying and the pursuers,

"John Brown's body lies a-mouldering in the grave,—
His soul goes marching on."

XXI

THE CAUSES OF SECESSION

ON a very momentous day in the annals of America a body of representative men were assembled to discuss the most vital issue of the time. In the chair was a man long venerated for his probity and wisdom. The crisis in the discussion of the critical issue had been reached; different opinions had been hotly maintained by excited disputants; and the matter then engrossing the minds of all was the cause of so serious a disagreement. The speaker addressing the assembly contended—to use the words of the record—"that the States were divided into different interests, not by their difference of size but by other circumstances, the most material of which resulted partly from climate, but principally from the effects of their having or not having slaves. These two causes concurred in forming the great division of interests in the United States. It did not lie between the large and small States: It lay between the Northern and the Southern."[1] Those words were spoken by James Madison in the Convention which framed the Constitution of the United States. The vital cleft of the country into North and South is older than the Constitution, older than States' rights, older than the cotton-culture, older than the anti-slavery movement.

Later in the debate, Gouverneur Morris declared that this distinction between the Northern and Southern States "is either fictitious or real; if fictitious, let it be dismissed and let us proceed with due confidence. If it be real, instead of attempting to blend incompatible things, let us at once take a friendly leave of each other."[2] With him agreed Luther

[1] Hunt's *Madison's Notes*, I, 278.
[2] Hunt's *Madison's Notes*, I, 351. What eventually happened was

Martin of Maryland. "He was for letting a separation take place if they desired it; he had rather there should be two confederacies than one" founded on such principles as those proposed.[3] James Wilson of Pennsylvania added that he knew some respectable, earnest men who preferred three confederacies, united by offensive and defensive alliances.[4] Such ideas, however, were far from new to the listeners. Half the earlier schemes for central government had provided for two, three, or even four confederacies. Nullification had appeared in the New England Confederacy when Massachusetts and Plymouth were hardly more than a score of years old. The right of secession had been openly proclaimed in the debates upon the adoption of the Declaration of Independence.[5] The infant nation, in fact, was suckled by secession and nourished upon States' rights. After the Convention had finished its work and the Constitution was before the country for adoption, Cyrus Griffin wrote from New York: "We are told that Mr. George Mason (of Virginia) has declared himself so great an enemy to the Constitution that he will heartily join Mr. Henry and others in promoting a Southern Confederacy."[6] Indeed so true was this prediction, that when the Virginia Convention had adopted the Constitution, Patrick Henry was invited by the minority to become President of a body to formulate plans for the formation of another Confederacy. Probably nothing but his refusal to countenance it prevented its success.[7]

foreseen. King said: "If they [the Southern States] threaten to separate now in case injury shall be done them, will their threats be less urgent or effectual, when force shall back their demands? Even in the intervening period, there will be no point of time at which they will not be able to say, 'Do us justice or we will separate.'" *Ibid.*, 345-6.

[3] *Ibid.*, 356; 253.

[4] *Ibid.*, 363.

[5] It was said that the delegates of such States as did not agree to independence must withdraw from Congress "and possibly their colonies might secede from the union." Quoted in Hazelton, *Declaration of Independence*, 112.

[6] Bancroft's *History of the Constitution*, II, 461.

[7] Rowland's *Life of Mason*, II, 274. The whole incident is fully described.

Not only were those ideas old when the Constitution was adopted, when slavery was believed to be dying a natural death, and when the cotton-gin had not yet made cotton-culture profitable in America; but in the succeeding generations these notions were held by Northern and Western States as well as by Southern. It is probably no exaggeration to say that when the great debates over the admission of Missouri in 1819 made clear for the first time the depth of the cleft between the North and South, every State in the Union had at some time within the preceding half century nullified some law or threatened to secede. North, South, West, East, had all planned secession before 1820, before the issues and factors prominent in the later struggle had unmistakably appeared.

In fact, the fundamental issues of the Civil War were old and not new. They were fundamental in the broadest sense, far transcending the influence or notions of any man or group of men, or indeed of any single generation. They were not produced by Calhoun, Davis, or Lincoln, and were of a nature which, in fact, forbade their conscious creation at all. No individual or body of individuals, no section of the country was in this sense to blame for the Civil War. It was, in the last analysis, the result of climate and of geographical conditions as old as the Glacial period, which began to exert their influence when the mammoth flourished in Kansas and when the cave bear still suckled her young in the Virginia mountains. We must very carefully separate the difficulty which created the possibility of a disagreement between two sections of this country from its own fundamental causes and also from those particular manifestations of it in the early nineteenth century about which men began to argue. We have even then only approached the situation where we find men drifting from disagreement into threats and from threats into defiance, and we must still make clear the specific factors and events which created two radical parties who could see no solution except in war. And even when we have found the cause of the determination to fight we are still far from the actual *casus belli* over which the fighting began. The technical *casus belli*, the firing on Sumter, no doubt grew out of a disagreement on the constitutional question of States' rights; and the student will on this ground agree with the position of Davis and of Stephens after the War that States' rights was the sole and only cause of the War. The issue, however, which brought States' rights to the fore in 1860 was unquestionably slavery, and the student can on this basis agree with Lincoln and many historians that a difference of opinion over slavery really caused the War. But if the student seeks the reasons why both slavery and States' rights were under discussion at all, he will see that sectionalism, the existence in the country of two strata widely differing in economic and institutional life, was the real difficulty, and he will find its existence adequately explained by the geographical and geological factors operating in America for uncounted millions of years. These conditions were found by the first settlers; they shaped colonial history when the white slaves in the South outnumbered the black; moulded the Constitution; produced tobacco, cotton, slavery, and the War; and are still to-day actively fashioning the issues of presidential campaigns.

The great events of American history have been attempts to reconcile the outward political form of the government with great existing economic and social facts. In 1776, the States were in all but law and name independent of England; the Revolution merely brought the political situation into conformity with the actual facts. In 1789, the Constitution set up a relationship between the States on the whole in conformity with their actual relations. But in the subsequent decades were developed two great economic forces utterly changing the situation; and men began to argue whether the superior economic power was the diversified industry of the North or the growth of cotton by slaves. Slavery, cotton, machinery, railroads, tariff, new territory, had been either very minor factors or not dreamed of when the Constitution was framed. Their constitutionality was therefore a most legitimate issue for debate, and the task of the Civil War was the adjustment of the legal fabric of central government to the obvious economic and territorial facts in existence.

At the same time that we recognize the fundamental character of the cleft between the sections and the absolute necessity of some sort of decision upon the fundamental constitutional relations of new economic forces to the older economic and political factors, we must not assume that their settlement by the arbitrament of arms was inevitable. Had the country developed more slowly and less, as it were, by spasmodic spurts, the adjustment of forces would perhaps have insensibly taken place in the course of their development.[8] The immediate cause of war was the impossibility of settling the issues by compromise or agreement. For fully forty years, the statesmen of the various sections successfully made compromise after compromise. Indeed, the period between 1820 and 1860 ought perhaps to be studied less as the growth of the war-spirit than as a time when the solitary object of all parties was the avoidance of hostilities. But this prolonged attempt to settle the fundamental relations of the two sections was frustrated by the very rapidity of the country's growth. No sooner had some compromise mutually satisfactory to all been made with much rejoicing than the whole situation, which it was intended to adjust, was entirely changed by the appearance of unforeseen factors of sufficient importance to produce a new situation, which raised the old fundamental questions with greater insistence. The Constitution itself was the first compromise and the only one to be lasting. The Missouri Compromise was invalidated (though not made void)

---

[8] "The question of the relation of the States to the Federal government is the cardinal question of our constitutional system. At every turn of our national development, we have been brought face to face with it, and no definition either of statesmen or of judges has ever quieted it or decided it. It cannot, indeed, be settled by the opinion of any one generation, because it is a question of growth, and every successive stage of our political and economic development gives it a new aspect, makes it a new question." Woodrow Wilson, in the *North American Review*, 187, 684.

by the astonishing growth of the cotton-culture and cotton-manufacture. The "American System," which was to provide for the interests of the various sections, was deemed unsatisfactory in the South as soon as it was adopted because of the severity of the commercial crisis in Europe just previous to 1830, whose influence on the price of cotton the South attributed solely to the tariff. The annexation of Texas and the Mexican War added so little land suitable for cotton to the existing area of the country that it was soon clearly apparent to the Southern leaders that the Compromise of 1850 was on the whole a victory for the North. Indeed, the extraordinary rapidity with which the available land in these enormous areas was occupied and in some fashion utilized made it literally impossible to foresee what the ensuing five years' growth would bring forward.

In 1860, the Southern leaders were still as sure as before that there was unlimited wealth to be had by the development of the cotton-culture, but they were certain that the degree of profit previously obtained would be inevitably reduced by the lack of new lands of the most fertile type, and by the enormous increase in the value of slaves from $600 in 1836 to $1400 in 1856. The reopening of the slave-trade would solve the difficulty by promptly furnishing such cheap labor that the fields already cropped and the less fertile soil in the South not yet utilized could be tilled at an enormous profit. The Constitution, however, stood squarely in the way of this remedy, for it definitely conferred on the Federal government the right, already exercised, to prohibit the slave-trade. New land could not be provided because there was no more land in the vast area of the United States which could be opened to cotton into which cotton was likely to go and, while the Southern States remained in the Union, there was no prospect of the annexation of land in the Gulf of Mexico. The extension of the influence of the United States in the Gulf and in Central America had been attempted in the decade following 1850, but England and France had determinedly interposed and had secured the signature of such treaties as practically forbade the United States to develop any vital interests in the Gulf except in concert with them. Secession would be a remedy and perhaps the only one. "I want Cuba," declared a Southern senator, "I want Tamaulipas, Potosi, and one or two other Mexican states; and I want them all for the same reason—for the planting and spreading of slavery. And a footing in Central America will wonderfully aid us in acquiring those states. . . . Whether we can obtain the territory while the Union lasts, I do not know; I fear we cannot. But I would make an honest effort, and if we failed, I would go out of the Union and try it there." [9] For, after the cotton States had split off from the Northern States, whose industrial and maritime growth England found dangerous to her supremacy, England might well look with favor on the scheme of a Southern Empire for the growing by slave labor in the Gulf of Mexico of that cotton on which the prosperity of northern England so entirely depended. It was the political tie, the Constitution,'which was the greatest incubus, and which saddled the suffering South with tariffs and diplomatic difficulties. Nothing else stood in their way, thought the Southerners; there were no economic, geographical, or institutional barriers in the way of Southern greatness and prosperity. It is this belief that the political bond was the stumbling-block of offense which is at the root of the belief in the possibility and expediency of secession.

Moreover, if the clash of arms was ever to come, it was eminently clear to the Southern leaders that they must move before the disparity in size of the North and South should become more pronounced. In 1828, in 1845, in 1850, with the Federal government really in their hands, with the wealth of the South increasing at a phenomenal rate, with a retarda-

[9] C. D. Drake, *Union and Anti-Slavery Speeches*, 184. Morton's *Southern Empire* has much evidence pro and con (mostly pro) this idea of expansion. "In the event of Southern secession, they contemplated a magnificent Confederacy of slave-holding States, including Cuba, Mexico, and Central America." Hodgson, *Cradle of the Confederacy*, 319. See his interesting account of the attempt of Lopez in 1850–51 to seize Cuba, pp. 314 *et seq.*

tion of that growth hardly likely, there was little to be gained by war which might not improbably be obtained by compromise. It seemed certain that their chances would be better at some future time. Calhoun had indeed solemnly warned the leaders in 1847 that the South was, in comparison to the North, stronger then than it would ever be again,[10] but the growth of the following decade was needed to bring that fact home to them.[11] The real genesis of the actual fighting is to be found in the history of the years 1854–1860. In the debates over the Kansas-Nebraska Bill in 1854, a Virginian had exclaimed in the House, "If you restore the Missouri Compromise, this Union will be dissolved," and from all sides had risen derisive mocking shouts of "Oh! No!" In the spring of 1860, the shadow of the coming crisis had already fallen athwart the floor of the House. The lack of new territory from which to make slave States; the rapid growth of new free States showed the Southerners that their control of the Senate was tottering, and to lose it meant to them the loss of the only benefit they derived from the Federal union,—the protection of their peculiar institution by the Federal government. With the free States in control at Washington, with Northern sentiment hostile to slavery, and with public opinion strong against the enforcement of the

[10] " Calhoun in a letter to a member of the Alabama legislature at this time, said that 'instead of shunning we ought to court the issue with the North on the slavery question'; that he would go one step farther and 'force the issue on the North.' 'We are now stronger, relatively,' said Mr. Calhoun, 'than we shall be hereafter politically and morally.'" Hodgson, *The Cradle of the Confederacy*, 273. The letter was not printed in Calhoun's *Works*. See also the quotations from the address of a convention to the people of Alabama on the danger of delay, pp. 331-2.

[11] "All admit that an ultimate dissolution of the Union is inevitable and we believe that the crisis is not far off. Then let it come now; the better for the South that it should be to-day; *she* cannot afford to wait. With the North it is different. Every day adds to her sectional strength and every day the balance of power becomes less proportionate between the two sections. In a few more years, . . . our doom will be sealed." *Charleston Mercury*, Sept. 18, 1860. Sherman's Southern friends told him the same. See the letters of W. T. Sherman.

Fugitive-Slave laws, every guarantee would disappear, and Mason and Dixon's line would become in very fact the boundary between two hostile confederacies. Nor did the North fail to perceive the real issue:—that the South dared not risk longer delay.[12] "The fault of the free states in the eyes of the South," wrote Lowell in the *Atlantic Monthly,* "is not one that can be atoned for by any yielding of special points here and there. Their offense is that they are free and that their habits and prepossessions are those of freedom. Their crime is the census of 1860. Their increase in numbers, wealth, and power is a standing aggression. . . . What they (the Southerners) demand is nothing less than that we should abolish the spirit of the age. . . . It is the stars in their courses that fight against their system." [13]

In 1860, the white population north of Mason and Dixon's line and of the Ohio River was about twenty millions and that south of the line about eight millions with four millions of negroes: and during the past decade the North had grown 41% and the South 27%. Not only were the whites at the North already more than double those at the South in number, but they were increasing nearly twice as fast (the more considerable part of the total Southern growth was among the negroes), and a decade hence the disparity might not be merely twice but thrice or even more! The census also re-

---

[12] As early as Dec. 14, 1843, George Ticknor wrote from Boston to Sir Charles Lyell, in London, "I would wait as a Northern man, because it is for my interest. The South is growing weak, we are growing strong. The Southern States are not only losing their relative consequence in the Union, but from the inherent and manifold mischiefs of slavery, they are positively growing poor. They are falling back in refinement, civilization, and power. Every year puts the advantage more on our side, and prepares us better to meet the contest . . . which can never be other than formidable and disastrous." *Life and Letters of Ticknor,* II, 218. On Nov. 27, 1860, he wrote again to Lyell: "The cry is that the South is in danger, because the South is in the minority and is weak; and they had better go out of the Union before they become weaker and more feeble by the constantly increasing power of the free States." *Ibid.,* II, 431. Ticknor gives this statement as something currently known and understood in Boston.

[13] January 1861.

vealed astonishing facts about the South which ill-compared with its list of populous cities and thriving towns at the North. In Alabama the census recorded fifteen towns, nine of which had a population of less than a thousand; in Arkansas, two towns; in South Carolina, three, besides Charleston, with more than a thousand people. To the arguments of Helper the census gave only too accurate and prompt confirmation. Only 10,781 families owned as many as 50 slaves; 1733 men owned the plantations on which more than 100 slaves were employed. In Virginia, out of a million whites, only 114 owned more than 100 slaves. Less than two million whites in the whole South were in any way concerned with slavery; over six millions neither owned slaves nor derived direct bene- fit from their labor. "That this body of three-fourths of the white men of the whole South should have fought stub- bornly for four years to fasten on more completely bonds which restricted them to every inferiority of life is one of the most extraordinary facts of history." Had not States'- rights feeling been so strong, had these poor whites not under- stood that the independent sovereignty of the States was at issue, their adherence would scarcely have been given to the new Confederacy.

The productivity of the two sections roughly divided on Mason and Dixon's line was amazingly different and showed clearly the results of the portentous development of varied industry in the North and the unexampled growth of popula- tion in the district west of Pennsylvania and north of the Ohio River. The South produced only one-eighteenth of the cheese and dairy products; one-quarter of the wheat, one- fifth of the oats, one-tenth of the hay, and half of the corn; but two-thirds of the swine, five-sixths of the tobacco and all of the cane sugar and cotton. The total value of the manufactured products indispensable to varied industry— agricultural implements, iron in all its forms, steam ma- chinery, coal, lumber, flour and meal, leather, all sorts of cloth, boots, shoes, nails, paper, ink, and the like—was valued at the South at about seventy-five million dollars, about one-tenth of the value of the products of the North. The grand total of all Northern products, $1,730,330,000, was eleven times greater than that of the South, $155,531,000. Two and one-half times as many fighting men! Eleven times the ability to produce everything needed for the prosecution of a war!

How could the Southern leaders with such facts staring them in the face begin a war with the only district within three thousand miles of them capable of supplying them with the manufactured articles they must have or of buying the only things they had to sell? Because they believed Cotton was King! For the best part of a century it had been dinned into American ears that the one absolutely indispensable thing upon which American prosperity rested was the possession of a medium of exchange with Europe. Cotton had been the only commodity the country had ever itself produced which had in any degree proved adequate, and in 1860 it was nearly fifty per cent of the total exports of the country and itself exceeded by twenty-five per cent the total exports of the North. In addition, the exports of manufactured goods which the North did make were believed to be dependent on the use of Southern cotton in the New England looms. With the proceeds of the sale of cotton in New England and in Europe, the South bought manufactured goods from New England, iron from Pennsylvania, food from the West. The Southern leaders could not credit, as a supposition even, that the North could avoid bankruptcy in case a war should deprive her at one blow of her raw material, her medium of exchange with Europe, and her market for manufactured goods in the South. And if the North could or would, was Europe willing to allow a war between the North and South to bring her looms to a standstill and turn the English and French operatives into the streets to starve? Where else was nearly ninety million dollars' worth of cotton to come from? The American market for European goods was by no means essential to European manufacturers; the raw material, cotton, was indispensable.

That the South did not produce the necessities of life, much less the essentials for the prosecution of a war, the leaders well knew. But food, leather, salt, medicines, iron, arms, lead, powder could all be secured in Europe in exchange for cotton. The possibility of effective blockade or of real interference by the Northern navy with the Southern freedom of intercourse with Europe, the leaders scouted. They counted definitely on the ease and rapidity of transportation. They also expected the foreign nations to recognize the new confederacy as an independent nation with promptitude and despatch as soon as the alternative of recognition or no cotton was appreciated.[14] As for food, mules, lead, leather, those could all be had in Missouri and in the Northwest, which was tied fast to the South by the Mississippi and its tributaries, and was effectually cut off from the Eastern coast by the mountains. The West might hesitate and haggle but in the end it would be forced by circumstances to join the South.[15] The adherence of the West, and recognition

[14] "The policy, or at least part of the policy of South Carolina is, after staving off war by non-action, to hold back cotton—omnipotent cotton—reduce the supplies in manufacturing countries—stop the thousands and tens of thousands of manufactories in the North and in Europe—until, by absolute force of circumstances, people will be driven to acknowledge the independence of the Confederacy," Quoted from the *Baltimore American* by the *St. Louis Republican*, Jan. 16, 1861.

[15] Mr. Uriel Wright in the Missouri Convention assembled to decide upon secession, said in March, 1861: "I see clearly that their [the Southern leaders'] idea is to secure the breadstuffs and provisions of the valley of the West, and get their manufactured goods from England. There is the whole desire. That is the desire and that is the wish that precipitated the cotton states into a revolution. It will be a formidable idea to meet in a readjustment. These people—I mean the leaders —have been in earnest about this matter for a great many years. The idea started in South Carolina under the dominion and power of such minds as McDuffie, Calhoun, and Hayne. . . . Still, in spite of the temptation—the glittering temptation—of a Southern Republic, whose basis is cotton, and whose policy is free trade with Europe and provisions from us— . . . I am satisfied . . . that ephemeral power will fade away into thin air." *Journal of the Missouri Convention*, 211.

Sam Tate, president of the Memphis and Charleston R. R., wrote to a prominent official in Richmond on May 1, 1861: "There are no provisions in the South—not enough for a full supply for 60 days. [And this was May 1861!] How are we to get it? The Government at Washington is making important arrangements to take St. Louis and

from Europe; the commercial crisis in the North evoked by
the loss of the southern market, of cotton as raw material,
and as a medium of exchange with Europe; the strength of
the States' rights party at the North, and of the Northern
democrats, would probably prevent the North from fighting
at all, and bring about a peaceful separation. In fact, the
Southern leaders were confident that the North would not
dare fight; it was widely reported that Jefferson Davis had
declared himself ready to drink all the blood that would be
spilled over secession.[16] The control by the South of the
Federal government would give them in the event of Lincoln's election fully four months for actual preparation;
would enable the Secretary of War to move into the Southern arsenals, where they could be seized, the supplies of
arms and powder owned by the Federal government, which
would thoroughly equip the first Southern armies put into
the field and deprive the Northern troops of the necessary
equipment. If still the war persisted, aid would come from
Europe by the time it was needed.

Constitutional, traditional, historical defenses were not
far to seek. Nullification, secession, States' rights had been
commonly proclaimed in every part of the country too often
and too recently to allow a scintilla of doubt as to the legality of secession to linger in Southern minds. Indeed, the
belief in the validity of secession as a constitutional right was
so widespread at the North as to make it doubtful for months

close the Mississippi effectually against us from Cairo up. This cuts
off our last hope for a full supply of provisions and lead. By efficient
action now we can save the State of Missouri to the South and keep
open an outlet to an abundant supply of provisions. . . . The first thing
we know we will be out of powder, lead, and percussion caps. They
can be had through Cuba alone at this time." *Rebellion Records*,
Series IV, Vol. I, 276.

William G. Eliot, of St. Louis, wrote later: "I doubt if the Southern Confederacy would have been attempted if the loss of that State
[Missouri] had been foreseen, and the plans of rebellion were as carefully laid at Jefferson City (of which there is now proof) as at Charleston." C. C. Eliot, *Life of W. G. Eliot*, 163.

16 *Personal Memoirs of U. S. Grant*, I, 178. Ed. of 1903. See also
Robin's *Sherman*, 56.

whether the people would support the Federal government, if war should break out upon that issue. From the fathers of the Revolutionary and Constitutional periods and in particular from Calhoun's writings, Hayne's speeches, and the incidents in South Carolina in 1828, the leaders of the South drew ample confirmation and justification of the step.

When the decision to secede was really taken, it is impossible to demonstrate without defining more accurately what is meant by secession. If we mean by secession the determination to establish a second confederacy based upon slave territory, the decision was taken in all probability some time just previous to the Mexican War and was constantly in the minds of the Southern leaders as a remedy to be applied with all speed whenever the probability of the loss of their control of the Federal government seemed imminent. Without that control it was generally conceded that the Constitution and all the statutes concerning slavery would be a dead letter at the North, and that, to continue the connection after that moment, would be merely to expose the South to the definitely hostile legislation which none of them doubted the North would at once utilize Congress to pass. On March 4, 1850, Calhoun solemnly stated the alternatives in the Senate: "There should be an open and manly avowal on all sides as to what is intended to be done. . . . If you who represent the stronger portion, cannot agree to settle them [the issues] on the broad principle of justice and duty, say so; and let the States we both represent agree to separate and part in peace. If you are unwilling we should part in peace, tell us so; and we shall know what to do when you reduce the question to submission or resistance. If you remain silent, you will compel us to infer by your acts what you intend."[17] Conventions in the South in 1849 and during the subsequent decade openly discussed the issue and as openly decided in favor of the legality and expediency of secession.[18] State cam-

[17] *Works of Calhoun*, IV, 572-3.
[18] Hodgson's *Cradle of the Confederacy* is wholly devoted to these abortive attempts at organized secession before 1860.

paigns were fought on the desirability of continuing longer in the Union; and the breach by the North of the Compromise of 1850, the failure to observe the Fugitive-Slave Law, the refusal to "repeal" the Missouri Compromise, to accept the Dred Scott "decisions," and the like, were continually brought forward in State after State and in general conventions as eventualities which would be regarded as the signal for secession, as proof that Southern control of the Federal government was already lost.   The election of 1856, like that of 1860, was fought over the issue of union or disunion.   Senator Mason declared that in the event of the election of Frémont "but one course remains for the South—immediate, absolute, eternal separation."   Buchanan, the Democratic candidate, wrote in a private letter, "I consider that all incidental questions are comparatively of little importance in the presidential election when compared with the grand and appalling issue of union or disunion." [19]   As in 1850, and later in 1860, the Southern leaders were assembled in 1856 concerting the final measures in case secession should become necessary.   Soon after 1850, the numerous military academies founded at the South and the resort to them of the youth of the planter class was significant proof of Southern determination.

Secession was certainly not hatched in a corner; it was no secret conspiracy.   The intentions of the Southern leaders had been solemnly and publicly announced so many times in such open fashion that the North had really come to believe them simply the cry of "Wolf, wolf."   In actuality, the election of Abraham Lincoln as President of the United States was merely the signal for secession, not its cause.   At the South this was well understood.   When, in the gray dawn, the waiting crowds in the streets of Charleston saw on the bulletins the complete returns and knew that Lincoln was elected, a rousing cheer spontaneously rose to their lips for a Southern Confederacy.

[19] See these and other quotations on this same point from most of the leaders, collected by Mr. Rhodes in *History of the United States,* II, 204-210; 227; and *passim.*

XXII

SECESSION AND COMPROMISE

A MONTH or more before the presidential election of 1860, a convention of Southern leaders was in session and the procedure of secession was thoroughly discussed, if not definitely agreed upon. It was apparent that each State must act individually and that formal action would take time; that the North would fight the leaders did not believe; and active preparation for that eventuality was postponed. In Alabama and South Carolina, conventions were called and sat just prior to election day to discuss the relations of the State to the Federal government. Before noon of the day following the election of Lincoln, the palmetto flag had been raised in Charleston amid ecstatic cheers; the legislature was taking measures for the military defense of the State; and the Federal officers had resigned. A convention was called for December 17 to act upon the crisis. This was of course defiance, and the leaders now proposed to wait until the attitude of the President and of the North became clear. Buchanan, after consultation with the Attorney General, made up his mind and advised Congress when it met in December of his determination to take no active steps. He declared secession unconstitutional and the election of Lincoln no valid excuse for the active measures undertaken in South Carolina against the Federal government, but he denied to both President and Congress any right to oppose secession by force. Practically this meant, and so the Southern leaders read it, that the South had until March 4 to complete its plans and organization without interference from Washington.

The desire to achieve their purpose without war, the belief that the North would in the end decline to fight, the practical certainty that they would not be actively opposed for several months caused the Southerners to act deliberately and to postpone for the time further overt measures. On December 20, South Carolina seceded and sent commissioners to Washington to treat with the Federal government. On January 5, a caucus of Southern leaders met at Washington in which the final measures were agreed upon. The States were advised to secede individually, to arm the militia with the weapons in the Federal arsenals and to seize the Federal forts in their territory; and a general convention was called to meet at Montgomery, Alabama, in February. With dramatic speeches and defiant declarations that they had been wronged, the Senators and Representatives of most of the Southern States "seceded" from Congress during January; six States adopted ordinances of secession during the same month and seized the Federal forts, arsenals, supplies, and property within their borders. There was much rejoicing; bells rung, guns fired, and a general carnival in the streets. In some States, the ordinance was solemnly signed before excited throngs in the open air.

February was occupied with the organization of the seven seceded States into a new confederacy. The delegates met on February 4 and impressed A. H. Stephens as the "ablest, soberest, most intelligent and conservative body" he had ever been in. Within a few days, they agreed upon an amended form of the Federal Constitution which explicitly provided for States' sovereignty, for the "delegation" of legislative powers, and for the recognition of slavery as a permanent institution. The President's term was made six years and he was to be ineligible for a second term; the imposition of a tariff and appropriations for internal improvements were explicitly forbidden; and a serious attempt was made to introduce certain administrative reforms which the experience of seventy years had shown to be desirable. On February 9, Jefferson Davis and Alexander H. Stephens were chosen temporary President and Vice-President, and were formally inaugurated on the eighteenth, though the Constitution was not ratified by all the States and did not become permanently binding until March 11. Toombs became Secretary of State and Walker, Secretary of War.

The real purpose of the new government and the "cause" of secession were proclaimed by Stephens in a notable speech. "The new Constitution," he said at Savannah, "has put at rest forever all the agitating questions relating to our peculiar institution, African slavery as it exists among us—the proper status of the negroes in our form of civilization. This was the immediate cause of the late rupture and revolution. . . . Our new government is founded upon exactly the opposite ideas: its foundations are laid, its corner-stone rests upon the great truth that the negro is not equal to the white man; that slavery—subordination to the superior race—is his natural and normal condition. This, our New Government, is the first in the history of the world, based upon this great physical, philosophical, and moral truth."[1]

Meanwhile, at the North and in the border States, Virginia, Maryland, Kentucky, and Missouri, all was consternation, turmoil, hesitation. A feverish anxiety to compromise and at all hazards avoid war was the dominant note. Scarcely had the intentions of South Carolina become plain when offers of compromise appeared in the North. Both Houses of Congress promptly appointed committees to consider the subject and upon them were placed the most prominent Northern and Southern men in each House. The Senate Committee introduced the Crittenden Compromise which provided for constitutional amendments to fulfil the Missouri Compromise by the exclusion of slavery from the Territories north of 36° 30'; to provide that when new States were to be admitted, the people should decide upon the question of slavery or freedom; but with a clause formally recognizing slavery as an institution entitled to protection by the Territorial and Federal governments. The amendments further explicitly deprived Congress of any power to interfere with the transportation of slaves to the Territories, or in any

[1] Putnam, *Rebellion Record*, I, Documents, 45.

way to effect the status of slavery in the States where it existed. Unless the Federal government returned the escaped slaves, it should reimburse the owner for his loss. The House Committee later proposed amendments safeguarding slavery in the States, the repeal of the Personal Liberty Laws, the revision of the Fugitive-Slave Laws, and the admission of New Mexico with or without slavery. Nor were the attempts at compromise confined to Congress. Late in December a conference of the Governors of seven of the largest Northern States met in New York and agreed to recommend to their legislatures the repeal of the Personal Liberty Laws. Had it been at all clear that this would have satisfied the South, every Northern State would probably have been willing so to act. The New York Legislature proposed to emancipate the slaves at national expense and deport them to Africa. After the publication of the Confederate Constitution, there was some sentiment in the North in favor of a general adoption of that document by the Northern States as the easiest way of settling the difficulty. In February, a conference, called by Virginia to discuss compromise, met at Washington, at which delegates from all the Northern and border States were present. Toward the close of the month, it recommended to Congress a series of proposals similar to the Crittenden Compromise, though somewhat less drastic in language. These were discussed in the Senate and attempts were made to refer them to separate State conventions and even to a national constitutional convention.

As it became more and more apparent that the formal proposals were not meeting with Southern approval, the Northern leaders privately offered the Southerners in January to pass at once an act organizing New Mexico as a slave State, if the people of the district would vote in favor of it. This was refused as inadequate on the ground that it did not cover the territory hereafter to be acquired. In February, the Northern congressmen offered to organize at once the rest of the Louisiana Purchase without any provision regarding slavery; to pay for all fugitive slaves not returned; to punish drastically any repetition of John Brown's attempts to rouse the slaves; to repeal all state legislation inimical to the Fugitive-Slave Act. They even offered an amendment expressly forbidding Congress to interfere with the status of slavery in the States.

The reason for these frenzied attempts to meet the objections alleged by the Ordinances of Secession is to be found in the realization, now keen at the North, of the commercial benefits of the Federal union and, above all, the splendor of nationality. The vision, which had entranced the fathers of the Republic and the framers of the Constitution, which Webster had so eloquently described, had now become a general possession. The North was utterly unwilling to renounce it in favor of the older ideal of two confederacies. The calmer minds, too, saw that the South was not unanimous upon the issue of secession: that the overt acts had been the work of the leaders and of conventions rather than of spontaneous agitation. The size of the vote against secession in several of the States made many conclude (and among them, Seward) that the numerical majority at the South was actually in favor of Union. They saw also the lack in the South of the necessities for the prosecution of a war and they could not believe that the leaders really proposed to try the issue of arms. Another large section in the North believed sincerely in States' rights, in the legality and validity of secession, and declined to admit the existence of a power in the Federal government to coerce a State. To them, unless a compromise could be agreed upon, the destruction of the Union was inevitable, for the South would secede beyond a peradventure and leave the North no resource but to accept its action. In the border States, this party was particularly strong and the sentiment against the constitutionality of coercion almost universal.

The Southern leaders seem, however, to have had from the first no intention of compromising. Until all should be ready, until they were assured that peaceful secession was impossible, they were resolved not to push matters to the extreme, but they were equally determined not to yield short of the complete legalization and protection of slavery. This attitude was clear as early as November. "I am daily becoming more confirmed," wrote A. H. Stephens on November 30, 1860, "that all efforts to save the Union will be unavailing. The truth is, our leaders and public men who have taken hold of this question do not desire to continue it on any terms. They do not wish any redress of wrongs; they are dis-unionists *per se,* and avail themselves of present circumstances to press their objects." His opinion explains the formal statement of the Southern Senators, made public on December 14, when the arguments regarding compromise were as yet hardly begun in either House. "The argument is exhausted. . . . In our judgment, the Republicans are resolute in the purpose to grant nothing that will or ought to satisfy the South." The only remedy was the formation of a confederacy. On December 22, Toombs of Georgia telegraphed his constituents that he had put the test fairly and frankly, that the Republicans had decided against the claims of the South, and that nothing was left but instant secession. This and other incidents soon convinced many that the South did not desire any settlement other than separation. Lincoln too was against compromise. "The tug has to come," he wrote, "and better now than later." "A year will not pass till we shall have to take Cuba as a condition upon which they will stay in the Union." And indeed, the sober, thoughtful men of both parties had long been coming to the opinion that "a proposition which in effect requires either party to surrender its convictions—to act in direct opposition to its principles—is not a compromise." Reluctantly on March 2, the leaders in Congress conceded the final defeat of the only proposition which had ever obtained much popular support, the Crittenden Compromise.

Though compromise had definitely failed, it was by no means clear that war would break out. The inauguration of Lincoln passed off quietly, and the new President's address, though firm and determined, was yet conservative in tone.

Nor during March did the situation outwardly change. The drilling and arming went on at the South; the clamor against coercion continued at the North, where a few States only mobilized their militia. Lincoln seemed as lacking in energy and decision as had Buchanan. The reasons are not far to seek. There were first of all dissensions in the Cabinet: Seward, and Chase, Lincoln's rivals for the nomination, had fully expected to take control of policy, and time was needed to convince Lincoln of their intentions and for him to show them conclusively who was actually President. A graver difficulty lay in the harrowing doubt whether or not the North would support the Government in an active policy of coercion of the seceded States. As yet the border States, with Arkansas and North Carolina, had not seceded and their hostility to a policy of coercion was only too manifest. Whether decisive action caused them actively to join the new Confederacy, or merely to decline to assist the Federal government, the result would be equally disastrous. In the first eventuality, the new Confederacy, thus strengthened, might conceivably be strong enough to win the war; in the second, a great strip of neutral territory would be interposed between the Northern and Southern States, which would either prevent the Northern armies from reaching the South or would compel them to occupy the border States as if they were actually hostile territory. Washington would be at once isolated from the loyal States, and it seemed scarcely probable that the Union would survive its capture.

Nor was it by any means clear that the North would support a war. *The New York Tribune*, edited by Greeley, by far the most influential paper in the East and the only paper much read in the Northwest, had for months openly advocated peaceful secession: "Let the erring sisters go in peace." The Mayor of New York had recommended the secession of that city from the State and the opening of her ports to the world. Late in January at a great public meeting in New York, a very influential man declared against coercion and was wildly applauded, while the Republican mayor of Philadelphia had pronounced publicly, amid very evident expressions of approval, against the hostility towards slavery. In March and April, the municipal elections in the North showed heavy losses from the Republican majorities of the previous fall. In Boston, in the home of Anti-Slavery, the Twenty-ninth Annual Session of the Massachusetts Anti-Slavery Society was broken up by a disorderly crowd and the Society next day disbanded. Indeed, it became evident that secession had almost produced a new alignment of parties. Until the attitude of the majority in the North became clearer, Lincoln had no intention of calling for troops.

Nor had Davis any intention of taking steps hostile to the Federal government until it was definitely established that negotiation, diplomacy, compromise, or whatever other forms of mediation or adjustment were available, had been entirely exhausted. The new Confederacy was of course desirous to secure recognition of its independence and sovereignty without resort to arms, and apparently deemed such recognition possible and probable, for in March commissioners appeared in Washington who desired formally to submit credentials to Seward and to discuss with him the relations of the two ''confederacies.'' Seward declined to commit himself or the administration by even communicating with them in his official capacity, but for some three weeks the inability of the Cabinet to decide to act upon their case one way or the other led the Southerners to believe that events and forces were working in their favor. The more warlike at the North even began to fear that the predictions of the Southerners would come true and that the North would not fight.

As usual, the larger issue presented itself in more concrete form. The Federal forts in Charleston harbor were garrisoned by Major Anderson and Federal troops. When South Carolina seceded, Anderson evacuated the fort and batteries on the shore and posted himself in Fort Sumter, which was located on an island and commanded the ship channels in and out of the harbor. Naturally, to the South Carolinians, drunk with the wine of their new found liberty, his presence was offensive and they had earlier protested to Buchanan and demanded the surrender of the fort. They had even dared fire upon a Federal supply ship which had attempted in January to reprovision the fort and which had in consequence returned without accomplishing its object. When Lincoln became President, the situation in the fort was critical: it was surrounded and commanded by the batteries erected on shore; the food was running low; and its surrender, reinforcement, or provisioning was a question of moment because the Southerners had repeatedly given warning that either of the latter would be treated as the signal for war. After weeks of indecision, Lincoln finally determined to provision the fort; he could not see the Union abandoned without at least trying the issue and certainly the provisioning of the fort was not from any reasonable point of view a hostile act, however the Southerners might choose to regard it. The commissioners of the Confederacy promptly sent a letter to Seward declaring the act a declaration of war; and at daybreak on April 12, the South Carolina batteries began the bombardment of Fort Sumter. The structure was old, and ill-equipped for resistance; and, after it had been shot to pieces, the powder exhausted and further resistance made useless, Anderson surrendered and evacuated it with the honors of war.

The sensation in the North is indescribable: blind rage and a desire to wipe out the insult to the flag replaced the lukewarmness and hesitation hitherto characteristic. The unanimity of sentiment in favor of war was as remarkable as it was sudden. Douglas at once waited on the President and promised his entire support. The publication of his message to the country had tremendous effect. A great crowd went out to his home in Chicago; he addressed them from a balcony, and besought them, his voice choked with emotion, to stand for the Union. "There can be no neutrals in this war; only patriots or traitors." Buchanan declared war inevitable and predicted that the North to a man would support the government.

He was right. On April 15, Lincoln called for seventy-five

thousand volunteers; on the next day the Massachusetts regiments mobilized in Boston, and on the following day, the Sixth Massachusetts left for Washington. Passing through Baltimore, the troops were mobbed by the Secessionists who controlled the town, but succeeded in getting through to the national capitol. Behind them the wires were cut and the railroad bridges burned. Maryland had risen and Washington was isolated!

The news came that Virginia had seceded; that Harper's Ferry with its arsenals and its control of the Potomac and Shenandoah Valley had been evacuated and the Navy Yard at Gosport destroyed. The legislatures of New York and Ohio voted large sums for the support of the government; a quarter of a million people held a rally in Union Square, New York, and solemnly pledged themselves to the defense of the Union, and the departure for Washington of the famous Seventh New York Regiment was the signal for scenes of enthusiasm and determination which beggar description. Rhode Island troops were already on the road. But the anxious President, marooned in Washington, in receipt of only occasional messages by couriers, could not believe in the actuality of this support. "I begin to believe there is no North," he said to the Sixth Massachusetts. "The Seventh Regiment is a myth. Rhode Island is another. You are the only real thing." The defenselessness of Washington was so apparent, the moral result of its loss so clear, that the watchword became "On to Washington!" Then Butler's Eighth Massachusetts Regiment landed at Annapolis, ignoring the protests of the Governor of Maryland against such an "invasion" of a sovereign State without permission, repaired the railroad trains disabled by the Marylanders, put the baggage on the cars, and marched on to Washington, rebuilding the track as they went. Over the same route, troops soon poured in; the connection with the North had been established and Washington was safe.

The city had never been in any real danger. The Confederates were not ready to move. In reality, the panic in Washington was equaled only by that in Richmond on Sunday, April 21. Word came that a Federal gunboat was steaming up the river. Bells rang; the congregations rushed out of the churches to arms; and not till late at night did the alarm subside and the people become thoroughly convinced of their safety. Meanwhile, in Charleston, the greatest joy reigned. Russell, the famous war correspondent of the *London Times,* wrote of "crowds of armed men singing and promenading the streets, the battle blood running through their veins— that hot oxygen which is called 'the flush of victory' on the cheek; restaurants full, reveling in barrooms, clubrooms crowded, orgies and carousing in tavern and private house, in tap-room from cabaret—down narrow alleyways, in the broad high-way. Sumter has set them distraught; never was such a victory; never such brave lads; never such a fight; . . . it is a bloodless Waterloo or Solferino."[2]

2 *Diary,* 98.

XXIII

THE CIVIL WAR AS A MILITARY EVENT

THE policy of passive resistance promptly adopted by the Confederacy had its solid basis in diplomacy and statesmanship rather than in military considerations; but its military result was to throw the war into the Southern States, to force the North to become the aggressor, and made the story of the war the tale of the progress of the Northern "conquest." The most important factor, then, in the military history of the Civil War is the strategical geography of the United States south of Mason and Dixon's line. This vast territory —about one-third of the total area of the country to-day, then nearly two-thirds of the settled States,—is divided by the Alleghany Mountains into two unequal parts, each of which promptly became a theater of war. During the first three years and more a series of simultaneous campaigns took place, all directed toward the occupation of the South, but carried on by Northern armies in the West and East which because of the mountains did not attempt to keep in touch with each other or carry out concerted movements. The campaigns in Virginia and the campaigns in the West were aimed at different strategic points. This same difficulty of communication through the Alleghanies, which so hampered the concerted action of the invaders, also made extremely difficult any coöperation of the Southern armies in either field and in particular clogged the wheels of the machinery intended to provide Lee's army in Virginia with supplies and munitions of war. Many of the first military movements were devoted to attempts to establish or prevent conjunction of forces in both armies, and it is not perhaps going too far to say that the character of the war as a whole was the result of the existence of the Alleghany Mountains.

The fact that Washington was situated a comparatively short distance from Richmond, the expectation entertained by both sides of a sudden collapse of the opposition under so striking a reverse as the seizure of its capital, the belief of each that the other was unprepared to resist sudden invasion, all combined to induce both to begin the war in Virginia and to conduct operations there with especial pertinacity in the face of all obstacles and reverses. Indeed, the enthusiasts on both sides could not comprehend why their general could not cross those few miles of territory and so end the War. The fact that the campaigns in Virginia, with the exception of a few brilliant successes for both sides, were for both a long series of striking reverses, which left the contending armies in the fall of 1864 no nearer the accomplishment of either's desire than when the War began, is the most significant aspect of this part of the War and is explained largely, if not entirely, by the character of the country. Military critics have unreservedly praised the generalship of Lee and have declared that his ability alone maintained the defense in Virginia and therefore prolonged the War for four years. Lee's defense, however, was based chiefly upon a detailed knowledge of the ground and a most skilful use of the natural advantages it afforded him.

Virginia is a plain, sloping southeast from the Blue Ridge Mountains to Chesapeake Bay and intersected by numerous parallel rivers, of which the Potomac, the Rappahannock, York, and James are the most important. So low is the land near the Bay that for a considerable distance the shore of the Bay and the sides of the rivers are marshy, and land firm enough for army manœuvers begins some miles from shore about the meridian of Fredericksburg. The possible field of war was thus narrowed and limited by nature. The rivers, moreover, all of them lying athwart an invader's path, afforded the Northern armies the maximum number of difficulties in their march overland on Richmond, and gave the

Confederates the maximum opportunities for defense and for assault at moments when the nature of the ground near the river fords made the deploying of any considerable part of the Northern army hazardous in the extreme. The district Lee had to guard was limited, and Nature herself had provided fortifications for him and obstacles for his enemies.

These same rivers had been since colonial times the highways of Virginia, for all commodities were moved to the Bay for export and were rarely sent overland from one part of the State to another. There had never been developed, therefore, any system of roads running north and south which was of real service to either side. Days were spent in making roads across river bottoms, swamps, and morasses, where more soldiers died of malarial fevers, dysentery, and camp diseases than were killed in battle. Then this part of Virginia had been normally devoted to growing tobacco; agriculture had declined; and food and fuel were scarce. Both armies were speedily dependent upon supplies brought to them and found it extremely difficult to procure in Virginia enough horses, mules, or wagons even, to get the supplies from the railroad to the camps. The invaders were compelled to carry everything. The war in the East indeed soon depended for its prosecution at all upon the smooth working of the immensely complicated administrative machine required to supply and move the Northern army under the geographical conditions. In fact, the comparative inaction of the first two years was almost entirely due to the imperative need of a machinery which only time and experience could render really efficient; and the operations undertaken were such as the limited resources of that machinery seemed to render possible. McClellan's continual complaint was that he was not given enough men properly equipped for the task assigned him. To the geographical difficulty of fighting at all in Virginia may be assigned much of the responsibility for the failure of the Union armies to wage war more successfully in the East.

This same configuration of the field of war, however, gave

both sides enormous natural advantages of which they were not slow to avail themselves, but which, as used by Lee, afforded the Confederates vastly more assistance than they did the Federals. The control of Chesapeake Bay and of the rivers gave the Federal gunboats and transports such ready access to the interior that the Union generals could land their armies where they pleased, in nearly any part of eastern Virginia and could maintain them there by provisions from the fleet. The early seizure of Maryland gave the Union control of a second side of the field of war, and maintained the indispensable connections with the North and West. This, however, was rather a possible advantage snatched from the Confederates than a positive assistance to the Federals.

Of a very different sort was the assistance derived by the Confederates from the Shenandoah Valley. The Blue Ridge occupied one whole side of the field of war and the numerous gaps made entrance to it or exit from it easy for both armies. Its northern end debouched in Pennsylvania and made it a protecting screen for an invasion of the North by the Confederates; from its center an army advancing through Manassas or Centerville and across Bull Run could menace Washington directly; while an army fleeing from pursuit could slip in one gap and no one know from which of the many others it would emerge. From this vantage point Jackson, Stuart, and Early threatened Washington or harried the rear of the Union armies till the last year of the War. Through it Lee twice attempted to invade the North; in its defiles, he twice eluded his pursuers, who were between him and the Confederate lines, and reached Richmond in safety. Aside from the beaten track of the contending armies, the pursuits of peace long went on uninterrupted and all through the years from 1861 to 1864 priceless loads of supplies were drawn from the fertile fields of the Valley for Lee's army. In addition, the Valley enabled the Confederates to threaten the communications of the North with the West via the Potomac River Valley and the Baltimore and Ohio Railroad, which crossed the river and the Valley roads at Harper's Ferry.

Indeed Harper's Ferry, Manassas, and Centerville, controlling the most direct roads from the Valley to Washington; and Fortress Monroe at the mouth of the James River were the only strategic points in the triangular field of the Virginia War. There were in fact no other strategic points of first importance to struggle for, and the long campaigns were a series of attempts by the Union armies to reach Richmond by passing a few miles west or east of the point of the last rebuff, or, on the part of the Confederates to try once more a dash on Washington or on Philadelphia through the Shenandoah Valley. The armies were too well matched; the valor of each too great; the skill of the generals too considerable to make the weary years of strife more than a draw. The War was not won by the Virginia campaigns, but, as Sherman early predicted, by the western armies.

The Mississippi Valley possessed many strategic points of the utmost consequence to the Union. The Ohio River, deep, swift, and almost fordless, flowing between steep banks across almost the entire width of the country would have been a splendid boundary for defense and would have given the Confederates a virtual fortification from which Ohio, Indiana, and Illinois could have been harried at will. Missouri controlled the junction of the Ohio, of the Missouri, and of the Illinois with the Mississippi, and paralleled the whole western side of the strong Union State of Illinois and the southern side of Iowa. Should it join the Confederacy, the South would control the whole of the navigable waterways of the Middle West and would be provided with splendid roads into the very heart of the anti-slavery territory. The loss of Kentucky, of West Virginia, and of Missouri to the South in the first months of the War was of far greater significance than has been supposed. While the military operations concerned with their seizure were slight in strategy and of little tactical importance, the result upon the general position of the South was equal to the winning of any single great battle of the War. The chance of meeting the Northern armies along the Ohio, far from the center of the Confederacy, was lost; and only

Forts Henry and Donelson kept the Federal gunboats out of the Tennessee and Cumberland, rivers which were navigable indeed far enough south to furnish a waterway into the very heart of the Confederacy. With the loss of Missouri went the control of the upper Mississippi, the Missouri, and the mouth of the Ohio. Practically, the great depth of the Mississippi cut the western part of the Confederacy into two parts, and prevented armies east of the river from coöperating effectively with the troops west of it. The hostility of Missouri kept Arkansas on the *qui vive;* while Texas and Louisiana were not sufficiently populous to maintain armies, even had the character of the country not made military campaigns in the marshes and bayous impracticable. From them must come supplies and recruits. The field of war in the West then was limited by Nature and by circumstances to the land south of central Kentucky, west of the mountains, and east of the Mississippi.

The strategic points were chiefly those controlling the lines of communication north and south, and east and west. The rivers first engaged attention. It became at once clear to the Northern generals that the possession of the Mississippi would prevent the South from drawing men and supplies from the Western States; and permit the provisioning and relieving of the western armies by the North much more safely than the railroads would have allowed. The moral effect of its loss could not fail to be tremendous. To advance along the Tennessee and Cumberland Rivers, however, was more likely to be decisive, for such a movement menaced the east and west connections of the Confederacy. The Civil War was one of the first to be fought with aid of the telegraph and railroad, and their value as military forces had not been entirely appreciated. It so happened that while the system of trunk lines running in all directions naturally developed by Northern trade were of immense strategic importance, the majority of Southern railroad lines were nearly valueless from a military point of view. There were only about 9,000 miles of track south of Mason and Dixon's line. Most of the lines were short spurs to the coast or to a shipping point on some river, and the majority of them were single track and narrow gauge. From Virginia no trunk line ran south to Charleston and Atlanta, and there was, indeed, only one trunk line running east and west that was likely to be of any consequence. The proximity of Washington and Richmond had, however, determined the chief field of war and the communications between Virginia and the country further south became at once of extraordinary military importance. The knowledge that the army in Virginia must be fed and clothed from a distance, and must be supported promptly by fresh troops in case of disaster, made the Cumberland Gap and its roads and railway seem almost as important a point to maintain as Richmond itself. Through this Gap ran the Danville and Ohio Railroad, the only east and west trunk line joining Memphis, Atlanta, Charleston, and Richmond. The railroads from Memphis to Richmond and from Charleston and Atlanta joined at Chattanooga; the roads north from Mobile and New Orleans crossed the line from Memphis to Chattanooga at or near Corinth. Through the Cumberland Gap supplies and troops must reach Lee or they would not reach him at all. Through that Gap the Southern army in the West must coöperate with the army in Virginia or the two would be separated and crushed singly. To maintain that connection it was absolutely essential to hold both Corinth and Chattanooga.

The campaign of 1861 in the West having given the Union troops the rivers and the States of Missouri, Kentucky, and Western Virginia (admitted as a State in 1863), Grant and Sherman prepared to move down the Tennessee, cut the railroad at Corinth and at Chattanooga, and thence invade Virginia from the rear through the Cumberland Gap. Simultaneously, the gunboat flotilla began the task of reducing the Mississippi from the north, while Farragut and the fleet assailed its mouth at New Orleans. By the end of April 1862, the river was in Northern hands as far south as Memphis; Grant had taken the forts guarding the passage of the Tennessee and Cumberland, had fought the battle of Shiloh and established himself in southern Tennessee ready to move on the railroad connections; and New Orleans was in the hands of Farragut and Butler. Grant and Sherman were now ordered to take Corinth and Memphis, which was soon done, and then were ordered to advance with Porter and his gunboats on Vicksburg down the river; coöperate with Butler and Farragut, advancing up the river; concentrate on Vicksburg and so clear the Mississippi of Confederates. Buell, soon replaced by Rosecrans, was at the same time ordered to lay siege to Chattanooga. But the success of the earlier months did not continue and the second half of the year 1862 saw the Northern armies everywhere at a standstill: McClellan outmanœuvered along the James, nearly defeated at Antietam, outgeneraled by Lee's masterly retreat, and the Army of the Potomac, now under Burnside, dreadfully cut to pieces at Fredericksburg; in the West, all the armies completely checkmated. Indeed, not until July 1863, did Grant and Sherman prevail at Vicksburg and secure full control of the river, and only the massing of troops at Chattanooga some months later under Grant, Sherman, and Thomas sufficed to clear the Gap and cut the communications of the South with Virginia. By this time, a direct line had been finished through North Carolina and the loss of the Gap was not so decisive a blow as it would have been a year earlier. Despite Vicksburg and Chattanooga, despite the decisive repulse of Lee at Gettysburg in July 1863, where his second attempt to invade the North was frustrated by Meade, it was clear that in Virginia at least the Northern army was not appreciably nearer Richmond, and that the losses in the West would not of themselves demolish the Confederacy. Military movements based upon the new position of the western armies became indispensable.

After much discussion, it was decided that Grant should, as before, advance on Richmond from the North; Sheridan should lay waste the Shenandoah, to prevent its further use as a base of operations and of supplies; Sherman should advance on Atlanta, march across Georgia to the Sea, proving the vulnerability of the Confederacy, and then, advancing north through South Carolina and North Carolina, take possession of the country on whose support Lee was depending, and so in the end reach his rear. Thomas was left behind in Tennessee to keep Hood's army in sight and prevent his interference with Sherman. Every campaign was successful except that of Grant, who was thrown back again and again by Lee's veterans in a series of battles which experts then and since pronounced bad generalship to have fought at all. So extended a series of operations, however, consumed the whole year and it was not until the spring of 1865 that the final moves of the game could be made. Grant, having already shifted his operations to the James, closed in on Richmond from the east and south; Sherman advanced through North Carolina, driving Johnston before him; Thomas's army scaled the Cumberland Gap, and Lee found himself completely surrounded. He abandoned Richmond and tried to retreat into the mountains, where he could have resisted indefinitely, but Grant was too quick for him, and in April 1865, the impending surrender took place at Appomattox.

XXIV

WHY THE NORTH WON

THE physical and economic preponderance of the North over the South—two and one-half times as many fighting men, eleven times the productivity [1]—could not fail ultimately to decide the issue, should the South be unable to beat the Northern armies or to obtain assistance from Europe. From the outset this was clear to the Southern leaders. Thanks to the Southern sympathies of the Secretary of War, the available supplies in the hands of the Federal government in 1861 were early seized by the Southerners; thanks to the hesitation of the North to believe in the reality of secession, the South, it was seen, was drilled, and prepared long before the North as a whole had decided to act. The expectation was that the Southern armies would be able to defeat the Northern and perhaps invade the North itself, while the failure of the supply of cotton and the lack of a medium of exchange with Europe would bankrupt Northern industry, bring Europe to the aid of the South, and compel the West to sell to the South on her own terms or face commercial ruin.

The first great blow to the Southern cause was the failure of the border States, Missouri and Kentucky, to secede or to defend themselves against the first movements of Union troops. The northern boundary of the swift, unfordable Ohio was lost to the South. With it went the control of the navigation of that great river, and the possibility of flanking the great State of Illinois, of threatening invasion of the West, and of thus weakening the Northern armies before

[1] *Supra*, p. 290-2.

Lee.   The whole aspect of the War was changed in a moment by the loss in May 1861, of Missouri, Kentucky, and Western Virginia.   The next crushing blow fell when it became evident that the growth of the railroads in the last decade had furnished the Ohio Valley and the Northwest a highway to the Eastern market as cheap and much more rapidly traversible than that which the Mississippi had afforded them to the South.   Moreover, the Eastern market was infinitely larger than the Southern and hence a better place in which to sell.   The East produced itself most of the manufactured goods the West desired and it was therefore a better market to buy in than the South, which could give its creditors only exchange on the East or on London and could furnish them goods only after the delay and expense of importation.   In 1850, the lack of adequate facilities for transportation to the Eastern markets must perforce have compelled the West to depend upon the Southern markets; in 1860, when the War actually broke out, the West was able for the first time to find a market for her own produce in the East.

Although the direct trade with the West helped the East, the outbreak of the War was a great economic blow, for the South had bought in the winter of 1860–61, with the usual arrangement for future payment, three hundred million dollars' worth of goods in the North.[2] The commencement of hostilities of course had the effect of a repudiation of the entire debt.   The New York firms alone lost one hundred and sixty millions as a result of secession; in 1861 six thousand Northern firms actually failed for sums over $5,000 and it was calculated that an equal number failed for liabilities less than that sum, with a total almost one-third as great.   The firms which did not actually fail were in every way crippled and found themselves almost as badly off as during the Panic of

[2] The financial and economic effects of the War have been adequately dealt with by Professor E. D. Fite in *Social and Industrial Conditions During the Civil War*. New York, 1910. Chapter V is devoted to the commercial conditions here referred to.

1857. Retrenchments of individual expenses due to fear of the War's results or possible failure were responsible for a great falling off of sales and for a consequent difficulty among wholesalers and manufacturers of placing new orders. Indeed, a commercial crisis of magnitude prevailed throughout the North during 1861 and 1862 and it combined with the inactivity of the Army of the Potomac and the "unconstitutional powers" exercised by Lincoln to make the War highly unpopular.

But the War itself set in motion economic forces which soon solved the chief difficulties. The army and navy absorbed many of the hands thrown out of work. The new factories needed to supply the army, the administrative offices at Washington, and other multifarious activities created by the conflict began gradually to provide for the rest. Everything it purchased the government paid for; nearly everything made in the North the government bought; the army, the navy, the clerks and officials of all grades and ranks received wages or salaries. The expense was enormous; the financing of the war [3] was a great problem on the whole skilfully handled; but the fact must not be overlooked that the whole North was employed by the Federal government directly or indirectly and was paid for its services at prices much higher than any which had ever been seen in the country before. Even those persons who themselves loaned the money found the government's bonds good investments and received at once high rates of interest. The individuals then alive benefited unquestionably from the War. "We are only another example," wrote John Sherman, "of a people growing rich in a great war. . . . This is not a mere temporary inflation caused by paper money but is a steady progress and rests almost entirely upon actual capital." Great sums were spent in luxuries: [4] "We are clothed in

[3] Any one who hopes to understand the financing of the War must read carefully the biographies of Jay Cooke.

[4] See the quotations given by Rhodes, *History of the United States*, V, 198-209; and the detailed evidence quoted by Fite, *opp. cit.*, 259-274,

purple and fine linen," said the *Chicago Tribune*. The South had expected the economic crisis caused by secession to bankrupt the North, and the War was actually making the North richer, stronger, larger than before! This incontestable prosperity enabled the North to bear heavy taxation without actually suffering. The great bulk of the cost of the War was foisted upon posterity, thanks to the very bonds whose sale provided capitalists with a good investment for their money in war-time and allowed the government practically to subsidize industry at the North on an enormous scale.

The expectations entertained by the South of assistance from England and France did not materialize, chiefly because cotton was not king. While large and influential sections of the English people favored the Southern cause, the government was loath to act until the ability of the Southern Confederacy to maintain itself was apparent. Unquestionably, too, the sagacity and ability of C. F. Adams, the United States Ambassador to Great Britain, was instrumental in preventing prompt action in favor of the South, and in delaying a decision until both England and France concluded, as the Confederate agents were compelled to report, that the probabilities of the restoration of the Union outweighed "the wisdom, energy, and completeness" of the administrative system established at Richmond.[5] The expected pressure upon foreign governments caused by the need for cotton was long postponed, because, in the spring of 1861, the

with the authorities cited. The *New York Independent*, June 25, 1864, said: "Who at the North would ever think of war, if he had not a friend in the army, or did not read the newspapers? Go into Broadway, and we will show you what is meant by the word 'Extravagance.' Ask Stewart about the demand for camel's hair shawls, and he will say 'monstrous.' Ask Tiffany what kind of diamonds and pearls are called for. He will answer 'the prodigious,' 'as near hen's-egg size as possible,' 'price no object.' What kind of carpetings are now wanted? None but 'extra.' Brussels and velvets are now used from basement to garret." The correspondent of the *London Times* was amazed to read the news in the papers of great losses at the front and yet find that "the signs of mourning were hardly anywhere perceptible; the noisy gayety of the town was not abated one jot." Cited by Fite, 259.

[5] Richardson, *Messages and Papers of the Confederacy*, II, 53.

European manufacturers had nearly a year's supply of cotton on hand. Long before this supply was exhausted, the general failure of the grain crops throughout Europe caused a demand for food-stuffs literally unprecedented since the Napoleonic wars.[6] England, even then unable to feed herself and dependent on importation, found her usual sources of supply either non-existent or inadequate and was forced to seek some new supply of food. In that very year of European scarcity, the West harvested the largest crops of its history;[7] the new railroads quickly and cheaply landed the crop at New York; whence it was shipped to England and found ready sale. The North possessed in fact the only available supply of a commodity which Europe needed far more than it did cotton.[8] The lack of cotton as a medium of exchange with Europe was scarcely felt. The Emancipation Proclamation, issued in September 1862, to take effect January 1, 1863, seems to have played an important part in deciding the European nations to decline to recognize the Confederacy. While the object of the War as stated by Lincoln and others was primarily and perhaps exclusively to perpetuate the political ties created by the Constitution, England and France had felt that the issue was chiefly one of expediency and not of principle. When, however, the Northern government pledged itself to the principle of emancipation, public opinion manifested itself too clearly in favor of the Union in Europe for the governments to disregard it. All hope of recognition was destroyed by the victories of Vicksburg and Gettysburg.

[6] The English wheat crop had averaged about 16 million quarters; fell in 1860 to 13 million, in 1861 to 11 million, and was in 1862 only 12 million, and in 1863 only 14 million. Fite, *Social and Industrial Conditions*, 18 note.

[7] The increase of the crop in the loyal States was 40 millions of bushels and the cessation of trade with the South added 10 millions more, available for export.

[8] W. E. Forster stated in the House of Commons: "When they were asked to go to war for merely selfish purposes, to procure cotton, it was allowable to ask, 'What would be the cost of the war in corn?'" Cited by Fite, p. 21.

Meanwhile, the expectation that the South would be able to buy in Europe with King Cotton nearly if not quite everything she would require also was crushed by the totally unexpected efficiency of the blockade of Southern ports established by the Northern navy. Although the South had neither navy nor merchant marine and had shipped her cotton to Europe in Northern or English bottoms, she knew that the Federal government had comparatively few ships in commission in the spring of 1861, and deemed it impossible for such a handful to blockade in a practical manner a thousand miles and more of seacoast. The administration at Washington set to work diligently to buy and build; developed shortly armor-clad boats and steam warships, both now introduced in naval warfare for the first time, and almost immediately "Uncle Sam's webbed feet," in Lincoln's odd but characteristic phrase, were leaving their marks "wherever the land was wet." It transpired that the numerous harbors along the Southern coasts were of no particular value, for only a few were connected by railways or roads with the interior, and none of them, outside of the Chesapeake region, were at the beginning of the War connected with the district where supplies were needed. In fact, the magnificent rivers had given each little district, each plantation, as it were, its own special waterway to the oceanic trade, and an elaborate network of roads and railroads had not been needed to ensure rapid economic growth. There was no system of intercommunication by land throughout the South which would have made one harbor as good a base of communication with Europe as another and therefore have rendered effective blockade of so many harbors as impossible as it first seemed. In reality, the investiture of a very few places closed the only ports through which any considerable volume of trade had flowed or which possessed any connection by rail with the interior. Even had the ports remained open, the deficiencies of transportation would still have sown formidable obstacles in the way of the speedy and regular transmission of supplies. The waterways were indeed a detriment to the

South, were simply so many roads to the interior which
Federal gunboats and transports were speedily utilizing to
land troops in the very heart of the Mississippi Valley and
to take possession of the seacoast and the river-bottoms
for many miles inland. In fact, the only system of transportation, which the South had consistently used between
plantations or with the outside world, fell into the hands
of her enemies. The normal intercourse with Europe ceased
even before hostilities were begun in earnest; by the summer
of 1861 the South was already finding it difficult to procure
lead, medicines, salt, and other necessities.[9]

Nor did the cotton famine attain anything like the proportions or have anything like the effect expected. The high
price and ready market encouraged exports of Egyptian cotton; the progress of the Northern armies in Tennessee and
Mississippi, the success of the navy along the Gulf coast,
enabled the Federal government to seize and confiscate considerable amounts of cotton, all of which was, of course,
instantly distributed to the hungry looms in New England
and Lancashire.[10] Both governments also connived at the
smuggling of cotton through the lines,[11] and Davis and some
of his cabinet were supposed to have agreed upon a scheme
for exchanging the idle cotton bales with the Northerners
for necessities.[12] This expedient was viewed with little favor:

[9] *Rebellion Records*, Series IV, Vol. I, 276.
[10] "It has been estimated that after Sept. 1863, England received
indirectly from the Confederacy an average of 4000 bales a week."
"The 'leak' was not a trickling stream, but a river, and the 'famine'
policy was a dream." Pendleton's *Stephens*, 305.
[11] C. A. Dana's *Recollections* are full of details about the system of
licensing trade through the lines. He was a government spy in the
western armies to investigate conditions and watch the generals. His
confidential letters to Stanton are full of the most valuable information.
[12] Jones, a confidential war clerk in the War Department at Richmond, handled the Secretary's private correspondence, including letters
from the Secretary and even from the President. With the consent of
the authorities, he kept a diary in which he recorded his impressions
of men and measures. *A Rebel War Clerk's Diary*, I, 180 (Phila.,
1866), and following, contains a good deal of information and con-
jecture about cotton speculation.

the North desired to exhaust the Southern supplies as soon
as possible; the South still believed that a real cotton famine
would be a great weapon in its favor and that the expected
results had not been obtained because there was really no
famine.　Blockade-runners plied a brisk trade and brought
invaluable cargoes of salt, medicine, cartridges, and the like;
but the vigilance of the Federal navy prevented any dependence on them as a regular source of supply.　On the whole, it
is no exaggeration to say that the blockade was so soon
effective that the South was compelled to fight the War from
her own resources, plus the very considerable supplies of
all kinds on hand in May 1861.

Her inability to utilize these resources was another cause of
the Northern victory.　When, in the first bitterness of defeat, the Southerners sought some explanation of it, many
concluded that Davis, his personality, his incapacity, the
inefficiency of his appointees, his stubborn refusal to remove
them were among the leading causes of disaster.[13] Men
like Pollard fiercely denied that the South was exhausted in
men or means;[14] the administration had simply proved itself
utterly incapable of utilizing and developing such resources
as it possessed.　Few will now deny that the difficulties were
too fundamental to have been overcome by human ability,
yet had Davis and his administration shown anything like
the consummate skill with which Lee utilized the meager resources at his disposal, the War might have been prolonged.
But the result could hardly have been changed.　Neither

[13] On Oct. 31, 1862, when he had had considerable time for observation, Jones asked himself whether Davis could ever become a second
Washington.　"I know not, of course; but I know what quite a number
here say of him now.　They say he is a small specimen of a statesman
and no military chieftain at all.　And worse still that he is a capricious
tyrant."　*Diary* I. 178.　Stephens declared in January 1864, after his
bitter quarrel with Davis had had time to cool, "Those at the head of
our affairs" seem to have had no policy, but to have trusted "to the
sublimity of luck and floating upon the surface of the occasion."　Pendleton, *Stephens*, 311.

[14] Pollard, *Life of Davis*, 445-447.　The whole volume is merely a
detailed elaboration of this charge.

logic nor skill could create something out of nothing, and the moment the gates to Europe were shut, it was clear that the resources of the South were hopelessly inadequate and that during a conflict of such magnitude with a foe so abundantly provided with every necessity, no foresight could develop in time a sufficiently diversified industry to produce what was needed.[15] Great efforts were made; more was accomplished than seemed in any way possible to the discouraged men when they first learned that the blockade would soon be effective; the straw was lacking and the bricks could not be made.

By the summer of 1861, the supply of volunteers in the South was exhausted. Conscription was begun and was perforce continued throughout the war in the face of a constantly increasing opposition. Careful search failed to uncover more than scanty supplies of nitre, salt, and saltpetre. There was not enough crude iron to keep at work the few foundries which the government did create, and very soon rails and old iron of all varieties had to be utilized. Cloth became scarce. All material for buttons gave out, and one prominent lady appeared at a Richmond ball in 1864 in a coarse homespun dress with buttons of gourd seeds. Paper and ink became particularly difficult to obtain, and the executive correspondence was in the later years written on old envelopes split open. Wood grew so scarce in Richmond that it was treasured and hoarded like gold.

Nothing was more serious than the effect upon transportation of the lack of iron, of machinery, and of skilled mechanics. The few trunk lines of the South had not been equipped to carry the commerce of the country: cotton had been shipped by water or by short spur-lines of narrow-gauge, single-track railroads to the nearest port. The rolling stock of the trunk lines was therefore too small and the rails were too light to bear the severe strain at once imposed upon

[15] The story of this struggle with economic difficulties is conveniently summarized with adequate citations in Schwab's *The Confederate States of America*.

them by the War Department.   Locomotives broke down; parts of the equipment wore out and could not be replaced because either the material for duplicating the damaged parts was lacking or no man understood how to turn them out.   Hence such supplies as there were could not be promptly and efficiently distributed.   Often the food collected by government agents spoiled before it could be moved; leather, desperately needed in Virginia, had been collected in North Carolina but could not be shipped.[16]   This deficiency of transportation facilities was one of the greatest difficulties with which the Confederate government had to cope.   It was due in the last analysis to cotton and to slavery, to the policy which had kept the South purely an agricultural country and which had regarded the development of diversified industry as needless.   This was not the fault of any individual, but of the very system which the Confederacy was created to defend, and which thus, by a curious poetic justice, demonstrated its unfitness to survive.

There was, however, at many periods during the war, strong feeling among Southerners, which later research has on the whole justified, that the men in control did not make the most of the facilities and supplies at their disposal.[17]   It is of course easy to criticize, and difficult to make sufficient allowance for the fact that the North enjoyed the use of the administrative machinery developed by the past seventy years

[16] Jones, *Diary*, I, 196.

[17] On such matters as this, Jones is an admirable witness, for he was purely an observer and had ample opportunities to learn the truth. The government has 50,000 pounds of leather in North Carolina, he writes. "This convinces me that there is abundance of leather in the South, if it were properly distributed.   It is held, like everything else, by speculators. for extortioners' profits.   The government might remedy the evils, and remove the distresses of the people; but instead of doing so, the bureaus aggravate them by capricious seizures and tyrannical restrictions on transportation.   Letters are coming in from every quarter complaining of the despotic acts of government agents." *Diary*, I, 196.   "From all sections of the Confederacy, complaints are coming in that the military agents of the bureaus are oppressing the people and the belief is expressed by many that a sentiment is prevailing inimical to the government itself." Nov. 29, 1862. *Ibid.*, p. 199.

and that the South was compelled to create a new administration and had perforce to fill many offices with men scarcely
competent because no better were available. But this will
not explain why Davis and his Cabinet so soon fell to loggerheads; why Stephens and many other ante-bellum leaders
went into implacable and at times violent opposition; and
why the impression became general that Davis was appoint-
ing favorites and not the best men available.[18] Jones, a
highly confidential clerk in Richmond, who knew nearly all
the secrets, wrote in his diary of his surprise to find the men
who had done the most to create the War offered clerkships
with hesitancy and relegated to "the lowest subordinate
positions, while Tom, Dick, and Harry, never heard of before,
young and capable of performing military service, rich and
able to live without office, are heads of bureaus, chief clerks
of departments, and staff officers flourishing their stars."[19]
Davis insisted upon retaining as generals Pemberton and
Bragg, in whom many placed no confidence at all after their
disasters of 1862 and 1863, and persistently refused to advance to commands of importance Beauregard, in whom the
people had implicit faith.

The clearest case seems to be nearly if not quite the most
important. It involves the Commissary General, Northrup.

"How does this speak for the government; or rather the efficiency of
the men who by 'many indirect ways' came into power? Alas! it is a
sad commentary." *Ibid.*, p. 204. "An exposé of funds in the hands
of disbursing agents shows that there are nearly 70 millions of dollars
not accounted for." *Ibid.*, 182.

[18] "*The Examiner* to-day [July 1863] in praising him [Yancey]
made a bitter assault on the President, saying he was unfortunately
and hastily *inflicted* on the Confederacy at Montgomery, and when fixed
in position, banished from his presence the heart and brain of the
South—denying all participation in the affairs of the government to
the great men who were the authors of secession, etc." *Ibid.*, I,
391.

[19] *Diary*, I, 205, 216. De Bow and Fitzhugh were offered clerkships
with hesitation. Might not De Bow's intimate knowledge of Southern
conditions and familiarity with financial and commercial questions
have been of value to the Treasury Department where the Secretary
seems to have had few to advise him competently?

Upon him fell the burden and responsibility of utilizing carefully the scanty supplies, and it is hardly too much to say
that by 1863 he retained the confidence only of Davis himself, and was cordially hated by the people at large.[20]   At
a time when shirts were selling for $12, Northrup issued an
order offering to buy shirts for the army at $1, an offer
widely commented upon as displaying something less than
average perception, to say nothing of common sense.   He
offered to carry clothing from the families and friends of
the soldiers to the men in the trenches, when, as Jones remarked, "the people will not trust him to convey the clothing to their sons and brothers, and so the army must suffer
on."[21]   This was in 1862.   Lee repeatedly complained of
the inefficiency of Northrup's work and more than once
categorically requested his dismissal; but Davis declined to
remove him.   It seems scarcely possible to justify the orders
forbidding the feeding of regiments on the produce of the
district in which they were located and compelling them to
depend upon irregular shipments of the regulation bacon and
corn.   Ugly charges, which received wide credit, were made
of speculations in food and cotton by individuals and even
by the commissary department,[22] of the use of the railroads
for transportation of private shipments of grain for specu-

[20] Elaborate discussions of Northrup's case will be found in all the
lives of Davis, in such books as Pollard's *Lost Cause*, and in the correspondence of the chief military men, especially cogent material being
found in the letters of Lee.

[21] Jones, *Diary*, I, 198, Nov. 29, 1862. "The Commissary General
to-day says there is not wheat enough in Virginia (when a good crop
was raised) for Gen. Lee's army, and, unless he has millions in money
and cotton, the army must disband for want of food. I don't believe
it." *Ibid.*, p. 183.

[22] "God speed the day of peace," wrote Jones in 1862. "Our patriotism is mainly in the army and among the ladies of the South. The
avarice and cupidity of the men at home could only be excelled by
ravenous wolves; and most of our sufferings are fully deserved."
Diary, I, 200. "We are already meager and emaciated. Yet I believe
there is abundance of clothing and food, held by the extortioners. The
government should wage war upon the speculators—enemies as mis-
chievous as the Yankees." *Ibid.*, II, 280. Sept., 1864. For cotton
speculations see *Ibid.*, I, 180-2; 187 *et seq.*

lative ends,[23] of the "loan" of army mules and horses for
months to wealthy gentlemen at a time when the army was
in desperate need and Northrup was complaining of a scarcity of transport animals; [24] of illegal exemptions from taxes
and food levies of the friends and relatives of Northrup.
After all allowances have been made, there seems to have
been in the commissary department much corruption and
inefficiency, whose immediate effect on the result of the War
was only too apparent and for which Davis in person must
largely be held responsible.

The finances of the Confederacy seem also to have been
mismanaged. The Secretary of the Treasury, Memminger, was
honest and well-intentioned, but totally unacquainted with
finance. He had, indeed, a fundamental difficulty to struggle
with which no skill could have surmounted—the lack of sufficient specie in the country to serve as an adequate medium
of exchange for domestic and foreign business. There seem
to have been about fifteen millions in specie in the South

[23] Jones, *Diary*, I, 182 *et seq.* "I believe the commissaries and quar-
termasters are cheating the government." "A gentleman in Alabama
writes that his [Northrup's] agents are speculating in food." *Ibid.*, 198.

[24] "Our cause is in danger of being lost for want of horses and mules,
and yet I discovered to-day that the government [i. e., Northrup] has
been *lending* horses to men who have but recently suffered some of the
calamities of war. I discovered it in a letter from Hon. *R. M. T.
Hunter* of Essex County, asking in behalf of himself and neighbors to
be permitted to retain the borrowed horses beyond the time specified,
October 1. Mr. Hunter borrowed two horses and four mules. He is
worth millions and only suffered his first loss by the enemy a few
weeks ago!" Sept., 1864. *Ibid.*, II, 279. A few days later he wrote:
"Over 100,000 landed proprietors and most of the slave-owners are
now out of the ranks, and soon, I fear, we shall have an army that will
not fight, having nothing to fight for. And this is the result of the
pernicious policy of partiality and exclusiveness, disintegrating society
in such a crisis, and recognizing distinction of ranks, the higher class
staying home and making money, the lower class thrust into the
trenches." Of course, the opinion of one man, however well informed,
is hardly conclusive evidence in so important a matter as this, but a
man in Jones's position of trust would scarcely believe such things
about his immediate superiors unless something was wrong. If his
testimony is worth anything on any subject, it certainly should be important on this.

at the outbreak of the War, which, carefully husbanded, would have served as the stable basis of issues of treasury notes or national bank notes, large enough for the needs of ordinary business. That the specie could not be replaced if exported; that the country would have no basis for a medium of exchange if it disappeared; that it was enough to support business at home but utterly inadequate to meet any of the needs of the War at home or abroad, seems never to have dawned on any one at Richmond. Hamilton had financed the United States with only two millions in specie, but this they either never knew or had totally forgotten. However that may have been, the specie in the South was with incredible difficulty collected by the government in the form of a loan, and with still more unbelievable stupidity was shipped to Europe to pay for supplies.[25] Then, notwithstanding the numerous examples offered by history of the futility of using unlimited paper money as a medium of exchange, the government began in 1861 a series of treasury note issues, and, whenever one issue was exhausted, printed more. The inefficiency of the administration is clear from the fact that within a couple of years the Secretary himself is believed not to have known how many notes had been issued or what the actual indebtedness of the government was.[26]

Taxes paid in money speedily became a farce; the people paid back to the government its own worthless paper. There was at the South no commercial fabric, no credit structure on which the government and the community might rely in the crisis. The government was promptly reduced to taxes in kind, the collection of grain, leather, and the like from the producer, and upon it was instantly forced the thousand and one burdens of transportation and manufacture which the Northern Government was able to turn over to private enterprise with admirable results. The Confederate ad-

[25] The financial history of the Confederacy, bonds, notes, and taxation, has been treated in detail by Schwab, in his *Confederate States of America.*

[26] Eggleston, *Rebel Recollections,* 79.

minstration, weak at best, compelled for the most part to work through inexperienced hands, had thrust upon it the almost insuperable task of utilizing the crude products of an agricultural community and of making them somehow or other meet the complex necessities of a civilized State at war. The failure of such an administration adequately to solve such a problem could be at best scarcely more than a question of time.

Out of such a situation grew inevitably centralized government, acts which seemed arbitrary to the people, infringements upon the liberty of States and of individuals. As at the North, the exigencies of the case forced the government to act and not pause very long over constitutional subtleties. Strangely enough, this very sort of centralized administration, this very readiness to override individual and State opinion in the name of expediency and of the general welfare, had been one of the causes alleged by the South for secession, and these very things the new constitution had been framed to prevent. South Carolina had inveighed against the tariff,[27] and the new Constitution had forbidden customs duties and declared for free trade; yet the Confederacy almost at once instituted a tariff of the most onerous and harassing type, a duty on exports which would have been extremely burdensome had there been any opportunity to collect it.[28] Worse than all others were the constant and obvious violations of State sovereignty and of individual liberty. In the fall of 1862, when only Virginia, the Carolinas, Georgia, and Alabama remained entire in the hands of the Confederates, Georgia and North Carolina were roused almost to the point of rebellion by their anger at what they deemed the disregard of the doctrine of States' sovereignty,[29]

[27] Her Ordinance of Secession declared the tariff one of her chief grievances.

[28] To ensure the payment of interest and principal on the $15,000,000 bond issue authorized Feb. 28, 1861, an export duty of one-eighth of a cent a pound was levied on all cotton exported, and was to be paid in specie or in the coupons of the bonds.

[29] Governor Brown of Georgia wrote to Davis that "no act of the

and the *Charleston Courier* called loudly for a convention
to depose or impeach the President.[30]   Many prominent men
considered it better to yield to the North and restore the
Union than to live under such a Confederacy.[31]   After Antietam, when Lee's regiments were melting away by desertion,
Governor Brown of Georgia put every possible obstacle in
the way of conscription in that State, and at the fall election, Vance, an open and avowed opponent of Davis's, was
elected Governor in North Carolina by a majority of forty
thousand.[32]   To connect Richmond and the field of war with
Charleston and Atlanta after the investiture of Chattanooga
had closed the only trunk line, it became necessary to join
together various short lines and build about forty miles of
road from Danville, Va., to Greensboro, N. C.   The latter
State declined to permit the Confederate government to build
it, and the road, a military necessity of the very first consequence, was built only when the war power was exercised
to override the prohibition of the State.[33]   In 1864, Governor Brown of Georgia flatly refused in an abusive and offensive letter, written at a crucial moment, to send the
militia of the State into the ranks in Virginia.[34]   "Gloom

government of the United States prior to the secession of Georgia had
struck a blow at constitutional liberty so fell as has been stricken [sic]
by the conscript acts. . . . The people of Georgia will refuse to yield
their sovereignty to usurpation." Dodd's *Davis*, 300.

[30] Issue of May 22, 1862.

[31] Stephens, the Vice-President, wrote in August 1862, "Better in
my judgment that Richmond should fall and that the enemy's armies
should sweep our whole country from the Potomac to the Gulf than
that our people should submissively yield obedience to one of these
edicts of our own generals." Pendleton's *Stephens*, 292.

[32] Dodd's *Davis*, 283.   Mr. Dodd, a Southern man, has temperately
dealt with the very large amount of material on the infringements of
States' sovereignty without denying their existence or importance and
yet without drawing conclusions of too sweeping a character.

[33] Dodd's *Davis*, 259-60.

[34] "A long letter was received at the [war] department to-day from
Governor Brown absolutely refusing to respond to the President's call
for the militia of that State.   He says he will not encourage the President's ambitious projects by placing in his hands, and under his un-
conditional control all that remains to preserve the reserved rights

and despondency rule the hour," wrote Cobb from Georgia, "and bitter opposition to the administration mingled with disaffection and disloyalty is manifesting itself." [35]   In fact, the Confederate government, like the Northern, found itself hampered continually by a bitter and active opposition among its own citizens, which not infrequently was carried to the point of flat refusal to act at critical moments although the prompt coöperation of all was needed to render the contest effectual.   "The cause was lost by our own dissensions," wrote a member of the Cabinet in later years.

The length of the War was due to a variety of reasons, but first and foremost to the military skill and personal magnetism of General Robert E. Lee and the able assistance he received from such men as Jackson and Johnston.   Indeed, the consummate skill with which Lee fought a losing contest for years has scarcely if ever been surpassed.   Certainly no general of equal skill was enrolled in the Northern armies; Grant's reputation was due to his success, which in its turn was the result of a combination of many factors, among which the superior resources of the North and other influences just enumerated ought to have prominence.   Much allowance must also be made for the fact that the South stood on the defensive and that to conquer her required the subjugation of an enor-

of his State. He bitterly and offensively criticizes the President's management of military affairs." Jones, *Diary*, II, 292-3. Sept. 26, 1864.

[35] *Rebellion Records*, Series IV, Vol. III, 1010. On Feb. 3, 1864, Davis sent the following message to the Confederate Congress: "Discontent, disaffection, and disloyalty are manifested among those who through the sacrifices of others, have enjoyed quiet and safety at home. Public meetings have been held in some of which a treasonable design is masked by a pretence of devotion to State sovereignty, and in others is openly avowed. . . . In certain localities men of no mean position do not hesitate to avow their disloyalty and hostility to our cause, and their advocacy of peace on the terms of submission and the abolition of slavery. . . . [Soldiers are taken from the ranks on the eve of battle by means of writs of habeas corpus. If this continues] Desertion, already a frightful evil, will become the order of the day. And who will arrest the deserter, when most of those at home are engaged with him in the common cause of setting the government at defiance?" Richardson, *Messages and Papers of the Confederacy*, I, 396, 398.

mous theater of war, which, even had the resistance been less able and desperate, would have required time for adequate occupation of the numerous strategic points. Furthermore, it must always be remembered that the South had very much the advantage in equipment in 1861, that the North required time to adjust itself to the situation, and was, moreover, hampered by the commercial crisis of 1861–2. Time was necessary to make the greater resources of the North in men and munitions of war tell decisively upon the outcome. Indeed, the very abundance of the Northern provision for the army was for a while an administrative problem of the first magnitude. There was too much food and clothing to be promptly and accurately distributed by the old machinery, and the creation of a new administration, undertaken by Stanton with admirable determination and energy and executed with consummate skill, required time to become effective.

Besides, politics at the North was constantly tying the hands of the generals and robbing them of discretion, and the activity of the opposition during the year 1862 made it long doubtful whether the conflict would not come to an end because of the refusal of the Northern people to countenance it longer. Lincoln found it difficult during the first two years to leave the conduct of the campaign in the hands of the men at the front. His idea that Washington needed fifty thousand men either within it or close at hand to insure its safety often prevented the undertaking or completion of any plan which depended for success upon the concentration of the Union forces, and the Confederates soon discovered that a feint at Washington invariably paralyzed the Union armies, because of the dispatch of so large a detachment to protect the city. Lincoln saw more clearly than the men in the field that the real object of the War was not so much to win battles as to crush the Confederacy, and that there were enemies at home almost as difficult to meet and whose defeat was even more imperative than that of Lee. From the first, there was a strong minority at the North opposed to the War, some because of a belief in the illegality of coercion or in the right to secede, the vast majority because they believed the conduct of the war reprehensible. The administrative corruption and confusion of the first year, the defeat at Bull Run, the long inactivity of the huge force of men at the front while McClellan was turning that "armed mob" into an army was interpreted at the North very much to the detriment of the government. It had been doubtful in 1861 whether the North would support a war at all; it continued to be doubtful as inactivity and bungling were succeeded by the reverses of 1862 whether the North would not make imperative the conclusion of an ignoble peace by the withdrawal of troops and supplies. Denunciations of Lincoln and of his generals were delivered by notable men in Washington and even in the anterooms of the Executive Mansion.[36] In September 1862, men said openly in Pennsylvania that they would be glad to hang Lincoln to the nearest lamp-post.[37] Men, waiting to see the President, maligned and abused him openly and went to lengths which were amazing.[38] A Democratic paper, the *New York World,* declared on June 9, 1864, after Lincoln had been renominated: "The age of statesmen is gone: the age of railsplitters and tailors, of buffoons, boors, and fanatics, has succeeded. . . . In a crisis of the most appalling magnitude, requiring statesmanship of the highest order, the country is asked to consider the claims of two ignorant, boorish, third-rate backwoods lawyers for the highest stations in the govern-

[36] Nearly all the books dealing with life in Washington during the War or with Lincoln as President will furnish numerous examples. Oberholtzer in his *Life of Lincoln* cites several characteristic cases.

[37] Oberholtzer, *Lincoln,* 237.

[38] So Riddle tells in his *Recollections,* 267. "The one most loud and bitter was Henry Wilson of Massachusetts. His open assaults were amazing." Lincoln would be renominated, said Wilson, and "bad as that would be, the best must be made of it." Chase, Secretary of the Treasury and later Chief Justice, wrote in 1864: "Nothing except the waste of life is more painful in this war than the absolutely reckless waste of means. . . . Contrary to all rules, the spigot in Uncle Abe's barrel is made twice as big as the bung-hole. He may have been a good flat-boat man and rail-splitter, but he certainly never learned the true science of coopering." Quoted by Rhodes, *History of the United States,* IV, 477-8.

ment." The Democratic party campaigned the North in 1862 and 1864 on the platform that the conduct of the War was a disgrace and demanded its prompt conclusion by a treaty with the South upon the best terms obtainable.

As Lincoln perceived, the defeat of the administration at the polls in the North would be even more disastrous than reverses in the field; and reverses in the field were the most powerful weapon in the hands of his political adversaries at home. Despatches poured into Washington from Northern governors and politicians: "Nothing but success, speedy and decided, will save our cause from destruction. In the Northwest, distrust and despair are seizing upon the hearts of the people." [39] Such was the refrain. The difficulties of the situation were nothing to Halleck and Lincoln; the armies must move forward at all costs, for inaction produced almost as unfavorable an effect on Northern opinion as did defeat. The generals must act so as to retain the confidence of the people at home; the war was no mere military event; it was a political and economic cataclysm of the utmost complexity. Its object was not to win victories but to destroy the Confederacy and military operations must be sacrificed to the exigencies of political campaigns, even if it became necessary to renounce the plans which seemed from a military point of view conclusive. Food, clothing, transportation, the need of elaborate preparations before opening the campaign, so invariably insisted upon by McClellan and other generals, made Lincoln impatient in the face of the feats accomplished by Lee without such resources or preparations. The President, wrote

[39] These sentences are from a despatch from Governor Morton of Indiana to Lincoln, dated Oct. 21, 1862. The Governors of Ohio and Illinois telegraphed at the same time in similar strain. The most instructive incident from this point of view was the removal of Buell and the appointment of Rosecrans, solely with a view to securing an immediate and successful advance. Rosecrans then declined to advance until his preparations were complete and for nearly a month remained at Nashville, furiously busy but apparently inactive, while President, Congress, and the Northern press raged and stormed. To all orders and demands he gave but one answer, his resignation. Rhodes has particularly well emphasized such issues as these in his account of the War.

Halleck, the General-in-Chief, to Buell, "does not understand why we cannot march as the enemy marches, live as he lives, and fight as he fights, unless we admit the inferiority of our troops and generals." [40]   But the generals, campaigning in the Alleghanies, knew that the mountain districts were at heart Unionist and that the surest way to throw them into the ranks of the enemy would be to forage there for the support of the Federal armies.[41]   The strength of the Unionist party at the South had been counted upon by many to aid as powerfully in the eventual reduction of the Confederacy as campaigns and armies.   Besides, the desperate expedients to which necessity drove Lee were scarcely measures to adopt from choice with a restless and suspicious public watching for mistakes.   The news that the troops were ragged, barefoot, and hungry because of an impetuous advance into a district where there was insufficient forage and to which supplies had not been brought, would have been a worse blow to the administration than inaction could possibly be.   In December 1862, the situation was darkest.   "Everything goes wrong," said Lincoln to Seward and Weed.   "The rebel armies hold their own; Grant is wandering around in Mississippi; Burnside manages to keep ahead of Lee; Seymour has carried New York and if his [the Democratic] party carries and holds many of the Northern States, we shall have to give up the fight, for we can never conquer three-fourths of our countrymen, scattered in front, flank, and rear." [42]

[40] *Rebellion Records*, XVI, Part II, 627. Lincoln wrote to McClellan, Oct. 13, 1862: "Are you not over-cautious when you assume that you cannot do what the enemy is constantly doing? . . . Change positions with the enemy, and think you not he would break your communication with Richmond within the next twenty-four hours? . . . We should not so operate as merely to drive him away. As we must beat him somewhere or fail finally, we can do it, if at all, easier near to us than far away." *Ibid.*, XIX, Part I, 13.

[41] Halleck telegraphed to Grant after the battle of Corinth: "Why not pursue the enemy into Mississippi, supporting your army on the country?" Grant replied, laconically, "An army cannot subsist itself on the country except in forage." Rhodes, *History of the United States*, IV, 181.

[42] Oberholtzer, *Lincoln*, 242. His authority is not cited.

Grant was more successful than other generals not so much because of superior military ability as because he alone fully grasped the relation of the military to the political situation. To retire along the railroad from Corinth and Iuka upon Memphis, there to pause to recuperate his army, to prepare a base of operations from which the following spring to advance down the river upon Vicksburg, would have been from a military point of view much better than an immediate advance overland on Vicksburg through Mississippi bayous and swamps, constantly exposed to the danger of losing touch with his base of supplies. But headlines in the Northern papers, "Grant Retreats on Memphis," would have been at that juncture fatal to the campaign and to his career as a general, and he knew it. An advance, which did not expose him to actual defeat, which would hearten the sinking and discouraged and give the administration papers a chance to print the scareheads, "Grant Advancing," would be potent material with which to conjure at home. Eventually, the victories at Gettysburg and Vicksburg "knocked the planks out of the Chicago platform" which declared the conduct of the War a failure. Not till then was it clear that the North would support the War to the end.

These difficulties were intensified by the wide disapproval of the interference with the right of free speech and of the press and of the arbitrary arrests made by virtue of the "war powers" assumed by Lincoln. It was thought at Washington inexpedient to allow speeches at public meetings which openly expressed sympathy for the South or declared the Federal government a despotism. Several men arrested for such utterances without the usual legal formalities were promptly elected by the people of their States to the legislatures, and in one case even to the United States Senate, at the very moment when they were in custody charged with treason. The large bounties offered by State and nation to volunteers failed to maintain the strength of the Union forces and the North was compelled to follow the expedients adopted months before at the South and have recourse to a draft to recruit the armies.

It aroused immediate and widespread opposition and in July 1863, caused in New York City a riot which assumed the proportions of a revolt against the government, held control of the city for three days, and was finally only reduced by troops hastily sent back from the front to coöperate with the navy. The amazing commercial prosperity at the North, which became evident in 1863, and was due to fundamental causes over which no one had control, greatly affected the attitude of the majority in favor of the administration and prevented anything more than sporadic and temporary opposition. The number of exemptions, the permission to pay substitutes, and the comparative ease of desertion also helped.[43] With this political opposition, Lincoln dealt with conspicuous success. The support of the government by a majority at the North was due more considerably than most men have realized to the personal character, influence, and tact of Abraham Lincoln, who in this sense was one of the important factors in the winning of the War by the North.

[43] The Draft of July 18, 1864, for 500,000 men resulted in the drawing of 231,918 names, of whom 138,536 reported; 82,531 were exempted outright; and the total draft amounted to 56,005, of whom more than half provided substitutes. In New York the accumulated county, state, and national bounties amounted to $677 for a new recruit and an additional $100 for a man who had seen service. Enlisting in one State, securing the bounty, deserting on the way to the front, enlisting again in order to receive a second bounty, became all too common a practice. Of a detachment of 625 recruits from New Hampshire for the Army of the Potomac in 1864, 137 deserted on passage to the front, 82 to the enemy's picket lines, and 36 to the rear, leaving a total of 370 men. Over 41 per cent deserted. Rhodes, *History of the United States*, IV, 429 *et seq.* The Southern armies experienced similar difficulties.

XXV.

THE RESULTS OF THE CIVIL WAR

THE Northern men who fought and won the War invariably declared that its purpose was the "preservation of the Union," the "maintenance of the Constitution," the defeat of those who were seeking to "destroy" both the Constitution and the Union. Yet, it is incontestable that the result of the War—the one permanent result of significance due directly to the War—was the alteration beyond recognition of both "Constitution" and "Union," as those words had been popularly and commonly understood in 1860. And every element in both was as unmistakably and unalterably changed—the people collectively, the individual, the idea of citizenship, the notion of a State and of its relation to its own citizens as well as to the Federal government, the idea of what was meant by the North, the South, the West.

The difficulty in comprehending this apparent paradox lies in the very general failure to remember what Lincoln meant by the words "Union" and "Constitution." The strong sentiment in the North in 1860 against the right of the Federal government to coerce a State will convince the student that the word "Constitution" connoted to most people North and South before the War a compact made by sovereign States, and that the "Union" denoted a league of units bound together by some tie not very exactly defined in any one's mind. Men had not yet rid themselves of the precedents and traditions of the anti-national movement which had received in Colonial and Revolutionary times the almost universal adherence of the people. To Lincoln, on the other hand, the word "Union" meant oneness, nationality; the Constitution had "created" a government of individuals and not of States.

340

He saw the issue of nationality as the vital concept behind the Revolution, and indeed credited the makers of the Declaration of Independence with national ideas which they would have denied with some vehemence.[1] But he correctly appreciated the fact that the Constitution had signified to its makers the conscious adoption of nationalism and in the debates of the Convention he found ample confirmation of his own beliefs and ideals.[2] States' rights and secession he saw

[1] On his way to Washington in 1861, Lincoln made many speeches whose tenor was substantially the same. "When the time does come [for action], I shall take the ground that I think is right—right for the North, for the South, for the East, for the West, for the whole country." Temporarily, he represented "the majesty of the nation"; so he told audience after audience. That phrase was new and pregnant with meaning. To the New Jersey Senate he said: "I am exceedingly anxious that that thing [struggled for in the Revolution]—that something even more than national independence; that something that held out a great promise to all the people of the world to all time to come— I am exceedingly anxious that this Union, the Constitution, and the liberties of the people shall be perpetuated in accordance with the original idea for which the struggle was made." His course would "tend to the perpetuity of the nation, and the liberty of these States and these people." Nicolay and Hay, *Complete Works*, VI, 147, 152, 154, 151, 155, respectively. What he found in the writings of Washington were probably such phrases as these. "Let us look to our national character and to things beyond the present moment." *Writings of Washington*, Ford's ed., XI, 81. "I have labored, ever since I have been in the service, to discourage all kinds of local attachments and distinctions of country, denominating the whole by the greater name of American, but I have found it impossible to overcome prejudices." *Ibid.*, V, 117. The wish and the impossibility of its realization are both significant for us.

[2] "A Union of the States is a Union of the men composing them, from whence a national character results to the whole. . . . If they formed a confederacy in some respects—they formed a Nation in others." Hunt's *Madison's Notes*, I, 186. See also I, 233, 248-50, 259, 263, 268, 274, 285, etc., etc., for clear evidence that both parties in the Convention were agreed as to what the document they were making meant. *The Federalist* and the debates in the various States over the adoption of the Constitution show that the leaders all understood that a conscious choice in favor of nationalism was being registered. Lincoln's doctrine of the Union as older than the States, as found in the First Inaugural and other state papers, will be found in this statement of Wilson's: "Mr. Wilson could not admit the doctrine that when the Colonies became independent of G. Britain, they became independent also of each other. He read the declaration of Independence, observing thereon

were, like Anti-Federalism, anti-national, striving openly for a confederation of sovereigns and denying the existence of a nation in the true sense of the word [2a] or the possibility or desirability of attempting to create one.[3]

We must not to-day, however, mistake the Declaration of Independence for a proclamation of nationality made by the people as individuals, nor confuse the affirmation of nationality as the ultimate basis for permanent central government, made in the preamble to the Constitution, with the existence of national sentiment among the people as a whole, and, least of all, with the flowering of national consciousness or with its realization of its own existence. The Constitution was a prophecy, a forecast of what would become true, and was startlingly accurate, for the framers saw that the social, economic, and geographical conditions in the country made eventual union inevitable.[4]   Webster saw what the Constitu-

that the *United Colonies* were declared to be free and independent States; and inferring that they were independent not *individually*, but *Unitedly* and that they were confederated as they were independent States." *Ibid.*, I, 188.

[2a] *The Salem Gazette* for October 18 and 21, 1814, contained long articles on States' sovereignty and denounced nationalism. "The truth is that the federal constitution is nothing more than a treaty between independent sovereignties." A war between the States would be a "public war between sovereigns . . . as much as in a war between Russia and France." *The Boston Daily Advertiser* in November, 1814, said: "We are too prone to think that there is a distinct sovereignty known by the name of the Government of the United States and that it exists independently of the several States. Whereas, in fact, the national compact is only an agreement entered into between the whole of the States and each individual State." *The Columbian Centinel* of Boston at this same time declared: "The individual States are 'free, sovereign and independent' nations . . . [To the Federal government] our allegiance is secondary, qualified, and conditional; to our State sovereignties it is primary, universal and absolute." See these and other extracts to the same purpose in the *Mississippi Valley Historical Association Proceedings*, 1912–13, VI, 176–188.

[3] General Quitman of Alabama in a public letter written in 1852, said: "If reorganized Democracy admits the absolute doctrines of the existence and sovereignty of a supreme national government, possessing power to coerce the States, nothing will be lost by its defeat and destruction." Hodgson, *Cradle of the Confederacy*, 335.

[4] The great question debated in the Convention was really what were

tion meant and his splendid affirmation of nationality as the true ideal of a democratic people, his orations eulogizing the Colonists and the Men of 1776 as patriots, his proof that the Constitution vested the sovereignty in the people as individuals [4a] are landmarks in the history of the achieving of American nationality. That the nation was becoming sentient, was really beginning to signify its existence by unmistakable signs, Webster comprehended. The greatness of the vision enthralled many of his listeners: ''Three or four times I thought my temples would burst with the gush of blood,'' wrote Ticknor.[5] But to the majority, nationality had not yet become a reality.[6] The logic of facts was too strong. Webster, however, was followed by a long line of historians, poets, and essayists—Bancroft, Sparks, Longfellow, Lowell, Whittier, Emerson, Thoreau—who apostrophized Freedom and Liberty as magnificent qualities and wrote of a great nationality ennobled by finding its expression through such concepts. Only by the fostering of such ideals in the popular consciousness could an aggregation of individuals become a people and attain nationality in the highest sense; only thus could an entity evolve worthy of national consciousness, and possessed of those fundamental virtues on which it could alone be nourished or sustained. Potent as was the written word, the spoken word was mightier, and the message of Webster and of the leaders of the intellectual world really reached the Northern people through the pulpit, the lecture platform, and the school

and what would be likely to be the social, economic, and geographical conditions in the country and was one national government or two or three confederacies the better solution. Again and again they reached the conclusion that union only would be feasible. Hunt's *Madison's Notes*, I, 255-7, 267, 269, 271 note, 274, 278-9, 288-91, 298-9, etc.

[4a] "That unity of government which constitutes us one people." Webster, Eulogy on Washington, *Works*, 1, 230. Chancellor Kent, introducing Webster at a public dinner in his honor to celebrate the 1830 speech, said: "It turned the attention of the public to the great doctrines of the national rights and national union." Webster, *Works*, I, 194.

[5] *Life and Letters of George Ticknor*, I, 330.

[6] See the quotation from De Tocqueville, *supra*, p. 226.

room, where the sermons, addresses, and text-books all breathed patriotism and nationality.

In the anti-slavery debates, in the searchings of conscience, North and South, over the issues that produced the War, we hear the first incoherent mutterings, the first attempts at connected thinking and at self-expression of the new giant, waking to consciousness of his own existence. The nation was seeking in mental anguish national ideals, moral standards, ethical concepts, policies—broad in scope, lofty in purpose, universal in application and meaning. From individuals here and there came something like utterance of the notions with whose mystic purport the national subconscious mind was full, the eager expression as conscious thought through a human and individualistic medium of the ethical and moral concepts of which the people as a whole were but dimly conscious. The greatness of such men lies not in themselves. They are vessels of the spirit, sensitive media for the apprehension and expression of the seething content of human sentiment struggling round them for utterance.

In Lincoln, the nation, North and South, grew to see itself. He was in the highest possible sense a representative man, making the nation conscious of its oneness of purpose and idealism, of the glory and splendor of nationality, and of the wondrous possibilities open to a great people who should be filled with the ideals of unity, democracy, and liberty. In him and through him, both North and South awakened to a consciousness of the meaning of American development, and realized that the War had actually been an attempt, all unwitting, to destroy this collective personality before it had attained consciousness. And in the last year of the War, as the consciousness of that great vital fact became universal, in the moment when the glorious conception of what nationality meant flashed upon the vast majority of Americans, a new nation was born. For a nation is; it springs into life, full fledged, in the imagery of the old Greek description of the birth of Minerva, and at once is possessed of sentient life and vast powers. Washington had made us free and independent; Lincoln became the father of American nationality. He was not the man who made it possible nor the man whose glowing words first carried the vision to men's minds, but the man in whom and through whom it became an actuality. Webster had made New England see the vision; Lincoln made the South, which neither saw nor believed, which was in arms against the very concept, not only realize that the object of the War was not conquest, the abolition of slavery, nor the abrogation of constitutional rights, but the creation of a nation out of a divided people. It was a great achievement to have convinced those whose own interests urged them to accept the idea of nationality; it was a thousand-fold greater to have convinced those whose interests were to be vitally injured by the acceptance of the idea, of its greatness and worth. The most immediate and most important result of the War was the creation of the American nation and this result we owe chiefly to Abraham Lincoln.

One is tempted almost to doubt the evidence of his own eyes and look upon this sudden "creation" of national consciousness as a miracle of that sort which cannot in its very nature be the work of one man. How could a nation, as it were, spring into existence? Is it true, after all, that nations are created by fighting, that great issues can be actually decided by battles? The "creation" of the new nation, in this particular instance, consisted in the achieving by the majority of a consciousness of facts and tendencies which had always been true. As a child takes form in its mother's womb and exists before it makes its entry into the world, so a nation grows, all unconscious of its own existence; and, as with the child, we date its life from its first moment of consciousness. The War made the people aware of what the Northern leaders had long seen; it convinced the South that the position of the North was the true one. The War showed the people, North, South, and West, what the President of the United States had meant by the Union and the Constitution, and that what he said was true.

In a sense, the War created the nation: it stimulated, as

nothing else could have done, the growth of common sentiment. The armies brought together men from the most distant sections and made them acquainted, showing them their common interests and beliefs, the essential identity of their democratic ideals, their common humanity and sympathy. The prisoners in both camps learned how superficial were the differences which they in their ignorance had assumed to be so great; with the vastness of the country and of its natural resources, most men became acquainted for the first time. The War gave the country a common aim for which to work and welded the North and the West tightly together, and made the Southern men more conscious of their similarities than of their differences.

Again, the War was a great social leveler and brought together in the trenches men hitherto sundered by wealth and social position. In the South especially, poor white and planter met on terms of equality and each learned to respect and admire the sterling traits of the other. Intercourse was stimulated and increased and the necessities of the struggle gave an immediacy to the attempt to agree upon the solution of common problems and difficulties which forced the process of the growth of a consensus of opinion. Gradually, the non-essentials became apparent and were discarded by both parties; gradually the really vital issue of nationality was pushed to the fore, almost entirely obscuring slavery and States' sovereignty.[6a] The average man thought perforce much about the reason for the War, about its purpose, about differences and similarities; and, as the essential nobility of each became clearer to the other, both North and South began to ask themselves why they fought at all. The simple presence of so many men in the various armies, the necessity of travel, the

[6a] "What was at first a struggle to maintain the outward form of our government has become a contest to preserve the life and assert the supreme will of the nation. Even in April 1861, . . . there was an instinctive feeling that the very germinating principle of our nationality was at stake and that unity of territory was but another name for unity of idea, nay, was impossible without it and undesirable if it were possible." Lowell in the *Atlantic Monthly*, October 1864, p. 566.

process of acquaintance was making the whole community aware that a nation existed, and this dawning of consciousness was in itself the process of birth. The War was the travail of the new nation. It proved all those things to the common man which he must otherwise have waited long to appreciate. It showed him what Lincoln meant and proved its truth.

The War had been literally won by the forces of nationality over those of separateness; by the geographical and commercial factors making the North comparatively stronger than the South. Here again the conflict merely made apparent the existing fact that the forces of union were and long had been predominant in the life of the people. They had produced the Constitution and the numerous compromises and had postponed the War for seventy years. The accidents of geography and of settlement had produced communities which were and are singularly interdependent. Only three natural divisions existed: the Atlantic Coast, the Mississippi Valley, the Pacific Slope. With these natural lines, other lines of heat and cold, of rainfall, of productivity of the soil, and the like, did not at all coincide. The geographical divisions ran north and south; the climatic and geological lines ran east and west. The accident of settlement, spreading westward across all of these natural areas, coinciding with none, forming successively small communities favored by this natural advantage, fettered by that natural obstacle, did create, as Gerry said, "neither the same nation nor different nations." No sectionalization of the country upon economic, political, racial, or religious lines was possible.[7] Nature had also failed to pro-

---

[7] Lincoln's Message to Congress of Dec. 1, 1862, contains a remarkably clear exposition of the facts described in these paragraphs. "That portion of the earth's surface which is owned and inhabited by the people of the United States is well adapted to be the home of one national family, and it is not well adapted for two or more. . . . Physically speaking we cannot separate. We cannot remove our respective sections from each other, nor build an impassable wall between them. . . . There is no line, straight or crooked, suitable for a national boundary upon which to divide. Trace through, from east to west, upon the line between the free and slave country, and we shall find a

vide any of the political entities with separate methods of communication with the outside world: the abundant waterways served of necessity many rather than one. All the tiny groups in existence in 1760, the different parts of the broad belt of settlement in 1789, the different sections of the continent east of the Mississippi in 1860, were interdependent, interrelated by economic, political, racial, and religious factors, whose potency was already appreciated by the leaders.

Yet, while the country remained sparsely settled, while the most pressing problems were local, States' rights, local sovereignty, were naturally paramount. They coincided best with actual conditions. But the growth of each succeeding decade, the resultant closer contiguity of States with States, of individuals with individuals, the rapid growth of the area of settlement, were creating common problems of constantly greater significance, whose settlement could not long be ignored or postponed, and which had necessarily to be settled by general discussion and compromise. The nationality of the common

little more than one-third of its length are rivers, easy to be crossed, and populated, or soon to be populated thickly upon both sides; while nearly all its remaining length are merely surveyors' lines, over which people may walk back and forth without any consciousness of their presence. No part of this line can be made any more difficult to pass by writing it down on paper or parchment as a national boundary. . . . As part of one nation, its people [in the Mississippi Valley] now find, and may forever find their way to Europe by New York, to South America and Africa by New Orleans, and to Asia by San Francisco. But separate our common country into two nations as designed by the present rebellion, and every man of this great interior region is thereby cut off from some one or more of these outlets—not perhaps by a physical barrier, but by embarrassing and onerous trade regulations. . . . These outlets, east, west, and south, are indispensable to the well-being of the people inhabiting, and to inhabit, this vast interior region. . . . Our national strife springs not from our permanent part, not from the land we inhabit, not from our national homestead. There is no possible severing of this but would multiply and not mitigate evils among us. In all its adaptations and aptitudes, it demands union and abhors separation. In fact, it would ere long force reunion, however much of blood and treasure the separation might have cost. Our strife pertains to ourselves—to the passing generations of men; and it can without convulsion be hushed forever with the passing of one generation." *Complete Works*, VIII, 110-116.

problems was growing each decade clearer and clearer. Withal, the benefits of nationality were becoming rapidly more obvious:—the freedom of intercourse between the communities so vitally dependent on each other for the continuity of economic life, unhampered by the artificial restrictions of frontiers and customs barriers; the untrammeled use of the natural highways by all; the freedom of the movement of individuals from State to State without loss of civil and legal privileges; trade with Europe on equal terms, all this the War made evident to the average man. Travel and military campaigns made clear the vastness of the country, its structure, its interdependence, and above all, the necessity of the common use of the lines of communication through the Mohawk Valley, the Baltimore and Ohio Railroad, and the Cumberland Gap. As never before men saw that the West was tied to New York and Chicago by the railroads; that the railroads of most consequence were interstate, not local; that the really profitable commerce was interstate and national; that the country was still dependent on its market in Europe and was therefore tied fast to the Atlantic seaboard by the necessity of contact with Europe through the ports. Even local trade was vitally dependent on the common use of the Hudson, the Delaware, the Mississippi, and the Great Lakes. Men began to realize that a central government strong enough to prevent individual States from interfering with each other's mutual rights was an absolutely indispensable political basis for the economic fabric upon whose solidarity and rapid development the prosperity of the country depended.

Indeed, it was slowly borne in upon the people by the experiences of the War that these natural conditions were the real difficulties with which the sections had been contending, and that they were immutable—to be conquered neither by fighting nor argument, factors to be recognized and to which all sections must adjust themselves as best as they could. They saw too that the pressure of these factors for settlement was increased by the growth of the country, by the growing density of population, and by the new complexity of the economic fabric. The existence of two confederacies would not solve the vital problems at all, would make their solution incalculably more difficult, and result constantly in issues which two sovereign nations could not with dignity compromise nor with indifference leave unsettled, and which they could, least of all, decide by an appeal to arms. The problems of North, South, and West were not different problems but different phases or complementary results of the same problems. The railroads and the telegraph were already knitting the country together and would in the future provide that close contact between all its parts and that ease of movement between them which would be certain to strengthen those forces making for nationality. As Lowell said, the very stars in their courses fought for Union.[8]

The result of the War upon the North had been striking. The commercial crisis of 1861 and 1862, the new contact with the West, the direct trade with Europe thanks to the western grain and the new railroad trunk lines, the new industries created by the needs of the army, and the new economic wants resultant upon the great prosperity of the years 1864 and 1865, had given industry in all its phases a jolt which had advanced it decades in development. The War made the North richer as a whole and laid the foundation of many individual fortunes. The causes are not far to seek. First and foremost, the North had been compelled to draw heavily upon its resources of capital and had loaned the government capital which would normally not have been invested in industrial securities. The Federal government then practically offered bounties to private individuals who were willing to utilize this capital for the production of military stores. Much capital that would normally have been invested for permanent returns and of which the community would have spent only the interest was spent in its entirety and posterity was to repay it. The high prices paid by the government enabled the people to bear heavy direct and indirect taxes, but the size of the debt at the end of the war, nearly three billions

[8] *Atlantic Monthly*, January 1861.

of dollars, indicates the amount of capital actually distributed among individuals then alive which posterity was to replace. Undoubtedly, too, the necessities of the War and the high prices stimulated production and investment and caused the spurs of ambition to urge the individual onward at a faster rate than before. The War created a new North, different in spirit, in temper, in ambitions, and wealthier, more confident, more complaisant than the North of 1860.

The War also made apparent the weakness of the economic and social structure at the South. The Confederacy had been constructed upon the belief that the slave States were independent of the North in fact, and that the political and constitutional separation would merely adjust theories to realities. The War proved the falsity of the notion. What had seemed enormous, fabulous wealth melted away the moment the blockade became effective, and the South saw only too clearly that its economic fabric was an artificial creation, dependent upon conditions whose continuance could not be assured by the simple political expedients of passing ordinances of secession and making a new constitution. Not the Constitution of the United States, not the tariff, not Congress, but the very character of Southern civilization was the true difficulty. The weakness of the Confederacy was less military than it was economic and social. There was no substructure on which the political entity could rest, no bricks out of which to build a new nation. The War did not itself destroy the slavocracy: it removed of necessity those props on which the slave power had depended and made apparent the frailty and artificiality of the structure. The old régime at the South was not destroyed; it collapsed. In the culture of cotton by forced labor there was no proper economic basis for an independent nation and the War proved it even before the fighting began in earnest.

The artificial factors were now evident. The high degree of profit obtained from the cotton-culture had been primarily due to the unexampled fertility of the virgin soil in the river-bottoms, which yielded enormous returns even to extensive

cultivation by the crudest of forced labor. The profit had
also depended on the growth of the demand for raw cotton in
the North and in Europe at the same rate at which the
planters had increased the supply. That the demand before
1860 scarcely ever failed to equal the supply was a remarkable fact, but there was no reason to suppose it would continue indefinitely to do so. Above all, freedom of access to
the Northern and European markets, a merchant marine and
cheap freights were even more essential. In the nature of
things, the continued coöperation of all these factors could not
be indefinitely assured. The amount of virgin soil was limited
by Nature. An increase in the value of slaves; a decrease in
the proportionate return; a falling off of the demand; the
discovery of a new source of supply; interference with freedom of intercourse; expensive freights; the alteration of any
single factor might destroy the profitableness of the investment, and such a change might be produced at any moment
by natural forces over which no human agency could exert
the slightest influence. The War stopped intercourse with
Europe and with the North by the interposition of a highly
artificial barrier, the blockade, which the growing of cotton
had not provided the South with any means to remove. The
whole fabric of the slave power instantly crumbled and died.
The South found itself pauperized, without any industrial
life at all. Its land and slaves, fabulously valuable on paper,
potentially valuable for growing cotton, were an utterly worthless encumbrance when one single factor in the artificial structure of Southern life was removed. The South was not independent; it was absolutely dependent upon the North, the
West, and Europe for existence at all. The War proved it.
The only arable land in use was not suitable for grain; the
only agricultural tools the planters had were inadequate for
the diversified intensive agriculture needed to sustain the life
of the community; the only skill the millions of slaves possessed was valueless in the crisis and they were too ignorant
and too lacking in adaptability to be forced into new industries in time to be of any avail. And even had they

possessed adaptability, the necessary raw materials were lacking.

It began to be evident to the Southerners that the cotton-culture had in its nature prevented the growth of a strong, well-knit community by locating the people on large plantations miles from each other, by putting a premium on the occupation of vast areas of soil only a tithe of which was in actual use. Towns and cities had not been able to grow; community life, the daily contact of the people, had been reduced to a minimum, and they had not acquired the habit of acting in concert nor learned the necessity of coöperation. States' rights had thrived; the individual had been unhampered by State and central government; and the very success of local government made difficult the sort of common action which the War made imperative. The social and political structure of the South did not furnish a proper basis even for strong State governments and still less afforded adequate support to a central government struggling with the administrative difficulties of a great conflict.

The separateness of the Southerners had also prevented the growth of a system of transportation which would adequately connect the various scattered communities with each other. The splendid river systems, eked out by a few miles of narrow-gauge railroad here and there, put every plantation into cheap and easy contact with the markets for cotton and made a network of railroads, east and west, north and south, needless for the ordinary daily life of the community before the War. But, when the Federal gunboats had occupied the seacoast and the rivers, the only universal system of transportation the South had possessed was lost, and it found itself without adequate means of communication and unable to utilize promptly and efficiently such resources as it did possess. The truth was that South Carolina, Alabama, Louisiana and the rest had been in contact with the North and with Europe far more than with each other; they were not even interdependent. Not the South as a whole, but literally every State and almost every plantation was dependent upon easy and direct contact with the North and with Europe. The Southern States had never actually coöperated with each other in economic, political, or constitutional life. While the leaders had lived together at Washington and had voted as a unit in the Senate, the States at home had gone each its own way. The Confederacy itself was an artificial aggregation of small isolated communities which were for the first time attempting life in common. The South was a geographical expression, not a nation, not even an entity. With its constitutional professions the facts did not agree. The War made strikingly apparent what had always been true.

The vital objection to slavery was that it was undemocratic and contrary to every legal and social principle of American life. It created obviously a three-caste system, the slave-holding whites, the non-slave-holding whites, and the slaves. Forced labor was and always will be nominally cheaper than free labor and the very existence of the slave deprived the poor white of economic opportunity. He could not compete in the cotton fields with the negro; so long as the degree of profit in the cotton-culture so greatly exceeded the profit of producing anything else at the South, he was excluded from any other industry, and would exist merely by the labor of his own hands on the small portion of less productive soil that might fall to his lot. Slavery, which robbed the poor white of his economic, political, and social freedom, put the power and wealth into the hands of a small oligarchy. In addition, slavery was undemocratic because it deprived the negroes and poor whites alike of opportunity for individual development and aggrandizement. From the lack of stimulus to progress, from the general lack of education, from the realization among the planters that any improvement of the slaves and poor whites threatened the extent and security of their own control, resulted that stagnation of community life which prevented any truly organic development. The Confederacy was a democracy whose fundamental principles were daily abrogated by its own life. It was an oligarchy which had theoretically renounced the use of those administrative and legal forms by which alone oligarchies had governed great masses of men. A democratic community in which four-fifths of the population was excluded by artificial restrictions from actual participation in the life of the community was a house built upon the sands, certain to perish under the first stress of unfavorable circumstances. An oligarchy under the forms of democracy carried the seeds of its destruction in its own constitution. Both were doomed. The actual social and political structure of the Confederacy was utterly inconsistent with and repugnant to its constitution. The War made the fact appallingly clear. The Southerners saw it the clearest, for the presence of the poor whites in the army side by side with the old ruling class had been a lesson in democracy for both and had opened their eyes to their common humanity. The willingness of the Southern Government to free the slaves who would serve in the army, the comparatively slight regret expressed at the South over the abolition of slavery, both showed the working of the leaven of democracy under the powerful stimulus of circumstances.

Above all, the realization that slavery was undemocratic and unprogressive convinced Lincoln, long before the war was over, that a democratic nation could neither be preserved, restored, or created unless this vitally undemocratic institution were abolished.[9] The South had not been one with the North because this "peculiar institution" had been undemocratic; and it could not become democratic and begin to develop in harmony with the genius of American institutions until slavery was destroyed.[9a] He saw, however, in 1865, that

[9] "He wished the reunion of all the States perfected, and so effected as to remove all causes of disturbance in the future; and to attain this end, it was necessary that the original disturbing cause [slavery] should, if possible, be rooted out." Nicolay and Hay, *Complete Works*, X, 353. Slavery "must be always and everywhere hostile to the principles of republican government; justice and the national safety demand its utter and complete extirpation from the soil of the republic." *Ibid.*, X, 119. See also 191, 193-7.

[9a] "The popular understanding has been gradually enlightened as to the real causes of the War, and in consequence of that enlightenment, a

the War had already done the work. The Planter class had actually been dethroned; the old social and economic structure had collapsed and had actually freed the poor whites from their shackles; many slaves had already left the cotton plantations; others would follow as soon as opportunity offered. The downfall of the old slave power was a fact and there remained only the declaration of the freedom of the negro from legal slavery to make the emancipation of the poor white a reality, the future development of the negro a possibility, and the building of a new South upon truly democratic principles a certainty. The obstacles hindering the growth of democracy had been artificial and not fundamental, and the War had removed them. Under any circumstances, a complete readjustment of economic and social life at the South would be necessary; the process might be long; the suffering to individuals would be considerable; but Lincoln felt that the North owed it to the true South to abolish by constitutional amendment the artificial fetters with which custom and tradition had hitherto allowed the oligarchy of great planters to hamper the development of the community at large. The North must not nullify the result of the War—the actual downfall of the old economic and social fabric built on slavery. It must insist that the New South should be a product of true democracy.

The War, nevertheless, resulted in an extreme economic exhaustion of the South. It had destroyed the old fabric and had put nothing in its place. Before the War there had been a few enormous private fortunes, a considerable number of well-to-do families, while the great majority of the poor whites and free negroes as well as the slaves had been on the very margin of subsistence. The great fortunes had flown in the first year of the War, and the produce taxes levied in kind and the forceable seizure of property

purpose has grown up, defining itself slowly into clearer consciousness, to finish the War in the only way that will *keep* it finished, by rooting out the evil principle [slavery] from which it sprang." Lowell in the *Atlantic Monthly*, October 1864, p. 572.

by the commissary department for the use of the army had pretty well deprived every one who had anything at all of nearly all he had. Though the South had never been wealthy except on paper, though its richest men had possessed large incomes rather than tangible wealth whose continued existence was assured, the War had taken from the community the little it had possessed. The Confederacy was bankrupt in 1861; its citizens had little left in 1865. Even the cotton, from whose sale once the War was over many had expected to recoup their fortunes, was confiscated by the Northern government. It should never be forgotten that the poverty of the individual Southerner, the dethroning of the planters, the enfranchisement of the poor white, the emancipation of the negro were direct results of four years of war. Reconstruction intensified the suffering but was not its cause. The inevitable difficulties of readjustment were certain to cause suffering to many individuals, though the community as a whole was benefiting from the change.

But upon the great constitutional and legal issues, out of which hostilities had arisen, the War decided nothing. The great fundamental issues of American development—the relation of the States to each other, to the individual citizen, and to the central government; the economic dependence of the country upon Europe; the questions of a sound and adequate currency, of the tariff, and of the public lands—the War did not settle at all. It could not; moral, ethical, legal, constitutional issues are not solved by fighting. The War simply decided that in the discussion and formulation of a solution, the North should play the preponderant part and that the solution should be in harmony with the principles of nationality and democracy as the North understood them. The War made the most important single element in the situation the opinion of the North. It was now necessary for the North to find out what its opinion was.

The logic of facts at the close of the War made the discussion and settlement of the great problems peculiarly difficult and the arrival at anything like a decision mutually agreeable to all parties in both sections practically impossible. The mere fact that in a great war, costing thousands of lives and billions of dollars, the Northern armies had been victorious, was to most men proof that a great issue had been at stake about which there was an ascertainable right and wrong. Did not victory in fact show that the North had been right? If there was no right and wrong about it, and if the South had not been wrong, why had the War been fought at all? It was unthinkable to the Northern men in 1865 that they had conquered in a fight for a principle and had espoused the wrong side. If so, the War was not only a mistake and a blunder, but a crime of unbelievable, horrible magnitude. It was inevitable that the men who won the War should have concluded, quite aside from history, precedents, morality, and law, that they had decided a great question in the right. Granting, then, as an axiom which few Northern minds questioned, that the South had been wrong, should she not be punished for it or at least forced to acknowledge that she had been wrong and compelled to take such steps as should prevent the recurrence of that wrong? Nothing else galled the South quite so much as this bit of logic. The very idea that they had been "wrong" rankled in the Southern mind; the very indefiniteness of the feeling, the entire lack of any specific thing which had been *the* wrong of wrongs, embittered the relations of the two sections. All of this feeling was intensified a hundred-fold by the assassination of Lincoln. Many at the North who had talked before of "securities" began to insist upon "punishment" and revenge.

To the Southern gentleman, who had governed the Confederacy before and during the War, there was also a logic of facts. For whatever reason, justly or unjustly, his estates were ruined and his fortune gone; he saw his friends in the same condition; he saw Northern soldiers quartered on the poverty-stricken and exhausted country and knew that, whatever legal excuse was offered, they were "conquerors" and held him and his in "subjection." There was too the undoubted existence of the negro and the poor white, whom he had despised and ruled; the War had raised the negro to the level of the poor white and had brought the old aristocracy down to the level of both. It seemed almost too much to bear that at this same time the North should be prosperous and reveling in luxury. At both North and South, the more sober and better informed men were anxious to return to amity and peace and to deal with one another like brothers, with a sympathetic forbearance on the one hand of taunts about the past and an eager acceptance on the other of the inevitable changes. It was perhaps too much to expect that it could have been so. Four years of war left behind a legacy that no one desired but of which none could rid himself.

XXVI

THE ISSUE OF RECONSTRUCTION

THE Civil War grew out of a misunderstanding [1] between honest and sincere men. So did the Reconstruction. Let us not deny that charity to the Northern Reconstructionists which the slave-holders of 1850 have received. Even the carpet-bagger and the scalawag had convictions. As we must renounce the idea that the War was caused by a conspiracy of Southern planters solely to extend and maintain slavery, so must we renounce the idea that the North intended Reconstruction to humiliate the South. Much that was done was unintentional, the result of the disagreement of honest men on both sides. Indeed, in the study of Reconstruction, there is scarcely another fact so conspicuous as the unexpected turn of events. The whole nation was groping around a problem whose real lineaments it did not know, like a blind man making his way about in an unfamiliar room. Reconstruction was an attempt to settle nearly all the great issues of American development, whose factors had been so altered by the War as to produce in each new features so radically different from the old as to change the problem itself beyond recognition.

Indeed, we are dealing with the construction of a new nation, not with the reconstruction, preservation, alteration, or restoration of the *status quo* before the War. The North,

---

[1] "I think very much of the ill feeling that has existed and still exists between the people in the section from which I came and the people here [Washington, D. C.] is dependent upon a misunderstanding of one another." Lincoln in reply to the greeting of the Mayor of Washington, D. C., Feb. 27, 1861. Nicolay and Hay, *Complete Works*, VI, 165.

the South, the Union, the Constitution, the States, the Senate, the House, the Presidency, the people had all been so vitally changed that the readjustment of each to the others required literally the construction of a new social and constitutional fabric. Nor was the necessity less because in the majority of instances the constitutional change was implicit rather than explicit; to be read into old phrases, not formally expressed; a difference to be applied in living rather than to be recorded in line and precept. All national politics and institutions were to be honestly tested for the first time by the concept of nationality, as Lincoln had made the nation conscious of it. In all social and economic problems at the South, the emancipation of the negro by proclamation and by the Thirteenth Amendment, ratified in 1865, had introduced a factor entirely unknown to every one. The political and economic emancipation of the poor white by the actual destruction of the older agricultural fabric had placed in the numerical majority in the South a class which hated the old planter class and the negro alike with vehemence.

Scarcely less important was the alteration in the relative prominence and authority of the executive as compared to the legislature. The exigencies of the War had compelled the use by Lincoln of extraordinary powers, which had been viewed with suspicion and downright hostility by Congress and by many individuals, and whose use had by the logic of facts completely reversed the traditional position of executive and legislature, robbing the latter of its preëminence and initiative. Nothing could have been predicted with greater certainty than that the close of the War and the consequent cessation of the imperative necessary for the recognition of executive discretion would father a determined attempt by Congress to deprive the executive of his new authority and to reassert once more the legislative supremacy. Without doubt, the doctrine of nationality abrogated the older concept of the State, as well North as South, and introduced in practice the theoretical notion of the paramount authority of the Federal government over the individual citizen as superior in obligation to that of his State. Whatever currency this idea had previously obtained, it had certainly never before been a precept upon which the actual working of the Federal system had been based and the close of the War clearly raised a series of most important practical issues which were to be adjudicated by the courts in the light of this new national reading of the Constitution. A difference of opinion with the States, so recently members of the Confederacy, was highly probable, and logic and precedent for several views of their status, past and present, were not long in appearing. In the guise of the payment of the Federal debt, and of the provision of a sound currency to replace the paper money adopted as an expedient during the War, rose all the old formidable financial issues— America's dependence on Europe, the necessity for a medium of exchange, the dependence of the South and West upon the commercial cities on the Atlantic coast, the necessity of distributing the specie evenly throughout the community and of the prevention of hoarding it. All of these vital factors reacted upon each other again and again and complicated still further a problem already difficult in the extreme. The construction of a new South in harmony with the new notions of nationality and democracy involved sweeping and significant changes in industry, in legislation, in substantive law, in administration, in social life which certainly could not be completed without tremendous difficulty and without suffering to many and many an innocent individual.

In studying this "great confusion, officially styled the Reconstruction of the Southern States,"[2] it is absolutely essential to read political and social movements in the light of the War. A situation, itself complex in the extreme, was tangled almost beyond the possibility of belief, by the actual conditions in the South and in Washington.

The presence of the Northern armies constantly reminded the Southerners that the new settlement was really being imposed upon them by the North, whatever legal or ethical grounds might be alleged in an endeavor to conceal the un-

[2] W. G. Brown in *Atlantic Monthly*, May 1901, Vol. LXXXVII, 634.

concealable. The only too evident ruin of all the wealthy, the certainty that the poor whites and negroes would be able to adjust themselves to the conditions of democratic freedom only slowly and painfully, the inevitable bitterness and rancor among the old planters at seeing themselves "degraded" to the level of the poor white and of the negro; the latter's equally inevitable elation, only too sure of blatant expression, at his elevation to an equality with the oligarchy, were all unfortunately insistent elements. The Southerners had embraced with real fervor and enthusiasm the new concept of nationality and had no intention of relinquishing it but were somewhat shaken in their belief that all would now be well by the discovery that the new nationality was bound tightly to a new concept of democracy which included the negro. That the United States should be one, they could believe expedient; but that the negro was industrially, legally, politically, socially the equal of the white man, they could not credit. This was a plain issue of fact and the evidence of their senses as well as the traditions of two centuries and a half forbade their accepting such a dictum without clear proof of its verity. The War had honestly made the North and South nationalists; but it was powerless to remodel, in a moment as it were, their social, moral, and ethical standards. The negro was no different after the War from what he had been before; if anything, he was less capable, less industrious, less honest, less moral; and he was surely not to be endowed with ability, education, and energy by making speeches in the Senate or by passing constitutional amendments. The logic of the situation was stronger than theory: the Southerners who had always known the negro saw that he could not be otherwise than he was; the Northerners, who had never known the negro at all, were able to believe honestly that the striking off of his shackles would as suddenly reveal hitherto unexpected qualities and his possession of the common heritage of humanity. To the Southerner, fundamental racial and economic facts stood in the way of the negro's actual freedom and equality; to many excited Northerners, only the artificial restraints of laws and constitutions had hidden the facts which had always existed, and which needed now merely to be made apparent. Here again was a clash of opinion certain to affect vitally the attitude of all parties and individuals to the new settlement.

Most apparent and important of all, the men in control at Washington naturally regarded as a national calamity the bare suggestion that they were not to direct the creation of the new national fabric, the hint that they were not the men best qualified to undertake it. Had not their winning of the War proved it? Should the results of the War be lost by taking the control of the settlement out of the hands of the friends of freedom? Indeed, it was difficult for them to believe that the opinions of Northern men who had opposed the War or criticized its conduct, of Southern men who had fought in the Confederate army, had any right to consideration upon the problems which the War had bequeathed, could be otherwise than inharmonious with the splendid principles upon which the War had been fought and won. It was clear that the most vital issues concerned the interpretation of the Constitution and statutes in the light of the new concepts, involved the passage of new legislation conceived in their spirit, and that all could be easily invalidated and the result of the War destroyed by hostile or unsympathetic interpretations. Thus was promptly injected into issues already too complex, the question of the balance of parties at the North, the personal reputation and reward of the men who had won the War, the importance of the army as a factor in politics at the polls and elsewhere, and the influence, interrelation, and interaction of all these upon each other and upon the old quarrels of the executive and legislature, of North and South, of the States and the Federal government.

The reorganization of the South was certain at best to cause suffering to many individuals, and required forbearance and consideration from the North. The actual conditions at the South and at Washington rendered almost inevitable mutual misunderstandings which could not fail greatly to

increase the sum total of suffering at the South and strain
almost to the breaking-point the new national bond which
the fighting of four years had been needed to create. The
manner in which Reconstruction was undertaken became a
new obstacle in the way of the realization of nationality.
To make it a permanent obstacle, the men who had won the
War seem to have unconsciously done their best; that it
caused only temporary difficulty, was due to the forbearance,
the splendid patriotism, and the statesmanship of the Northern conservatives who had opposed the War and of the
Southern men once enrolled under the Stars and Bars. We
should never forget that if the War was won by a part
of the nation to create nationality, the nation as it now
stands is nearly as much the work of those who loyally
accepted the true results of the War after it was over and
who narrowly managed to prevent the destruction of the
new nation at the hands of its friends as soon as it had
been created. The South as well as the North, the Reconstruction as well as the War, played a vital part in making
us one people, bone of our bone, flesh of our flesh.

As was inevitable, an issue of so many sides and significant
aspects, none of which in any sense were mutually exclusive,
none of which could by any possibility be settled except in
relation to the rest, presented for that very reason, even to
the honest and energetic, one aspect so much more vital in
its effect on their personal predilections, ideals, and ambitions
that it stood in their minds for the whole complex tangle
of needs and desirabilities. The issue of Reconstruction was
neither political, constitutional, legal, social, ethical, nor economic, but an extraordinarily complicated network created
by the interrelation and interaction of all. The first criminal
error committed, therefore, in all honesty and good faith,
was the attempt to deal with it from only one point of
view. Presidential Reconstruction assumed that the question
was legal and formal, to be decided by the constitutional
theories upon which the War had been fought. Congress
promptly saw that there were political questions of the utmost

consequence involved and that the South would be hard pressed to deal alone with the numerous temporary difficulties growing out of the conditions actually in existence. The social reformers soon appreciated that the presidential plan really left the South nearly complete discretion in the rebuilding of the economic and social fabric and they instantly objected to such a "sacrifice" of the negro. To them, the transcendent issue was social and ethical, the negroes the most important class of the community to be protected and assisted over the transition from bondage to freedom. Each of these plans was based upon an important element in the situation; each committed the pardonable blunder of assuming that element to be the only issue of real consequence. None, therefore, met the prerequisite of statesmanship,—the open recognition that the problems were interrelated and must be solved together with due regard for each other. All three remedies were applied in succession, and as each left unsolved important problems, another sovereign emollient was brought forward. The result was almost indescribable confusion and the intensification and prolongation of the natural difficulties of adjustment at the South, and the trebling of suffering for many individuals.

The greatest trouble of all rose out of a misunderstanding. During the War, Lincoln had announced a theory of executive "reconstruction" of the seceded States which he applied before the end of the War to those States in the hands of the Union armies. He assumed that secession was unconstitutional; no State could "get out of the Union;" no State had ever been a State at all "out of the Union;" and the mere fact that the Southern States had attempted to secede upon this mistaken theory had not in the least altered their constitutional status. The Southern States were still members of the Union, and the process of their reinstatement would therefore be simple in the extreme. So soon as the President was assured that a loyal State government was peaceably performing the usual civil functions, he should by proclamation make that fact known to the country and to

Congress, and thus by an executive announcement of the actual fact, the State would once more take its place among its sisters. No "reconstruction" would be necessary, for there had been no legal breach of the constitutional fabric; the States would merely recommence their old life and the President should announce the moment when it began. Naturally, the President should exercise his discretion in deciding what tests should indicate its beginning.

This theory was certainly that on which the War had been fought and that approved by all parties at Washington during the first years of its continuance. The Democratic slogan had even been "Restore the Union as it was." On the whole, the terms proposed by the Federal government in the various abortive negotiations with the Confederacy had in view the "restoration" of the Federal bond as the North understood it. Lincoln recognized Tennessee and Louisiana as States in 1864, and, though a clash of opinion between the President and Congress was already apparent before Lincoln's death, Johnson continued his policy. The measures he prescribed in May 1865, were of the simplest. A proclamation offered amnesty to all taking an oath of future loyalty to the United States, and the prominent Confederates, who were excepted from the amnesty by classes, were to be pardoned by the President when they had taken the oath and petitioned for executive clemency. The President next appointed provisional governors in the various Southern States, who caused an election of delegates to a constitutional convention by such of the electorate qualified to vote at the date of secession as had already taken the oath of loyalty. By proclamations the civil departments of the Federal government once more began the execution of the Federal laws in the several States. When Congress met in December, all the Southern States had in pursuance of this plan repealed the ordinances of secession, had adopted new constitutions abolishing slavery, and, with two exceptions, had repudiated the war debt of the Confederacy. The legislatures had met, the executive officers had taken their seats, the Federal officers were executing the United

States statutes. United States senators and representatives had been chosen, and, with two exceptions, all had adopted the Thirteenth Amendment abolishing slavery. In view of these facts, the President had by proclamation declared the cessation of armed resistance, the restoration of intercourse, and the end of the blockade. The troops had not been withdrawn nor the right to the writ of habeas corpus restored, but, in his message to Congress of December 1865, Johnson made it clear that, in his opinion, nothing remained to be done to complete the process of restoring the States to their former places but the acceptance of the newly-elected senators and representatives by Congress.

XXVII

CONGRESSIONAL RECONSTRUCTION: ITS CAUSES AND ITS METHODS

To the Congressional leaders, the issue was by no means so simple. They saw obvious objections on political, constitutional, and social grounds to any recognition of the presidential solution. Their overwhelmingly important objection was that the process was entirely executive and created or assumed powers extending an executive authority already too large. Congress had always been jealous of the President. The enormous accession of power thrust upon him by the War had been flatly contrary to the general tradition since the earliest Colonial times of the supremacy of the legislature over the executive, and Congress had during the War ill concealed its impatience and hostility. While the crisis actually existed, it was felt that constitutional scruples should be pushed to one side; but now that the War was over the pent-up wrath, suspicion, hatred which had accumulated during the long four years burst forth over Johnson's demand that Congress should tamely accept at his dictation the settlement of all the questions bequeathed by the War. That the executive should have fought and won the War galled Congress inexpressibly; that the Presidency had drawn from the War and from Lincoln's personal prestige an extraordinary accession of power and an importance as compared to the legislature which could never be entirely regained, the angry senators and representatives fully appreciated. But that the executive should already have issued his fiat upon the results of the War, should not have consulted them even as a formal courtesy as to the proper course to be pursued in the numerous constitutional difficulties involved, was more than the men who had repressed their hatred so long could have been expected to bear. They viewed all of Johnson's acts and decisions with supercilious suspicion, simply and solely because they were executive acts. Of the facts of the situation at the South, of the probable consequences of a quarrel between Executive and Congress, they recked little. To them, the whole structure of the Federal Constitution, which the North had fought the War to preserve, was being destroyed by the usurpations of the executive. States' rights was a specter; presidential domination of Federal policies and means was stalking abroad as a giant whose head topped the clouds. Lincoln had taught Congress only too well that the legislative power could deal only with new policies, and now if this greatest subject for new legislation, the results of the War, could thus coolly be dealt with by Johnson by proclamation and fiat, the President could literally usurp by a similar process of interpretation all the functions of Congress and reduce that body to a nonentity. The members of the House felt themselves called to be the saviors of the country from a new and greater peril than States' rights and slavery. With them agreed thousands both North and South who had been alienated and disgusted by what they considered the arbitrary and unconstitutional acts of Lincoln and Davis, and who had impatiently awaited the end of the War as a time when such "usurpations" would certainly cease. The strength and intensity of the determination to put an end to the extension of executive authority is a chief factor in the drama of Reconstruction, and in Washington it almost certainly dwarfed all others.

The other objection to the presidential theory was its failure to take into account the actual situation at the South. It was all very well to declare that the States were what they had been, but the actual facts contradicted the theory; the Southern States had been actually out of the Union for four years;[1] the civil administration, the economic and social

[1] In a Eulogy on Lincoln delivered by Sumner in Boston in 1865, he took issue squarely with the presidential plans. "There can be no question here whether a State is in the Union or out of it. This is but

structure had been literally destroyed by the War, and new State governments upon a new national and democratic basis were to be set up. Furthermore, it was entirely clear that the roving negroes and rascally thieves then thronging many parts of the South were not to be successfully restrained by the sort of loosely-organized civil government which had formerly existed there. Excited orators denounced Johnson for closing his eyes to the obvious facts of the situation, and, to their logic and reasoning, the Northern interpretation of the Southern efforts to grapple with the most imperative problems lent only too much color. Johnson had handed over to the men, who had seceded to preserve slavery, discretion to deal with the freedmen, and they had used it as he should have anticipated.

Needless to add, the excited enemies of the President in Washington and throughout the North had only a faint adumbration of the practical difficulties of the negro problem at the South, and, with the almost universal exaggeration of the negro's capacity, virtue, and honesty then prevalent, they quite inevitably misinterpreted the experiments the Southerners based upon the practical difficulties whose very existence the glorification of the negro forbade the North to credit. The Emancipation Proclamation of 1862 and the Thirteenth Amendment did not contemplate the need of instruction to the negroes concerning the use of their new freedom. It was, indeed, inconceivable to the enthusiasts that a man should not know what to do with freedom, should be incapable of applying freedom to the problems of life as he himself had to live it. There was no insurrection or universal outbreak of anarchy and bloodshed as the ante-bellum slavery advocates had predicted; but the millennium of freedom anticipated by the anti-slavery men was patently unrealized. Many negroes, especially the house servants, remained with their old masters, faithful, loyal, contented; but thousands

. a phrase on which discussion is useless. Look at the *actual fact*. Here all will agree. The old governments are *vacated*, and this is enough." Charles Sumner, *Eulogy on Lincoln*, 59. Boston, 1865.

had enlisted in the Union armies, or had followed as laborers, digging in the trenches or driving baggage wagons, and were now stranded by the cessation of the War. Many thousands had left the interior of the cotton States, as food grew scarce, or had wandered around merely to find out whether they could, and had congregated along the rivers where the Federal government had attempted to feed them in contraband camps controlled by the army. These roving thousands had somehow to be provided for and it was perfectly patent to any one in contact with them that, as long as the government would feed them, they had no intention of working. Other crowds like them clustered in the cities and towns, restless, lazy, shiftless, committing freely innumerable minor crimes, a constant menace to the peace of the community. On the plantations, petty crimes and thieving had been personal offenses against the master only and were still to the negroes not offenses against any law involving trials in courts. The removal of the master's authority left them almost uncontrolled by any legislation then in force. To control their criminal propensities was essential, but to force them to do enough work to support themselves and relieve the white community of the hardship of doing the work necessary to support everybody, was the very first and most important step in the economic construction of a new South. The chief source of labor for growing the only commodity of value had not only ceased to be available in the cotton fields, but had become an overwhelming economic burden. That the bulk of the negroes had not the slightest intention of working was evident; that it would ruin the South beyond repair to be forced to feed between two and three million mouths from the labor of the whites and a million or so of blacks was eminently clear.

The Federal government had seen the difficulty and had created the Freedman's Bureau in March 1865, to care for the blacks and their interests, to shield them from the speculators and sharpers, white and black, already imposing on their inexperience, and to allot to them the abandoned plantations and furnish enough tools and seeds to start them on the new life. To facilitate the work, jurisdiction was given the Bureau over all controversies to which a negro was a party, including family relations and marriage. In particular, the Bureau was to take cognizance of all the means and methods by which the whites sought to secure the labor of the freedmen and was to guarantee them against contracts which should be the equivalent of slavery for life. Most of the appointees of the Bureau were military officers who worked in conjunction with the army in the district. To the Southerners, the Bureau was a diabolical device to perpetuate the military control of the South and humiliate the whites before the negro, a method of compelling by force recognition of the social equality with the blacks which the whites were determined not to concede.

The resentment and reaction at the South caused the insertion of clauses in the new constitutions denying with vehemence the equality of the white and black races and affirming that negroes could not be citizens of the United States. To coerce the negroes into working, "vagrancy" acts were passed in several States in the fall of 1865 which declared it an offense for negroes over eighteen years old to be without "lawful employment or business" or to be found "unlawfully assembling themselves together either in the day or night time." For this offense the negro was to be fined $50, and, if he should not pay his fine within five days, he should be hired out by the sheriff to the man who would pay the fine and costs, in return *for the shortest period of service,* preference being given to the negro's previous "employer." Negroes under eighteen years of age, "orphans or the children of parents who could not or would not support them," were to be apprenticed until twenty-one years old by the Clerk of the Probate Court at his discretion, preferably to the former owner. Mississippi made a similar provision for negroes who did not pay their taxes and then levied a poll tax of $1 a head on all negroes "for the support of the poor." The criminal statutes provided fines and compulsory work to be done by the criminal for the man who would pay the fine in return for the shortest period of service in such elastic offenses as "malicious mischief," "insulting gestures," "seditious speeches," or "any other misdemeanor."

Granting that these acts were necessary to replace the negro in the economic fabric and secure his coöperation in supporting the community of which he was now a citizen, they were certain to create the impression in the North that the Southerners intended to restore actual slavery under the guise of apprenticeship or as a punishment for debt or crime, and, to hasten and facilitate the completion of the process, had put acts on the statute-book defining vagrancy and crime in broad and inclusive terms which *ipso facto* made every negro guilty. They had provided compulsory work for negroes in debt and had then passed laws which instantly put every negro into debt. Nor could the constant reference to his "former employer" or owner as the fittest person to become his guardian or jailor fail to lend verisimilitude to all these charges of a revival of slavery.

Such statutes seemed to Congress evidence that the spirit in which the South proposed to interpret the Thirteenth Amendment was by no means that in which it had been passed. To this unfortunate misunderstanding, fuel was added by the election of men, who had been especially prominent in the administrative and military service of the Confederacy to be senators and representatives of the United States from the new State governments reconstructed by the President. If such men could at once return to Congress to begin over again the old debates, why had the War been fought? Could the North ask less recognition of the defeat of the Confederacy, demand less evidence of an honest intention to accept the result, than the choice by the Southerners of senators and representatives for the national councils who had not been connected with the "rebellion"? The reply, that nearly every man of ability or character had been in some way identified with the Confederacy and that their disqualification would deprive the South of the services of its natural leaders, did not seem to the North really valid. Stephens, Brown, and their ilk again in Washington! This was surely defiance.

Moreover, with some astonishment, many Northern men learned that the South would now be proportionately stronger in the House of Representatives than ever before. The adoption of the Thirteenth Amendment had changed the basis of representation from the whites plus three-fifths of the negroes to the whites plus all the negroes. The South was entitled to more votes in Congress, and these would certainly be thrown against the Republicans and in favor of the Northern Democrats, who had already so large a minority that the addition of the increased Southern vote might give them a majority. Already the vivid fears of the Republicans saw the men who had won the War ousted from office; the men who had opposed the War, North and South, in control of the national government; the War debt of the North repudiated and that of the Confederacy paid; the negro enslaved once more; the results of the War entirely lost. Why should the War have ever been fought if the men who had won it were thus supinely to allow its results to be evaded? Before the white South should be allowed to elect representatives to Congress for the negroes, the suffrage must be extended at the South to include the negroes, who would of course vote for Republican representatives.

In addition, came the news that the uneasiness and fear of the Southern whites at the presence of such large numbers of negroes, insufficiently restrained from the commission of crime by the scattered Federal troopers, had resulted in the formation of State militia by the new Southern governments, in whose ranks were naturally to be found a large proportion of Confederate veterans. Was this not clearest evidence of all, insisted the excited Northerners, of an intention to reimpose slavery by force and to protect the South from the natural ire of the North at this evasion of the War legislation? Lee's army enrolled again under the guise of State militia! The Confederate Vice-President again in Congress! The negroes serving out by forced labor sentences for crimes which their very existence compelled them to commit! "To my mind," declared Sumner of Massachusetts, "it abandons the freedmen to the control of their ancient masters and leaves the national debt exposed to repudiation by returning rebels." "We tell the white men of Mississippi," vociferated the *Chicago Tribune*, "that the men of the North will convert the state of Mississippi into a frog-pond before they will allow any such laws to disgrace one foot of soil over which the flag of freedom flies." At Washington, the sentiment was general that the political reorganization of the old States ought to be postponed until the continued ascendency of the Republican Party could be assured. For such purposes and in such a spirit was Congressional Reconstruction undertaken.

The first measures passed were intended to increase the power of the Freedman's Bureau to protect the negro and ensure him equality of civil rights. Johnson vetoed the acts and, on the failure of Congress to repass one of them over his veto, exulted openly over his victory, declaring that the leaders in Congress were striving as hard to undermine the principles of the Constitution as had the Confederates. The Northern Democrats and the whites at the South promptly and not unreasonably concluded that the President and the administration at Washington were on their side and consequently were encouraged to go further than they otherwise would have. At the same time, Congress discovered an ally in Stanton, the Secretary of War. He was of course *ex officio* in control of the army in the South and of the Freedman's Bureau, of the only administrative arms of the Federal government which could effectively enforce either executive or legislative decisions. With his assistance, the Congressional leaders hoped to nullify the President's orders and secure the adequate enforcement of their own.

The denunciation of the Congressional policy as unconstitutional set the leaders at once to work in the spring of 1866 upon the Fourteenth Amendment which was to settle firmly and decisively the results of the War. It was to secure to the negro full equality in civil rights and before the courts;

to define the term "citizen of the United States" and include the negro; to guarantee the payment of the Federal debt and repudiate the Confederate debt; to repudiate forever all claims to indemnification for loss by reason of the emancipation of the slaves; and to disqualify all Confederates for election to Federal office. Above all, it was intended to prevent the Southern States, when reorganized, from taking advantage of the increase in representation, to which the Thirteenth Amendment entitled them, without enfranchising the negro. The "Federal ratio," the chief compromise of 1787, had permitted the South to count in computing its population, on which direct taxes and representation were to be apportioned, three-fifths of the negroes. The whites at the South had always, therefore, voted for a part of the negroes as well as for themselves. The new amendment provided, as finally passed, that the population of each state for representation should be decreased in proportion to the number of male inhabitants, "being twenty-one years of age and citizens of the United States," who were denied the suffrage. Practically, this deprived the Southern States of the partial representation of the negroes they had had and gave them representation only for those male inhabitants over twenty-one who were actually allowed to vote. The language of the amendment applied it to all the States of the Union, but conditions in the North made it of no consequence there. In the States where the negroes equaled or outnumbered the whites, the effect of the amendment was materially to decrease the old representation of the State in the House of Representatives and thus to ensure the control of that body by the Republicans, for any increase could be obtained only by the enfranchisement of the negroes, who could be depended upon to vote for the Republicans. "Loyalty must govern what loyalty preserved" became the new slogan.[2]

---

[2] The phrase was coined by Colfax, Speaker of the House of Representatives during the War. "If it be said that the colored people are unfit, then do I say that they are more fit than their recent masters or even than many among the poor whites. They have been loyal

In the Congressional Campaign of 1866, with this confused jumble of issues, the Republicans certainly swept the country; Johnson was clearly unpopular at the North; and, when by spring all the Southern States had rejected the Fourteenth Amendment by overwhelming majorities, Congress felt itself thoroughly justified in proceeding with the plan elaborated by the Joint Committee on Reconstruction during the year 1866.

In February 1867, the new measure was passed and without doubt was brutal, tyrannical, foolish, inexpedient, unjust, and probably unconstitutional. Admitting that there was much justification for hesitation in accepting at once presidential reconstruction, and that the Southern acts were not unnaturally misinterpreted by the North, it is still impossible to defend the method by which Congress proposed to reconstruct the South on any other basis than a determination to ensure the preponderance of the Republican Party under all conditions for at least a generation, and to humble the executive and render Congress supreme in the Federal government at all costs. Congress had found fault with presidential reconstruction because it failed to recognize the fact that the Southern States had actually been out of the Union for four years, and it now proceeded to declare that those States were to be punished for seceding, though the War itself had been fought expressly to prove that no State could by any legal act constitutionally secede. It declared them liable to a penalty for doing something which the War had proved they had not done. The preamble spoke of the "rebel States," though they were patently no longer in rebellion and the contention of Congress was that they were no longer States at all. It declared the absence of civil government and the existence of conditions to be controlled only by the military to be the reasons for the bill, when it was notorious that a reasonably efficient civil government had successfully preserved the

always, and who are you, that under any pretence, exalt the prejudices of the disloyal above the rights of the loyal?" Charles Sumner, *Eulogy on Lincoln*, 57. Boston, 1865.

peace and administered the statutes of the United States in all the Southern States since the summer of 1865. To supply this lack of civil government until conditions should make it possible to restore it, the act created five military districts, to be governed by martial law enforced by the Federal troops. Any semblance of civil government which might be in existence was to be utilized or not by the general in command of the district at his discretion. These districts should continue until the State should enfranchise all males over twenty-one years old without regard for race, color, or previous condition of servitude; until a convention should be elected by the males not disfranchised for participation in rebellion or for crime, which should frame a constitution in conformity with the laws of the United States; and until a majority of the electorate, voting at the election, had accepted the constitution and the Fourteenth Amendment. When the constitution had been accepted by Congress and the Fourteenth Amendment by three-fourths of the other States, the State should be readmitted to the Union.

To this measure, were joined others intended to prevent the President from removing executive or army officers loyal to Congress without the consent of the Senate; to force Johnson as commander-in-chief of the army to issue all orders to the generals in command of the military districts in the South only through the general of the army, whom Congress believed loyal to it, and who was not to be removed without consent of the Senate. Congress then passed a bill calling a new session of Congress for March 4, when the long recess would normally have left the President supreme, and thus perpetuated itself in office. All of these measures Johnson vetoed with masterly arguments, and all were derisively passed by huge majorities over his head.

To save the South some of the humiliation and suffering which these acts involved, Johnson interpreted them in the most favorable sense. Congress, to insult the President, promptly made an explicit interpretation to the opposite effect and rendered the legislation even more stringent. Attempts to examine the constitutionality of the acts, to secure an injunction to prevent their enforcement were frustrated by the decision of the Supreme Court that it had no jurisdiction, and when a case was found which the Court could consider, Congress in a panic repealed the act in question and quashed the suit. There seemed literally to be no method of restraining the unlimited authority claimed by Congress; the President's veto was no check; the Supreme Court could not properly interfere with instances of executive or legislative discretion and could under any circumstances consider only contentious cases brought to its bar by private citizens.

But the injustice and bad faith of Congress even more than the inconsistency and unconstitutionality of the scheme roused bitter opposition both North and South. During the summer and fall of 1867, the elections were held and the "Black and Tan" Conventions chosen, chiefly of Northern "carpetbaggers," poor whites, and negroes. "No such hideous bodies of men had ever been assembled before upon the soil of the United States" to assist in constitution-making. In Alabama, the General in charge ordered the election of State officers to be held at the same time as the vote on the adoption of the Constitution; for this Johnson recalled him. Moreover, a majority of the citizens stayed away from the polls in order to defeat the Constitution, because the Reconstruction Act required an affirmative vote by a majority of the electorate, voting at the election. Congress now capped the climax of injustice and shameful dealing by voting that the holding of elections at the same time as the vote for ratification of the Constitution was valid, and that the approval of the Constitution by a majority of those voting would be sufficient to secure its adoption. This legislation was applied *ex post facto* to the Alabama election. The crisis between the President and Congress resulted in the winter of 1867 and 1868 in the attempt to impeach Johnson, a scandal which was a fit companion to the drama being enacted at the South. In the summer of 1868, with the presidential election approaching, with the Northern Democrats rapidly growing in strength on account of the open disapproval of Congressional Reconstruction, the Republicans saw that, even with Grant as a candidate, they would almost certainly lose the election unless they could secure the votes of the Southern States. With undue haste and unseemly inconsistency, seven States were reinstated in time to vote and the Fourteenth Amendment was declared a part of the Constitution. This reinforcement, coupled with Grant's candidacy, the promise of bountiful pensions and the payment of the debt in sound currency, enabled the party to weather the storm of Northern disapproval. The acme of inconsistency was reached, however, when the Republican platform announced that negro suffrage was not to be required of the Northern States—a stand too obviously unjust to be maintained and in the following session the Fifteenth Amendment was passed. It did not actually confer suffrage upon the negro but prevented his exclusion on the ground of his race, color, or previous condition of servitude, and in particular, it prevented the amendment of the new Southern constitutions and thus guaranteed the continued existence of the Republican Party in the South. By 1870, all the Southern States had complied with all the exactions of Congress and had been readmitted, but the Reconstruction which should have been the birth time of the new nation had very nearly resulted in its disruption.

XXVIII

THE SOLID SOUTH

THE results of Congressional Reconstruction were only too soon apparent in the growing hostility of the South to such measures. Fortunately for the new national consciousness— that greatest of the results of the War, the resentment of the Southern whites was not visited upon the North as a whole but rather upon the men then in control at Washington and upon their more selfish and individual aims. For the most part, however, the broad humanitarian aspect of the movements after the War, which made so much impression upon the North, was totally lost upon the South. The latter saw in the Congressional measures the work of a cabal striving at whatever cost to both South and North to ensure the ascendency of the Republican Party over the Democratic opposition throughout the country, and to increase by fair means or foul the relative authority and prestige of the legislature as compared with the executive. The tools of the Congressional leaders were the reconstructed governments, without whose votes they could not continue in control of the Federal government, and of which they could retain control only by such desperate expedients as negro suffrage and unfair interference with the attempts of the whites at the South to free themselves from the bondage of negro ascendency. Indeed, the Southerners felt sure that the negro governments would have lasted but a short time (and Congress thoroughly agreed with them) but for the support furnished by the army and the Freedman's Bureau acting under the radical measures directed or sanctioned by the Enforcement Acts. The purpose, the method, the result, all were to the Southerners vile beyond the power of language to describe.

That the military and negro governments meant the postponement for as long as they might last the construction of a new legal, social, and economic fabric for a new South was to the leaders the most burning wrong they could have suffered. The losses of the War had been hard to bear, but these losses, so unnecessary and so much more taxing to the shattered resources of the South, seemed almost beyond human endurance. The new South must be built upon truth, not upon falsehood. The exaltation of the negro, "loyalty under a black skin," as more trustworthy and as capable and virtuous as the white man, was to them a flat contradiction of existing facts.[1] Upon such a foundation nothing could be built. Its falsity and iniquity were demonstrated by the almost inconceivable badness of the work of the reconstructed governments. "The lion had had his turn," wrote Francis Parkman,[2] "and now the fox, the jackal, and the wolf took theirs."

South Carolina, which furnishes us with probably the worst case of negro domination, is also the best case to study because the negroes were largely in the majority, and because the army, the Freedman's Bureau, and the Enforcement Acts effectively prevented any interference with their rule. The majority of the legislature and of the most important officers were negroes and the rest were rascally whites from the North or even more unsavory characters from the South. A "Band of Forty Thieves" unblushingly sold themselves to the highest bidder. The barbarous luxury and extravagance at the Capitol were unexampled—$1600 was paid for two hundred imported china spittoons, $750 apiece for French mirrors for the Speaker's Room, while a bar and restaurant dispensed free food and drink to members and their friends. Hundreds of pardons were openly sold to criminals by the Governors. Nearly $600,000 was spent on worn out rice-fields and sand hills, for the relief of negroes. The land was not worth $100,000; not a hundred negroes were ever settled on it; the Committee drew $100,000 more than its appropriation and

[1] *Supra*, p. 370-2.
[2] Farnham, *Life of Parkman*, 275.

never accounted at all for the expenditure of more than a quarter of a million dollars. So much for black philanthropy! In 1860, the taxable property in South Carolina had been $316,000,000, which had shrunk in 1871 to $184,000,000; the taxes had risen, however, from $392,000 to $2,000,000. The valuation had decreased 40%; the taxes had risen 500%; and the State debt increased 400%. The taxes were levied by the negroes, of whom scarcely 20% had any property at all and of whom 80% were totally illiterate, and were paid by the whites the vast majority of whom were disfranchised for participation in the War.

To the Southerners, the worst part was the forcible maintenance of such a régime by the Federal troops, by the Freedman's Bureau, by negro militia, for the most selfish of political purposes, as they conceived it, the continued supremacy of the Republican Party. If slavery had been anti-democratic and was for that reason alien to the spirit of American institutions, what name should be applied to the maintenance of the Republican Party in power by means of ignorance and incapacity supported by fraud and violence in defiance of the expressed will of the Democrats, North and South? D. H. Chamberlain, the white Governor of South Carolina who rescued that State, many times met the Congressional leaders in Washington. No less Northern a periodical than the *Atlantic Monthly* [3] published his gently worded but crushing arraignment of Stevens and his colleagues. "Not one of these leaders had seen the South or studied it first hand. Not one of them professed or cared to know more. They had made up their minds once for all and they wished only to push on with their predetermined policy. . . . The personal knowledge of the writer warrants him in stating that eyes were never blinder to facts, minds never more ruthlessly set upon a policy, than were Stevens and Morton on putting the white South under the heel of the black South." It was told of Stevens, and believed to be a characteristic story, that, when informed both applicants for a certain office in the South were thorough ras-

[3] Vol. LXXXVII, p. 474.

cals, he vociferated, "What do I care for that? Tell me which is *our* rascal." On the whole, the men who had really been the backbone of the North during the War did not approve of the Congressional policy of Reconstruction. There seems to be little reason to doubt that after 1867 the popular majority at the North was Democratic and thoroughly hostile to Reconstruction. Indeed, this very fact must be appreciated to understand why certain features of the Congressional policy were devised and adopted at all.

The South was saved by the moderation and real devotion of the Southern whites aided by the Northern Democrats. The methods used were empirical and were discovered almost by accident. To deal with the arrogant negroes and protect the lives and honor of the whites, which the Southern men were afraid to entrust solely to the scattered Federal troops, secret organizations were devised and had their greatest currency and success between 1868 and 1872. Unable to organize publicly because of the attitude of the authorities at Washington, "it was therefore necessary in order to protect our families from outrage and preserve our own lives to have something that we could regard as a brotherhood,—a combination of the best men in the country to act purely in self-defense, to repel attack in case we should be attacked by these people. That was the whole object of this organization," testified General Gordon in later years.

In 1870, the Freedman's Bureau was abolished, the corps of the army soon after entirely withdrawn, and the artificial support of the carpet-baggers and negroes disappeared. Gradually, too, the whites who had been disqualified for participation in the War were qualifying as voters, and, as the negroes were in the numerical majority in only three States, it was clear that the whites would control the other States as soon as they could be reinstated. It was seen, however, that the white vote must be cast for the Democratic party and its candidates. Hence arose the Solid South, a white South based upon the exclusion of the negro from political power. To secure the election of the first white candidates, and to anticipate as much as possible the day when the restoration of the vote to the whole white electorate should entirely place the power in their hands, it was seen that the intimidation of negroes to prevent them from voting would be useful, if not actually essential. The superstitious terror of the negroes for the Ku Klux Klan and similar societies suggested their use to keep enough of them from the polls to allow the whites to succeed in choosing their candidates. Much exaggeration and vilification of the influence and purpose of these mysterious orders has been common and probably many rascals took advantage of the familiar disguises to perpetrate crimes which were wrongly ascribed to the orders. In South Carolina, where the negroes formed a majority of the population, salvation came through the splendid honesty and ability of a white man, elected by the negroes themselves, who turned upon them and, after a hard fight, led the whites to victory.

The greatest problem lay in the maintenance of the whites in the ascendency, and, in the States where the negroes formed the majority, this could be permanently assured only by the disfranchisement of enough negroes to leave the whites in the majority. It was soon clear that the Fifteenth Amendment was not mandatory: it did not provide that negroes should vote, but that they should not be excluded from the electorate by a constitutional or statutory provision which in express words or by necessary implication excluded them solely on the ground of race, color, or previous condition of servitude. Any limitation of the suffrage by educational or property qualifications, applicable to all classes and races, would effectually and constitutionally exclude the negroes from the electorate. It was also apparent that the national government was not empowered to investigate the manner in which each State's officials exercised such discretionary authority as might be conferred upon them in applying such statutes to individual cases. If the officials declared the white man literate and the black man illiterate in defiance of the facts, there would not be any remedy. The official's right to decide could not be taken from him nor his use of it investigated by Federal authority. If the white man was invariably asked to prove his ability to read by "reading" a short phrase which could be easily learned beforehand, and the negro was required to show genuine intelligence, it would be a simple matter to qualify even the ignorant whites and exclude all but the educated blacks, for the vast majority of the negroes were utterly illiterate. By such measures, enforced by such a use of the discretionary authority of the executive, all the Southern States soon reduced the negro electorate to a safe minority.

Meanwhile, it had become apparent that the severe pressure of circumstances would not permanently prevent vital differences of opinion among the whites on other questions of policy than white supremacy, and that soon some method of debating other issues among the whites would be imperative to avoid any possible split in their ranks and any consequent loss of the election to the Black Republicans. Then they resorted to the machinery of the Democratic Party. The qualifications for membership were not affected by the Fifteenth Amendment because the Party was not legally in existence. Within its organization the whites might disagree, debate, and finally reach some decision as to candidates and policies, which they could then make effective at the legal election by a solid vote. The negroes have been excluded from the Democratic Party; they still are a minority of the legal electorate in all the Southern States; and they have thus been effectually robbed of all the real exercise of political power which the humanitarians and politicians sought to give them, but which they were not as a race qualified to use.

By 1870, all the Southern States had in one way or another been restored to their places in the Union; by 1877 the whites had recovered control of the State government in all and the period usually known as the Reconstruction was over. In reality, the struggles of the twelve years following the War had merely enabled the Southern whites to remove the worst obstacles sown in the way of the construction of a really new South by the pernicious activity of Congress. The building of the New South did not begin anywhere much before 1870 and in some States not till 1877.   Nor has the North in any proper sense been responsible for the making of the new South: the Southerners themselves have solved their own problems with the assistance of mighty factors whose operation no one foresaw.

The Southerners have aided economic forces in solving the economic problems which conditions both before and after the War had created.   The insistent cry for more land had been chiefly due to the fact that only the most fertile soil yielded large returns to the crude labor of the slaves and that its virgin productiveness was so soon exhausted that the planters must be constantly clearing new land.   Moreover, only land along the rivers was wanted because the river furnished an easy, cheap method of transportation, while the cultivation of the land a few miles away, and in particular of the uplands, required transportation of the crops, the expense of which greatly reduced the amount of profit and prevented competition with the river-bottoms.   Nor was the quality of the cotton grown outside of the river-bottoms as good.   The upland soil lacked certain necessary chemical constituents and the product was less in amount and difficult to prepare for market. Modern scientific agriculture and modern machinery plus the railroad have completely obviated these fundamental difficulties.   It is now possible cheaply to fertilize the fields and crop them year after year; it is possible to till fields never before profitable and to cleanse cheaply by machinery cotton which before the War could not have been used at all.   The network of railroad trunk lines, growing constantly throughout the South, has put thousands of acres into close contact with the market which were before the War hopelessly isolated. With the introduction of better tools and better methods, of fertilizers and intensive agriculture, a larger crop has been constantly grown with fewer hands.

On the whole, too, even "unreconstructed" Southerners are compelled to admit that the free negro is a more intelligent and industrious worker than the old slave, that there is to-day less labor wasted than there used to be.   The experience of the South since the War has conclusively disproved the Jeremiads of 1858 that cotton could not be grown without slaves and that emancipation would destroy the industry. Indeed, far from interfering with its development, free labor, aided by a great number of other powerful factors, has produced cotton at an even faster rate than before. The old assumptions of profitable cultivation—fertile land and cheap labor— have been proved true, but experience has shown that virgin soil is not necessarily the most fertile cotton land nor ignorant slave-labor necessarily the cheapest.

At the same time, the negro has not shown himself as capable, industrious, and energetic as the eager humanitarians assumed he would be once his shackles had been struck off. Men are not changed by legislative fiat nor by the good intentions of other people. Whether the result of inherent racial deficiencies or of the environment provided by slavery, the negro as a race has not been capable of self-development, and the more intelligent negroes themselves now realize that their fathers were economic as much as legal slaves, and that emancipation did not strike off the economic shackles welded by the negroes' own ignorance, laziness, and lack of personal ambition and moral strength. Educational and religious organizations have accomplished much and will undoubtedly accomplish proportionately more each decade, but the solution of the negroes' difficulties has been found in the exercise by most employers of a sort of patriarchal authority. Nothing else has saved the more superstitious and more ignorant from the clutches of the loan shark, from constant imprisonment for petty offenses, and from chronic beggary and want. It has been necessary to pay the negro in food and clothes because he nearly invariably gambled away the money or bought with it valueless and useless trinkets at extortionate prices. Naturally, this situation has permitted the unscrupulous employer to exact "contract labor," to create permanent debts at his "truck" store, and terrorize the unfortunate negroes with impossible penalties for trivial crimes. In an infinitely greater number of cases, it has compelled the white employer to advance supplies to the negro and his family far in excess of the value of the labor performed and constantly to care for them through sickness and hard times. It should be more generally and more generously admitted that the vast majority of Southerners have conscientiously and nobly acquitted themselves of their responsibility toward the negro. At the same time, despite the assistance of the better class of employers, between the loan shark, the unscrupulous poor whites often chosen to judgeships and legal offices, thieving agents, and unjust employers, the negroes as a class have enjoyed anything but ideal economic freedom since 1865 and have in many cases been less contented and less well cared for than the slaves were on the more humane plantations before the War. The negro is indeed his own greatest problem.

Yet, while the Southern sentiment is still strong against any recognition of social equality, the best opinion is now insistent upon the strict enforcement of laws which will ensure even the most ignorant and credulous negroes from exploitation at the hands of the unscrupulous of all sorts, varieties, and shades, and give them actual civil and economic equality with white men of the same capacity. The most serious aspect of the negro problem was and still is the existence of these millions of an alien race compelled by circumstances to live in the midst of the white South. Slavery was no remedy because it meant the perpetuation of the evil. Emancipation was the only possible permanent remedy because it alone could provide the negro with the possibilities of unlimited development and change. The only permanent solution will of course be the gradual transformation of the ignorant, shiftless, and superstitious cotton-hand into such intelligent, industrious, capable, colored men, really as well as nominally the equal of the white man in all civil and political pursuits, as have developed in some number since the war. The latter are yet only a bare handful and in the nature of things, as normal processes of evolution are slow, will become the majority only in course of generations. Emancipation spelled opportunity, not fulfilment.

Again, while emancipation and the War provided opportunities, removed artificial obstacles, they did not and could
not create the economic forces which have caused so remarkable a transformation of the poor white as the years since
Reconstruction have seen. Natural forces have been freeing
him from his economic slavery by the creation and wide development of diversified industry and of improved agriculture.
Cheap steel has meant more railroads, better and cheaper
transportation facilities, cheaper machinery, and the possibility of transporting it cheaply, cheap coal and the certainty
of a steady supply for factories operated by steam in loca-
tions where the lack of water-power and of raw materials had
hitherto prevented their development. The factory, spinning
and weaving cotton in the South at the source of the supply of
cotton and labor, has successfully competed with older
Northern and European firms, better organized and with more
skilful but higher paid labor. The new agriculture, the use
of fertilizers, of selected seed have made again fertile lands
long considered to have been worn out. Access to the railroads has made it possible to market the crop to advantage,
and, though cotton is still the great source of income in most
Southern States and still prevents the adequate development
of agricultural and mineral resources in general, the change
for the better is very marked. In this as in every other direction the factors solving the Southern problem have been economic and social, not political and legal,—the application of
science to the fundamental geological difficulties which made
the South in 1850 what it was.

Best of all, the railroads, the telegraph, the press, schools
and education are welding the Southern people to each other
and to the nation at large. The country is truly interdependent for the first time and is realizing more and more that its
future is interlocked with that of the nation at large. While
the wounds of the War, augmented by the trials of Reconstruction, are not yet entirely healed, there are now few, if
any, who do not feel themselves Americans and not Southerners.

XXIX

NATIONAL PROBLEMS

THE truly fundamental and difficult problems, which had for so many generations caused concern and anxiety to American statesmen and merchants, were finally solved in the decades succeeding the Civil War, but neither the War itself nor any of the political or constitutional developments resultant from it or subsequent to it had more than a subsidiary influence in consummating the settlement. As the problems were themselves economic, the result of the character of the new country, of its people, and of its natural backwardness in development, so the solution was itself the work of economic forces, which solved the problems by literally obviating the economic difficulties out of which they arose.

The dependence of America upon Europe had colored the whole of Colonial history and had largely shaped political and constitutional events before 1860. Free trade with the West Indies had been the fundamental condition of Colonial economic development and to secure it political and constitutional relationships had been created or rejected. The disobedience to the Navigation Acts, the outbreak of the Revolution, the War of 1812, the protective tariff, the "American System," and much more had been the direct result of American economic dependence on Europe. With the development of the cotton-culture, a medium of direct exchange with Europe appeared, and with the concomitant growth of diversified industry in the North and the use of machinery and fertilizers by the West in agriculture, the dependence on European manufactured goods and the lack of a home market for American produce were no longer so pronounced. Before 1860 a beginning had been made, but the economic development of the country since the War finally and decisively freed us from the old economic shackles hitherto binding us to Europe. America and Europe are now fairly interdependent. Our "infant industries" have disappeared; the old tariff problem has disappeared with the cessation of the economic dependence whose disastrous effects it was intended to mitigate. The growth of the country,—and not the Revolution, the Civil War, or the tariff,—has made us economically independent of the rest of the world.

The second greatest problem in American development, the lack of a medium of exchange between sections of the country, has been similarly solved by the growth of the United States. The disappearance of the problem has ended the internal quarrels in America which were such striking factors in 1776, in 1812, and in 1861. One fundamental cause of the difficulty had been the lack of a domestic supply of specie from which or on which a sound currency could be based, for the dependence of the country on Europe prevented us from retaining here enough of the world's supply of the precious metals to serve our purpose. Another basic difficulty had lain in the existence of highly developed communities along the coast and of primitive districts in the interior, the latter being necessarily and inevitably in debt to the former. Thus had grown up debtor and creditor classes in all parts of Colonial America, and debtor and creditor sections in post-revolutionary America, which, as the belt of settlement extended westward, ceased to be a source of discord within each State and produced an alignment of States and then of sections of which the Western were always the debtors of the Eastern States or sections. The favorite remedy for this difficulty of domestic exchange throughout American history has been plenty of money, or cheap money, and it has appeared in various guises from the land banks and paper money crazes of Colonial times to the repudiation of debts during the Critical Period and the Greenback and Free Silver agitations in 1876 and 1896. Always the problem has been the same: a fundamental difficulty in maintaining the equilibrium of exchange between the various parts of the country and consequently a very serious pressure on individuals in the debtor sections the moment an economic crisis like the Panics of 1837, 1873, or 1892 existed. It has always been necessary for coin or currency to "flow" from the East to the West and South "to move the crops," and, when during a panic the demand for Western and Southern products decreases, the scarcity of demand manifests itself usually to the farmer and planter as a scarcity of currency. Hence the widespread belief in the debtor districts in 1873 that enough greenbacks would remedy their particular troubles, and in 1896, that silver coined at a ratio of 16 to 1 would relieve the distress.

The difficulty is now almost, if not entirely, obviated. In the first place, the discovery of gold in California in 1849, of silver in Nevada shortly after, and of gold in Alaska, has provided the United States with an indigenous supply of specie more than adequate to meet the demands for specie as currency. We now dig out of the ground a commodity which Hamilton had to husband with the greatest care for fear no more would be procurable in case the little he had were hoarded or exported. But the more vital difficulty, the dependence of America upon Europe, the dependence of the West and South upon the East, has been itself fundamentally altered by the increase of wealth and population throughout the country and in particular by the rise in the Mississippi Valley of a strong diversified economic life, by the growth of the New South, by the development of the Pacific Coast States. The disappearance of the frontier, the extraordinary increase of population from about thirty-one millions in 1860 to seventy-six millions in 1900 and to over one hundred millions in 1914, the rapid immigration, the distribution of land by the government, either free or for nominal payments only, have effectively destroyed the peculiar "frontier" conditions which in themselves were the most difficult aspects of this particular problem. As the country has become more and more truly interdependent, the independ-

ence of each section has become more and more marked and
its dependence less and less apparent. To-day, no section is
altogether self-sufficing; no section is wholly dependent; all
therefore mutually benefit from the constant interchange of
commodities. The rate of exchange and the amount of currency needed are after all results of the comparison of actual values, and such difficulties as America had struggled
with were due to fundamental differences in the degree of
economic development in various parts of the country which
nothing short of fundamental economic forces could remedy.
Financial policies and measures like those of Hamilton and
Gallatin might obviate some of the worst difficulties or partially
mitigate the seriousness of the consequences, but only an actual
economic equality between America and Europe and between
different parts of the United States could really make the conditions of foreign and domestic exchange essentially similar.

The third problem of magnitude with which American history had been concerned was the constitutional and political
relationship of individuals to each other, and to the local,
State, or central government. It had appeared in various
guises and forms: democracy, States' sovereignty, nationality, personal liberty, slavery, and in the crowding corollaries
of each and of their interaction and interrelation. The
operation of the economic forces making for union and
nationality and for the abrogation of local independence and
States' rights has in no period produced as marked results
as in the decades subsequent to the Civil War. The disappearance of the frontier and of those conditions which had
hitherto strongly fostered localism; the rapid attainment of
something like contiguity of settlement throughout the country by the natural growth of population and by immigration;
the increasing economic interdependence of the sections; the
absolute dependence of the urban population upon the nationalization of trade and industry; all are rapidly erasing the
old State lines as boundaries marking vital differences of interests and ideas. With the cheapness of transportation by
rail came an ease of the movement of population and a con-

stant shifting of individuals from one State to another and from one section to another, which, coupled to immigration, is fast obliterating the racial, religious, and social characteristics hitherto regarded as typical in the older sections and States. The population is becoming homogeneous both in blood and in traditions; sectionalization and segregation are already becoming improbable and even impossible.

In this work of unifying and equalizing the population, schools, universities, newspapers, magazines have played a conspicuous part. The evident attempt to produce books, papers, and literature which should be acceptable to all interests, sections, races, and creeds, and the consistent avoidance of what would be likely to appeal to a part only has had an influence towards nationality and uniformity which is exceedingly clear in the present generation of children. Sectionalism, localism, States' sovereignty, traditional notions of class, creed, or race are disappearing with an astonishing rapidity and truly national ideas are taking their place. The growth of the country has given us a national idea of the relations of individuals to each other, of the individual to his own State, of the States to each other, and to the Federal government. Our old hatred of England has disappeared with the change in our economic condition. The antipathy between East, and West, and South is gone because of the new economic interdependence. The abolition of slavery has removed the only thoroughly undemocratic institution in America and the negro problem is slowly but surely solving itself by economic and educational methods. The difficulties and problems are still great but they are no longer State or sectional; they are in the broadest and truest sense national.

The old problems have disappeared and the very growth which dissipated them has caused new problems, and this time national problems to be solved by the nation as a whole. Those were the problems of growth, these are issues of development; those were of childhood and youth; these are of manhood; those concerned with the strengthening of the phys-

ical body of the nation; these with the expression of its conscience and the development of its corporate mentality.

We are confronted with a nationalization of industry in the
growth since the Civil War of transcontinental railroads, of
enormous trusts and combinations controlling production or
distribution or both throughout the country of some commodity as important to the welfare of the people as steel, beef,
or oil. We must understand the attempt of every manu-
facturer to reach a national market and so to standardize and
make uniform his product as to meet the demand in all parts
of the country. We have also seen the national political
parties and national political issues completely dominate, as
probably never before, local, municipal and State parties and
policies. The new nationalized industry has influenced the
new national politics and parties, and this vast wealth centralized in a few hands, these organizations of thousands of
men controlled by railroads and trusts, have not unnaturally
exerted great influence in politics, resulting, as many believe,
in corruption and wrong. With power and wealth has come
national ambition and a desire for expansion. The United
States has acquired the Philippines and Porto Rico, is building the Panama Canal, and has now so expanded the Monroe
Doctrine as to claim a right of interference (and perhaps control) in the Central and South American States, which some
believe to portend political domination of the Western Hemisphere. The new nation is at work as a nation, and thinking,
feeling, aspiring as a nation. In the new reform movements,
in the widespread protests against graft and corruption, in the
denunciation of the white-slave trade, we hear the national
conscience speaking. By writing, speaking, organizing, we
are attempting to arrive at something like a national consensus of opinion as to the problems, their causes, and the
best remedies.

But this stupendous growth of the country in wealth and
in population, this nationalization of industry, of politics, of
education, of literature, of reform, has vitally changed every
aspect of American life as Hamilton, Jefferson, and Jackson

knew it.   It has altered beyond recognition every fundamental factor in the structure of democracy as they built it and has created a problem of living of which even the basic conditions are different.   American democracy is not what it was meant to be because America is no longer what it was in the times of Jefferson and Jackson.

The old theoretical assumptions, from which were derived a belief in the adequacy of democracy to govern and administer efficiently the community's affairs, premised the possession by the electorate of sufficient ability to pass upon the qualifications of candidates and upon the expediency and justice of measures.   Jackson indeed based manhood suffrage and the reign of the people upon a deep-rooted faith in the simplicity of governmental issues.   It was to him therefore a truism that every man in the community possessed the political intelligence requisite for a just decision about measures or for holding offices, to formulate or execute them.   On the whole, their observation of conditions taught the early democrats that government was no peculiarly difficult art to be performed by experts, but an obviously simple matter of which every man was capable as soon as he became of age.   Problems were really few and simple in 1787 and had not greatly changed in 1830; the average man did understand them and did know the candidates nominated for office in the relatively small agricultural community in which he lived.   The conditions were those under which democracy works best, and from the conditions the theorists drew the premises on which they built the larger structure of central government.   But they naturally did not perceive the effect which the constant doubling of the population generation after generation has had on the electorate and on administrative issues.   It has become almost impossible for a well-educated public-spirited citizen to vote intelligently, as Jefferson and Jackson assumed as a matter of course he would, from his own knowledge of candidates and issues.   The premises of democracy are no longer true: government is now a difficult art and the average "well-educated" man does not normally possess the information or experience needed to qualify him either to participate in elections or to hold office.

As the country has grown in size, as States have multiplied, as cities have swollen in size till Greater New York now contains more people than the whole of America held in 1789, the problems thrust upon State and municipal governments have changed utterly in character from those familiar in 1830. The every-day work of city government—sanitation, water, sewage, lighting—can be adequately performed only by the application of scientific knowledge by experts and by the use of administrative skill of a high order in organizing the work of thousands of men, whose daily coöperation in tasks most men performed for themselves in 1830 is now a prerequisite of public health and safety. City problems have become engineering difficulties which even experts do not always successfully handle; State problems require a detailed knowledge of conditions in a large community which no individual normally possesses at all; and national issues like the tariff and the trusts are so complex and difficult that years of study and experience are necessary even to comprehend the problem itself. Though education has spread wider and wider throughout the community, though the standard has risen with each generation of school children, yet the growth of the community has been robbing the electorate bit by bit of that ability to understand conditions and of that familiarity with candidates which were the foundations on which democratic government was built. The average man cannot of his own knowledge judge measures or select from among the candidates nominated. The mere size of the community has made personal information about its needs or its members impossible for the vast majority. Upon this fact have been based the national and State parties to judge measures and select candidates for the electorate.

The old concept of democracy adequately satisfied the individual's craving for a share in the direction of affairs because the notion of one man, one vote, rested in 1830 upon an actual substantial equality of ability, education, and wealth.

Something like an aristocracy of wealth had appeared along the seaboard in Colonial times, had been destroyed by the Revolution, and an equality of fortunes created. In the South, slavery and the cotton-culture produced another un-democratic social and political oligarchy which was destroyed by the Civil War. During the last generation has appeared once more a wealthy class, whose personnel constantly changes, but whose existence is once more creating an oligarchy of property whose influence on social life in the larger cities and in national business and in politics is only too clearly great. "Big business" is contrary to the principles of Jacksonian democracy. The justice of assigning each individual only one vote depended upon an essential identity of individual interests, and huge aggregations of capital, a radical divergence of interests between labor and capital, are contrary to the old premises of democracy. The facts do not coincide with the theory; a man's legal rights clash with his economic status. The vast majority of the electorate are to-day non-taxpayers, but they control the appropriation and assessment of taxes. A majority of the electorate are in the ranks of labor. Shall the small minority which capital and the taxpayers form be contented with an influence in the affairs of the community commensurate with the count of heads? The magnate feels that preëminent ability and phenomenally large economic interests affected by the policy of the State entitle him to more consideration in politics than is accorded a man who has in the world at large neither influence, interest, nor position. Shall the numerical majority already in control of the State refrain from using the administrative, legislative, and judicial branches of the government to further its aims in the economic and social war with capital?

The danger of the situation lies in the fact that neither side can claim the support of the original democratic premises. If these assumed an essential equality of wealth, ability, and social position, they also founded universal suffrage on the assumption that the property of the numerical majority was greater in amount than that of the minority; and that the almost universal possession of taxable property (a literal fact in 1830) would give practically every one a direct interest in avoiding extravagance and guarding against corruption. Both are no longer true. Not only has the usable capital of the community become concentrated in a few hands, theoretically entitled by reason of their scanty numbers to no political consideration at all, but the control of the political organs of the community lies necessarily in the hands of those who as non-taxpayers, non-property owners, have no direct interest whatever in an economical, efficient utilization of the resources of the country. What seemed the worst of all possible eventualities to the fathers of American democracy has actually come to pass—the control of the State is now in the hands of those who have no immediate financial interest in its continued existence or proper administration. Every man originally received a share in the management of affairs because he possessed a tangible financial interest in their right conduct. The growth of the industrial fabric, of trusts and railroads, the growth of cities, have literally destroyed that vital premise of democracy.

Hence we have seen attempts, on the whole, successful, by the minority chiefly interested in the good conduct of affairs, to exert through party machinery and subservient officials and legislatures more influence on the policies of the State and the daily conduct of affairs than the democratic tenet of equality entitles them to exercise. This minority has denied the justice and equity of permitting the numerical majority to decide great issues, involving the status of property and investments, in accordance with what the majority has conceived to be its particular interest, where its interest obviously clashed with theirs. On the other hand, the majority have inveighed against the existence of large aggregations of capital as "illegal," meaning of course undemocratic, and have viewed as corruption and wrongdoing the attempts of capitalists to exert an influence upon the affairs of the State commensurate with the size of their interests. Here the difficulty lies—not in the existence of a battle between prejudice and honesty, between democracy and oligarchy, but in a clash of interests and a war of prejudices. Both minority and majority are prejudiced; each is anxious to advance its interests to the exclusion of the other; neither is unprejudiced or disinterested; to each political power in the other's hands seems a menace to its own existence.

The fundamental difficulty lies in the fact that the economic power in the community no longer rests with those who nominally control the state; the fundamental assumption of democracy was that the two would naturally be in the same hands. Unquestionably, some satisfactory decision of this oldest of governmental issues is the most important question before the nation to-day. Because it involves of necessity all possible relations between man and man, it concerns not only the happiness of the community but its very existence. It is first and foremost a question of the relation of undoubted economic forces to the political fabric and calls for an adjustment of constitutions and theories to a clash of interests which is as old as the Pyramids and as difficult of solution as the Riddle of the Sphinx. The real question to be debated is whether property and wealth as such have a right to any influence in a democratic community, whether efficiency, ability, and the undoubted control of the physical resources of the country are to count for naught in deciding the more immediate issues before the community. It is a question as broad as the conception of morality, as vital as the possession of individual liberty, as deep as the foundations of civil life.

As the result of these changes and as the necessary ideas upon which any solution must be based, we see emerging gradually various new notions of the purpose and powers of the existing parts of the constitutional fabric. Where Jefferson looked upon government as a negative force which would be more useful the less it interfered with the life of the individual, the present tendency is to insist upon the positive, directive, formative influence the state may exert upon the lives of its citizens. We are agitating for corrective and regulative legislation on every conceivable subject from the public health and the public morals to the hours of labor and the minimum wage. The assistance of the community is to be invoked to settle all the perplexed issues between individuals or between groups of individuals. Gradually, too, we find the authority of the central government gaining in the public estimation and believed to possess more adequate powers and to be better able than State or city to deal efficiently and promptly with most problems. The great increase of governmental authority, which the era of regulation demands, will apparently accrue almost entirely to the Federal government, to the exclusion of State and local governments. And it will, furthermore, break another precedent of democracy and accrue to the executive rather than to the legislature. Commission government, expert advice, autocratic power in the hands of the mayor have already robbed the municipal legislatures of prominence and now the State legislature and Congress seem likely to lose both power and prestige in their turn.

In still another point, the new democracy is the antithesis of the old. Jefferson and Jackson built their society on the individual, for whose welfare the state itself existed, and who had perfect freedom to follow his own desires or advantage, so far as the law did not explicitly restrain him nor some other individual sue him successfully in the courts. The welfare of the majority of individuals was the highest aim of statecraft; the policy of the state should be based on the views and interests of the majority which cared to vote at the polls; the minority had no rights as against the majority, nor the community as a whole against the individual. This excessive individualism, which in an agricultural community was afforded few chances for harm, found in the new economic developments astounding opportunities for self-aggrandizement at the expense of other individuals and of the state at large. To rob the nation of lands and mineral rights, to rob posterity of its forests and water privileges, to burden posterity with huge debts, to destroy competition with the aid of the tariff, all was easily sanctioned by the notion that the community had no rights as against individuals because its rights were merely the sum of theirs.   We have come to see that the truly national ideal, the truly democratic ideal, is the good of the whole people and that only by the fullest protection of the rights of the minority and of that greater entity, the State itself, can a great and free people attain in the highest degree, ''Liberty and Union, now and forever, one and inseparable.''

THE END

INDEX

INDEX

Adams, John, 56, 97, 98, 113, 114, 117, 120, 126, 141, 180, 194.

Adams, Samuel, 96–99, 101, 179.

Anti-Slavery, rise of, 245–6; compared with pro-slavery argument, 246–8; relation to the outbreak of war in 1861, 246; escaping slaves aided by advocates of, 264–5.

Armada, significance in American History of defeat of, 18–19.

Balboa, 12.

Boston, settlement of, 25; in colonial times, 50–54, 56, 62–7; in the Revolution, 93, 94, 96–106.

Brown, John, in Kansas, 273; raid of, 280–1.

Bunker Hill, battle of, 94, 97, 98, 104–106, 137.

Calhoun, John C., in the War of 1812, 206; views upon conflicting interests of sections, 215; *Exposition* of, 221–2; democratic ideas of, 234; against Compromise in 1850, 267; counsels war with the North, 266, 289 and note, 295; death of, 268.

Canada, French colonies in, 74–6; results of conquest of by the English, 78–9; attempts to annex to United States, 199 and note, 206; boundary settled with United States, 262.

Capitalists, part played by in colonization, 20; origin of in colonial America, 43–4; attacked during Revolution, 95–6, 111–116; difficulties of during

Critical Period, 140–5, 152–7; support strong central government, 1787–90, 160, 184–5, 196–7; support protective tariff, 215–219, 221; alone profit from slavery at South, 241–5; strength of at the North due to manufactures, 249–250; effects of Civil War upon, 350–9; effects of nationalization of industry upon, 399–403.

Civil War, 1861–65, place in American History of, 9–10, 18; fundamental causes of, 282–6; immediate causes of, 284–296; outbreak of, 297–307; military aspects of, 308–316; why won by the North, 317–339; results of, 340–359; results on the North, 340–351; on economic condition of the South. 351–9.

Clay, Henry, in War of 1812, 206; responsible for the "American System," 216–218; on union in 1820, 220; on elections of 1824 and 1832, 232–4; creator of legislative system in House of Representatives, 236–7; on slavery in border States, 244; on Compromise of 1850, 267; death of, 268.

Colonists, character of, Spanish, 13–14; French, 16; English, 26, 33–7; Dutch, 27–8.

Columbus, 11, 17.

Commerce, colonial, 38–44, 73, 81–4, 93; after the Revolution, 152–5; interstate commerce after 1783, 155–6; foreign commerce after 1783, 163–4, 183, 196–200, 205, 211–216.

LaVergne, TN USA
04 February 2010

172054LV00008B/269/A

9 780548 005293